# How to Invest in
# E-Commerce Stocks

## Other Titles from CommerceNet Press

# How to Invest in E-Commerce Stocks

Bill Burnham

## McGraw-Hill

New York   San Francisco   Washington, D.C.   Auckland   Bogotá
Caracas   Lisbon   London   Madrid   Mexico City   Milan
Montreal   New Delhi   San Juan   Singapore
Sydney   Tokyo   Toronto

Library of Congress Cataloging-in-Publication Data

Burnham, Bill.
    How to invest in E-commerce stocks / Bill Burnham.
        p.    cm.
    Includes index.
    ISBN 0-07-009238-9
    1. Electronic commerce—United States.
HF5548.325.U6B87      1999
658.8'00285'4678—dc21                            98-10373
                                                 CIP

# McGraw-Hill

*A Division of The McGraw·Hill Companies*

1 2 3 4 5 6 7 8 9 0    FGR/FGR    9 0 3 2 1 0 9 8

ISBN 0-07-009238-9

*The sponsoring editor for this book was Susan Barry, the editing supervisor was Curt Berkowitz, and the production supervisor was Claire Stanley. It was set in Palatino by North Market Street Graphics.*

*Printed and bound by Quebecor Fairfield.*

Product or brand names used in this book may be trade names or trademarks. Where we believe that there may be proprietary claims to such trade names or trademarks, the name has been used with an initial capital or it has been capitalized in the style used by the name claimant. Regardless of the capitalization used, all such names have been used in an editorial manner without any intent to convey endorsement of or other affiliation with the name claimant. Neither the author nor the publisher intends to express any judgment as to the validity or legal status of any such proprietary claims.

 This book was printed on recycled, acid-free paper containing a minimum of 50% recycled, de-inked fiber.

# Contents

# Tables and Figures

## 3. The Security Sector: Too Important for Its Own Good?                        **43**

## 4. Electronic Payments and the Death of "The Switch"                        **97**

## 5. Financial Software and the Rise of the Integrator     151

## 6. Business Commerce and the Rise of the Distributed Extraprise
**199**

## 7. Commerce Content: Brands Battle Intelligent Agents    241

# Preface

In the spirit of "you either do it right or you don't do it at all," this report is a long one. Don't worry though, we recognize that very few readers will have the time or need to read this report from cover to cover.

*For those truly pressed for time, we suggest reading the separate eight-page summary* that we have produced in conjunction with this report and then returning to the full report once time permits or the need to develop a more in-depth perspective arises.

All readers should take note that *Chapter 2 is optional* and only intended for those who do not have a background in the fundamental security technologies that underlie Electronic Commerce ("EC"). Chapters 3–7 each address a separate "sector" of the EC industry in detail and are all laid out in a largely identical form comprised of 11 separate sections (see table on page xiv).

Although we have written each chapter to logically flow from one section to the next, *readers can pick-and-choose* amongst the sections depending on their knowledge and interest in the subject at hand.

Finally, *we have created an extensive index* at the back of the report that should allow readers to quickly find particular information that is of interest to them. Hopefully these measures will make the report readable and relevant to both EC experts and novices alike.

## Description of the Standard Sections Found in Chapters 3–7

| Section | Description |
| --- | --- |
| Structure | Provides basic background on the structure and operation of each sector of the EC industry. Readers with advanced knowledge may want to skip this section. |
| Sub-Sectors | Groups and details the different players in each particular EC sector. |
| Market Size | Provides current estimates of the size of the sector. |
| Drivers | Describes the specific drivers that are influencing the growth of the sector. |
| Potential | Estimates the future size of the sector and the amount of revenues that it is likely to generate. |
| Trends | Reviews the trends that are currently impacting the sector and discusses their potential affect. This section is the most topical part of each chapter. |
| Success Factors | Establishes the key success factors that will likely help determine whether or not individual firms succeed in the sector given the current trends. |
| New Opportunities | Explores a few of the new opportunities being created by the ongoing development of the sector. |
| Investment Considerations | Reviews the historical investment performance of companies focused on the sector and puts this performance into perspective. |
| Risks | Delineates the risks that could have a substantial impact on the future growth prospects of companies in the sector. |
| Conclusion | Provides a very brief wrap up of the chapter. |

# Acknowledgements

Thanks to everyone who generously took the time to share their thoughts on the Electronic Commerce industry in preparation for this report.

| | |
| --- | --- |
| Stephen Aldrich | *Insuremarket* |
| Gary Anderson | *St. Paul Software* |
| Doug Braun | *Intelidata* |
| John Carlson | *Office of the Comptroller of the Currency* |
| Casey Carter | *Office of the Comptroller of the Currency* |
| Jim Chen | *V-ONE* |
| Amour Cheung | *Client Server Computing* |
| Lynne Colvin | *Integrion* |
| Christos Cotsakos | *E\*Trade* |

| | |
|---|---|
| Richard Crone | *Cybercash* |
| Bob Crowell | *Elcom* |
| Tom Dittrich | *Home Financial Network* |
| Frank Donny | *Sanchez Computer Associates* |
| Dan Drechsel | *EC Partners* |
| Lucinda Duncalfe | *Destiny Software* |
| Eric Dunn | *Intuit* |
| Bart Foster | *Connect* |
| D. R. Grimes | *Atlanta Internet Bank* |
| Steven Hagen | *U.S. Senate Banking Committee* |
| Paul Harrison | *MECA Software* |
| Jim Heerwagen | *V-ONE* |
| Charles Herel | *Edify* |
| Jack Hwang | *Client Server Computing* |
| T. Stephen Johnson | *Atlanta Internet Bank* |
| Gina Jorasch | *Verisign* |
| Xenia Kwee | *Home Account Network* |
| Sam Kinney | *Freemarkets Online* |
| Joe Koshuta | *Online Resources* |
| Peggy Kuhn | *U.S. Senate Banking Committee* |
| Matt Lawlor | *Online Resources* |
| John Lopez | *U.S. House Banking Committee* |
| Julie Lorigan | *Open Market* |
| David Lytel | *Lytel Consulting Group* |
| Chip Mahan | *Security First Network Bank* |
| Robert Majteles | *Ultradata* |
| Jeff Marquardt | *Board of Governors of the Federal Reserve* |
| Deepesh Misra | *Integrion* |
| Charles Ogilvie | *Security First Network Bank* |
| Jim Omura | *Cylink* |
| Andy Reidy | *Visa Interactive* |
| Rob Rosen | *Vertigo Development* |
| Fernand Serrat | *Cylink* |
| Don Shapleigh | *Atlanta Internet Bank* |
| Pete Smith | *Intelidata* |
| Bill Soward | *Edify* |
| John Stafford | *Office of Senator Alfonse D'Amato* |

| Tom Steding | *Pretty Good Privacy* |
| Bob Weinberger | *Open Market* |
| Susan Weinstein | *Wells Fargo* |

Thanks also to those who helped whip the final draft into shape including Chuck, David, Navtej, Tim, and Tom. And a special thanks to the A-Team of editing: Barbara, Elana, Tami, and Brent.

—BILL BURNHAM

# How to Invest in E-Commerce Stocks

# 1

# The Electronic Commerce Industry

## Introduction

In 1991, the Internet was considered by many to be little more than an amusing academic backwater used by researchers to exchange e-mail and computer files. Then in late 1991 a computer scientist in Switzerland developed a system for easily displaying words and pictures on the Internet called the World Wide Web. Almost overnight the World Wide Web, with its ease of use, simple navigation, and widespread availability, transformed the Internet from academic backwater into potentially one of the most important technological advances of the 20th century. Indeed, while at the beginning of 1991 there were a total of just 376,000 computers on the Internet, today, over 500,000 computers are added to the Internet *each month.*

The Internet's explosive growth has not only changed the daily lives of millions of people, but it has also changed the fortunes of hundreds of companies. Starting in 1992, companies providing the basic infrastructure of the Internet, including network equipment (Cisco, Ascend, Cabletron), modems (US Robotics, Hayes), software (Netscape, Spyglass, FTP), and access services (Netcom, PSI Net, UUNet) all jumped aboard the Internet train and began to see tremendous growth as consumer and business interest in the Internet began to take off.

As the growth of this first wave of Internet companies began to stabilize, a second wave of companies dedicated to providing information over the Internet began to emerge in 1993 and 1994. These so-called "content" firms, such as Yahoo!, Lycos, Excite, and CNET, made their living by helping users find what they were looking for on the Internet and by providing customers with new sources of Internet related information.

But throughout all of this growth there was something missing. For despite all of the attention that the Internet was getting there was still a widespread reluctance to use it for the activity that occupies much of our daily lives: commerce. While fears about the reliability and security of the Internet were partially to blame, perhaps the biggest single inhibitor to the growth of the Internet as a medium for commerce was the lack of products and services that allowed businesses and consumers to easily conduct commerce over the Internet.

What some people saw as problems, others saw as opportunities and starting in late 1995 and 1996 a third wave of companies emerged each claiming to solve different elements of the "commerce" problem. Today, this third wave of companies is rapidly coalescing into a full-fledged industry of strategically and financially related companies that are all focused on just two words: Electronic Commerce.

As this new "Electronic Commerce" industry begins to enter its growth phase, it is creating a tremendous amount of excitement both in the popular press and in the investment community. Unfortunately, along with this excitement has also come a good deal of confusion. From grain processors to utilities, a confusing array of companies have suddenly recast themselves as "leaders of the EC industry." Such a wide variety of firms claiming to be involved in EC has made it very difficult for investors to determine which companies are truly in position to capitalize on the potential of EC and which companies are simply trying to expand the multiples on their stocks. This situation has also made it difficult for investors to determine which companies are competitors versus partners and what indicators should be used to judge the health and direction of the industry. This book attempts to clear up the confusion surrounding Electronic Commerce and the investment opportunities created as a result of its growth by answering a few basic questions about the EC industry including: What exactly is "Electronic Commerce"?, How does it work?, and What are the real prospects for the EC industry?

Answering these questions will hopefully shed some light not only on the structure and operation of the EC industry, but also on the key success factors and major areas of opportunity going forward.

While this book is written primarily with investors in mind, it contains a great deal of general industry background and information and therefore should prove useful to anyone with an interest in the growth and development of Electronic Commerce.

## What Is "Electronic Commerce"?

Perhaps the first question that bears answering in any examination of the EC industry is just what constitutes "commerce." While there are many potential definitions, Commerce is perhaps best defined as the transfer of value through four basic types of activities: buying, selling, investing, and lending. To support these activities in the physical world an elaborate infrastructure has been developed to allow businesses, consumers, and governments to efficiently provision, pay for, and finance each commercial transaction.

Taking its cue from the traditional definition of commerce, Electronic Commerce simply involves the transfer of value over the Internet through one of the four basic activities: buying, selling, investing, and lending.

It is important to keep in mind though that while this definition is fairly simple, making EC a reality is not a simple undertaking. Specifically, several points about the EC industry should be kept in mind. First, in order to make the concept of EC a reality, a massive infrastructure must be built that mimics the infrastructure provided in the physical world. What's more, while the physical infrastructure has been built up over many decades, companies in the EC industry are under pressure to build the EC infrastructure in just years or even months.

Second, it is important to keep in mind that EC spans a broad range of commercial activities. There has been an unfortunate tendency in the popular press to reduce EC to solely the conduct of business-to-consumer activities, such as buying books or records over the Interent. The fact of the matter is that EC involves much more than just selling trinkets over the Internet. EC encompasses not only business-to-consumer commerce (such as book store sales), but also business-to-business commerce (such as jet engine sales), and government-to-business/consumer commerce (such as distributing benefits or filing taxes).

Finally, EC includes not just the actual transfer of value, but all of the communication, collaboration, and information that has to be exchanged in order to complete that transfer. Therefore EC involves not just the transaction, but the entire process that leads up to and follows the transaction.

Taken together these three points make it clear that while the definition of EC may be simple, its role and structure is not.

## Structure

In the physical world, the conduct of commerce requires an elaborate infrastructure. For example, take a grocery store. Before a grocery store can open for business, it not only needs to find a location, build a store, and stock the shelves, but also to install cash registers, place advertisements, and establish bank accounts. In addition, it also needs to buy a safe, put locks on its doors, install video cameras and hire a security guard to ward off robbers and shoplifters. However, even if the grocery store is built and operated perfectly, it is still dependent on other infrastructures, such as the highway system, for its success. After all, if the food can not be delivered to the store on time then there will be nothing to sell.

Just as a grocery store requires a large and complex physical infrastructure to support its business today, businesses conducting EC also require a large infrastructure composed of hundreds of different pieces. Building these pieces and connecting them together is the job of the EC industry.

### Foundations of the EC Industry

As Figure 1.1 makes clear, in the same way that the grocery stores are dependent on the highway system, the EC infrastructure is dependent on three other infrastructures including:

1. *Internet Software and Tools:* The basic software languages, technologies, and development tools that are used to develop Internet software. These are used by the EC industry to create EC-specific applications and services.

2. *Internet Infrastructure:* The set of open standards, protocols, and network interconnection points that make up the Internet. This infrastructure gives the Internet its wide reach and universal appeal.

3. *Telecommunications Infrastructure:* The plain old telephone lines (POTs), leased lines, and fiber optic cable that make up the telephone system. Increasingly include wireless, cable, and satellite components. This infrastructure provides the basic electronic links that make the Internet, and by extension, EC possible.

### The Five EC Industry Sectors

As for the EC industry itself, like most other industries, the EC industry is not a single, homogenous entity, but rather a collection of distinctly sepa-

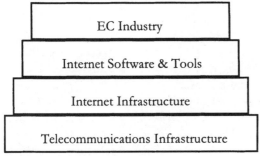

**Figure 1.1**   EC Industry Foundations

rate, yet interdependent industry sectors. Each sector is comprised of a group of firms that are all focused on providing one of key products or services that are required to make EC a reality.

From an investment perspective, properly defining these sectors is a very important exercise. By their very nature, industry sectors establish a framework for evaluating the competitive positions, market structures, and potential growth opportunities for the companies within each sector. Incorrectly defining these sectors creates a skewed and inaccurate picture of the industry's competitive and market dynamics which can in turn lead to unpleasant investment "surprises" as companies are affected by industry events in unanticipated ways. With this in mind, we have examined the market and competitive dynamics within the industry and defined five separate sectors (see Figure 1.2):

1. *Security Sector*[1]*:* Provides the software, hardware, and services that enable businesses and consumers to securely use computer networks. Examples of products/services sold by this sector include: firewalls, encryption tool kits, payment security software, and digital certificates.

2. *Electronic Payments Sector:* Initiates, processes, and analyzes all forms of electronic payments on behalf of businesses, consumers, and financial

---

[1] The first reaction of many readers may be to consider security a horizontal rather than a vertical sector. Please see the beginning of Chapter 3 for a discussion of why we believe Security is a separate but vertical sector in the EC industry.

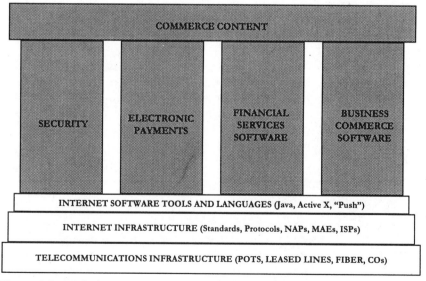

**Figure 1.2** EC Industry Structure   *Source: Piper Jaffray*

institutions. Examples of products/services sold include: payment processing, electronic bill payment/presentment, and electronic cash.

3. *Financial Services Software Sector:* Develops software that enables businesses and consumers to electronically access, manage, and analyze their financial accounts over the Internet. Examples of products/services sold include: Internet banking software, on-line trading software, and financial management software.

4. *Business Commerce Software Sector:* Provides the software and services that businesses need to link their internal payment, remittance, inventory, and order systems to the Internet. Examples of products/services sold include: electronic catalog software and Electronic Data Interchange (EDI) software/services.

5. *Commerce Content Sector:* Comprised of the companies that are *actually conducting* retail and wholesale commerce over the Internet. The stores and businesses in this sector use all of the products and services produced by the previous four sectors to create services that allow consumers and businesses to transfer value over the Internet. Examples of products/services sold include: books, CDs, wine, industrial supplies, and plastic resin.

## Differences Between the Sectors

While one of the clear differences between these sectors is that they offer different products or services, there are a few less apparent differences between the sectors that are even more important, including:

- *Different Capabilities:* While scale and operating experience may be critical in one sector, creativity and human capital may be more important in another. For example, firms in the Electronic Payment sector rely on scale and operating efficiency to compete while firms in the Financial Services Software sector rely on programming talent and relationships with financial institutions.

- *Different Resources:* Different sectors need different resources to power their success. For example, while applied mathematicians might be nice to have in the Business Commerce sector, they are an absolute necessity for many firms in the Security sector.

- *Different Customers:* Different sectors sell to different customers. The type of customer a firm sells to influences the firm's sales and marketing structure as well as its revenue model, product cycle, and development priorities.

## Importance of the Structure

*These differences are important because they form "hard walls"* or barriers to entry between the different sectors that make it very difficult for the same company to successfully compete in multiple sectors.

Another important point to note is that each of the five major sectors has its own set of sub-sectors (see Table 1.1). These *sub-sectors have inherently "soft walls,"* that is, companies in one sub-sector have many of the capabilities, resources, and customers necessary to compete in another sub-sector. Therefore, it is logical to expect that these "soft walls" will dissolve over time and that companies will eventually compete across all of the different sub-sectors within a particular sector.

**Table 1.1**   Definitions of the Five EC Sectors

| Sector | Definition | Sample sub-sectors | Examples |
|---|---|---|---|
| Security | Securing of computer networks. Identification and authentication of parties involved in network-based purchases and payments. | ■ Network Security Conglomerates <br> ■ Encryption Tool Providers <br> ■ Certificate Authorities | ■ Security Dynamics (#) <br> ■ Verisign <br> ■ Checkpoint |
| Electronic payments | Initiating, transporting, processing, and analyzing electronic payments | ■ Card Payment Processors <br> ■ Bill Payment and Presentment <br> ■ Payment Support Providers | ■ First Data <br> ■ Checkfree <br> ■ Gemplus |
| Financial services software | Software and services designed to give consumers and businesses on-line access to their financial accounts and information. | ■ Consumer Software <br> ■ Business Software <br> ■ Middleware | ■ Intuit <br> ■ EC Partners <br> ■ Integrion |
| Business commerce software | Software and services that enable businesses to link their internal payment, remittance, order, and inventory systems to the Internet. | ■ Open Commercial Exchange (OCE) <br> ■ EDI Software and Services <br> ■ Direct Data Interaction (DDI) | ■ Sterling Commerce <br> ■ Open Market <br> ■ Crossroute |
| Commerce content | Comprised of the companies that are *actually conducting* retail and wholesale commerce over the Internet. | ■ Shopping <br> ■ Financial Services <br> ■ Industrial Purchasing | ■ Amazon.com <br> ■ E*Trade <br> ■ Onsale |

Finally, it is also important to note that while the five sectors are separate, they are also *interdependent*. For example, a major problem with security will affect all of the other sectors; likewise, if the Business Commerce sector fails to release important software on time, it will have an impact on the growth of the other sectors.

Perhaps the best way to demonstrate this interdependence is to look at the correlation in stock price movements between the five different sectors. As Table 1.2 demonstrates, daily stock price movements in four of the five sectors are highly correlated with each other, indicating a strong degree of interdependence from (at the very least) an investment perspective. This correlation is underscored by the fact that four out of the five sectors are also negatively correlated to the S&P 500, indicating a true degree of independence from the influence of the overall market. The only sector that is not consistent with this trend, Commerce Content, is actually so small and immature that its negative correlation is more than likely not significant. As this sector grows and matures, we expect that it will also "fall in line" with the other sectors, providing even greater evidence of the interdependence between the sectors.

Our approach to the EC industry is driven by this theoretical and observed interdependence. We strongly believe that unless investors have a perspective on the full breadth and depth of the EC industry, they will be unable to exploit the true opportunities in the industry and incapable of avoiding its inherent risks.

## The Four Commandments

To sum it all up, it is important to keep the following four key points about the EC industry's structure in mind at all times:

**Table 1.2**  Correlation of Daily Stock Price Changes in the Five EC Industry Sectors

|                        | Security | Electronic payments | Financial software | Business commerce | Commerce content |
|------------------------|----------|---------------------|--------------------|-------------------|------------------|
| Security               | 100.0%   | 58.6%               | 67.9%              | 76.5%             | −69.8%           |
| Electronic payments    | 58.6     | 100.0               | 6.2                | 55.5              | −74.0            |
| Financial software     | 67.9     | 6.2                 | 100.0              | 45.7              | −87.5            |
| Business commerce      | 76.5     | 55.5                | 45.7               | 100.0             | −38.3            |
| Commerce content       | −69.8    | −74.0               | −87.5              | −38.3             | 100.0            |
| Overall EC industry    | 86.9     | 87.4                | 51.4               | 77.7              | −75.4            |
| Overall vs. S&P 500    | −48.6    | −13.7               | −83.0              | −26.7             | 74.7             |

### The Four Guiding Principles for Investing in the EC Industry

1. The *"hard walls"* between sectors generally mean that firms from one sector will find it very difficult to successfully enter another sector.

2. The *"soft walls"* between sub-sectors mean that firms within a sector are generally capable of successfully entering other sub-sectors.

3. Firms currently trying to compete in more than one sector will eventually be *forced to focus* on a single sector due to the specialized capabilities required.

4. The *interdependence* of the sectors makes it critical to have a perspective on what is happening in all five of the different sectors.

These four points provide some simple but important rules to live by for investors in the EC industry. That's not to say that there won't be exceptions to the rules (for example, Microsoft has a good shot at breaking #2 *and* #4), but these exceptions should be few and far between.


## Moving On . . .

As the structure of the industry makes clear, the EC industry covers a tremendous amount of ground. Indeed the bulk of this report (chapters 3–7) is dedicated to covering that ground by stepping through each of the five sectors and explaining how they are structured, what their potential is, and what the major opportunities are likely to be.

Before we delve into these sector-specific discussions though, we want to discuss two aspects of the EC industry at the aggregate level: market drivers and investment considerations.


# Market Drivers

While each sector has its own unique drivers, there are a few "macro-level" drivers powering the industry's overall growth, each of which deserves some upfront discussion.


## The Growth of the Internet

Clearly, the Internet's explosive growth is perhaps the single most important driver behind the EC industry. As almost everyone knows, the Internet has been growing at a fantastic rate, with the number of computers or hosts connected to the Internet almost doubling every twelve months to a recent level of just under 30 million hosts. Likewise, the number of Internet users has grown from just several million in 1994 to almost 70 million in 1997. By 2000, this number is expected to reach 163 million (see Figure 1.3).

When put into perspective, this growth is even more impressive. Indeed, the World Wide Web portion of the Internet may well be one of the faster growing consumer electronic devices of all time (see Figure 1.4).

The growth of the Internet is being propelled along by a phenomenon known to economists as "network externalities." Network externalities are the negative side-effects associated with not being part of a network. Put another way, network externalities mean that the larger a network gets, the greater the imperative there is for people to join it.

David Metcalf, the inventor of the Ethernet network protocol, coined a "law" to describe network externalities with regard to the Internet.[2] Called Metcalf's Law (what else?), it states that the "power" of the Internet is equal to the square of its nodes. Stated otherwise, Metcalf's Law means that every computer added to the Internet doubles the overall power of the network and, therefore, makes it that much more imperative for businesses and consumers to join the Internet. Like a snowball rolling down a hill or a rapidly forming planet, the mass of the Internet simply attracts more mass. Given that the Internet is now adding millions of computers each year, its overall attractive "power" is growing at a spectacular rate.

[2] Actually, Metcalf's Law refers to networks in general, not just the Internet.

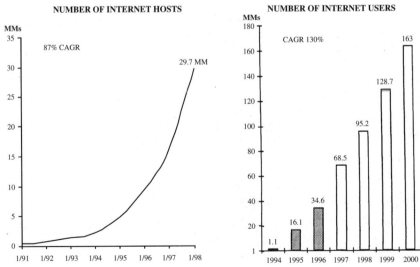

**Figure 1.3**  Growth in Internet Hosts and Users  *Source (left): Network Wizards Source (right): International Data Corporation*

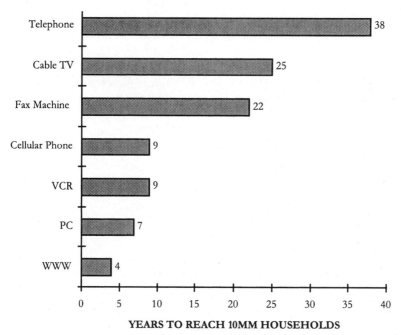

**Figure 1.4** Growth in Internet Relative to Other Electronic Devices *Source: Booz, Allen & Hamilton*

As the Internet grows in size and power, it is dramatically expanding the potential market of the EC industry and increasing the likelihood that the Internet will not only become a viable channel for commerce, but perhaps a preferred one.

## Improved Technology

Improving technology is also driving the EC industry forward. The most familiar technology law of all, Moore's Law, continues to work its magic, doubling the density and thereby the power of computer processors every 18 months (see Figure 1.5). This law is expected by most observers to stay on track for the next 7 to 10 years. Another law, coined by the columnist George Gilder (that we'll term Gilder's Law), holds that bandwidth, or the communications capacity of networks, will triple every year for the next 25 years.[3] These increases in functionality are being accompanied by significant decreases in costs. For example, the cost per megabyte of disk

[3] See Gilder, George, "The Bandwidth Tidal Wave," *Forbes* ASAP 12/5/94. A powerful essay on the impact of bandwidth on technology and society.

TRANSISTOR DENSITY

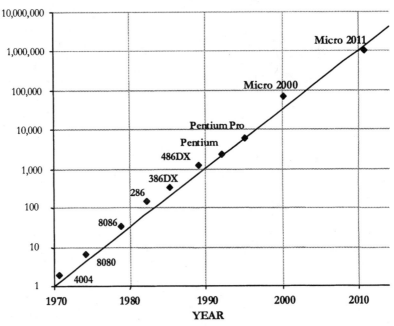

**Figure 1.5**  Progress of Moore's Law    *Source: PC Magazine*

storage space has plummeted from $10,000 a megabyte in 1957 to just $0.10 a megabyte in 1997 and should approach just $0.03 per megabyte by 2000[4] (see Figure 1.6). These radical decreases in costs combined with just as radical increases in functionality have made technology far more accessible, attractive, and useful to the average consumer and business. Access has improved as decreased prices have lowered the barriers to entry and encouraged both small businesses and consumers to buy their own computers. Attractive graphical user interfaces have taken the place of command line interfaces, and cheaper, more abundant, bandwidth has made it possible for businesses and consumers alike to communicate in real time.

These are familiar refrains to anyone following the computer industry and they are driving many other trends outside of EC, but they do have particular relevance to EC because they are not only making it dramatically cheaper for business and consumers to use the Internet to conduct commerce, but they are dramatically increasing the functionality that can be offered. With all of these powerful trends expected to continue unabated

---

[4] See "Future: Mass Storage," *PC Magazine,* 3/25/97. 182. The 15th anniversary issue and a generally outstanding one at that. The 1992 figure is from a separate issue.

**COST/MEGABYTE**

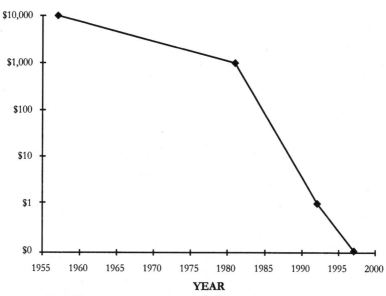

**Figure 1.6**  Cost per Megabyte of Storage for Selected Years
*Source: PC Magazine*

for at least the next 7–10 years, they should prove to be a powerful driver for the EC industry, enabling features and functions that are not even contemplated today.

Outside of these rather obvious and well understood technology trends, there are a couple of other trends that, while not as noticeable, are just as important to the long-term growth of the EC industry.

## Business Process Redesign

Intensifying competition due to deregulation, the lowering of trade barriers, and the increasing price transparency are encouraging businesses to fundamentally reexamine how they conduct their business. While many businesses initially went through large-scale, one-time business processing "reengineering" projects in the early 1990s, they are still continuing to seek out new ways to redesign their business systems and capture additional savings. EC, with its paperless processing, ability to integrate directly into a company's computer systems, and emphasis on technology, offers the promise of substantial savings. The lure of these potential savings should prove a strong driver for EC adoption.

## Improved Logistics

The last twenty-five years have witnessed a series of improvements in the cost and time that it takes to deliver goods and services to consumers and businesses. This improvement is due to advances in technology as well as the deregulation of the airline, trucking, and railroad transportation industries. Together, these two factors have had a significant effect on transportation costs, with airline fares 9% lower and railroad costs almost 40% lower than they were in 1980. As these costs have decreased, delivery times have actually improved due to increased flexibility and better operational designs.[5]

Improvements in the cost and time required to deliver goods and services are reducing the need for businesses to be geographically close to their customers. Without these improvements in logistics, EC would lose a lot of its appeal. After all, who wants to order a book over the Internet if it takes two weeks to arrive? But if the book can arrive in a day or two and at a reasonable price, many businesses and consumers will find EC to be a compelling proposition. Therefore, further improvements in logistics should help drive the entire EC industry forward.

## All Systems Are "Go"

Like a rising tide lifting all boats, all four of these "macro-level" drivers will help grow each of the five individual sectors that make up the EC industry. What is most interesting about these drivers is that to a large extent they are already predetermined. The technological improvements are coming. Early versions are already in the labs and the basic technologies are already proven. These improvements, along with Metcalf's Law, to a large extent predetermine that the Internet will soon expand to be many times its current size. Debating whether or not the Internet will grow to be three or five times its current size over the next five years misses the point; in either case it will be tremendously bigger and much more powerful than it is today. Improvements in logistics and business process design, while less dramatic, will no doubt continue their steady pace as technology improves and as an increasingly global and deregulated economy forces businesses to become more productive.

So at the macro level, dramatic future growth in EC seems almost a lock. Even if the industry just sits on its hands between now and 2001, the market would still expand to be at least three times as big as it is today. Of course there are a few potential problems which could derail this train,

---

[5] See "Changes in Airfares, Service, and Safety Since Deregulation," Government Accounting Office. 4/96 and "Government Regulation and American Business," Center for the Study of American Business. 12/92.

one of the most obvious being security problems (which we discuss in Chapter 2), but for now all systems are "go."

## Investment Considerations

There are two extremes when it comes to opinions on investing in the EC industry, both of which are dangerously wrong. The first extreme holds that EC will never take off due to consumer and business reservations about the security of EC. Similar arguments were made by the railroads about air travel during the first half of the twentieth century. The railroads maintained that consumer concerns over the safety of air travel would prevent the airline industry from growing. While consumers were concerned about security, the convenience of air travel proved to far outweigh the potential risks. So just as consumers and businesses overcame their "fear of flying" they will more than likely overcome their fear of EC. That's not to say that security concerns are not important, but as Chapter 2 will make clear, the basic technologies required to make EC as secure as, if not more secure than, current modes of commerce, are already in place.

The other extreme holds that the EC industry is the modern day equivalent of the Oklahoma Land Rush or the California Gold Rush. In this scenario, any firm with a hot idea and a business plan can set up shop, sit back, and make a fortune as eager prospectors plunk down thousands of dollars to take their chances. This vision of the EC industry as a land of limitless investment opportunity overlooks the fact that far from an uninhabited open plain, the EC industry is already populated by large, experienced, and well-capitalized players who are all looking to get their fair share of the action.

### It's a Jungle Out There: Watch Out for the Elephants

The industry is perhaps better characterized as a jungle: tremendous natural resources and potential, but filled with skilled predators and populated by more than a few "elephants." Among the elephants are such firms as Microsoft, IBM, and Oracle (#). These elephants are the most worrisome part of investing in the EC industry and present the industry with several major problems (see Table 1.3).

While the elephants are indeed substantial competitors worthy of respect, they are not all powerful. Indeed, many of the same characteristics that make the elephants such fearsome competitors also create numerous opportunities for other firms in the EC industry. As Table 1.4 demonstrates, the elephants have their own weaknesses that, when properly exploited,

**Table 1.3**  Negative Impact of the "Elephants" on the Industry

| Elephant characteristics | Impact on the EC industry |
| --- | --- |
| They are pretty much unstoppable | If an elephant decides to enter the market for a particular EC product or service there is little if anything that incumbent firms can do to prevent a loss of market share. |
| They can inadvertently crush other jungle inhabitants | In the drive to control a particular product or service, the elephants can create a lot of "collateral damage," whereby companies that they really had no direct intention of hurting are inadvertently "stamped" out of existence. |
| They have no natural predators | The elephants roam the industry with impunity. Their only real threat comes from other elephants. This makes them particularly bold and brazen competitors. |
| They have a tremendous appetite | The elephants not only have significant revenues but they also have high P/Es. This creates a tremendous appetite for growth that can propel them to try to dominate almost every revenue opportunity they encounter. |

can lead to a relatively peaceful coexistence between the elephants and the rest of the industry.

So the elephants are not all bad news for the EC industry—they are just one more factor that has to be carefully considered when evaluating the range of investment options in the EC industry.

**Table 1.4**  Positive Impact of the "Elephants" on the Industry

| Elephant characteristics | Impact on the EC industry |
| --- | --- |
| They can't fit in many places | The sheer mass of the elephants prevents them from easily pursuing smaller "niche" opportunities This leaves the playing field wide open for smaller, specialized services and products. |
| They aren't incredibly agile | Smaller competitors can often "turn on a dime" and react quickly to market changes and customer demands. Most elephants can't muster this kind of agility. |
| They operate on a wide plain | EC firms can optimize themselves to solely deliver a single product or service while the elephants must necessarily focus on a broad range of opportunities, many far afield from EC. |
| You can hear them coming | It is very difficult for an elephant to sneak up on a sector and launch a surprise product or service. This inability gives EC firms the opportunity to develop a response well in advance of an elephant's eventual offering. |

As we noted in our description of the industry's structure, we suggest that investors keep four main points in mind when investing in the EC industry:

1. *Don't worry* about firms from one sector entering another sector—the "hard walls" between sectors will generally prevent them from accomplishing this.

2. *Do worry* about firms from one *sub-sector* entering another sub-sector—the "soft walls" between sectors virtually guarantee that this will happen over time.

3. *Expect* that firms currently trying to compete in more than one sector will eventually be forced to specialize in a single sector—experience in industries such as retailing and financial services indicates that specialization is inevitable.

4. *Do* develop a perspective on what is happening in all five sectors—their *interdependence* demands it.


## Long-Term Outlook

Before we move on, we should note that in chapters 3–7 we talk a good deal about long-term industry evolution. A lot of this talk may seem inappropriate—after all, we're dealing with stocks, not 30-year bonds. But discussions of the long term (that is the 3+ year evolution of the industry) are absolutely necessary in an industry where valuations are based on earnings that are often 3+ years out. By discussing the long-term outlook, we are establishing a framework or "early warning system" which should allow investors to rapidly assess the impact of short-term events and trends on a particular company's long-term growth and earnings potential. Given that many of the EC stocks are highly sensitive to even slight changes in long-term expectations, such an early warning system is critical for investors to have in place.


## EC Index

We have put together an index of the leading firms in the EC industry in an effort to try and put the overall investment performance of the industry into perspective. The index includes public companies from each of the five sectors in the EC industry. We set two broad criteria for inclusion in the EC index:

1. Companies must have a significant focus on one of the five areas of electronic commerce.

2. Companies must be committed to maintaining or expanding their presence in these sectors.

A detailed appendix of the 48 firms in the index can be found in the back of this report. It is important to note that while several of the firms in the index derive a significant portion of their revenues from outside of the five EC sectors, we believe that, over time, these firms will generate an increasing amount of their revenues from activities related to EC and thus warrant inclusion in the index. Notable companies that are *not* part of this index (due to their broader market focus) include Cisco Systems, IBM, Microsoft, Netscape, and Oracle.

### Recent Investment Performance

In general, the EC industry has been on a roller coaster ride since the beginning of 1997 (see Figure 1.7). During the few months of 1997, fears about competition from the elephants, as well as a general downturn in small capitalization stocks, drove most EC stocks down to 52-week lows. In late April, however, EC stocks rebounded on the strength of solid second quarter earnings reports and an upturn in the overall market. The stocks seemed to coast through much of the summer but fell hard in October as fears about slowing economic growth in Asia depressed the overall market in general. EC stocks didn't seem to recover until fourth quarter earnings

**Figure 1.7**   EC Index Versus S&P 500: 1/97–5/98   *Source: Piper Jaffray*

reports in mid-January when they went on a sustained bull-run until mid-March, due largely to renewed enthusiasm for both Commerce Content and Business Commerce stocks. Just before the mid-way point of 1998, EC stocks went on another run, with Commerce Content stocks leading the way.

Despite this run, it is tough not to notice that the EC index has still underperformed the broader market. Indeed, since January 1, 1997, the EC index has only appreciated 29% compared to the S&P 500 index's return of 54% (the S&P 500 index provides a broad-based measure of overall stock market performance). Investors should take heart though that the poor performance of the EC index over this period is largely due to problems in the Electronic Payments sector. Excluding the Electronic Payments sector, the EC index actually appreciated 70% (compared to the S&P 500's 54%), which, overall, is very nice return indeed.

## Market Characteristics

There are 49 companies in the EC universe. These are the firms largely focused on the respective sectors in the EC industry. Over half of these firms went public in either 1996 or 1997 (see Table 1.5). Key statistics for this group as of 7/1/98:

*Market Capitalization:* $53.4 billion in market capitalization as of 7/1/98. A single firm, First Data Resources represents 28% of the total capitalization.

*Liquidity:* On an average day, $646 million in EC company stock trades hands. At this rate, market capitalization in the industry turned over every 83 days.

*Volatility:* The EC industry is significantly more volatile than the larger market, but roughly comparable to the high tech industry. On a capitalization weighted basis, daily S&P 500 prices moved an average of 0.80% from 1/97–7/98. During that same period, daily EC industry prices moved on average by 1.27%, or 59% greater than the S&P.

Compared to the high tech-dominated Pacific Stock Exchange (PSE) index's average daily price change of 1.21%, the EC industry's aggregate price volatility appears about equal to the rest of the high tech industry; however, this comparison masks the fact that several of the smaller EC sectors (Security, Financial Services, and Commerce Content) have average daily price changes well in excess of 3%.

*Revenues:* Total revenues for the EC universe were $11.4 billion in 1997. This represents a very healthy 24% increase in total revenues from 1996.

**Table 1.5**  Initial Public Offerings in the Electronic Commerce
Industry: 1/96–6/98

| Company | Ticker | Sector | IPO date | IPO price | Current price | % Δ |
|---|---|---|---|---|---|---|
| Raptor | RAPT | Security | 2/7/96 | 15.00 | 15.00 | 0% |
| CyberCash | CYCH | Electronic Payments | 2/15/96 | 17.00 | 12.19 | −28% |
| Ultradata Corp. | ULTD | Financial Services | 2/16/96 | 10.00 | 5.25 | −48% |
| Cylink | CYLK | Security | 2/16/96 | 15.00 | 12.00 | −20% |
| Sterling Commerce | SE | Business Commerce | 3/8/96 | 24.00 | 48.50 | 102% |
| Paymentech | PTI | Electronic Payments | 3/22/96 | 21.00 | 20.56 | −2% |
| Axent Technologies | AXNT | Security | 4/24/96 | 14.00 | 30.36 | 117% |
| Edify | EDFY | Financial Services | 5/3/96 | 15.00 | 10.13 | −32% |
| Security First | SFNB | Financial Services | 5/23/96 | 20.00 | 14.94 | −25% |
| Open Market | OMKT | Business Commerce | 5/23/96 | 18.00 | 18.88 | 5% |
| Broadvision | BVSN | Business Commerce | 6/21/96 | 7.00 | 23.88 | 241% |
| Checkpoint | CHKPF | Security | 6/28/96 | 14.00 | 32.75 | 134% |
| National Process | NAP | Electronic Payments | 8/9/96 | 16.50 | 10.69 | −35% |
| Connect Inc. | CNKT | Business Commerce | 8/15/96 | 11.00 | 2.06 | −81% |
| E*Trade | EGRP | Commerce Content | 8/16/96 | 10.50 | 22.94 | 118% |
| Trusted Info. Sys. | TISX | Security | 10/10/96 | 13.00 | 21.50 | 65% |
| V-One | VONE | Security | 10/24/96 | 5.00 | 3.63 | −27% |
| First Virtual | FVHI | Electronic Payments | 12/13/96 | 9.00 | 3.06 | −66% |
| Ameritrade | AMTD | Commerce Content | 3/3/97 | 15.00 | 27.00 | 80% |
| On-Sale Inc. | ONSL | Commerce Content | 4/17/97 | 8.00 | 24.75 | 209% |
| Amazon.com Inc. | AMNZ | Commerce Content | 5/15/97 | 9.00 | 99.75 | 1008% |
| Peapod | PPOD | Commerce Content | 6/11/97 | 16.00 | 6.00 | −63% |
| Net B@ank | NTBK | Commerce Content | 7/29/97 | 12.00 | 29.50 | 146% |
| N2K | NTKI | Commerce Content | 10/17/97 | 19.00 | 19.63 | 3% |
| Preview Travel | PVTL | Commerce Content | 11/20/97 | 11.00 | 34.38 | 213% |
| Versign | VRSN | Security | 1/30/98 | 14.00 | 37.38 | 167% |
| CD Now | CDNW | Commerce Content | 2/10/98 | 16.00 | 20.13 | 26% |
| Internet Security Sys. | ISSX | Security | 3/24/98 | 22.00 | 37.63 | 71% |

SOURCE: Company financial reports

Revenue growth in smaller sectors was even more impressive with
Security Sector revenues growing 120% and Commerce Content Sector
revenues growing 202%.

*Earnings:* Earnings fell from $430 million in 1996 to a loss of $26 million
in 1997, or over 100%. There are two main causes for this negative
growth. First, many of the firms that went public in 1996 and 1997 were
still generating substantial losses at the time they went public, and second, several firms had substantial one-time charges in 1997, including
First Data (#) and Cylink.

*Valuations:* Collectively, the EC universe is valued at 5.0 times 1997 revenues and 47 times 1998 estimated earnings. This is 70% higher than the
S&P's estimated 1998 P/E of 27.6. While valuations cooled off dramatically in 1996 and 1997, they have picked back up in early 1998.

# Risks

With such impressive valuations, also come substantial risks. While later chapters will discuss the specific risks confronting each sector in detail, there are a few industry-wide risks which deserve their own special treatment upfront.

## Slowdown in Internet Growth Rates

It almost goes without saying, but EC industry valuations are highly dependent on the continued growth and development of the Internet. Any significant slowdown in the growth of the Internet relative to current expectations would have a dramatic and wide-ranging impact on industry valuations. While all EC firms would suffer from a slowdown, it is likely that well-established payment processors, such as First Data and First USA, would be able to weather such a storm with minimal damage due to their current low exposure to the Internet.

## Security "Meltdowns"

The fact that the next two chapters of this report are dedicated to the issue of security belies the issue's tremendous importance to the success of EC. There are numerous potential security "events" that could have a chilling effect on the entire EC industry, including:

- A leading EC Internet site is broken into and its business operations are disrupted;
- A major bank or brokerage is broken into via the Internet and significant customer funds are stolen; or
- Methods to easily "break" encryption algorithms are developed.

**Table 1.6**  Financial Profile of the Five EC Sectors

| Sector | # of firms | 1997 revs ($MMs) | Revenue growth | Market cap (BN) | Cap/Sales |
|---|---|---|---|---|---|
| Security | 12 | $1,034 | 120% | $10.4 | 10.0 |
| Electronic Payments | 12 | 8 | 11 | 24.1 | 3.2 |
| Financial Services | 7 | 754 | 19 | 4.3 | 5.1 |
| Business Commerce | 9 | 457 | 36 | 7.1 | 10.9 |
| Commerce Content | 4 | 156 | 202 | 8.0 | 13.5 |
| Total | 46 | $10,214 | 21% | $38.8 | 3.8 |

SOURCE:  Company financial reports

While we believe that the basic technology is sound, investors should be prepared to weather several security "scares" over the next few years as confidence in the system is momentarily shaken.

### Beware the Elephants!

Microsoft's market capitalization alone is almost four times that of the entire EC industry. Other major players, such as IBM and Oracle, are no slouches either. These companies are like elephants: they go where they like, do what they please, and anything in their way gets flattened. Investors in the EC industry should keep careful track of the elephants and avoid any companies that appear to be in their immediate paths.

### One Last "Minor" Point . . .

It is incumbent on us to point out that like most high-growth stocks, when bad news hits, EC stocks don't correct, they "blow up." Price declines of over 50% in a single day are not unheard of. *Investing in the EC industry is a high-risk proposition, especially at this early and rather immature stage. Investors uncomfortable with such risks may want to avoid this sector in the short term.*

## Conclusion

With the Internet highly likely to triple or quadruple in size over the next five years and with technology costs continuing to fall while functionality improves exponentially, the EC industry appears poised for explosive growth over the next few years. Indeed, the industry's high valuation levels indicate that many investors share this belief. The challenge for the *industry* is to execute against the opportunity without exposing itself to major security risks or needlessly antagonizing the "elephants." The challenge for the *investor* is to identify those companies focused on the key success factors that will position firms for long-term growth and profitability within their sector.

# 2

# An Introduction to Electronic Commerce Security

*This chapter provides some basic background on the key security technologies underpinning the EC industry. Readers familiar with public key encryption, digital signatures, digital certificates, and certificate authorities will want to skip this chapter and go straight to Chapter 3. Readers who are unfamiliar with these technologies or who want to brush up on their knowledge should read on.*

In poll after poll, both businesses and consumers cite security as the #1 inhibitor to the use of Electronic Commerce. Given the high profile of security, we thought it might make sense to provide a quick introduction to the technologies that are being used to help solve the security problems facing the EC industry.

Ironically, many of the security problems facing the EC industry can be traced back to some of the Internet's most "useful" and "advanced" features. The two specific features of the Internet that are causing the most problems are:

1. *Routed Infrastructure:* Messages on the Internet are passed from network to network until they reach their intended destination. This "routing" process reduces communication costs by limiting the total number of network connections needed. However, during the routing process, the contents of a message are typically exposed to a number of intermediary networks. In the absence of security precautions, it is possible for the intermediary networks to observe, record, and even alter messages as they pass through. In addition, the very nature of the routed infra-

structure dictates that each network has access to every other network. This creates the potential for a given network to not only examine the messages passing through it, but to also examine the contents (files and databases) residing on the other networks.

2. *Open Standards and Protocols:* Open standards and protocols ensure that messages can be transported by and interpreted on widely disparate hardware and software platforms. For example, the Simple Mail Transport Protocol (SMTP) enables any properly formatted e-mail message to be read by any SMTP capable e-mail software. Unfortunately, the "open" nature of these standards and protocols also makes it possible for third parties to make messages appear to have originated from one location when they have in fact originated from another. Using knowledge of the SMTP standard, it is possible to change the "From" field on an Internet e-mail message to indicate that the message came from someone other than the actual sender. Thus without some type of security system in place, it is impossible for Internet users to be 100% confident that a message is not a forgery.

These are very serious security problems. They not only expose sensitive information to prying eyes, but they also make it possible for that information to be altered and the identity of its author to be forged, all without the knowledge of the recipient or sender. This is not exactly an ideal business environment and it is, therefore, no wonder why both businesses and consumers alike are so apprehensive about using the Internet for Electronic Commerce.

Fortunately, the EC industry is well aware of these problems and has been working diligently to overcome them. In order to meet the goal of greater security while still maintaining the Internet's universal and spontaneous nature, the industry has been focused on delivering security solutions that ensure:

| | |
|---|---|
| *Privacy:* | Ensuring that transactions remain private even when handled by intermediary networks. |
| *Spontaneity:* | Enabling two parties to spontaneously but securely conduct Electronic Commerce. |
| *Trust:* | Providing assurances that a specific transaction has not been tampered with since it was sent and came from the party who appears to have sent it. |

The road to meeting these three requirements has been a long and winding one with a variety of technologies being used to get the industry a step closer to a vision of secure, unfettered EC.

## Rules-Based Security: A Good Start

The first technology deployed in an attempt to meet these requirements consisted of so-called "rules-based" security. Rules-based security technology uses a set of rules to determine who gets access to a particular network and what service they can use once they gain access.

Using this security technology, companies can prevent unauthorized parties from entering their network and thereby gaining access to the company's private files and databases. To implement rules-based security, companies install so-called "firewalls." Firewalls are actually specialized software programs that can be programmed with a set of rules by the company. Firewalls increase security by limiting and controlling *access* to a company's *internal* network.

While rules-based security is better than no security at all, it has many limitations. For example, because rules-based security often results in blanket rules such as "keep all strangers out of this company's network," it can often run counter to the need for spontaneity in Electronic Commerce. In addition, rules-based security does not address concerns over privacy and trust as it focuses solely on *access* and not the content of a message or its sender's identity.

## Encryption: The Next Level

Recognizing the limitations of rules-based security, the EC industry has instead focused much of its efforts on the development and deployment of encryption technology. Encryption technology essentially scrambles a message before it is transported and then de-scrambles the message after it is received. This process ensures that the message remains private no matter who has access to it while it is in transit.

At its heart, encryption simply involves changing the patterns by which information is arranged. For example, the word "buy" can be encrypted to "yrv" by simply moving each letter of the word back three places in the alphabet. An entire message could be written in this pattern and only those people who knew the "key," that is, to shift all the letters back three places, would be able to read it. Most early encryption schemes used the same key to "encode" each message. While this type of encryption scheme was easy to develop and administer it also had two severe weaknesses:

1. It was fairly easy for any reasonably intelligent and determined intermediary to figure out or "break" the key.

2. Once the key was broken, every message encrypted using that same key could then be read.

Indeed, during World War II, the Japanese and the German governments learned this lesson the hard way when the U.S. and Great Britain successfully discovered the key or encryption pattern for the Enigma encryption machines. Breaking just one key allowed the allies to "listen in" on hundreds of their adversaries' most sensitive communications.

### "One-Time" Encryption

The weaknesses of these "static" encryption schemes led to the development of "one-time" encryption technologies. These technologies used each key only one time to ensure that if any one key was broken, only a single message would be compromised.

While "one-time" encryption increased security by limiting the amount of damage that could be done by breaking a single key, it did not make it any more difficult to break a given key. The solution to this problem was to use complex mathematical formulas to generate encryption keys. These large, complex, and seemingly random keys made it extremely difficult for adversaries to guess the correct key.

### Symmetric Encryption

Today, the most widely deployed encryption systems use a single, mathematically generated, one-time encryption key to encrypt messages. These systems are often called symmetric or single key systems. They are called "single key" encryption systems because the same key is used to both encrypt and decrypt the message.

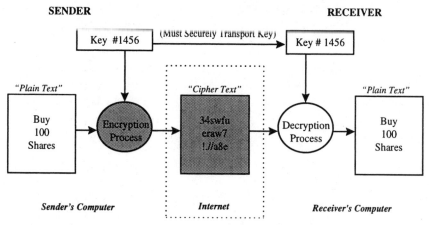

**Figure 2.1** Symmetric Key Encryption Process Flow

## Data Encryption Standard

The best-known single key encryption system is the Data Encryption Standard (DES). DES was developed by IBM in the mid-1970s and was adopted by the U.S. government as its official encryption standard in 1977. Since that time, DES has been widely deployed and is used extensively throughout the public and private sectors. DES's wide adoption is due to some basic strengths:

*Fast Operation:* DES uses relatively simple mathematical calculations to encrypt and decrypt messages. These straightforward calculations make DES a very fast encryption algorithm. This speed makes DES an ideal algorithm for encrypting high-volume information streams such as financial transactions.

*High Security:* There is no known way to "break" DES other than repeatedly trying to guess the correct key. The process of guessing every possible key is known as a "brute force" attack. While "brute force" attacks are technically possible, they are usually prohibitively expensive (see the Sidebar on Key Lengths for more detail). That said, there have been successful brute force attacks against DES.[1] To thwart these attacks, a technique called "triple DES" was developed. Triple DES encrypts a message three times with three separate DES keys. It is believed that "triple DES" currently is, for all practical purposes, unbreakable.

That said, the government is currently working on a replacement for DES called the Advanced Encryption System or AES. AES will probably be adopted in 1998 when the DES standard comes up for recertification by the government.

## SIDEBAR: KEY LENGTH

### Key Length: How Long Does a Key Have to Be?

During almost every discussion of Internet security, someone will undoubtedly bring up the subject of key lengths. Key lengths are important because the longer the key, the greater the number of possible keys. The greater the number of possible keys, the harder it is for an adversary to guess the correct key.

Given that most modern encryption algorithms cannot be broken by using a mathematical formula (at least that's the belief), simply trying to guess the key is often the only feasible attack.

---

[1] U.S. intelligence agencies are believed to have supercomputers dedicated to breaking DES keys. The first public break of DES occurred in mid-June 1997. See the *Wall Street Journal* 6/19/97. A2.

As we pointed out in our discussion of the Data Encryption Standard (DES), attempts to break a key by guessing are generally known as "brute force" or "exhaustive search" attacks. Anyone who has ever forgotten the combination to their briefcase or suitcase and then tried to open the case by trying every possible combination is familiar with the concept of a brute force attack. Most briefcases have 3 dials with 10 numbers each (0 through 9). This means that there are $10^3$ or 1,000 possible combinations to try.

In the world of computers, the equivalent of the briefcase dial is called a "bit." A bit has only two possible values, 0 and 1. So for a key X bits long, the total number of possible keys is simply $2^x$. For example a "2 bit key" has $2^2$ or 4 possible keys (0,0), (0,1), (1,0), (1,1).

Modern encryption algorithms use keys that are considerably longer than 2 bits. For example, DES uses 56 bit keys. This means that there are $2^{56}$ or roughly 72 quadrillion ($7.2 \times 10^{16}$) possible keys for any given DES message. It is important to note that increasing the key length by just one bit doubles the number of possible keys. So in the case of DES, increasing the bit size by just 1 bit from 56 to 57 increases the number of possible keys by 72 quadrillion to 144 quadrillion possible keys.

With so many keys, the only hope of ever breaking a DES message is to figure out a way to guess keys as fast as possible. This is where computers come in. Using existing computer technology, it is possible to create specialized, high-performance computers that can guess billions, even trillions of keys per second. In a highly publicized incident, a student at a French University did exactly this by linking together some of the university's computers and having them guess keys during their "free time." Using approximately $6 million worth of computer hardware, the student was able to break a single 40 bit key from Netscape's popular Internet browser in 30 days. A similar effort was organized in the United States to break a 56 bit DES key. That effort took five months and hundreds of separate computers.[2]

While these achievements might not be all that impressive, using a network of highly specialized "key guessing" computers, it is possible to reduce the time to break a 40 bit key to as little as .0002 seconds. The only problem is that this type of capability does not come cheap. In fact, it is estimated that building a computer capable of breaking a 40 bit key this fast would take a mere $300 million (see Table 2.1).

### So How Long Should a Key Be?

At first it might seem as though the natural answer to this question is "as long as possible." But, deciding on a key length is not so simple because it involves a series of trade-offs including:

**Value of Information vs. Cost of Acquisition:** It doesn't make sense to spend $300 million or for that matter $300,000 to steal a credit

[2] *Wall Street Journal* 6/19/97. A2.

**Table 2.1**   Cost and Time to Break DES Keys

| Type of attacker | Budget | Time to break key | |
|---|---|---|---|
| | | 40 bit key | 56 bit key |
| Pedestrian hacker | $400 | 5 Hours | 38 Years |
| Small business | $10,000 | 12 Minutes | 556 Days |
| Major corporation | $10 Million | 0.7 Seconds | 13 Hours |
| Intelligence agency | $300 Million | .0002 Seconds | 12 Seconds |

SOURCE: "Minimal Key Lengths for Symmetric Ciphers to Provide Adequate Commercial Security." Blaze et al. 1/96.

card number that has a maximum credit line of $3,000–$5,000. Generally speaking, the less valuable the information being protected, the smaller the key that can be used.

**Security vs. Speed:** The longer the key, the longer it takes to encrypt and decrypt the message. While most people would be happy to wait a couple of extra seconds for the additional peace of mind that comes with a longer key, many businesses cannot afford to wait that long. Take payment processors for example. They process thousands, sometimes millions, of payments a day. In this environment, every second counts and there may well be an incentive to reduce key length if it improves processing speeds.

**Shelf Life:** Information that only needs to be secured for a short amount of time does not need a long key. For example, dated information that will change the next day (and therefore be of little value to someone else) only needs a key long enough to ensure that it will remain secure until the following day. In contrast, information that needs to remain secure for long periods of time, such as contracts and company secrets, require keys that are long enough to not only withstand sustained attacks from existing computer technology, but to withstand attacks from future computers as well. Given that computing power continues to double every 18 months and will continue to do so for at least the next 7–10 years, selecting key lengths that are secure against future computing power is especially important. It is estimated that in order to keep a key secure for the next 20 years, at least 14 bits should be added to the key length.[3]

The bottom line is that for commercial information that needs to be kept secure over a long period (20 years) the current consensus is that it should be protected by a symmetric key of 75–90 bits in length. Public keys and certificates (which are discussed in greater detail later in the chapter) should be at least 128 bits while particularly important certificates should probably be over 1,000 bits long.

---

[3] Blaze et al. "Minimal Key Lengths for Symmetric Ciphers to Provide Adequate Commercial Security." January 1996.

## Is DES the Answer?

DES has a number of advantages including strong security, fast operation, and wide-spread acceptance. In fact, these attributes make DES an ideal solution to certain security problems such as securely storing information on a disk drive.

However, DES has two major problems which prevent it from fully addressing the security concerns of EC industry:

1. *DES lacks spontaneity.* Because it is a "single key system," DES requires that a copy of the key must be transported from the sender to the receiver. Not only does this requirement expose the key to possible discovery during transport, but it also requires people to coordinate their actions in advance so that they know which key to use for each message they receive.

2. *DES does not ensure trust.* While DES does a terrific job of ensuring privacy, it does not provide any guarantees about the integrity of the contents of the messages or the identity of its sender. Without these guarantees, it fails to address the trust concerns.

### Public Key Encryption

Luckily, there is another type of encryption system that has the potential to address both of these problems. Called an asymmetric or "two-key" system, this technology is based on "one-way" mathematical functions. One-way functions are very easy to compute in one direction, but very hard to compute in the opposite direction. By building trapdoors, or secret ways to easily reverse one-way functions, it is possible to create encryption systems that address the three major security concerns of the EC Industry: privacy, spontaneity, and trust.

Two-key encryption systems are more popularly known as "public key" systems. In public key systems, each party has a unique "key pair" consisting of a *private key,* which they must keep secret, and a *public key* which they make available as widely as possible. Each "key pair" is similar to a Social Security number or passport number in that every person has a unique key pair.

### SIDEBAR: PUBLIC KEY SYSTEMS: TAKE YOUR PICK

There are actually three different public key systems. These systems are often mentioned during discussions of public key systems so a quick discussion of them is warranted.

## RSA

The RSA algorithm was invented in 1977 and is named for its founders Ron Rivest, Adi Shamir, and Leonard Adleman. Today, RSA is arguably the most widely deployed public key algorithm and many people (mistakenly) use "public key system" and "RSA" interchangeably. Even so, given that RSA is indeed the dominant algorithm, when we explain how public key systems work in this chapter, we are actually describing how the RSA variant of public key systems works. RSA's security is based on the difficulty of factoring large prime numbers into their component parts. As such, any improvement in factoring theory could seriously weaken the security of RSA. RSA is patented and the patent is owned by RSA Inc., which is a division of Security Dynamics (#). RSA's patent expires in September 2000.

### Diffie-Hellman

The Diffie-Hellman algorithm was invented at Stanford in 1976 by Martin Hellman and Whitfield Diffie. The Diffie-Hellman algorithm differs from RSA in that each party uses its public and private keys to create a "shared" secret key. No shared keys are calculated in RSA. Diffie-Hellman is not used as widely as RSA, but it has found substantial use in specific industries such as financial services. Diffie-Hellman's security is based on difficulty of taking logs in finite fields, which mathematicians call "the discrete logarithm problem." Diffie-Hellman is also patented. The key patents were owned by Cylink Inc. (#@), but they expired in September of 1997. For years, RSA and Diffie-Hellman forces sparred in court over patent rights. It was not until early 1997 that they both decided to "let by-gones be by-gones" and cross-license each other's technology. While RSA and Diffie-Hellman use different mathematical algorithms, it is generally agreed by experts that there is little difference between the two when it comes to the two most critical factors: speed of operation and security.

### Elliptic Curve

Not as well-known as either RSA or Diffie-Hellman, elliptic curve encryption systems were first theorized by Victor Miller and Neal Koblitz less than 15 years ago. The elliptic curve system is based on the same discrete logarithm problem as Diffie-Hellman, but uses geometric rather than integer math for its calculations. The up-shot of this is that elliptic curve systems are actually considered to be both stronger and faster than both RSA and Diffie-Hellman. Stronger security means that elliptic curve keys can be shorter in length than RSA and Diffie-Hellman keys, yet still provide the same level of security. Proponents of elliptic curve claim that a 160 bit elliptic curve key has the same security as a 1024 bit RSA key. In addition to shorter keys, the mathematical operations required to solve elliptic curve equations are generally easier for computers to perform. As a result, proponents claim that elliptic curve systems can operate up to ten times as fast as equivalently secure RSA systems for certain encryption operations. As elliptic curve systems have not yet been widely deployed, it remains to be seen whether or not they will live up to their promise; but if they do, elliptic curve systems could well replace RSA and Diffie-Hellman algorithms, especially in transaction processing intense areas such as payment processing (see the Sidebar on SET in the next chapter). The basic elliptic curve algorithm is not patented, but several firms including Certicom and Cylink own patents for specific implementations of elliptic curve algorithms.

To send a secret message to someone in a "public key" system, the sender uses the recipient's *public key to encrypt* the message. The recipient then uses their *private key to decrypt* the message (see Figure 2.2).

From a mathematical perspective, the sender uses the public key to encrypt the message via a one-way function. The recipient uses the private key (or trapdoor) to decrypt the message. The security of public key systems is therefore highly dependent on the difficulty of figuring out the recipient's trapdoor key.

The most obvious advantage of a public key system over the symmetric systems, such as DES, is that *public key systems allow for both privacy and spontaneity at the same time.* Anyone can send a secure message to anyone else at any time, provided that they know the person's public key. Unlike single key systems, there is no need to exchange keys beforehand and coordinate which key is used for each message.

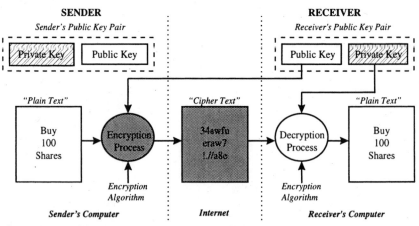

**Figure 2.2**  Public Key Encryption Process Flow

Based on these advantages alone, public key systems might appear to be the panacea the EC industry is looking for, but there are still a few problems:

*The same keys are used repeatedly.* Remember the lessons learned during World War II? Using the same key over and over again means that if one message is broken then all of the messages sent using the same key can be broken. Fortunately, this problem can be overcome in public key systems by simply increasing the size of the public key to point where even the most determined enemy would find it almost impossible to break.

*Longer keys take longer to process.* While longer keys may increase security, they also cause additional problems. Longer keys require more complex computations which means that public key messages generally take much longer to decrypt than symmetric key systems. This problem is especially acute in Electronic Commerce. For example, take First Data Corporation. First Data processed an average of 260 card transactions per second in 1996. If increasing the size of a public key were to add just 1/10 of 1 second to each transaction, it would increase the daily processing time required by 2.2 million seconds or 26 days!

In a novel twist, the solution to this problem is to use both symmetric key systems and public key systems together. In such a "dual use" scheme, the public key system is used to encrypt the message "envelope" as well as a symmetric key. The symmetric system is used to encrypt the message. To read the message, the recipient uses the public key system to decrypt the envelope and then uses the attached symmetric key to decrypt the letter itself (see Figure 2.3).

Using both systems enables users to maintain the privacy and spontaneity benefits of a public key system while enjoying the speed of symmetric systems.

### What About Trust?

Even with this clever work around, there remains one problem: trust. Sure no one but the recipient can read the message (privacy) and sure the message can be sent to anyone who makes their public key available (spontaneity), but how do recipients know that the message has not been tampered with or that the person who sent the message is really who they claim to be; that is, how do they know they can trust the message?

Surprisingly (and quite conveniently), public key technology also provides the solution to this problem. Specifically, two applications of public key technology, called digital signatures and digital certificates, provide the solution.

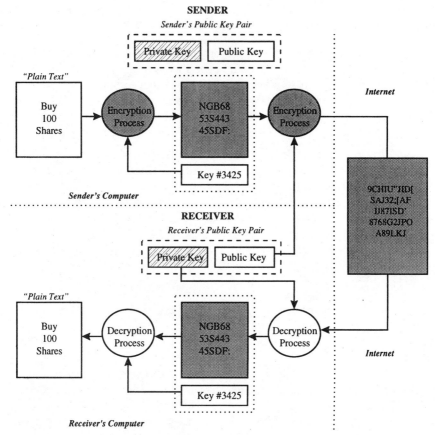

**Figure 2.3**  Dual Use Encryption Process Flow

## Digital Signatures

Digital signatures are just what they sound like. They are an electronic way to "sign" a message so that recipients can determine who exactly sent the message. As an added bonus, digital signatures can also be used to confirm that the contents of a message have not been changed since the message was signed.

How do digital signatures accomplish such magic? The process is actually pretty straightforward (see Figure 2.4). First, something called a hashing algorithm is used to create a condensed summary of a message, called a "hash."

The hash is then *encrypted by the sender with their own private key*. The encrypted hash is then attached to the message itself and the whole package is then encrypted with the recipient's public key. This process is anal-

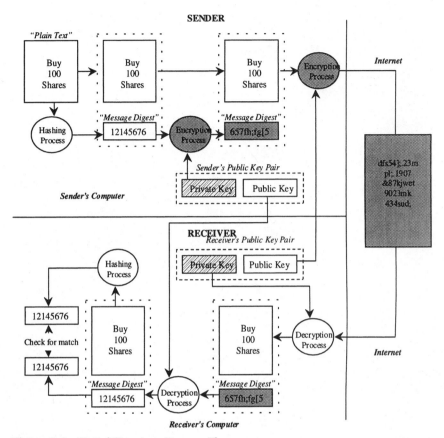

**Figure 2.4**  Digital Signature Process Flow

ogous to sending a letter in the real world. First you write the letter (or message in this case), then you sign it (attach a digital signature), and finally you put the signed letter into an envelope (you encrypt it).

When the recipient receives the message and the attached hash, they perform a three step process. First they decrypt the message itself with their own private key and then create a hash of the decrypted message. They then decrypt the hash that was attached to the message using the sender's public key. Finally, they compare the hash they created on their own with the hash they received from the sender. If two hashes match then the recipient knows:

1. *That the message has not been altered since it was "signed."* If the two hashes match that means that not one single piece of the message has changed since it was signed. Even the slightest alterations to a message, such as

adding a space or changing an upper case letter to a lower case letter, will change the hash and thus "invalidate" the signature.

2. *That the message was created by the same person who signed it.* The recipient used the sender's *public key* to decrypt the hash. Because each public key pair is unique, only the person with the proper private key could have created the hash.

Given these benefits, it's easy to see that in many ways digital signatures are actually far superior to written signatures:

**Much Tougher to Forge.** Any sixth grader worth his lunch money can probably produce a pretty good written facsimile of his mother's signature, but in the future the sixth graders of the world are going to need more than a steady hand if they want to get out of gym class. Digital signatures can't be mimicked or copied the way written signatures can and a computer can spot even the slightest fake in almost no time at all.

**No Wiggle Room.** Cryptographers like to say that digital signatures provide for "non-repudiation." This is a fancy way of saying that once someone digitally signs a document, it is next to impossible for them to claim that they didn't sign it or that the document was altered after they signed it. This means that with digital signatures in place, a lot of contract disputes will never get started and there would be very little "wiggle room" for people to back out of a deal once they "signed" it.

**Can "Sign" Just About Anything.** An art collector's worst fear is that he/she will purchase a "signed original" Monet only to discover that it is in fact a knockoff. With digital signatures, anything that can be digitized can be signed. Photos, artworks, software programs, they can all be digitally signed so that purchasers can be 100% sure that they are getting the real thing. On the flip side, digital signatures identifying not only who produced the item, but who purchased it, can be "hidden" within the item. This feature allows digital signatures to become the equivalent of watermarks and copyrights. With this feature in place authorities can trace copied software back to the original owner to either return the lost or stolen property or arrest the person for copyright violations.

**One Last Problem . . .**

There is one last problem though. Because digital signatures are solely based on the private key, if that private key is lost or stolen then the signature is itself lost or stolen. Once a key is lost or stolen, all of the added protections provided by modern encryption technology can actually be turned against someone. In an adversary's hands, a private key can be used to create perfect forgeries and to "perfectly" impersonate someone. Worse yet, if an adversary secretly copies a person's private key, the adversary might be able to impersonate that person without that person ever knowing it.

If this can happen, and it has happened, aren't we back at square one in a situation where no one can trust anyone? After all, an encrypted message that appears to be from a business partner or customer may have been sent by someone who has stolen their private key. How are we to know?

The answer to this question is Digital Certificates. Today the average person has lots of paper certificates. When we're born, one of the first things we get is a birth certificate. Soon after follows a social security card and thereafter many more certificates of all shapes and sizes (diplomas being some of the largest). In fact the average person carries 10–15 paper certificates in their wallet in the form of driver's licenses, credit cards, checks, etc.

## Digital Certificates

Digital certificates are simply the electronic version of paper certificates. They are pieces of identification in the form of electronic messages issued by third parties which vouch for a person's identity and affiliation with a particular state, company, or organization. While paper based certificates can be forged fairly easily (just ask any college student with a fake ID), digital certificates are much harder to forge because they are based on the

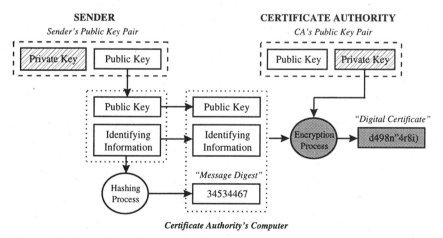

**Figure 2.5**  Digital Certificate Production

same public key technology that makes it almost impossible to read private messages or forge someone else's signature. Digital certificates contain the person's name, public key, and any other relevant information. This information is digitally signed by the third-party. Together, the message and the third party's digital signature make up the "certificate."

## Issuing Digital Certificates

Because certificates are really just specially formatted, digitally signed messages, just about anyone can issue them to anyone else. However, the idea behind a certificate is to have a *credible* third party vouch for a person's identity, so it doesn't do someone much good to have a digital certificate from "John Doe."

Therefore, the third parties that issue digital certificates tend to be very well-known entities, such as the government or major banks. The certificate issuer is known as the Certificate Authority or CA. Digital certificate authorities, just like their real world equivalents, require people to prove their identities before they issue a certificate. Some issuers require more proof than others. For example, to get a passport from the government, you typically need a lot of formal documentation such as a birth certificate, while to get a library card you usually only need to fill out an application.

The same goes for digital certificates. To get a digital certificate from the government you will probably have to go to a government office (wait in line no doubt), fill out all sorts of forms, and provide all sorts of I.D., and only then will the digital certificate be issued to you. The reward for suffering through this process will be that just about anyone will feel comfortable accepting your government-issued digital certificate as proof positive of your identity. On the flip side, a library-issued digital certificate might be good for on-line browsing of the library's catalog, but don't expect anyone else to honor the certificate.

Today there are actually very few active certificate authorities, but many organizations, including most banks, the U.S. Postal Service, and hundreds of companies, have big plans for issuing their own certificates. Chances are that everyone will still have 10–15 separate digital certificates (if not more). The only difference is that they will be stored in a virtual wallet instead of a real one.

## Using Digital Certificates

To use a digital certificate, a person simply attaches a copy of a certificate to their message and then sends the message along with the attached certificate to the recipient. The recipient decrypts the message in the manner we discussed earlier in Figure 2.2. The recipient then takes the attached certificate and verifies the digital signature of the third party, just as they would any digital signature (see Figure 2.6). With the third-party's signature validated, the recipient then compares the name and public key in the digital certificate to the name and public key in the original message. If the two match then the recipient knows that, according to the certificate authority, the public key:

1. belongs to the person who sent the message.

2. has not been stolen or lost.

While this may seem like a complex process, it's really not all that different from what happens in the physical world today. Take writing a check for example. Today, most stores require consumers to present two forms of valid I.D. when they write checks, usually a driver's license and a major credit card. These two extra certificates (the driver's license and

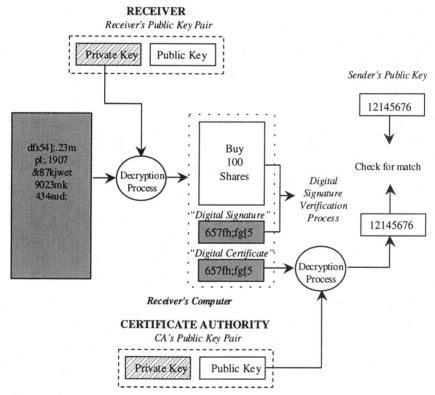

**Figure 2.6** Digital Certificate Verification

the credit card) are being used to validate the message (the check). Often the store will check the signature on the certificates against the signature on the check to make absolutely sure that the check is not being forged.

## Revoking Certificates

While it's easy to see how this process validates a legitimate person with a valid certificate, what if the certificate is lost? Can't someone still pass themselves off as someone else, but with even greater ease?

In the physical world this a big problem. Anyone who has ever lost their wallet has spent a lot of time "revoking certificates" in the form of calling credit card companies and government agencies to let them know that the "certificates" have been lost. In response, these agencies revoke or cancel the certificates. Credit card companies cancel the credit card accounts, while state governments add lost licenses to their databases.

One big advantage of digital certificates is that *if you lose the certificate, it's no big deal;* the certifying authority can just issue you a new certificate. Unlike the physical world where a thief can use a stolen credit card without much trouble, in the digital world, without the private key or password associated with that certificate, a stolen certificate is useless.

However, *if you lose your private key, the consequences can be quite serious.* Now someone cannot only impersonate you, but they will have a note from a reputable third party vouching for their legitimacy.

When people lose their private key, they must contact all of their certificate authorities who have issued certificates for that key, just as people do today when they lose their wallet. The certificate authorities in turn then add the compromised certificate to a Certificate Revocation List, or CRL. The CRL is simply a list of all the certificates that are no longer considered valid by the certificate authority. This list not only includes certificates of people who have lost their private key, but also includes people who have had their keys revoked for other reasons, such as moving, canceling their account, or dying.

In order for this whole process to work, there has to be a step inserted into the process in which the recipient checks a certificate authority's CRL to see if the certificate in question has been revoked or not.

While digital certificates are a great way to once and for all solve the "trust" problem, they do have a few drawbacks.

1. *They lack portability.* Typically digital certificates are stored on a person's computer hard drive. If the person uses another computer, these certificates will not be available. It's sort of the real world equivalent of having one's wallet permanently attached to one pair of pants. Computer types refer to this problem as "a lack of portability." The good news is

that this may prove to be a temporary problem as many companies are developing a number of ways to make certificates portable, mostly by putting certificates onto so-called "smart cards" (which are discussed in greater detail in Chapter 4).

2. *They wear out.* Just as paper and plastic certificates wear out, digital certificates also wear out. The difference is that digital certificates wear out because as time passes and computers get more powerful, digital certificates become less secure due to increases in computing power. The solution to this problem is to issue certificates with as long a key as possible, but this has certain trade-offs that may prove unacceptable (see "Key Length: How Long Does a Key Have to Be?" [p. 27]).

3. *They get lost and keys get compromised.* Just as people lose their credit cards, they will lose certificates and they will lose private keys. This will require a large and costly administrative structure to revoke keys, issue new certificates, and replace "worn-out certificates."

Despite these drawbacks, when properly implemented and administered, digital certificates provide all parties with the confidence they need to fully trust the communications they are receiving from one another. In doing so, they provide the final piece of the EC security puzzle: trust.

*So taken together, public key encryption, digital signatures, and digital certificates enable private, spontaneous, and trustworthy Internet transactions, all of which just happen to be the key prerequisites for Electronic Commerce.*

## Risks

Unfortunately, no security system is perfect, and despite all of this great technology, there are still some major potential security risks for Electronic Commerce that, at least for right now, no one can do anything about. These risks include:

*Someone could lose their private key.* This is not so much a risk as it is a certainty. Just as people lose their car keys, they can be expected to lose or inadvertently reveal their private key. Every time someone compromises their key, there's a decent chance that someone else will use it to do something criminal. This is no different than what happens in the physical world today, but given the heightened sensitivity of people with regards to EC security, a particularly high-profile theft may slow the adoption of EC.

*Someone could "break" the key of an important certificate authority.* There is always the possibility that someone could steal or otherwise obtain the secret key of a major certificate authority, such as the government, VISA, or MasterCard, even though extraordinary precautions are taken to prevent this from happening. While this would not be a catastrophic event, if it happened fairly soon it could stunt the growth of EC by making a lot of people very nervous about conducting their business over the Internet.

*Someone could "break" public key encryption.* It is not an understatement to say that this would be a catastrophe. There is always the possibility that advances in mathematical theory could make it much easier to break public key systems. The good news is that many of the best minds in the world have been spending the last 20 years and billions of dollars trying to do this and have yet to make much progress. Still, there is always the risk that someone will make an amazing mathematical discovery and the entire public key infrastructure could crumble overnight. While today that wouldn't be a huge deal, ten years from now it could be the equivalent of Black Monday for the EC industry. All would not be lost, however, as we could switch over to another "non-broken" public key algorithm, or at the very worst, we could go back to using only symmetric systems, but the transition would be quite painful and very uncomfortable for a lot of companies.

## Conclusion

Despite the best attempts of everyone involved, the EC industry will never be 100% safe. However, there is a very real chance that when the entire security infrastructure is put into place, the EC environment may well be more secure than our existing modes of commerce. For example, today's system of paper certificates and written signatures allows over $1 billion in credit card fraud and $800 million in check fraud to occur each year. All of the technologies described in this chapter will make it much more difficult for check frauds, credit card thieves, forgers, and the like to practice their trade. That's not to say that these new security technologies will eliminate crime, but they may very well take a big bite out of it while, at the same time, making private, spontaneous, and trustworthy Electronic Commerce a viable reality.

# 3

# The Security Sector:
# Too Important
# for Its Own Good?

Where there is no security, there is often little, if any, commerce. Fear, uncertainty, and the potential for bodily harm are generally not the ingredients for a robust market. That's not to say that commerce cannot continue in the face of little or even no security; indeed, there are plenty of examples of quick-witted merchants making fortunes during wars, uprisings, and insurrections. However, the transaction costs of doing business in such an insecure environment are often so high that there is little, if any, market growth and often wholesale economic decline.

The EC industry is well aware of the crucial role that security must play in its development. In evidence of this awareness, an entire Security Sector has sprung up within the EC industry. This sector itself is based on the fundamental technologies outlined in Chapter 2 and is focused on providing businesses and consumers with the tools, products, and services that they need to create a secure environment for EC.

We should note that in order to successfully conduct EC, the Security Sector must not only secure information as it travels over the Internet, but it must also secure the private networks that store information before and after it is transmitted. Indeed, in the spirit of "first things first," most firms in the Security Sector are currently more focused on securing private company networks than they are on securing the communications over the Internet. This focus will balance out over time as EC becomes more prominent, but for now it is important to note that the Security Sector (quite rightfully) is spending the majority of its time securing private networks.

## Structure

Moving at a lightning-fast pace, the Security Sector is building a complex infrastructure "on the fly" in an effort to secure both private networks and the messages sent between them. This infrastructure can appear bewildering at first as it contains numerous interconnected pieces that all play a specific role (see Figure 3.1). Using Figure 3.1 as a guide, the first part of this chapter will explore and explain the different pieces of the infrastructure and just what role each plays in helping to create a secure infrastructure.

Later on in the "Trends" section of this chapter, we will explore how industry forces are driving a simplification of the security structure and fusing together the disparate pieces into just a few separate "systems," but before we do that, a detailed explanation of the current structure is warranted, starting with one of the most well-known pieces of the network security infrastructure, firewalls.


## Firewalls

Firewalls use "rules-based" security (i.e., a set of rules) to make decisions about what messages should be let into and out of a network. Firewalls have traditionally focused on a procedure called "packet filtering." Every piece of information that travels across the Internet is first divided up into hundreds, if not thousands, of packets. These packets are then "routed" across the Internet from network to network until they reach their final destination. Each packet contains information on where it came from and where it is going. "Packet filtering" involves examining each packet that is attempting to enter a network and then determining whether or not that packet should be granted access. Firewalls use rules such as, "Don't let any packet from Internet Address X enter the network," to determine which packets to let in and which packets not to. Using packet filtering, firms cannot only deny access to packets from a specific Internet address, but they can also block outbound access to Internet addresses such as non-work-related World Wide Web (WWW) sites.

A relatively busy firewall must be able to scan thousands, even millions of packets per second. Because firewalls must process packets quickly, they cannot spend a lot of time trying to analyze each packet, so the rules must be fairly simplistic and straightforward.

Just a short time ago, most firewalls were actually separate computers with their own specialized software. Firewalls were typically located just behind a company's Internet routers and/or servers. Today, an increasing number of firewalls are actually just software programs or pieces of software programs that are tightly integrated with system software residing on either the Internet server or the router.

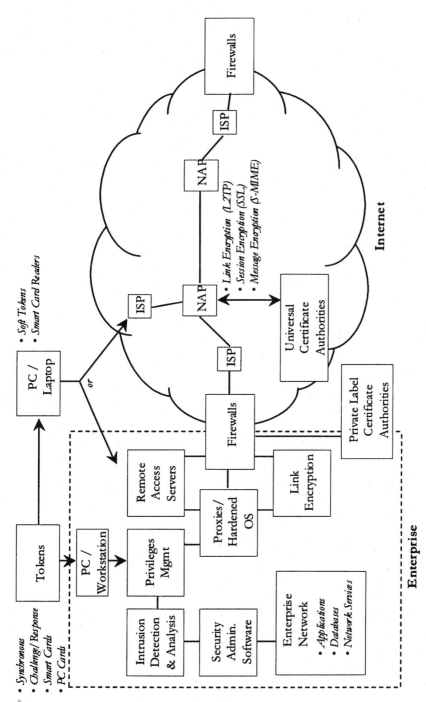

**Figure 3.1** Security Sector: Current Day Structure  Source: Piper Jaffray

While many firewalls were initially deployed in an effort to keep *all* Internet traffic out of a company's internal network, the Internet's increasing importance as a channel for business and commerce has forced firewalls to become much more selective and elegant in the ways in which they "filter" access to a network. Firewalls are increasingly using advanced statistical processes and historical experience to make more intelligent decisions about what packets should be granted access. For example, by examining the patterns of packets created when unauthorized parties are attempting to gain access, firewalls can learn the pattern and be able to recognize it the next time the activity is in progress. Firewall vendors have come up with a variety of terms such as "stateful inspection" and "type enforcement" to describe these advanced techniques.[1]

Firewall manufacturers are also trying to increase their overall value by incorporating previously stand-alone products and services, such as proxy servers and link encryptors, into their core product offering. For the purposes of explaining the different areas of the Security Sector, we have decided to keep these products and services separate, but the reality is that these three products are all rapidly coalescing into a single product (see the "Trends" section of this chapter).

**Proxy Servers**

Also known as "application proxies" or "guards," proxy servers are used to control communications between internal applications and outside networks. They accomplish this control by limiting the types of internal applications that are available via the Internet and by "masking" the structure of the network so that Internet users cannot determine the location of specific computers or hosts on a company's internal network. Proxy servers allow a company to safely let their applications and databases interact with the outside world, but in a carefully controlled manner that prevents outside users from performing any unauthorized activities.

Proxy servers provide an extra layer of security above and beyond packet filtering. Most firewall vendors have embedded proxy server capabilities into their products, and it appears as though these two pieces of the security infrastructure are rapidly merging together. However, for sites with particularly sensitive security concerns, it is generally agreed that separate proxy servers are required.

---

[1] Checkpoint Systems lays claim to "stateful inspection" technology while Secure Computing (#@) developed its "type enforcement" technology. Both of these advanced techniques actually include elements of application proxies in them as well.

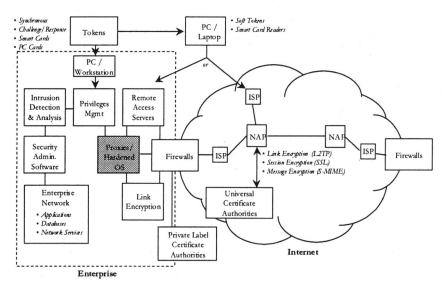

**Figure 3.2**

## Link Encryptors

Link encryptors secure all of the communications traffic traveling between two points by encrypting all information before it leaves Point A and decrypting it after it reaches Point B. Link encryptors create the equivalent of a "concrete tunnel" that protects all of the communications "traffic" that passes between two points. To create one of these "tunnels," a business or organization simply places link encryptors on either end of a network segment.

Link encryptors have two important characteristics: they encrypt all traffic traveling between two points, not just specific messages; and they operate "on the fly," that is, they encrypt and decrypt traffic as soon as they receive it. In a busy "tunnel," the link encryptor must encrypt and decrypt hundreds, if not thousands, of pieces of information a second. In order to avoid becoming a bottleneck and thereby creating the computer network equivalent of a "traffic jam," link encryptors must, therefore, be as fast as possible.

While it's possible to perform all of the necessary encryption and decryption routines in software, for high-speed communication links with heavy traffic loads, it is still necessary to conduct these activities on specialized hardware devices with custom-designed Application Specific Integrated Circuits (ASICs).

Cable TV boxes are good examples of a very primitive link encryptor. If you've ever seen all those channels on cable TV that appear to be nothing

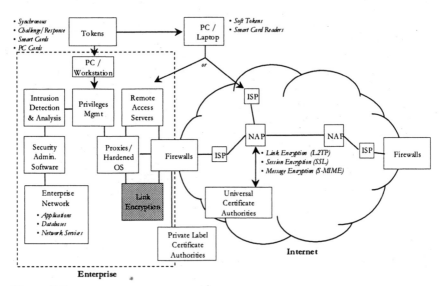

**Figure 3.3**

more than a jumble of scrambled lines, then you've seen a very basic form of link encryption in action.

Recently, many link encryption manufacturers have begun to offer "packet-" and "cell-" level encryptors. Rather than building a "tunnel" between two points, packet and cell encryptors secure communications traffic by essentially providing armor plating to all of the different "cars" or packets/cells in a "traffic" flow.

Packet/cell-based encryption is different from link encryption in that the individual packets can be mixed in with other non-encrypted packets as they travel from Point A to Point B. This increases the flexibility of link encryption solutions and makes them more efficient for companies which want to secure specific communication streams but still enjoy the cost and technological advantages of packet-based transmissions. Significant packet-based transmission standards include X.25, Frame Relay, and TCP/IP (the key packet protocol that underlies the Internet). Cell-based encryption products secure Asynchronous Transfer Mode (ATM) transmissions. ATM is a very high-speed, cell-based switching standard popular for transporting multiple data types over network backbones.

As CPU speeds increase, it will be possible to do more and more link encryption using software rather than hardware. This shift will transform low-end link encryptors from hardware devices into software programs and will make them available to a larger portion of the market.

## Hardened Operating Systems

Hardened operating systems are versions of operating systems that have been specially modified in order to eliminate potential security "holes" or problems. The process of eliminating any potential security holes is called "hardening" the operating system. Most hardened operating systems are variants of the Unix operating system. Many variants of the Unix operating system have been extensively modified to improve performance and add features. Security was often not the foremost consideration when these changes were being made as many of the Unix systems were being optimized to perform dedicated tasks within closed networks. With the growth of the Internet, enhanced security became an important focus of Unix development.

Hardened operating systems pay particular attention to limiting "root" or "super user" access to Unix machines. Root access typically allows someone to perform many basic administrative functions on a Unix computer, including setting security privileges. As a result of its importance, gaining "root access" is typically one of the main goals of network intruders. By making special modifications to Unix's security architecture and privileges, hardened operating systems attempt to eliminate the potential for non-authorized users to get root access.

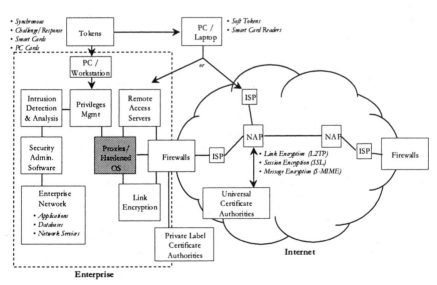

**Figure 3.4**

## Remote Access Servers

Remote access servers are composed of a dedicated computer, some software, and a group or "bank" of modems. While the computer and modems are typically provided by networking and modem companies, such as 3Com (COMS) and Ascend Communications (ASND), the Security Sector typically provides a few crucial pieces of software that are needed to help protect the servers from intrusion by unauthorized parties. The most common users of remote access servers are company employees who happen to be traveling or working from home and need to gain access to the company's network.

In general, remote access servers are very similar to firewalls. The main difference is simply that remote access servers interface with the telephone system, whereas firewalls interface with the Internet.

Initial remote access security software focuses on establishing a system for securely managing a system of user I.D.s and passwords. These kinds of identification systems were widely deployed and well understood by users. Unfortunately, they also had some major problems, including:

*Weak Security:* User I.D. and password schemes have an inherently low level of security for a variety of reasons. First, because user I.D.s are usually assigned according to a set convention and because many users choose non-random passwords, it is often fairly easy for an intruder to break into such a system. For example, many people choose the name or

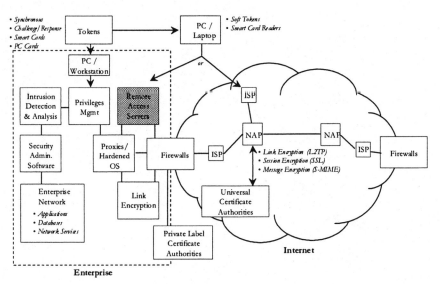

**Figure 3.5**

birth date of a close relative as their password. Intruders with knowledge of a user's family therefore have a decent chance of guessing the correct password. Second, because these systems typically use the same I.D. and password over a prolonged period of time, they provide a long "window of opportunity" for intruders to attempt to steal a password. Finally, because I.D.s and passwords are not physical objects, when they are stolen or otherwise compromised, there is often no immediate evidence of the theft. It is therefore possible for user I.D.s and passwords to be compromised for long periods of time without the user or network administrator ever realizing it. These types of undetected security violations can be some of the most serious.

*High Maintenance:* Administering a system of user I.D.s and passwords is often cumbersome and time consuming. When users forget or lose their passwords, which they often do, existing accounts must be canceled and new ones must be created. In addition, employee and customer turnover requires constant updates to the I.D. and password files. Finally, in order to keep the system secure, I.D.s and passwords must be periodically reissued, creating yet another administrative burden. While there are a number of software programs that help alleviate some of these burdens, administering a password and I.D. access scheme is still relatively time consuming.

Even though most organizations are well aware of the weaknesses of user I.D./password schemes, they continue to use them. They appear dirt cheap because most of the administration costs are hidden within normal support costs, and they are readily available. As a result, user I.D./password schemes are still supported by many vendors of remote access security software.

## Tokens

Tokens were developed in an attempt to address some of the shortcomings of the user I.D./password systems. Tokens are hardware or software devices that help establish the identity of a user and allow the user to securely gain access to a private network through the Internet, a remote access server, or a local area network (LAN). Many tokens are about the size of a credit card and look like very small calculators. Tokens have three main advantages over user I.D./password systems:

1. *Dynamic Random Password Generation:* One of the key advantages of tokens is that they generate dynamic or changing passwords. By switching to a system of "one-time" passwords, tokens dramatically increase security and decrease administrative burdens. Security is increased because passwords are constantly changing. This dramatically shortens,

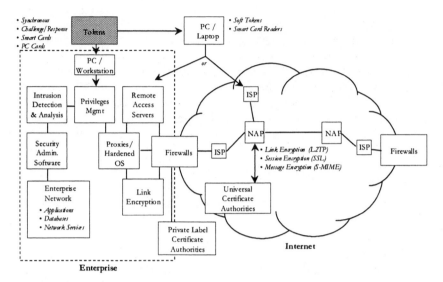

**Figure 3.6**

and in some cases eliminates, the "window of opportunity" for intruders to steal valid passwords. Dynamic passwords also lower administrative burdens by eliminating the need for users to remember their passwords or for administrators to keep a password file.

2. *Theft Indication:* Because many tokens can be seen and observed by users, it is fairly easy for them to determine when they have been lost. Just as when you lose your ATM card, you know you should call your bank; when someone loses their token, they know they should contact their security manager. The ability to easily recognize when the token has been lost greatly limits the risk of a security breach going undetected.

3. *Transferability:* Tokens can be easily transferred from one person to another. For example, if there are two shifts in a corporate treasury department, the clerk from the first shift can simply hand the token to a second shift clerk. This makes tokens ideal for environments where one or more persons need to share access to the same system at different times (of course, the companies that sell tokens would recommend that you buy two tokens instead of sharing one). The reverse of transferability is that if the second shift clerk quits, they cannot easily break into the system using the general department I.D. and password they learned, because with tokens the password is constantly changing.

Today, most tokens are used by companies to enable their employees to remotely access their corporate network. The portability of tokens (most fit in a wallet) makes them ideal for traveling, and their high level of security allows a company to offer remote access services without exposing its networks to unacceptable security risks. Even though remote access is the major driver of token use today, some companies also use tokens to secure access within their internal networks. In the EC industry, tokens are often used to give suppliers and customers access to a company's web site or internal network. Some financial institutions are also using tokens to provide a higher level of security to their electronic banking customers.

While at a high level most tokens operate in much the same way, there are actually quite a few different types of tokens that warrant a bit more discussion:

**Synchronous Tokens.**    Synchronous tokens work by generating the exact same password at the exact same time as a special computer server. To make this scheme work, when the tokens are first created they are synchronized with the computer server. This means two years later on Wednesday afternoon at 3:17 p.m. both the server and the token will be generating the same password. If someone attempts to get access to the computer network at that time, they will have to input the password currently displayed on the token. If the token and the server are "in synch," then the passwords should be the same and the user will be granted access. The most popular synchronous token is something called *SecureID* from a company called Security Dynamics (#). The *SecureID* token looks like a credit card-sized calculator except for the fact that it has no number pad and only a small LCD screen. Synchronous token passwords change every 45 to 60 seconds. While synchronous tokens are a fairly elegant and straightforward solution, they have a few major drawbacks:

1. *They can get out of synch.* Even computers can have a hard time staying exactly in synch over several years; just ask anyone with a digital watch. Slight differences in processor performance and power supply can gradually move the token and the server "out of synch." Once these two parties are out of synch, users are out of luck and they must typically replace their token with one that is "in synch."

2. *They can run out of gas.* Most tokens require their own power source to change passwords. These power sources are usually the equivalent of a watch battery, so they have a life of a few years. Some tokens have non-replaceable batteries, so if the battery runs out, then the token has to be replaced. This is probably not a big deal because within a few years a new and improved technology usually comes along, but customers do consider this when looking at tokens.

3. *They still present a window of opportunity.* While synchronous tokens greatly enhance security by dynamically changing passwords, they only do so every minute or so. During this "window of opportunity," it is possible for anyone who knows the correct password to gain access

to the system. Because of this, synchronous tokens are not considered to be true "one-time" passwords schemes (i.e., each password can be used only once). Theoretically, the lack of a true one-time structure allows intruders to monitor the password being sent and then use the same password to gain access to the system, all during the minute-long window of opportunity. This kind of attack is tough to pull off, but some organizations would rather not risk it.

4. *They aren't cheap.* While it's hard to find someone who will argue that tokens are not a major improvement over user I.D./password systems, it's pretty easy to find someone who will argue that tokens cost too much for the level of security they provide. To just deploy a token-based security system can cost upwards of $100/user. In organizations with tens of thousands of employees or customers, this cost can add up quickly.

**Challenge and Response Tokens.**    Challenge and response tokens work on the principle of "testing" someone by asking them a question to which they should know the answer. For example, when credit card companies ask for a cardholder's mother's maiden name, it's a form of challenge and response.

Challenge and response tokens use mathematical algorithms to generate the appropriate responses to specific challenges. To use a challenge and response token, the user first asks the network to generate a challenge. The network then generates the challenge and sends it to the user. The challenge is received by the user and entered into the token either via a keypad, a direct link to the computer, or some other method. The token then automatically generates a response which, in turn, is either automatically transmitted by the token back to the network or entered by the user and then sent to the network. Challenge and response tokens suffer from some of the same problems that synchronous tokens do: they cost a lot and they require new batteries every few years. However, challenge and response tokens do have some major advantages over synchronous tokens in that they generate true "one-time" passwords. This eliminates the "window of opportunity" to steal other people's passwords. Challenge and response tokens also do not have to be synchronized with the server so there's no risk of things getting "out of synch."

**Smart Cards.**    Smart cards are most often associated with the credit card industry and electronic cash, but they also make surprisingly good security tokens. Smart cards, also known as chip cards, look like credit cards with a small computer chip on them. The computer chip can store information on it. In the case of electronic cash, the computer stores currency serial numbers. In the case of security, smart cards typically store digital certificates and public key pairs. To use the smart card, users insert it into a smart card reader that is either part of or attached to a computer. The user is then authenticated using the same public key encryption sequences described in Chapter 2. The smart card has many advantages as a token for public key systems.

- *It's secure.* With smart cards, public key pairs and digital certificates spend most of their time in someone's wallet, not sitting on a computer network waiting for some hacker to steal them. This "off-line" storage capability increases security. In addition, smart cards store their information inside proprietary computer chips which are harder to access than file servers or PC disk drives.
- *It's portable.* While most tokens are portable, the smart card is exceptionally so. It is the same basic size and weight as a credit card, so most of us are already quite used to carrying one around.
- *It's simple.* The card itself is basically just a plastic card with a computer chip. It does not need a battery and it has no LCD screen or keypad to break.

This is not to say that smart cards don't have a few drawbacks. Chief among these drawbacks:

- *They require a "smart card reader."* One big advantage of both synchronous and challenge and response tokens is that they don't require any special equipment to work. Smart cards, on the other hand, require a specialized card reader. In order for smart cards to be used as remote access tokens, these smart card readers would have to be installed in either public telephones or laptop computers. Unfortunately, outside of Europe, there are very few smart card readers installed.[2]
- *The readers aren't cheap.* While in the future smart card readers may be a dime a dozen, today they are pretty expensive. When you include the cost of the smart card reader in the equation, smart cards are currently not much cheaper than other alternatives.

Until smart card readers are widely deployed in PCs, public telephones, and point-of-sale locations, it is likely that they will be largely limited to securing closed environments, such as office buildings and high-security Local Area Networks (LANs). Over the long term, smart cards face a "chicken or the egg" problem in that companies will probably not buy many smart cards until smart card readers are widely deployed, but smart card readers will not be widely deployed until manufacturers are sure that there is a market for using them.

One company that is trying to solve the "chicken or the egg" problem is Hewlett-Packard (#). Its recent acquisition of Verifone, the leading credit

---

[2] Not to mention that the smart card readers installed in European public telephone systems would have to be upgraded before they could handle identification and authentication duties.

card reader manufacturer and a producer of several smart card readers, indicates that HP is convinced that smart cards are going to be "the next big thing." With its experience in computer peripherals and its growing PC business, it is not hard to imagine HP selling smart card readers through its existing sales channels and embedding smart card readers into its own and other OEM's PCs.

**PCMCIA or PC Cards.**  PC cards are small hardware cards that fit into the expansion slots found on most laptop computers. PC cards are about as wide as a credit card, about 1.5 times as long, and about 1/8- to 1/4-inch thick. The purpose, functionality, and use of PC cards are very similar to that of smart cards. However, PC cards differ from smart cards in a few important ways:

1. *They are more capable* due to their ability to carry much more memory and processing power than smart cards. This means that PC cards can often be used to not only store public key pairs and certificates, but the card itself can perform the encryption and decryption process.

2. *They are already widely available.* Almost all laptops currently being sold have some type of PC card slot. The availability of these slots means that PC cards can be easily used by employees as a remote access token without the need for a separate card reader.

3. *They are, unfortunately, more expensive.* Along with the added functionality and size of PC cards comes a higher cost. Today, most PC card implementations are more expensive than challenge and response or synchronous tokens.

Until the price of PC card tokens comes down substantially, it is unlikely that they will be widely deployed as a security token. One interesting twist that appears to be gaining steam is combining PC cards and smart cards. The PC card serves as the smart card reader, while the smart card serves as the token.

### Software Tokens

Software tokens are simply software versions of their hardware equivalents. Software tokens can operate as synchronous, challenge and response, or smart card equivalents. They are used in much the same way as the other tokens only they are carried around in either a disk or within a personal computer. Software tokens have two main advantages over hardware tokens: they are very cheap to install, distribute, and maintain; and they are very flexible. They are cheap because the marginal cost of producing an additional software token is almost zero and the token can be easily distributed over a network. They are more flexible than hardware tokens in that they can be easily updated to incorporate new improvements in technology or changes to a company's security architecture. On the minus side, software tokens are not as portable as hardware tokens and they are not as secure. The lack of portability stems from the fact that they must be stored on a computer or diskette, both of which are more fragile and more difficult to carry around. The lack of security derives from the fact that software can be modified by hackers, whereas hardware cannot be easily modified once it has been created.

### Biometric Tokens

Fingerprints, voiceprints, retinal patterns, and our own DNA all uniquely identify each and every human being on this planet. Human beings, therefore, represent the ultimate development of token technology: we never forget ourselves; we are very difficult to copy; and when we run out of "power," computer security is no longer an issue for us (unless, of course, St. Peter is demanding some form of token these days).

Biometric tokens are already starting to make some in-roads. For example, the U.S. Immigration Service offers a service called *INSPass* that allows selected U.S. travelers to enter the country by using their hand as a biometric token. The *INSPass* service uses a machine to essentially take a picture of a passport holder's "handprint."[3] Every time the traveler is entering the U.S., he/she places his/her hand in the machine. The machine then takes a picture of the hand and compares it to the one in its records. If they match, the person is automatically admitted into the country.

Another application of biometric tokens is being tested by Chase Manhattan Bank in New York. At a few test bank branches, depositors record "voiceprints" and every time they make a withdrawal from their account, they verify their identity by speaking into a machine which compares the new voiceprint with the one in their records. If the pilot goes well, Chase could possibly even extend the "voiceprint" service to its ATM machines which would eliminate the need for depositors to memorize and protect their Personal Identification Number (PIN #).

Unfortunately, the differences between humans are fairly subtle from a computer's perspective. Recognizing a human being requires a computer to efficiently "interface" with a human, collect a large amount of data, and

---

[3] Handprints differ from fingerprints. Fingerprints are the unique two-dimensional patterns on a person's palm and fingers. Handprints are three-dimensional pictures of a person's hand. Handprint machines use sound waves, whereas fingerprint machines use optical scanners.

perform complex processing; whereas, recognizing a numeric token is a relative "lay-up" for computers. As a consequence, it usually costs relatively more money to implement a biometric token solution and once it is implemented, there is no guarantee that it will work 100% of the time.

The good news is that these limitations will gradually decrease as computing power increases and as biometric technology improves, but for the near future, the cost and capability limitations of biometric tokens are likely to limit them to very specific and/or very high-security applications.

### Certificate Authorities

Certificate Authorities (CAs) generate, issue, and maintain digital certificates. CAs also maintain Certificate Revocation Lists (CRLs) (see Chapter 2 for more detailed descriptions). Some CAs may also extend legal or financial guarantees to parties that use their certificates. There are three general types of CAs:

1. *Universal CAs:* Universal CAs issue digital certificates that are designed to be used as widely as possible. Today, there are very few universal CAs in operation that issue digital certificates. There are, however, a number of universal CAs that issue paper certificates, the best example of which is the government. The government issues paper certificates, in the form of passports, social security cards, and driver's licenses, that are universally accepted as proof of identification. While the government does not issue equivalent digital certificates today, it's a safe bet that it will do so. Indeed, the U.S. Postal Service has already announced a plan to do just that. While governments are probably the most natural candidates to be universal CAs, there are some other organizations, such as VISA and MasterCard, that already issue paper certificates (or, in this case, plastic certificates) and have plans to shortly begin issuing digital certificates (see the SET sidebar later in this chapter). Other firms, such as Verisign, are also attempting to establish themselves as a universal CA.

   The key to being a successful universal CA is *credibility*. The whole idea of a digital certificate is that a third party is lending its credibility to a transaction or message by vouching for someone else's identity. If the person or computer examining the certificate does not know the CA or does not have confidence in the CAs' ability to properly identify people, the digital certificate is worthless. For example, when traveling to another country, many paper certificates, such as drivers' licenses and social security cards, become worthless because people and organizations in other countries do not recognize the CAs that issued them. In contrast, passports are accepted around the world because most people are familiar with names and reputations of different countries. The same goes for digital certificates. If the computer or user is unfamiliar with, and does not have confidence in the CA, the digital certificate becomes worthless. While this is true for any certificate, it is especially true for universal CAs.

2. *Private Label CAs:* Private label CAs issue and manage "branded" certificates on behalf of other organizations. The complex and costly nature of the CA infrastructure creates a natural incentive for firms to outsource production and management of certificates to other firms that know what they are doing and have the scale to do it efficiently. In recognition of this, a number of firms are offering to act as private label CAs, including GTE's Cybertrust, Nortel Entrust, and Verisign.

3. *In-House CAs:* In-house CAs are staffed and operated by the organization that issues the certificates. For example, a large bank such as Citibank could decide to set up and run its own in-house CA. It could use the CA to not only issue certificates to its employees (so that they could securely access Citibank's global computer network), but it could also issue certificates to its customers, suppliers, and correspondent banks. For a bank as large and as distributed as Citibank, issuing its own certificates probably makes a lot of sense in the long term because its customer base is large enough to warrant the expense and controlling the issuance of the certificates gives Citibank the freedom to customize and improve its services quickly.

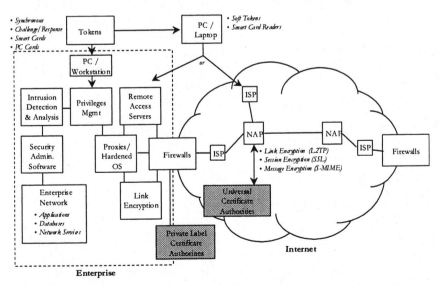

**Figure 3.7**

While it's possible for any firm or individual to act as their own CA, being a successful CA requires a number of strengths, including:

1. *Technical and operational expertise:* CAs must be able to efficiently and effectively operate a very complex technical infrastructure. As the Internet grows, many CAs will find themselves having to process hundreds, perhaps thousands, of certification requests a second. The potential for such high volumes means that CAs must also be able to grow or scale their operations quickly and efficiently in order to handle additional growth. They must also be able to achieve close to 100% availability. Being down for even a minute could expose the CA's customers to loss of revenue and could expose the CA to legal action.

2. *Rock-solid security:* CAs need to take extensive technical and operational security precautions in order to protect the viability of their services. Protecting a CA's private keys is of paramount concern. If the private keys of a CA are compromised, all of the certificates issued by the CA immediately become invalid and must be reissued. Protecting the key generation process is also a major concern. CAs must have elaborate precautions in place to prevent the issuance of fraudulent certificates by rogue employees or intruders. CAs must also protect the privacy of the information they are storing. Some people may not want the information contained in their certificates or information about the use of those certificates to become public knowledge. As a result, CAs must take precautions to guard this data with the same intensity that they guard their private keys. Finally, CAs must protect the availability of their services by protecting their premises from intrusion as well as their network connections from technical and physical attacks.

3. *Credibility:* We have already mentioned this once, but it's worth mentioning again. *Without credibility, the certificates from the CA are useless.* Credibility comes not only from the visibility of the CA, but also from its financial resources, operational record, and certificate issuance process.

CAs that can successfully deliver a well-run, secure, and credible service will look forward to a successful future. Those that can't will be looking for another line of work.

## Privileges Management Software

This is software that is used to micro-manage user-level access to specific network services, applications, and databases. Privileges management software determines whether or not a user can use a specific printer, run specific applications, or access specific data, such as the latest sales results. Some operating systems, such as *Windows NT* and *NetWare,* incorporate many features of privileges management into their basic operating

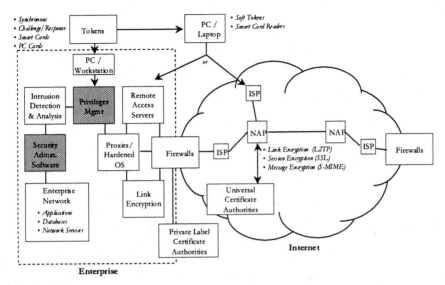

**Figure 3.8**

system, but true application-specific or file-specific privileges management is still the province of specialized "privileges management" software. This software must be closely integrated with remote access, firewall, and proxy software to ensure that once a user is permitted access to the network, the user's access is limited to appropriate areas.

As companies begin to allow suppliers, customers, and partners to directly access their networks, privileges management will become an increasingly important part of the Security Sector.

## Security Administration Software

Security Administration Software is software designed to enable network security managers to configure, monitor, and manage their company's entire security infrastructure from a central location.

It should be clear by this point in the discussion that the security infrastructure is rapidly increasing in size and complexity. As security networks become more extensive and more complex, the need for a cohesive way to centrally manage all of the different security resources within an enterprise is also increasing in importance. Security administration software's goal is to fill this need by making the successful management of this complex infrastructure as painless and straightforward as possible for network security managers.

However, before this software can work as intended, it must be able to communicate with all of the different security devices and software programs within a network's security infrastructure. To date, there are no standards in place to enable such "inter-operable" management of products and services, but the Security Sector is beginning to form these standards. In the meantime, vendors are rushing to offer a full range of cross-compatible products in a race to fulfill the promise of centralized, hassle-free network security management (see the "Trends" section of this chapter for further discussion of these points).

## Intrusion Detection and Analysis Software

Intrusion detection and analysis software alerts network security managers to potential security breaches and helps them analyze the root cause of the problem so that they can take corrective actions in order to prevent future intrusions. While security administration software helps configure and maintain the infrastructure, intrusion detection software helps ensure that the infrastructure is successfully doing its job. Many individual components of the security infrastructure, such as firewalls, have their own intrusion detection software. As the security infrastructure expands in size and complexity, it will be increasingly important for network security managers to have a centralized way to monitor all components of the network.

While in the past intrusion detection and analysis have largely been a retrospective process, the latest generation of such tools seeks to provide "real-time" intrusion detection that allows network security managers to respond to an intrusion while it is in process.

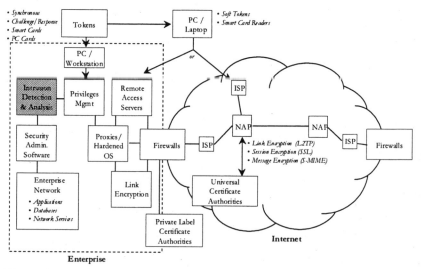

**Figure 3.9**

## Encryption Standards

Encryption standards are the glue that holds much of the security infrastructure together. There are several security-specific Internet standards that play an especially important role in rounding out the security infrastructure. A few of the most important standards include:

- *S-MIME:* The Secure Multi-purpose Internet Mail Extension (S-MIME) is an emerging standard for sending and receiving secure Internet e-mail. Today, most Internet e-mail travels unencrypted across the Internet, making it ill-advised to discuss sensitive topics or substantive business matters via Internet e-mail. Both Microsoft and Netscape have announced their intention to incorporate S-MIME into their Internet browsers, ensuring that the standard will be rapidly disseminated and widely supported. With S-MIME in place, a major hole in the Internet's security infrastructure will be plugged. The S-MIME standard has recently run into some opposition as it is based on the patented RSA encryption algorithm and therefore developers must pay royalties to use the standard.

- *SSL:* The Secure Sockets Layer (SSL) has been implemented by both Microsoft and Netscape for some time now. SSL allows for secure "sessions" to be conducted between two SSL-enabled applications. A session is a series of message exchanges. There is no set time for a session; it can be "set up" and "torn down" at the discretion of the application. SSL is essentially a low-end form of software-based link encryption that operates at a higher level than link or packet encryptors.

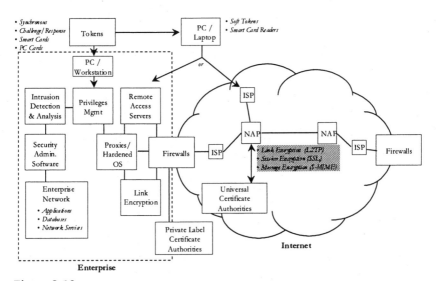

**Figure 3.10**

On the Internet, users often move in and out of several secure sessions over the course of their browsing. With SSL in place, businesses and consumers can interact with each other in real time within a completely secure "session." SSL is largely what enables consumers and businesses to securely send their credit card numbers and other vital information over the Internet today.

- *L2TP:* The Layer 2 Tunneling Protocol (L2TP) automatically establishes a fully encrypted link between two Internet sites. Unlike the SSL standard which can be "set up" and "torn down" at will, the L2TP protocol creates a "tunnel" across the Internet that can only be exited if the Internet session is terminated. L2TP is an emerging standard for link encryption over the Internet and will probably find its greatest use as a new way for travelers and telecommuters to establish what appears to be a remote access connection with their company's network via the Internet instead of a remote access server. This will allow companies to greatly reduce the telecommunication costs associated with employees dialing long-distance to reach remote access servers.

## Sub-Sectors

While there are a myriad of pieces that make up the security infrastructure, from a competitive perspective, it's possible to group the industry into just a few major competitive sub-sectors. As we will explain in the "Trends" section of this chapter, we see even fewer sub-sectors in the future, but we are describing the current state of the industry in order to give investors a framework for assessing each company's likely "migration path."

**Network Security Conglomerates.**   Companies that are all in the process of attempting to build "enterprise security solutions." Most of these companies started out making firewalls or remote access software and are now trying to broaden their product lines in an attempt to provide their customers with a complete solution.

**Token Vendors.**   This sub-sector is focused on providing different types of hard and soft tokens. The number of stand-alone token providers has been falling rapidly due to acquisitions by network security conglomerates (see the "Investment Considerations" section).

**Encryption Tool Providers.**   Encryption tool providers represent a small but elite niche of the Security Sector. Companies in this sub-sector develop basic encryption technologies and provide other developers with the tool kits they need to build these technologies into their own hardware and software.

**Certificate Authority Providers.**   Companies in this sub-sector compete with each other to deploy, maintain, and enhance the certificate authority infrastructure. This sub-sector includes companies that act as either uni-

**Table 3.1**   Selected Network Security Conglomerates

| Company | Description |
| --- | --- |
| Axent Technologies (AXNT) | OMNIGUARD product line is focused on administration and privileges management. Recently merged with Raptor, a major firewall vendor. |
| Checkpoint (CHKPF) | Its FireWall-1 product is the #1 firewall in the market. Use patented "stateful" inspection technology. Founded OPSEC alliance to encourage interoperability with other vendors. |
| Cyberguard (CYBG) | Firewall provider that is expanding to provide enterprise solutions. Recently purchased Tradewave for its CA products. |
| Cylink (CYLK) (#) | Traditionally strong in link encryption products. Moving into network security administration with its SecureManager products and taking a more "market-focused" approach. |
| Information Resource Engineering (IREG) | Traditional provider of link encryption and token products. Heavy focus on enabling Virtual Private Networking. |
| Milkyway (MLK) | Canadian firewall provider with strong ties to Canadian government. Recently added SecureACCESS VPN solution. |
| Network Associates (NETA) (#) | Formed by the late 1997 merger of virus detection software maker McAffee Associates and network management software developer Network General. Now focused on providing full range of network security and network management services. |
| Racal Data Products (RACL) | Subsidiary of British defense and electronics firm Racal Electronics. Strength in link encryption. May be sold shortly. |
| Secure Computing (SCUR) (#@) | Began as a firewall provider but now focusing on building a broad product range. Purchased token vendor Enigma Logic and firewall provider Borderware in 1996. |
| Security Dynamics (SDTI) (#) | Leading token and encryption provider. Its SecureID is the leading token in the market. Purchased RSA Data Security in 1996. Minority interests in Verisign, VPNet Technologies, and others. |
| Trusted Information Systems (TISX) | Provider of the Gauntlet firewall products. Moving out from its traditionally strong presence in the government sector. Recently acquired by Network Associates. |

versal or private label CAs, as well as companies that sell software to create "in-house" CAs.

**Privilege Managers.**   These companies produce network- and application-level systems designed to control user access to network resources. These systems often employ some form of token, such as a smart card, to authenticate users.

**Niche Application Vendors.**   These companies are focused on providing security applications that are highly specialized or have vertical market focus. While this sub-sector will never get as big as the others, it will be difficult for other sub-sectors to subsume it.

As we said before, in keeping with our overall thesis, we anticipate that competition across sub-sectors will continue to increase and that the "soft

**Table 3.2**   Selected Token Vendors

| Company | Description |
| --- | --- |
| ActivCard | Hard token manufacturer. Has both time synchronous and challenge and response versions. Listed on the EASDAQ in Europe. |
| Biometric Access Corporation | Produces a biometric finger print scanning device and processing software. |
| CRYPTOCard | Provides challenge and response tokens as well as Unix and *Windows NT* remote access management software. |
| Gemplus | World's largest manufacturer of high-security magnetic stripe and smart cards. Recently sold stake to GE Capital's Consumer Finance Group. Generated an estimated $440 million in revenues in 1996. |
| Schlumberger | Large diversified conglomerate. Also a major smart card manufacturer. |
| Indentix (IDX) | Maker of pattern-based finger print imaging and recognition systems. Strong law enforcement presence. |
| Indenticator Technology | Developer of minutiae-based finger print imaging and recognition systems. Contract with SWIFT. |
| Vasco | Provider of VACMan challenge and response token systems and remote access software. Introduced Internet-based version in 1996. |

**Table 3.3**   Selected Encryption Tool Providers

| Company | Description |
| --- | --- |
| Certicom | Canadian company that specializes in Elliptic Curve encryption algorithms. |
| Cylink (CYLK) | Recently acquired an Israel-based firm called Algorithmic Research, which has its own encryption tool kit. |
| RSA Data Security Inc. | Subsidiary of Security Dynamics. Provides basic encryption tool kits for the implementation of the RSA, the leading public-key encryption algorithm. |
| Spyrus | Focused on providing development tool kits for payment security. Recently acquired Terisa systems in a bid to focus on the SET market. |

**Table 3.4**   Selected Certificate Authority Providers

| Company | Description |
| --- | --- |
| CertCo | Certificate authority spun off from Bankers Trust. Received contract from Visa to produce root key for SET. Focused on financial institutions. |
| Entrust Technologies | Spin off from Canada's Nortel. Private label certificate authority and software tools provider. |
| GTE Cyber Trust | Spin off from GTE. Private label certificate authority and software tools provider. |
| Verisign (VRSN) | Highly visible certificate authority. Committed to acting as both a universal and a private label CA. Issuing digital certificates directly to consumers. |
| Xcert Software Inc. | Developing certificate authority and digital rights management software. |

**Table 3.5** Selected Privilege Managers

| Company | Description |
| --- | --- |
| CKS | UK-based developer of "MyNet" client/server based, application level, secure single sign-on and privileges management software. |
| EnCommerce | Developer of web-focused privileges management software that can be used to control access to specific web servers, databases, and other specific network services. |
| Gradient | Hardware/software solution for enterprise wide access security, transmission encryption, and privileges management. |
| V-ONE (#@) | Smart card-based SmartGate solution allows for fully authenticated network wide access security and privileges management. Product basically serves as a proxy between application and presentation layers. |

**Table 3.6** Selected Niche Application Providers

| Company | Description |
| --- | --- |
| Argus Systems | Creator of trusted operating systems. Main product is a "trusted" version of Sun's Solaris operating systems. |
| Entegrity | Start-up developer of a universal security "toolbox" that will allow companies to easily incorporate different security technologies into both custom and packaged applications. |
| GlobeSET | Formerly named Interval. Creates payment and digital rights software. Renamed itself to signify its intent to focus on SET software including wallets, gateways, and CAs. Spun off from Banker's Trust. |
| Internet Security | Leading developer of intrusion detection and analysis software. Can use Systems software to proactively test network for security vulnerabilities. |
| Inter-Trust Technologies Inc. | Developer of a digital rights management technology that enables businesses to establish secure, distributed, and trusted control over various forms of content. |
| Netect | Developer of Netector and Netective real-time intrusion detection and analysis software. |
| PGP Inc. | Provider of public key-based e-mail encryption software. Branching out into network access control with acquisition of Zoomit. Acquired by Network Associates (#) in late 1997. |
| Pilot Network Services | Focused on providing secure electronic commerce hosting services. Hosts client web sites within a secure network environment protected by a dynamic firewall. |
| RedCreek | Creator of the Ravlin family of remote access and link encryption hardware and software. Integrating products into Cisco's PIX firewall. |
| VPNet | Dedicated to providing hardware and software based Virtual Private Networking (VPN) solutions. Has a resale deal with Bay Networks. |
| Wave Systems | Focused on enabling secure distribution of digital content. Creating payment and accounting systems to enable metered usage of content. |

walls" between the sectors will largely dissolve over time. Indeed, the rise of the "network security conglomerates" provides clear evidence of this trend. While the evolution of any particular firm is difficult to predict, we have put together a table which details the specific products offered by each firm (see Table 3.7). Over time we believe that many firms will attempt to "fill in their gaps" through acquisitions and/or partnerships.

**Table 3.7** Products Offered by Selected Firms in the Security Sector

| | Firewalls | Application proxies | Hardened oss | Link encryptors | Remote access | Hard tokens | Soft tokens | Encryption tool kits | Privileges mgmt | Intrusion detection | Admin. software | Universal CA | Private label CA | CA tools | Digital rights | Message encryption |
|---|---|---|---|---|---|---|---|---|---|---|---|---|---|---|---|---|
| **Network Security Conglomerates** | | | | | | | | | | | | | | | | |
| Axent Technologies | X | X | X | | X | X | X | | X | X | | | | | | |
| Checkpoint Software | X | X | X | | X | | | | | | | | | | | |
| Cyberguard | X | X | | | | | | | | | | | | | | |
| Cylink | X | | | X | X | X | X | | | | | | X | X | | |
| Information Resource Eng. | X | | | X | X | X | X | X | | | | | | X | | |
| Network Associates | | | | | | | | | | X | X | | | | | X |
| Secure Computing | X | X | X | | X | X | X | | | | X | | | | | |
| Security Dynamics | | | | | X | X | X | X | X | | X | | | X | | X |
| **Token Vendors** | | | | | | | | | | | | | | | | |
| ActivCard | | | | | X | X | | | | | | | | | | |
| Crypto Card | | | | | X | X | | | | | | | | | | |
| Vasco | | | | | | X | | | | | | | | | | |
| **Encryption Tool Providers** | | | | | | | | | | | | | | | | |
| Certicom | | | | | | X | | X | | | | | | X | X | |

| Company | 1 | 2 | 3 | 4 | 5 | 6 | 7 | 8 | 9 | 10 | 11 | 12 |
|---|---|---|---|---|---|---|---|---|---|---|---|---|
| CertCo | | | | | | | | | | X | X | |
| Entrust Technologies | | | | | | | | | X | X | X | |
| GTE Cyber Trust | | | | | | | | | X | X | X | |
| Verisign | | | | | | | | X | | X | X | |
| Xcert Software | | | | | | | | | | X | X | X |
| **Privilege Managers** | | | | | | | | | | | | |
| CKS Software | | X | | | X | | | | | | | |
| EnCommerce | | | X | | X | | | | | | | |
| Gradient | | | X | | X | | | | | | | |
| V-One | | | X | X | X | | | | | | | |
| **Niche Application Vendors** | | | | | | | | | | | | |
| GlobeSET | | | | | | | | | | | | |
| Internet Security Systems | | | | | | X | | | | | X | X |
| Inter-Trust Technologies | | | | | | X | | | | | X | X |
| Netect | | | | | | X | | | | | | |
| RedCreek | | | X | X | | | | | | | | |
| VPN Net | | | X | X | | | | | | | | |
| Wave Systems | | | | | | | | | | | X | X |

SOURCE: Piper Jaffray

## SIDEBAR: SET: SETTING THE STAGE FOR SECURE ELECTRONIC COMMERCE

As Internet usage began to explode in 1993 and 1994, it became increasingly apparent that the Internet would soon become an important channel for the purchase of goods and services. At the same time, it also became apparent that one of the easiest and most accessible ways to pay for these purchases would be with credit cards.

While the credit card industry was excited at the prospect of playing an important role in the emergence of Electronic Commerce, it was also deeply worried that the Internet's lack of security would expose the industry to substantial fraud losses, which even without the Internet's help were already running at over $1 billion a year.

### Creating SET

In response to these concerns, several rival groups began to develop standards for securing credit card transactions on the Internet. One group, composed of VISA and Microsoft, proposed a standard called Secure Transaction Technology (STT), while a group composed of MasterCard, IBM, and Netscape proposed another standard called the Secure Encryption Payment Protocol (SEPP). After much bickering, these two groups finally agreed in February of 1996 to combine their different approaches into a single standard called the Secure Electronic Transaction standard, or SET.

SET uses most of the technologies we outlined in Chapter 2, including symmetric keys, public key pairs, digital signatures, digital certificates, and certificate authorities, to create a system for making secure credit card purchases over the Internet. This system is so complete and so secure that when fully implemented, SET will arguably be the single most secure way to purchase something with a credit card.

Digital certificates form the foundation of SET's advanced security. Under the SET scheme, every merchant, bank, credit card processor, and credit card holder will be issued their very own digital certificate. During a SET transaction, these digital certificates will make absolutely sure that every participant in the transaction is legitimate. Symmetric keys, public key pairs, and digital signatures will keep the details of the credit card transaction private as it travels over the Internet and validate that each party has in fact authorized the transaction. Certificate authorities oversee the whole process, issuing certificates and maintaining CRLs.

### How SET Works

Briefly, a SET transaction starts with the customer verifying that they are dealing with a legitimate merchant (see Figure 3.11). The customer then sends their order and payment information to the merchant who in turn checks to see that it is dealing with a legitimate credit card holder and then sends back a message to the customer confirming the order.

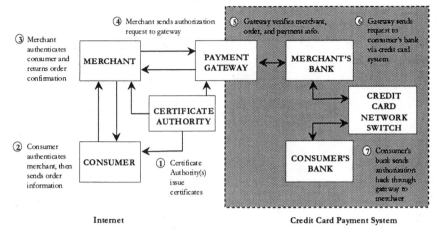

**Figure 3.11** SET Payment Authorization

The merchant then sends a payment authorization request to a "payment gateway." The payment gateway is operated by either the merchant's bank or its third-party processor. The gateway decrypts the message, verifies that the transaction is from a legitimate merchant, and checks to see that it contains the proper information. It then sends a traditional authorization request over the existing credit card network to the customer's credit card company (see Chapter 4 for a description of how a credit card transaction works). The credit card company sends its response to the request back across the credit card network to the merchant's bank or third-party processor. It then sends the approval (or denial) to the gateway which encrypts the response and sends it back to the merchant via the Internet. The merchant then lets the consumer know whether or not their purchase has been approved.

## Better Than What We Use Today

This complex scheme of "checks and balances" will actually make SET even more secure than almost all other types of credit card transactions. Specifically, SET will have several advantages over traditional transactions:

1. *The merchant will never see the customer's credit card number.* Instead, the merchant will only know the name of the credit card company that issued the card. This feature will eliminate the risk of unscrupulous employees or merchants stealing credit card numbers from customer charge slips.
2. *The customer will be able to have complete confidence that they are dealing with a legitimate merchant.* Today, criminals can set up fake stores or catalogs and then steal credit card numbers by taking orders from customers. SET's use of digital certificates ensures

that only Internet sites with a valid merchant account will be able to accept credit card orders.

3. *The credit card company will have greater confidence that the transaction is legitimate.* Today, credit cards can be used without passwords or PIN numbers, making it easy for them to be used by thieves. SET will require both the merchant and the customer to use passwords, which should give the credit card company greater confidence that the transaction is legitimate.

With the support of the world's two largest credit card associations as well as some of the most important Internet software firms, the support for SET has been almost overwhelming. Not only has just about every software firm and credit card issuer in the world agreed to support it, but some companies have even changed their names to more closely associate themselves with SET.

With so many organizations committed to the success of SET and with SET's vastly improved security, many people believe that the deployment of SET will be a defining event which finally convinces both consumers and businesses alike that the Internet is truly safe for Electronic Commerce.

## Some Rough Edges

SET may eventually fulfill these prophecies, but, in the interim, it has a few rough edges which could pose some problems for its rapid deployment and acceptance. These problems include:

1. *Compatibility:* SET is just a standard. It is up to individual software providers around the world to build the SET standard into their software. While the whole idea of a standard is to create interoperability between different hardware and software, companies can take different approaches to implementing the standard which, in turn can create incompatibilities. To deal with this issue, the original SET partners have set up a process to certify software as "SET-compliant." However, this process takes time and there is no requirement that every software maker has to get the "SET-compliant" seal of approval. As a result, a number of people have concerns about the "interoperability" of different types of SET-compliant software.

   Apparently, VISA and MasterCard share these concerns. They have very carefully selected SET demonstration sites in order to avoid any interoperability problems. The good news is that these are relatively short-term problems. Software vendors all want to be "SET-compliant" because otherwise they will not sell much software. So this is really only a problem in terms of the speed of deployment and adoption of SET, not a fundamental problem with the standard.

2. *Portability:* Today, credit cards are "portable" in that they are very easy to carry around. The same cannot be said for SET's digital certificates, the digital equivalent of a credit card. While this is

not an issue for merchants or credit card companies (their certificates will likely stay on their SET servers 24 hours a day), it is potentially a big issue for credit card customers, especially those customers that use more than one computer.

As the SET digital certificates are stored on a specific computer's hard drive, if a customer tries to use a different computer, the SET certificate will not be available and the customer will be out of luck. The SET partners are well aware of these problems and are in the process of developing a system for loading SET certificates on to smart cards. With the certificates on a smart card, customers will be able to use any computers in the world to make a SET-compliant purchase provided that their computers: A) are connected to the Internet; and B) have smart card readers. While it is getting increasingly easy to find A, it is still almost impossible to find B. Thus, until smart card readers are widely deployed, SET will continue to lack easy portability. While this will not stop adoption of SET, it may slow adoption by making SET less appealing to some customers, especially heavy computer users (many of whom are already making purchases over the Internet without SET).

3. *Latency:* SET may be secure, but as currently implemented it is not fast. Every single payment authorization request using SET generates over 30 separate encryption and decryption processes. (Not to mention the fact that each SET message must negotiate at least three separate parties as well as two separate networks.) All of that encryption, decryption, and authentication takes time. While most point-of-sale card transactions are easily completed in less than ten seconds, it looks like SET transactions will have major difficulties being completed that quickly. Computer types refer to these time delays as "latency" problems.

SET's latency problems are centered at the so-called "gateways." Early reports have these gateways struggling to keep up with even moderate transaction volumes. The latency problems are enough of a concern that the SET partners have begun quietly looking for ways that might be able to speed things up. One idea on the board is to use a newer encryption algorithm called the elliptic curve (see Chapter 2 for description). Messages encrypted with elliptic curve can potentially be encrypted and decrypted ten times as fast as messages using the SET encryption algorithm (which is RSA).[4]

The good news is that most people are so used to waiting on the Internet (if they can even get access to it) that they will probably blame any delay in processing their purchase request on the Internet and not the SET standard. That said, the latency

---

[4] For certain cryptographic operations which are critical to SET, such as digital signature verification, elliptic curve is actually slower (for keys of the same length). In addition, most encryption experts feel that elliptic curve has not been subjected to enough testing, so replacing RSA with elliptic curve is not a "slam dunk."

problems with SET will have to be addressed at some point or they will prevent the SET system from "scaling" properly in order to meet rising demand.

4. *Cost:* While SET is called a *standard,* it is in fact an entirely new and very complex *system* for securing and transporting credit card transactions. SET not only requires tens of millions of digital certificates to be issued, revoked, and otherwise managed, it also requires new software such as payment gateways to be built, tested, deployed, and operated. None of this is going to come cheap. While the Internet is widely hailed as perhaps the lowest cost transaction channel ever, all of the overhead associated with a SET transaction may actually make it just as costly as the average point-of-sale credit card transaction. Of course, some of SET's additional costs will be recouped through lower fraud losses and communication costs, but still, any way you look at it, SET does not come cheaply.

Taken together, all of these problems raise the very real prospect that SET is going to take a good deal longer to deploy than previously thought and that customer acceptance may be a bit less robust than first thought.

This delay, in turn, would take quite a bit of the luster from the SET standard and could have quite a number of interesting consequences, including:

- Given the high expectations for SET both within the marketplace and the stock market, companies that have closely attached themselves to the SET train may be in for a rough ride in the near term.
- Concerns over the pace of SET adoption may eventually prompt the major credit card associations to lower their interchange fees for SET transactions in order to spur adoption.

While these events may put a pretty large hole in the side of the SET ship, they still don't stand a chance of sinking it. With so many major organizations investing so much time, money, and credibility in SET, no matter what happens, SET will be deployed. Just like a money center bank, SET is in many ways now too big to fail.

## Pandora's Box

One interesting thing to note about SET is that it ever so casually opens up the equivalent of "Pandora's Box." When most people look at a SET diagram, the one thing they tend to notice is that SET still uses the traditional credit card network to actually authorize and settle credit card transactions. "Why not just do the whole transaction over the Internet?" they inevitably ask. Good question.

In fact, at least one credit card processor agrees. American Express actually encourages merchants on the Internet to send its transactions directly to American Express, by-passing third-party processors and other transaction networks in the process.

In theory, MasterCard and VISA banks could do the same thing. Rather than passing an authorization request on to an issuer through the credit card network, the bank could simply send the request directly to the issuing bank over the Internet. Why bother? Because VISA and MasterCard charge for every message sent over their networks. Using the Internet instead of the credit card network could thus save the bank a healthy sum of money.

As for VISA and MasterCard, SET raises the real possibility that credit card processors could use the Internet to bypass the credit network or "jump the switch," not only depriving VISA and MasterCard of their fees but also the information contained in the transaction (which they use today to create ancillary products and services).

Taking things a bit further, it doesn't take a lot of imagination to see SET and the Internet creating a much more level playing field throughout the credit card association "business." Today these associations are infamous for their somewhat heavy-handed tactics and market clout. So, in an ironic twist, SET, a mechanism created in part to ensure VISA and MasterCard's dominance of consumer Electronic Commerce, may ultimately undercut the influence of its creators.

## Market Size

Despite its complex structure and numerous competitive sub-sectors, the Security Sector is still quite small relative to other established markets. During 1997, the 14 public firms dedicated to the Security Sector generated just $934 million in revenues. We estimate that private sector firms generated another $150 million and large systems software and hardware firms like IBM, Digital (#), Computer Associates, and NEC generated another $150–$200 million. Therefore, the total revenues generated by the Security Sector in 1997 amounted to just $1.2–$1.3 billion. Put another way, it took the Security Sector an entire year to generate the same amount of revenues that General Motors (#) generated in just over two days.

Granted, this number is a bit misleading. It represents the total revenues that commercial firms generated selling products and services expressly devoted to network security. This narrow definition leaves a number of areas out, including:

- *Revenues from "built-in" security.* Most operating system software, such as Microsoft's *Windows NT*, has "built-in" security features. In addition, many manufacturers of networking equipment, such as Cisco Systems and Ascend Communications, are increasingly building basic features of firewalls and remote access security software directly into their products (see the Trends section for more on this).

- *Money spent on "in-house" development.* Some companies just cannot seem to let anyone else touch their systems. As a result, they use their in-house development staffs to add security features to their networks and applications. While this activity does happen, only a few large corporations have the time, resources, and confidence necessary to build their security solutions "in-house."

- *Money spent by governments.* While most companies don't have the time, money, or inclination to try to develop their own security solutions, a lot of governments do. For example, the United States admits to spending a mere $28 billion on "intelligence activities" in 1996. Of that $28 billion, about $3.5 billion was spent on the National Security Agency (NSA). The NSA is responsible for securing U.S. government communications and "unsecuring" other government's communications. While the NSA does a number of other things, it's safe to say that about a third of its budget in 1996, or at least $1 billion, was spent on information and network security activities. In total, governments around the world probably spent close to $2 billion on similar activities in 1996.

It's important to note that part of this government money finds its way back into the private sector in terms of revenues and R&D funding. For example, government spending accounted for 42% of Secure Computing's (#@) 1997 revenue. This close connection between the government and the Security Sector can be seen in the fact that many security firms, including V-ONE (#), Trusted Information Systems, and Information Resources, are all located within close proximity to the NSA.

From an investment perspective, these indirect revenues should be excluded because they create the illusion of a much larger market than what actually exists.

## Drivers

It's a bit of a let down to find out that the Security Sector is so small, when it appears to get as much, if not more, attention than market sectors that are 100 times its size. While part of the reason the Security Sector gets so much attention is that it is new, mysterious, and related to the Internet, the main reason it gets so much attention is its enormous growth potential.

Indeed, a number of powerful drivers are propelling the growth of the Security Sector, guaranteeing that it will be a good deal larger than it is today. The biggest drivers of this growth include:

### Internet Usage

The Internet itself, warts and all, is currently one of the biggest, if not the biggest driver of the Security Sector's growth. Each new computer added to the Internet increases the size of the security market, because sooner or later whoever owns that computer is going to have to think seriously about securing it. Given that the number of computers or hosts connected to the Internet has grown at a compound annual growth rate of 83% over the last three years (from 3.2 million to 19.1 million) and that this number is expected to expand to at least 50 million within just a few years, it's quite evident that Internet usage should continue to be a forceful driver of the Security Sector.[5]

## Need for Remote Access

Corporations look a lot different today than they did thirty years ago. They are more decentralized, more international, and less vertically integrated. These changes, combined with falling travel and communication costs, have, among other things, resulted in: increased travel, the rise of telecommuting, the increasing use of partnerships, and the geographical dispersion of corporate offices. All of these factors have in turn increased the need for employees to access their company's network remotely. Like Internet usage, remote access creates a new entry point to a network and thus adds another security worry to a company's plate. In the recent past, remote access has been a strong driver of the security market. For example, remote access has been the primary driver of the token market for a number of years. As the remote access market continues to grow, it in turn will continue to drive the growth of the security market.

## Rise of Virtual Private Networking (VPN)

VPN enables companies to securely provide remote access services via the Internet. By using the Internet instead of expensive leased lines or private networks, VPN allows companies to dramatically reduce their communication costs. The security industry is working feverishly to put together turnkey VPN solutions. As these solutions mature and as companies become comfortable with the concept of VPN, the entire market should start to take off. The growth of VPN should, therefore, prove to be a powerful driver of the Security Sector going forward.

## Increasing Network Complexity

As networks become more complex, they not only become more useful, but they also become more vulnerable because complexity makes net-

[5] See Network Wizards 1/97 Internet host survey at www.nw.com

works harder to manage, harder to monitor, and harder to control access to. It is in this way that network complexity is inadvertently helping drive the growth of the Security Sector. While the Internet is one of the most visible elements driving network complexity, there are a number of other drivers worth mentioning, including:

- *Increasing connectivity:* They say no man is an island, but ten years ago most computer networks were. Today, prodded on by the example of the Internet and the power of Metcalf's Law, networks are trying to connect themselves to just about everything with a wire on it. In addition to the Internet, connections for remote access, wide area networks (WANS), and value added networks (VANs) are all being added at a furious rate. While this increased connectivity is creating value, it is also creating new ways to illegally gain access to a company's network. Thus, as network connectivity increases so does the need for security.

- *Multi-tier architectures:* In the old days, everything you needed to run a software program resided in one place, either on a mainframe at the company headquarters or on a personal computer or workstation. During the 1980s, many computer programs were split in half, with some of the program residing on a personal computer and the rest residing on a server, which could be either a mainframe, minicomputer, or sort of "super" personal computer. Computing types called this client-server arrangement a two-tier architecture. From a security perspective, splitting the application in two meant that there were two tiers to secure instead of one. Lately, many software programs are being split yet again, this time into "multi-tier" architectures that have three or more tiers. This split is again helping to drive the Security Sector by creating new tiers to secure.

- *Distributed computing:* Multi-tier architectures, along with increased bandwidth, network connectivity, and new software protocols, are making something possible called distributed computing. Distributed computing "spreads out" databases, applications, and servers across different networks instead of co-locating them all in one place. This "distributes" processing loads and allows for the optimal location of each computing resource. The World Wide Web is perhaps the most well-known example of a distributed (and multi-tier) computing "system."

    The move toward distributed computing increases network complexity by spreading out the different elements of a computing "system" across multiple networks. As distributed computing becomes more widespread due to increases in bandwidth and improved software tools, it will become an increasingly important long-term driver of the Security Sector.[6]

## Security Breaches

As every insurance salesman knows, nothing does wonders for business like a death in the family. In much the same way, widely publicized accounts of security breaches help drive demand for security products and services. After all, the last thing an information systems manager wants to do is lose his/her job because some 12-year-old broke into the company web site and put a fake mustache on a picture of the company chairman.

That said, *systemic* security breaches that result from fundamental technological problems can have the opposite effect. They can encourage companies to withdraw from the potentially insecure activity altogether. Thus, security breaches can be either boon or bane to the security industry.

We believe that while there will indeed be more systemic problems, the momentum toward the Internet, remote access, and network complexity will be almost impossible to stop short of some catastrophic event (like the "breaking" of public key encryption). We also believe that more than a few IS managers will lose their jobs over the coming years because they failed to take the proper security precautions. Net/net we believe that security breaches will be a positive, though difficult to quantify, driver of the Security Sector growth.[7]

## Improved Technology

Beyond improving the cost and functionality of network security products, new technology will also help drive the growth of the security market by improving the ability of crooks and thieves to break into networks. For example, faster computers will enable criminals to break public key systems more easily, which will in turn drive the need for more complex and more efficient encryption algorithms as well as longer digital certificates and public keys.

---

[6] In many ways, distributed computing is already the single most important driver of the Security Sector's growth (witness the World Wide Web), but it will truly come into play as corporations use distributed object technology, such as CORBA and DCOM, to mesh their internal applications and databases with those of their suppliers and customers which will effectively eliminate the distinction between internal and external network security.

[7] It's interesting to note that when the *Wall Street Journal* reported that a group of hackers successfully decrypted a DES message, the stocks of Security Sector firms generally rose, indicating the market believes these events to be a positive driver. See the *Wall Street Journal* 6/18/97 page A2.

With Moore's Law predicted to hold for at least another seven years, the security industry seems to be guaranteed a technology-driven "Arms Race" over the foreseeable future, and as any weapons manufacturer will tell you, there's nothing like a little arms race to stimulate the market.

## Market Potential

Given these powerful drivers, it's tempting to ask: just how big will the Security Sector get? In order to estimate the sector's potential growth, it's important to look at a few important factors:

*Internet access:* Of direct importance to the Security Sector is the number of computers or hosts attached to the Internet, as each of these computers will technically need some sort of security solution. Estimating the future number of hosts is a difficult undertaking, but a conservative assumption would have them increasing at the same rate as the number of Internet users or at a CAGR of almost 50% over the next four years.

*Certificate issuance:* As companies and organizations begin to deploy public key security solutions, they will have to start issuing certificates. The more certificates issued, the more resources needed to manage them. We expect that billions of certificates will be outstanding by the year 2001.

*Installed base turnover:* Technology has proven to have a fairly short, useful life and, as a result, the installed base tends to be replaced or turned over fairly quickly. Using the PC industry as a guide, we estimate that about 12% of the security infrastructure will turn over every year.

While these three factors will all have a positive influence on the growth of the Security Sector, two other trends will decelerate the sector's growth:

*Pricing trends:* Falling prices are a well-known phenomena in technology markets. For example, computer memory chip prices fell as much as 70% over the course of 1996. This price crash lowered projected industry revenues by billions of dollars in one fell swoop. Closer to home, the prices of firewalls also fell dramatically in 1996 in response to higher scale, improved technology, and greater competition. Using long-term PC software prices as a proxy, we estimate that prices will decrease about 5% a year over the next five years.

*Cannibalization by "embedded" solutions:* If anything has the potential to put a hole in the hull of the Security Sector this factor does. Unfortunately, it is one of the hardest factors to project. By isolating those revenues that are most at risk and then decaying them at 25% a year, we estimate that this factor will decrease total growth, on average, by 10% a year.

Taking both the positive and negative factors together, we estimate that the security market should grow from its current base of just over $900 million to $2.8 billion in size by 2001 (see Figure 3.12). By 2001, we expect that 14% of the sector's revenues will come from the provision of security services, and that upgrades and enhancements to the installed base will drive about 70% of the industry's revenues.

## Trends

### The Search for Simplicity

Earlier in this chapter, we noted that the increased complexity of computer networks is helping to drive the Security Sector. We also noted that the Security Sector is creating an increasingly complex series of products and services in order to solve the different security problems. The task of managing all this complexity typically falls on the shoulders of one person: the network manager. This manager must not only make sure that he/she has plugged every potential security hole in his/her rapidly growing network, but they must also maintain, upgrade, and monitor the whole network security "system" to make sure that it is actually doing its job.

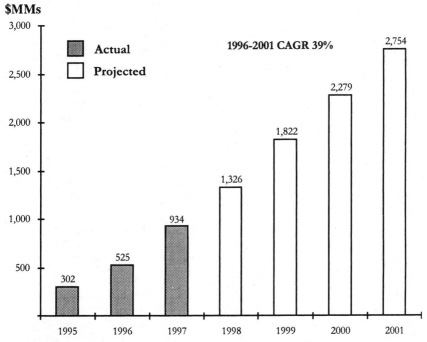

**Figure 3.12** Projected Security Sector Revenues—1998–2001
*Source: Piper Jaffray*

Today, most network managers must buy their tokens from one vendor, their firewalls from another, and their encryption software from yet another. Once they buy all of these separate products, they must then try to get them to work together peacefully without disrupting the whole system. Administering such a heterogeneous system of products and services can be a nightmare, as very few firms produce products that are compatible with rival products, and each product typically comes with its own separate administration software.

As a result, network managers are increasingly looking for security "solutions" that not only plug all of the potential holes in their network, but that also simplify the administration and maintenance of the entire security "system" by providing a centralized way for the manager to set up, monitor, and maintain all of the different security elements.

### The Advent of Consolidation and "One-Stop Shops"

The Security Sector took note of this demand and began to aggressively respond to it in 1996 and early 1997. The most visible evidence of this response was the attempt by a number of firms to create "one stop shops" by acquiring firms that offered complementary products (see Table 3.8). In

**Table 3.8**  Recent Mergers and Acquisitions in the Security Sector

| Date | Buyer | Seller | Seller's focus |
|------|-------|--------|----------------|
| 4/96 | Security Dynamics | RSA Data Security Inc. | Encryption Tool Kits |
| 5/96 | Secure Computing | Border Technologies | Firewalls |
| 6/96 | Vasco Data Security | Lintel | Tokens |
| 6/96 | Secure Computing | Enigma Logic | Tokens |
| 6/96 | Vasco Data Security | Digipass | Tokens |
| 7/96 | Pretty Good Privacy Inc. | Lemcon Systems | Message encryption |
| 11/96 | Pretty Good Privacy Inc. | Privnet | Privacy software |
| 1/97 | Axent Technologies | Digital Pathways | Hard tokens |
| 4/97 | Cyberguard | Tradewave | Certificate authorities |
| 5/97 | Spyrus | Terisa Systems | Encryption tool kits |
| 7/97 | Security Dynamics | Dynasoft | Single sign-on |
| 9/97 | Cylink | Algorithmic Research | Internet remote access |
| 10/97 | Trusted Information Sys. | Haystack Labs | Intrusion detection |
| 12/97 | Network Associates | Pretty Good Privacy | Secure e-mail |
| 12/97 | Axent Technologies | Raptor Systems | Firewalls |
| 1/98 | Bay Networks | New Oak Communications | VPNs |
| 2/98 | Network Associates | Trusted Information Systems | Firewalls |
| 3/98 | Security Dynamics | Intrusion Detection Inc. | Intrusion detection |

SOURCE:  Company Press Releases, Credit Suisse First Boston

addition, a number of firms "fast-tracked" internal R&D projects that would allow them to expand their product offerings, and many firms also began to aggressively seek partnerships with other firms.

In fact, it's hard to find a firm in the Security Sector today that doesn't claim to somehow be offering "an enterprise-wide solution" to security. The reality of the situation is that while many firms offer a fairly broad range of products, very few have successfully integrated these products in a way that has reached the goal of significantly simplifying the entire security system. That said, many firms are devoting tremendous energies to this goal of offering a truly integrated "one-stop shop."

## Standards: The Other Option

At the same time that many firms have been racing to build "one-stop shops," another group of firms has been working on an alternative solution. Rather than trying to offer an entire "solution," these firms have been working on setting standards that will allow products and services from different vendors to work together seamlessly. The idea is that network managers can have their cake and eat it too. Not only will standards greatly simplify the managers' task of monitoring and managing the security "system," but they will also give managers the freedom to choose "best-of-breed" products and services for each particular security problem.

To date, a few sets of standards have been proposed. Cisco Systems, the dominant producer of network routers, is proposing something called the Enterprise Security Alliance, while Checkpoint Software, the leading firewall provider, is proposing something called the Open Platform for Secure Enterprise Computing (or OPSEC). Finally, Hewlett-Packard (#) is pushing a standard "architecture" it calls "Presidium."

While both of these efforts are still quite young, they highlight a coming battle in the industry over simplicity and integration versus choice and flexibility. Clearly, having one set of engineers produce a single "solution" has the greatest potential for actually fulfilling the goals of a seamless security system. But just as clear, many companies would not be comfortable implementing a solution which made them entirely dependent on one vendor.

However, the weight of history favors standards. For example, in the telephone industry, a very similar battle ended in the development of the SNMP/FMIS standards, which allow telephone companies to mix and match equipment from different vendors. Not to be forgotten, the Internet itself in many ways represents the ultimate triumph of open standards.

Given the almost inevitable establishment of standards, we believe that the important points to watch in this battle between "one-stop shops" and standards is not so much which side will win, but how the different firms position themselves to compete in the likely end game.

## Security as Part of a Larger Puzzle: Too Important for Its Own Good?

With the battles within the Security Sector providing such good fare, sometimes it's easy to lose perspective and forget that the Security Sector is just a very small piece of a very large puzzle.

In fact the most interesting and perhaps the most ominous trend in the industry has not been consolidation or the battle of one-stop shops versus standards, but the move by the elephants (i.e., large software and networking firms) to build security solutions directly into their own products (see Table 3.9).

For example, the next version of Microsoft's *Windows NT* software will include a built-in version of MIT's Kerberos security system. *Windows NT 5.0* will use the security system to help manage access to network resources, such as file servers and other network domains. Kerberos will not only control access to these services, but it will also be used to ensure the privacy and integrity of messages sent between network resources and clients. It will

**Table 3.9** Examples of Embedded Security Solutions

| Company | Embedded security solution |
| --- | --- |
| Ascend | Ascend has introduced a series of remote access network equipment products that have embedded security features including support for tokens and elements of remote access software. |
| Cisco | Cisco has been embedding an increasing amount of firewall functionality into its products and has its own line of PIX firewalls. It recently purchased Global Internet Software Group, a *Windows NT* firewall specialist. |
| Microsoft | Microsoft is building a version of MIT's Kerberos encryption and key management system into version 5.0 of *Windows NT*. It will allow *Windows NT* servers to identify and authenticate *Windows* clients and to encrypt communications within and between LANs. In addition, it is heavily rumored that Microsoft will shortly be revealing a new enhanced version of its *Proxy Server* (Version 2.0) that includes a full-blown firewall. The *NT* market was supposed to be the biggest growth market for the firewall sector. |
| Sterling Software | Sterling is a major EDI firm that has licensed elliptic curve encryption technology from Certicom to provide embedded security for transport of documents across VANs and the Internet. Sterling's products threaten Security Sector firms focused on message encryption. |
| Sun Microsystems | Sun has developed its own line of "Sunscreen" firewall products that are closely integrated with its Solaris operating system. Sun's actions put other firewall vendors at a decided disadvantage when selling to SPARC users. |

also authenticate each copy of *Windows* on the network to make sure it belongs there.

It is not hard to imagine that Version 6.0 of Microsoft *NT* might include an even broader range of security services, such as support for user-level, token-based authentication, file-level privileges management, and system-wide security management features. With *Windows NT,* a lot of companies in the Security Sector could be just one version away from extinction.

As Microsoft expands into the Security Sector from the system software side, Cisco is expanding into the sector from the networking side. Cisco's customers (most of whom are also Security Sector customers) are demanding an integrated system for managing the massive collection of switches, routers, hubs, and wires that make up the modern network. Cisco's solution, similar to Microsoft's, is to build as much functionality as possible into its routers and switches, including support for such network security functions. Cisco has already built "basic" firewall capabilities into its products, and it's not hard to imagine them building in more advanced features as well. Other Security Sector products that are candidates for integration into Cisco's products include application proxies, link encryptors, and remote access software.

### Can't We All Just Get Along?

Having Microsoft and Cisco bearing down on the Security Sector from either side raises the very unpleasant specter of the sector being trampled to death by the two biggest elephants in the jungle as they race toward world dominance.

While this scenario is possible, it is not inevitable. It's possible that rather than trying to build absolutely everything on their own, these giants will simply take the pieces that are most critical to the success of their own products and let their "partners" fight over what's left. Cisco's Enterprise Security Alliance appears to be an early attempt at just that. Partners can join the alliance, as long as they simply cede the entire networking market to Cisco.

These partnerships don't have to be one-sided. Checkpoint Systems provides a good example of a win-win situation. Checkpoint entered into a partnership with Sun Microsystems, whereby Sun agreed to bundle its firewall product with the Sun operating system. Not only did this alliance allow Sun to quickly offer an "integrated" firewall solution for its customers, but it allowed Checkpoint to establish a leading position in the firewall market which it successfully leveraged into partnerships with other hardware and operating system providers.

Still, any security firm that enters into a partnership with such giants as Sun, Microsoft, and Cisco will always have to worry about their much larger partner's true intentions. In the case of Checkpoint, Sun is now planning on selling its own firewall software and thereby potentially cutting Checkpoint out of the action. Luckily for Checkpoint, it was able to leverage its early leadership position with Sun to branch out into other platforms, so Sun's decision to sell firewall software will not cause irreparable harm to Checkpoint, but it demonstrates the uneasy tensions between Security Sector firms and their "partners."

## Government Regulation and Involvement

If worrying about the intentions of Cisco and Microsoft weren't enough, the Security Sector must also worry about the intentions of the biggest firm of all, the U.S. government. From the government's perspective, security technology has the potential not only to do a lot of good, but to also allow terrorists, criminals, and rogue nations around the world to hide their malicious activities. In the minds of the government, this elevates security technology to a "national security" level issue.

The government's concern manifests itself most obviously in its steadfast objection to the export of so-called "strong encryption" technology. "Strong encryption," according to the government, is any kind of public key encryption system that uses keys of greater than 40 bits in length. This means that U.S. firms, which dominate the Security Sector and hold most of the patents, have not been allowed to export any products with public key encryption systems that use anything bigger than a 40-bit key.

Given that a French university student was able to break a 40-bit key by simply stringing together a bunch of computers and having them work on the problem in their spare time, most businesses and consumers outside of the U.S. feel as though the U.S. companies are shipping them second rate, insecure products. This has forced non-U.S. firms looking for "first rate" encryption to turn to non-U.S. suppliers. While there are not many non-U.S. suppliers today, the longer the U.S. prohibits the export of the technology, the greater the window of opportunity for non-U.S. firms to lock up the market outside of the U.S.

As a result of this situation, the U.S. Security Sector, along with the rest of the EC industry, has put tremendous pressure on the government to change its policies. The government's law enforcement and intelligence agencies, led by the NSA, adamantly oppose the export of strong encryption, principally because it will make their jobs much harder, if not impossible, to do. While for years the government refused to budge its position, recently it has started to be a bit more flexible.

First off, it has agreed to allow the export of strong encryption for very specific applications, such as securing payment transactions, so long as it is not possible to use the application for anything other than its very narrow purpose.

Second, the government has agreed to allow firms to export programs with 56-bit keys so long as they have a "key escrow" feature. Key escrow systems provide a way for a third party (i.e. the government) to decrypt a message if they get the proper permission, such as a wire tap order or search order. There are a variety of ways to implement a key escrow system but almost all of them involve something called a "trusted third party." The trusted third party keeps copies of a key that will allow someone to read a message sent between two parties.

Originally, the government wanted to be the trusted third party, but this plan met with strong resistance from the business community and technology firms. In a compromise, the government has agreed to companies acting as their own trusted third parties. Under these so-called "key recovery" systems, companies could recreate a particular key if the government asked for it and had the proper authorization (i.e., a search warrant).

Several Security Sector firms, including V-ONE, Trusted Information Systems, Cylink (#@), and Hewlett-Packard (#), have applied for and received permission to export their own "key recovery" systems to companies operating outside of the U.S.

Over the long term, the government is fighting a losing battle and it knows it. While it's illegal to export strong encryption, the Internet makes it almost impossible to stop it from happening. For example, Pretty Good Privacy's (now part of Network Associates) popular e-mail encryption program can use keys of over 1,000 bits in length. When the latest version was released in the U.S. earlier this year, it was available for download from an Internet site in Norway on the same day. At some point, all of the people that the U.S. government is worried about are going to have access to this technology. When that point is reached, the only real effect of the U.S. prohibitions against export will be to deprive the U.S. Security Sector of the international market.

By most accounts, that point is fast approaching. While our conversations with government officials in both Congress and the Executive Branch indicate that opposition to relaxing export restrictions on general message encryption remain strong, there also appears to be a wide ranging recognition that within the next five years these restrictions will have to be dropped.

## Legal Recognition

Outside of encryption export policy, the Security Sector has two other concerns. The first concern is whether or not the government will make digital signatures legally binding. Today, most official documents can only be executed by physically writing a signature on a piece of paper. This dependence on pen and paper to create legally binding documents has put a bit of a crimp in the stride of the EC industry. For example, while banks can use their Internet sites to solicit new accounts, and customers can even electronically fill out new account applications, the government still requires banks to get a signed form in order to actually open a new account. This means that the customer has to print out their electronic application form, sign it, and mail it to the bank before an account can be officially opened. Not exactly the ideal of real-time paperless EC. Before this ideal can be reached, the government will have to recognize signatures as legally binding and put in place the systems and processes it needs to track and verify these new signatures should the need arise.

Developments on this front look more promising for the industry in the short term. The government has shown no real opposition to using digital signatures and has even endorsed a standard for digital signatures. Some state governments have actually gone so far as to approve digital signatures as legally binding. Slowly but surely, this issue will be worked out over the coming years.

One final government issue is the question of the government's involvement in the Certificate Authorities (CA) business. Traditionally, the government has been the largest and most important provider of certificates. It is logical to assume that at some point the government will either want to, or be forced to, issue digital versions of passports, driver's licenses, and birth certificates.

The government's entry into the Certificate Authority business could upset the plans of other private CAs. As the thinking goes, "Why use a private certificate from a company that may not be recognized and accepted, when you can use a certificate from the government, which everyone, both nationally and internationally, will likely recognize and accept." There's a lot to be said for that line of thinking, but it doesn't mean that private CAs are out of a business. After all, the average person's wallet today has more private certificates in it than public. So as we have said before, even if the government enters the CA business, there will still be a healthy and vibrant business issuing and managing private certificates.

## The End Game?

The government. Microsoft and Cisco. One-stop shops versus standards. Trying to determine how any one of these trends will play out is hard enough, but trying to make sense of them all can make your head spin. However, on closer inspection, there are already some pretty clear indications as to how the industry will evolve over the next few years and what opportunities this evolution might create.

Today, the industry is a motley collection of product- and service-specific providers. The added complexity that this dispersion creates, along with the need to more closely integrate security into operating systems and network equipment, has made the current structure untenable. Over the near term, we see these trends driving a simplification of the industry structure (see Figure 3.13). Several main structural components will arise out of this drive for network management simplicity:

- *Perimeter Security Devices:* These devices will incorporate firewalls, remote access software, link encryption, and application proxies into one package that will be tightly integrated with the network switches and routers. Hardened operating systems will largely disappear as these features are built directly into the shipping versions of major operating systems.

- *Security Administration Software:* The need to create a single control center for managing the entire security system will push privileges management, security administration, in-house certificate authorities, and intrusion and detection management software into tightly integrated suites that enable network managers to control their entire security system from a single user interface. This suite will have to

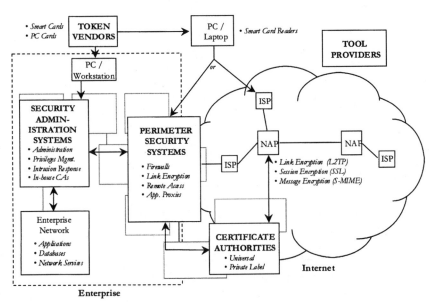

**Figure 3.13** Security Sector's Likely End Game   *Source: Piper Jaffray*

interface tightly with the network operating system and will have to add value above and beyond the basic security features provided by the operating system.

- *Token Vendors:* A group of manufacturers will continue to produce a variety of hard tokens to help authenticate users both at the network and operating system level. However, over time smart cards will become to dominant form of token.

- *Certificate Authorities:* Scale, combined with operational and financial requirements, will drive the sector toward a small collection of large CAs. Many CAs will serve in both universal and private label roles. Some private CAs will operate on behalf of governments at the state and/or local levels, but the federal government and the larger states will operate their own CAs, much as they do today.

- *Tool Kit Vendors:* A small group of firms will work to create the basic tool kits that enable other software vendors to build encryption features directly into their applications. The tool kits will not only cover encryption algorithms such as RSA, but also payment standards such as SET and digital rights management.

The formation of this structure is already clearly under way. Firewall vendors are in the process of creating the perimeter security device, and the "one-stop-shop" firms are assembling all of the pieces necessary to create the Security Administration System. With this migration already under way, the question facing companies in the industry as well as investors is not so much "Where are things going?" as "What will it take to be successful in this new environment?"

## Success Factors

Nothing can assure a company of success in this changing environment, but given the way things are going, it's fairly clear that a number of important factors will go a long way toward ensuring that a company not only survives, but thrives, as the security sector matures.

**Complete, but modular solutions:**   No one knows whether or not one-stop-shops will rule the world or a standards-based environment will create product-focused competition among best-of-breed providers. The best companies will bet on both by building complete, yet modular solutions that can either be bought as an entire system or as individual piece parts. This way, no matter which way the battle goes, they will be in position to capitalize on the outcome.

**Partnerships:**   Partnerships with hardware and system software providers will become increasingly important as these firms look to more tightly integrate security features into their core product offerings. Security Sector firms that build partnerships with such firms will benefit from their established customer bases and distribution channels.

**Market-focused management:**   In the past, many Security Sector firms focused more on technology and mathematics than they did on market shares and competition. Going forward, successful firms will focus on the business problems of their customers and their strategic position within the sector. These firms will combine aggressive marketing, partnerships, selective acquisitions, and an emphasis on making technology accessible to create "market-focused" firms that are truly in position to capitalize on the market's growth.

**Intellectual capital:**   A group of rocket scientists may not be needed to produce security technology, but what is needed is many applied mathematicians, some very talented programmers, and an in-depth understanding of the operational and technical intricacies of network and information security. It also doesn't hurt to have a few key patents on emerging technologies. At the end of the day, these requirements may be the saving grace of the industry, as there just aren't that many people in the world who really understand how this stuff works. Firms with a strong stable of this "intellectual capital" have less to fear than others because even if the industry is taken over by Microsoft and Cisco, chances are these firms will be able to walk away with a healthy premium for all their human talent.

# New Opportunities

The evolution of the Security Sector is no doubt going to create some new opportunities. Some of the most significant that will emerge over the next six to twelve months include:

- *Certificate Authorities:* There will no doubt be a significant need for firms that issue and then manage digital certificates. While numerous firms, such as Verisign, Entrust, and Cybertrust, are already active in this area, the CA market should be big enough to support many more players. In the long run, the key factor in this market is likely going to be customer service and flexibility in designing a certificate issuance and maintenance scheme. We suspect that there are plenty of opportunities left in this market for firms with the right approach to the market.

- *Niche Applications Market:* Applications focused on specific needs and markets will become increasingly viable as the sector grows in size. These applications will also be protected from encroachment by the networking and OS firms as they are too specialized to warrant particular attention. Payment security, digital rights management, and security "system design" software should prove to be small but lucrative niche markets.

- *Security Services Market:* The complexity of integrating and maintaining a "state-of-the-art" security solution will intensify the need for a "security services" market. While much of this market will be dominated by traditional systems integrators, we expect that several security services firms will emerge over the next year. Pilot Network Services is an early example of this trend.

## Investment Considerations

Of course even well-positioned firms that take advantage of these emerging opportunities may not make good investments. It is with this in mind that we would like to briefly review the investment performance of the Security Sector and discuss the sector's investment characteristics.

### Recent Investment Performance

As Figure 3.14 demonstrates, since the beginning of 1997, the Security Sector has performed slightly better than the entire EC industry. However, the sector has generally tended to be more volatile than the overall EC industry. During the early part of 1997, the Security Sector was particularly hard hit by the downturn in small capitalization stocks, with the sector falling by over ⅓ in the space of just a few months. Fortunately, the sector soon rebounded on the strength of strong first quarter earnings reports by Checkpoint, Security Dynamics, and others. For the rest of 1997 though, the sector seemed stuck in a holding pattern, never capable of sustaining a series of brief run-ups.

The Security Sector started with a bang in 1998, with the Security Index leaping forward by almost 40% in just the first three months of the year. However, just when this run-up appeared as though it would continue, several firms announced poor first quarter results, including (quite ironically) Security Dynamics and Checkpoint. These poor results helped drive the sector back down from its heights.

**INDEX**

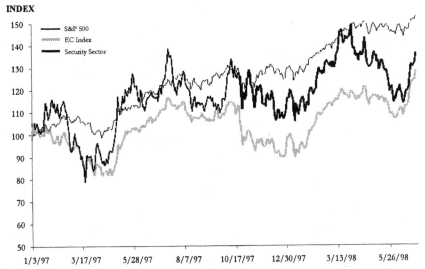

**Figure 3.14**  Security Sector Performance Versus the EC Index and S&P 500
*Source: Piper Jaffray*

## Market Characteristics

From an investment perspective, our definition of the Security Sector includes those public firms that are *focused* on providing network security services and products. We do not include the elephants (such as Microsoft or Cisco Systems), nor do we include file protection firms, such as Symantec.

This process of elimination leaves just thirteen U.S. public firms that are focused on the Security Sector today (see Table 3.10). Eight of these firms, or 62% of the sector, have gone public since 1996. Key statistics for this group as of 12/31/97 include:

*Market Capitalization:* The 12 firms command a market value of $10.4 billion. This makes the Security Sector the second largest sector in the EC universe behind the Electronic Payments Sector and in front of the Business Commerce Sector.

*Liquidity:* While this sector is small, it is active. In 1997, total daily trading volume averaged $208 million/day. Capitalization in the sector, therefore, turned over an average of every 50 days compared to 83 days for the entire EC universe. This makes the Security Sector the second most actively traded sector in the EC industry.

*Volatility:* As is clear from Figure 3.14, the Security Sector was even more volatile than the already volatile EC industry. On a capitalization

**Table 3.10**  Firms in the Security Sector Index
as of December 31, 1997

| Company | Ticker | Mrkt cap | $Vol/ day ($MMs) | % price △/day | 1997 revs ($MMs) | 1997 earn ($MMs) | 1998E P/E | 1999E P/E | 1997 P/S |
|---|---|---|---|---|---|---|---|---|---|
| Network Associates | NETA | $5,492 | $126.1 | 2.9% | $612 | ($28.4) | 29.4 | 22.7 | 8.3 |
| Checkpoint | CHKPF | 1,086 | 26.0 | 3.5 | 83 | 40.2 | 21.7 | 18.7 | 10.8 |
| Versign | VRSN | 775 | 11.6 | 4.1 | 9 | (19.2) | NA | NA | 64.0 |
| Security Dynamics | SDTI | 756 | 14.9 | 3.4 | 136 | 16.4 | 27.2 | 18.0 | 5.1 |
| Axent Technologies | AXNT | 750 | 10.0 | 3.0 | 45 | (19.7) | 40.8 | 29.7 | 13.2 |
| ISS Group Inc. | ISSX | 634 | 11.9 | 3.8 | 13 | (3.9) | NA | 250.8 | 47.1 |
| Cylink Corp. | CYLK | 348 | 2.3 | 3.4 | 49 | (63.3) | 35.3 | 17.9 | 6.2 |
| Secure Computing | SCUR | 158 | 2.2 | 3.3 | 47 | (4.3) | 31.9 | 16.2 | 3.2 |
| Vasco | VASC | 109 | 0.2 | 4.3 | NA | NA | NA | NA | NA |
| Wave Systems | WAVX | 91 | 1.2 | 3.2 | 0 | (13.9) | NM | NM | NM |
| Cyber guard | CYBG | 85 | 1.7 | 3.3 | 16 | (12.5) | NM | 13.8 | 4.1 |
| V-One | VONE | 50 | 0.2 | 4.1 | 9 | (9.4) | NM | NM | 5.3 |
| Info. Resource Eng. | IREG | 41 | 0.2 | 2.9 | 16 | (3.6) | NM | 18.4 | 2.3 |
| Total | | $10,375 | $208.4 | 2.1% | $1,036 | ($121.6) | 39.2 | 5.5 | 10.0 |

SOURCE:  Company reports, First Call, and Piper Jaffray

weighted average daily basis, Security Sector stocks were twice as volatile as the overall industry, changing 2.1% per day compared to 1.3% per day for the EC sector and 0.8% for the S&P 500. This makes the Security Sector the third most volatile sector in the EC industry.

*Revenues:* Revenues for the sector totaled over $1 billion in 1997 but they grew 120% from 1996. The Security Sector's revenue growth rate is the second highest in the EC universe.

*Earnings:* As a whole, the industry actually lost $122 million in 1997 thanks, in part, to charges associated with acquisitions and divestitures. As a group only 2 of the 13 firms were profitable in 1997. However, the market leaders proved quite profitable, with Checkpoint Software posting a 48.5% *net* margin and Security Dynamics posting a profit of $19.7 million (excluding acquisition charges) on revenues of $136 million for a net margin of 15%.

# Risks

Going forward, consistent with the industry's continued evolution, we see four major investment risks for stocks in the Security Sector:

1. *Competition from Networking and OS Firms:* The major networking and operating system firms have a vested interest in the progress and development of security technology. To date, these firms have, more often than not, chosen to expand their security offerings by partnering with existing Security Sector firms. However, decisions by these powerful firms to pursue their own "built in" solutions could seriously impact the sector's long-term growth and even its ultimate independent viability. Of particular note, an acquisition of a Security Sector firm by any of these firms would likely depress the values of the remaining players. Given these companies' massive cash flows and demonstrated comfort with growth through acquisition, this is a real possibility. At the end of the day, the real risk that the Security Sector faces is that it may be too important for its own good.

2. *Margin Erosion:* Current product margins may prove unsustainable as competition intensifies and as the market becomes big enough for established networking and operating system companies to consider developing their own solutions. In the summer of 1996, concerns over the sustainability of firewall margins resulted in heavy stock price declines. There is a possibility that these trends will be repeated in the encryption markets as several patents in this area will expire over the next few years and these expirations may intensify competition in this new area as new entrants seek to establish market share.

3. *Regulatory Risk:* There is a general expectation that the U.S. government will continue to relax its export restrictions and will probably repeal them before the turn of the century. Strong indications from the government contrary to this belief could have a serious impact on the market. In addition, there is always the possibility that the government could subject firms to regulatory requirements which could impact their operating expenses and market flexibility. Also, the government's plans for its participation in the Certificate Authority market are not yet formed. There is a small chance that the government could preclude private companies from acting as CAs (possibly due to the large key sizes required by CAs) which would obviously have a negative effect on the sector.

4. *SET Deployment:* As we pointed out earlier in the chapter, there are high expectations in the market for the deployment and acceptance of SET. Many Security Sector firms are creating products expressly for the SET market, and expectations for forthcoming sales have been built into

their stock prices. Material problems with the deployment and/or acceptance of SET could, therefore, have a negative impact on the Security Sector as a whole.

## Conclusion

Over the past few years, several powerful drivers have propelled the Security Sector to impressive growth and tremendous visibility. The fundamental drivers of the market should remain strong over the course of the next several years. The Security Sector's main challenge is to make the transition from a collection of disparate products and services into a set of business-focused security solutions that simplify the inherent complexity of security technology. Companies within the sector are undergoing their own metamorphoses as they strive to become more focused on their customers and the market than they are on technology and engineering for its own sake. The key challenge for these companies will be successfully positioning themselves to effectively complement and coexist with the inevitable security product offerings of the major network equipment providers and operating system developers.

# 4

# Electronic Payments and the Death of "The Switch"

## Introduction

Without the ability to electronically transfer value, EC would be merely little more than a fancy form of window shopping. Luckily, the Electronic Payments Sector has been electronically initiating, processing, analyzing, and supporting electronic payments for quite some time and is eager to apply these capabilities to the emerging world of EC. With the rise of EC, the Electronic Payments Sector will finally get its chance to shine as it moves out from the shadows of back office processing centers and into the center stage of the EC industry.

The Electronic Payments Sector is very different from the security sector. Whereas the security sector is a small and relatively nascent sector, the Electronic Payments Sector is large and established. Whereas the security sector's role and position are somewhat tenuous, the Electronic Payments Sector occupies a defined and largely unassailable position. These differences mean that the Electronic Payment Sector's structural and competitive dynamics are also considerably different.

Investors in the Electronic Payments Sector need to understand these differences in order to identify where the real opportunities will be as the Electronic Payments sector enters the age of EC.

## Structure

The Electronic Payment and Security Sectors do share two things in common: networks and complexity. In the Electronic Payments Sector, the source of these two factors is something called "the payment system."

A basic understanding of the payment system is critical to understanding the Electronic Payments Sector because changes in the payments system can have a major impact on almost every firm in the sector.

## Payment System Basics

The "payment system" is actually a complex collection of several different payment systems, some of which, but not all, are linked together. In the U.S., depending on how you count, there are at least seven different payment systems that in turn make up the "payment system." Each individual payment system is basically a private computer network that has been optimized to handle specific types of financial transactions. As a rule, payment systems must be fast, highly reliable, and secure.

While payment systems differ greatly in their size and structure, each system serves the same basic role: to authorize and settle payment transactions. Authorization is the act of providing permission for someone to make a particular payment. Settlement involves actually transferring funds from one party to another. Some payment systems authorize and settle payments at the same time, while others do each separately. For example, credit card transactions are authorized at the time the sale is made, but they are typically settled separately, at the end of the day. Settlement is the most important function of a payment system and it is also potentially one of the riskiest. "Settlement risk," or the risk that one person in a payment transaction will not have the money needed to make payment, is a major preoccupation of payment system managers.

Another important concern of payment systems is float. Float is the income produced by a payment while it is "in transit." Whoever is holding onto the payment while it is in transit gets to keep that income. Different payment systems have different levels of float. Checks can take several days to process so they generate a significant amount of float; whereas, wire transfers between large banks are completed instantaneously and therefore have no float.

Most payment systems can be broken out into four generic piece parts (see Figure 4.1). Each part plays a defined role in completing a transfer of value:

- *Certifying Authority:* Certifying Authorities establish and maintain the guidelines and standards that all of the participants in a system must abide by. They also typically certify new participants to join the system and adjudicate disputes between existing members. Certifying Authorities also often manage the brand and public relations for the payment system. Most certifying authorities are owned or controlled by financial institutions. VISA, MasterCard, and the National Automated

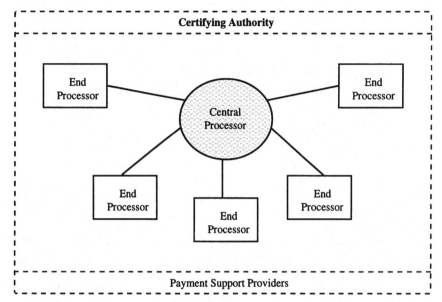

**Figure 4.1**  Generic Payment System Structure    *Source: Piper Jaffray*

Clearing House Association (NACHA) are all examples of Certifying Authorities.

- *Central Processors:* Central processors transfer or "switch" payments between the different parties in a payment system. In this way, central processors are quite similar to the "routers" that make up the core of the Internet's infrastructure. Unlike simple routers, most central processors don't just simply forward transactions on to the appropriate party, rather they "net" payments against each other. "Netting" payments is the process of keeping score of how much each participant owes each other on a net basis. "Netting" enables parties to make one "net settlement" instead of having to settle each transaction. Most, but not all, central processors are owned or controlled by financial institutions. The Federal Reserve Banks (checks) and VISA (credit cards) are two examples of central processors.

  Central processors and Certifying Authorities are often, though not always, part of the same organization. For example, VISA and MasterCard serve as both central processors and Certifying Authorities in the credit card industry.

- *End Processors:* End processors initiate, receive, and process payments on behalf of businesses and consumers. End processors are not necessarily owned by financial institutions. In fact, some of the largest end processors are non-financial institutions such as First Data Corporation (#), Deluxe Inc., and EDS. That said, these companies typically sell their processing services to financial service firms on an outsourcing basis.

■ *Payment Support Providers:* These firms do not process payments, but provide the hardware, software, and services that make payment processing possible. Many high technology firms such as Verifone [now part of Hewlett-Packard(#)], Gemplus, and Transaction Systems Architects, can be found in this sector.

## Different Types of Payment Systems

To simplify our examination of the "payment system" we have grouped the seven different U.S. payment systems into three main categories:

1. *Wholesale Systems:* Wholesale payment systems are designed to make large dollar (i.e., multimillion) payments between financial institutions. Membership in these systems is typically tightly controlled and almost all of these systems are owned by either central governments or bank associations. These systems account for the vast majority of payments in terms of total dollar volume. Most countries have two types of wholesale payment systems: a central bank system and an Inter-bank system. The central bank system is used by banks to make payments directly to the central bank as well as indirect payments to other banks while the Inter-bank system is used by banks to make payments to each other.

2. *Retail Electronic Payment Systems:* These payment systems handle small dollar payments from consumer-to-business, business-to-consumer, and business-to-business. These systems can be generally used to make either scheduled payments or point-of-sale payments. Scheduled payments are payments that can be authorized well in advance of their due dates, such as paychecks or mortgage payments. Point-of-sale payments are payments that are completed spontaneously at a location other than a financial institution. Retail electronic payment systems are distinguished by their wide availability and direct usage by consumers and businesses.

3. *Paper Payment Systems:* Paper payment systems are configured to efficiently collect, transport, process, and distribute paper payment instruments, primarily checks and cash (bank notes). Paper payment systems are used for all forms of commerce, but dominate consumer to consumer payments.

## Primary Payment Systems for EC

While all three of these payment system categories are likely to play at least a minor role in EC, the category most important to EC will be Retail Elec-

**Table 4.1**　Different Categories of Payment Systems

|  | Wholesale | Retail electronic | Paper |
|---|---|---|---|
| Description | Make payments between financial institutions | Make business-to-consumer and business-to-business payments | Make business-to-consumer, business-to-business, and consumer-to-consumer payments |
| Value of payments | ■ High | ■ Low to high | ■ Low to medium |
| # of users | ■ Low | ■ High | ■ High |
| Examples | ■ FedWire<br>■ CHIPS | ■ Credit card<br>■ Electronic Funds Transfer (EFT)<br>■ Automated Clearing House (ACH) | ■ Checks<br>■ Cash |

SOURCE: Piper Jaffray

tronic Systems. These payment systems have the ability to handle everything from $10 to $10 million payments, are almost completely electronic, and are heavily used by both businesses and consumers (see Table 4.1).

Within the Retail Electronic Systems category, three payment systems in particular [the credit card system, the Electronic Funds Transfer (EFT) system, and the Automated Clearing House (ACH) system] are likely to play the most important roles in EC and therefore warrant further discussion.

**Credit Card Payment System**

With its ubiquitous, international reach and well understood operation, the credit card payment system is well positioned to play an important role in EC. The credit card payment system includes several different entities, each of which roughly corresponds to one of the four generic roles we laid out earlier in the chapter (see Table 4.2).

One important feature to note is that while the VISA and MasterCard associations only serve as Certifying Authorities and central processors, other card brands, such as Discover, American Express, and Diner's Club, issue cards and acquirer merchants in addition to acting as the Certifying Authority and central processor.[1]

A typical credit card transaction (see Figure 4.2) starts at the "Point-Of-Sale" (POS), which is usually the cash register of a merchant. The merchant runs the credit card through a payment terminal (provided, more

[1] It should also be noted that American Express and Diner's Club (which is owned by Citibank) are primarily charge card operations (i.e., they do not grant credit lines and require payment in full each month).

**Table 4.2** Credit Card Payment System Description

| Entity | Generic role | Brief description | Examples |
|---|---|---|---|
| Associations | Certifying Authorities | Approve firms to issue a specific brand of credit card. Set rules for members to follow. Build brand of credit card. | ▪ VISA<br>▪ MasterCard<br>▪ American Express |
| National switches | Central processors | Relay authorization and settlement requests between end processors. Facilitate net settlement. Manage payment network. | ▪ VISA<br>▪ MasterCard<br>▪ American Express |
| Issuers | End processors | Grant credit lines and issue cards to consumers and businesses. Authorize credit card purchases. Bill customers for purchases made. | ▪ Citibank<br>▪ MBNA<br>▪ American Express |
| Acquirers | End processors | Sign up merchants to accept credit card. Relay merchant authorization requests. Capture and process payments from issuing banks. | ▪ Bank of America<br>▪ First USA<br>▪ American Express |
| Third-party processors | End processors | Perform either all or part of issuer and/or acquirer duties as an outsourcer. May work directly for merchant. | ▪ First Data Corp<br>▪ National Processing<br>▪ SPS Transaction Systems |
| Terminal, software, and service vendors | Payment support providers | Provide credit card terminals, software, network services, etc., to all of the above parties. | ▪ Verifone (HP)<br>▪ Transaction Network Services |

SOURCE: Piper Jaffray

than likely, by either Verifone or Hypercom). The terminal then contacts the merchant processor which in turn initiates an authorization request. This request is sent to the national switch which routes it to the issuing bank (i.e., the bank that gave the credit card to the cardholder) where it is either approved or denied. The response is relayed back through the switch to the merchant acquirer and then back down to the point of sale. Later in the day the process is repeated when the various processors (issuers and acquirers and/or third-party processors) settle on a net basis with the national switches.

The credit card payment system is large and growing. According to *The Nilson Report*, in 1996 the credit card payment system included 6,800 issuers, 2.8 million merchants, and 98 million cardholders. These parties generated transactions with a total value of $870 billion (see Figure 4.3). In addition, the issuing banks held about $366 billion in outstanding debt by year-end 1996.[2]

[2] The Nilson Report. 3/97.

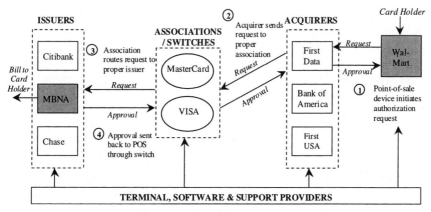

**Figure 4.2** Credit Card Transaction Example *Source: Piper Jaffray*

Merchants pay for credit card transactions through something called the "discount fee." The discount fee generally ranges from 2% to 4% of the purchase price and is paid to the merchant's processor/acquiring bank. The discount fee covers the acquirer's/processor's expenses. These expenses include losses due to fraud which amounted to only $670 mil-

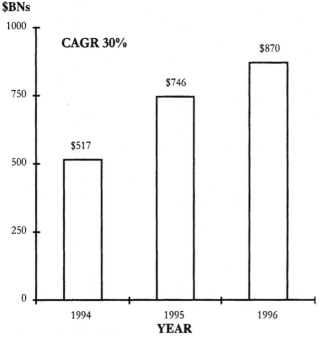

**Figure 4.3** Credit Card Dollar Volumes 1994–1996
*Source: The Nilson Report*

lion, or 0.1% of total volume in 1996.[3] The processor in turn pays "interchange fees" (also a set percent of the transaction) to the credit card associations and the issuers which use the fees to help defray network, advertising, and other costs. While the issuers get to participate in the interchange fees, they earn most of their money by charging interest on debt balances carried by their cardholders.

### Electronic Funds Transfer (EFT) Payment System

The EFT payment system is structured somewhat like the credit card payment system, but unlike credit cards, where there are just five major associations and Certifying Authorities, the EFT system has over 50 separate Certifying Authorities or "Regional Network Switches" as they are known (see Table 4.3). The reason for this regional structure is that most EFT net-

[3] This includes VISA and MasterCard only.

**Table 4.3**   EFT Payment System Description

| Entity | General role | Brief description | Examples |
|---|---|---|---|
| Regional switches | Certifying Authorities and central processors | Switch EFT transactions between regional members and national switches. Sign up new issuers and acquirers. | • Electronic Payment Systems (MAC)<br>• NYCE<br>• Star |
| National switches | Central processors | Switch EFT transactions between regional EFT networks. Build connections to international EFT networks. | • Plus (VISA)<br>• Cirrus (MasterCard)<br>• Express Cash (Amex) |
| Issuers | End processors | Issue online debit cards (ATM cards) to account holders. Authorize and process account transactions. Provide customer service. | • Citibank<br>• Wells Fargo<br>• Bank of America |
| ATM deployers/ acquirers | End processors | Deploy ATM terminals and/or sign up new POS merchants. Process authorizations and settlements on behalf of merchants. | • Bank of America<br>• EDS<br>• NationsBank |
| Third-party processors | End processors | Perform either all or part of issuer and acquirer duties as an outsourcer. Some merchants may run their own or "drive" their own networks. | • Concord EFS<br>• Deluxe Data |
| ATM, terminal, software, and service vendors | Payment support providers | Provide ATMs, POS terminals, software, network services, etc., to all of the above parties. | • Interbold<br>• Transaction System Architects |

SOURCE: Piper Jaffray

works were built as extensions of local bank branch networks, primarily in order to distribute cash via ATMs.

That said, there are several big National Switches in the EFT payment system, the biggest of which are Plus and Cirrus, which are owned by VISA and MasterCard, respectively. By leveraging their existing payment networks, VISA and MasterCard have made it possible for consumers to use their local bank's ATM card not only throughout the U.S., but throughout the world.

A typical EFT transaction starts with the consumer putting his/her ATM card into an ATM machine. The consumer then enters a Personal Identification Number (PIN) code into the ATM as well as the transaction he/she wishes to make. The acquiring processor then contacts the Regional Network Switch which forwards the transaction onto the appropriate issuing bank or national EFT switch. The issuing bank then verifies the PIN number and determines whether or not the cardholder has sufficient funds in the account to process the transaction. Authorization for the transaction travels back through the network to the ATM, which (assuming the transaction was approved) dispenses the cash.

The EFT market is actually bigger than the credit card market in terms of total transactions and dollar volume. According to *Bank Network News,* in 1996 there were about 11.6 billion EFT transactions (see Figure 4.5). The dollar volume of these transactions was about $725 billion, almost 20% higher than total credit card volumes.

The economics of ATM transactions are fairly straightforward. The issuing bank pays the regional switch a per transaction fee that is dependent on the total volume of transactions that the issuer generates. These fees

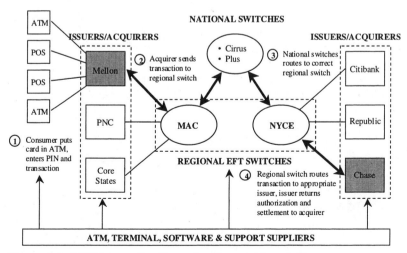

**Figure 4.4**  EFT Transaction Example   *Source: Piper Jaffray*

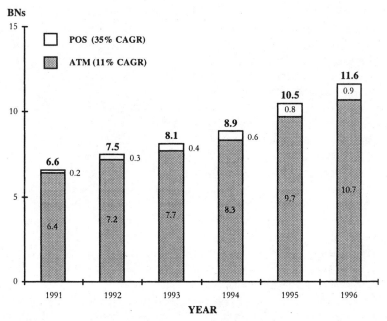

**Figure 4.5**  EFT Transaction Volumes 1991–1996   *Source: Bank Network News*

can range anywhere from $0.10 to $0.50 per transaction. If the transaction originated outside of the regional network, the issuer pays the national switch a fee in addition to the regional switch fee. This fee also depends on volume as well as the location of the transaction, but it can range up to $1.00. It is up to the issuers whether or not they pass any of these fees along to their customers. Transactions by an issuer's customers at the issuer's own ATMs are called "on-us" transactions. The issuing bank pays no fees for these "on-us" transactions, but must absorb the expense of operating the ATM. One new wrinkle in ATM economics is called "surcharging." Surcharging involves directly charging consumers an extra $0.50 to $2.00 for a transaction. Banks do not surcharge their own customers, so surcharging creates an incentive for consumers to use only their own bank's ATMs.

The EFT system could potentially play a major role in the EC industry as it is the only major *real-time* retail electronic payment system in the U.S.

### Debit Transactions

Initially, the EFT payment system could only be used to withdraw cash from ATMs. In an attempt to expand the EFT payment system, the

Regional Network Switches installed what were in effect "mini-ATMs" inside individual stores. These mini-ATMs, called Point-Of-Sale (POS) terminals, allow consumers to pay for items such as groceries and gas using their ATM cards.

This type of payment is called a debit transaction. For all intents and purposes, debit transactions are almost identical to ATM transactions: consumers still use an ATM card and enter a PIN, transactions are still processed using the EFT system, and the funds are still debited from accounts immediately. The only real difference is that the *merchants pay* for the transaction (between $0.05 to $0.30 per transaction) instead of the issuing bank. Merchants are willing to pay for the transactions because electronic payments reduce their cash handling and check processing costs.[4] Consumers like debit transactions because they are faster than writing a check and they eliminate the need to carry around excessive amounts of cash. While debit transactions got off to a slow start, they have since become an increasingly important source of volume for the EFT payment system.

This would be where the story ends if it wasn't for a new type of transaction called "off-line" debit. At a high level, off-line debit transactions are very similar to traditional debit transactions (now called "on-line debit" transactions) in that both types of transactions allow consumers to pay at the point of sale using their checking account.

At a detailed level though, there are a number of important differences (see Table 4.4). The most important difference is that while on-line debit is controlled by the Regional Network Switches, off-line debit is controlled by VISA and MasterCard.

In its raw form, off-line debit is an attempt by VISA and MasterCard to take control of the debit transaction business from the Regional Network Switches. The main obstacle to this attempt is that off-line debit transactions cost merchants much more per transaction than on-line debit transactions. This higher cost has made most merchants, including Wal-Mart (#), Sears (#), and The Limited, bitterly opposed to off-line debit. In fact they have filed lawsuits to try to gain the right to refuse to accept off-line debit cards.[5]

Meanwhile, most banks have become big boosters of off-line debit because, unlike on-line debit cards, off-line debit cards generate inter-

---

[4] Actually, at first merchants wanted nothing to do with debit transactions as they required a hefty investment in payment terminals and communications gear. As a result, most banks either ate the cost of debit transactions or charged consumers.

[5] MasterCard and VISA have contract agreements which force merchants to accept any MasterCard or VISA branded card. The merchants contend that this violates banking industry "anti-tying" laws which prohibit banks from requiring customers to give them deposit business in return for the extension of credit.

**Table 4.4**   On-Line and Off-Line Debit Card Description

| Card type | AKA | Certifying authority | Key characteristics | Economics |
|---|---|---|---|---|
| On-line debit | "Cash Cards" | ▪ Regional network switches | ▪ Similar to ATM transaction<br>▪ Requires PIN<br>▪ Can only be used within the Regional Switch's operating area<br>▪ "On-line" authorization from bank<br>▪ Same Day Settlement<br>▪ "Good funds" | Per transaction ($0.05–$0.30) |
| Off-line debit | "Check Cards" | ▪ Major credit card associations (VISA/MC) | ▪ Similar to Credit Card transaction<br>▪ No PIN required<br>▪ Can be used anywhere VISA/MC accepted<br>▪ Authorization from VISA/MC<br>▪ Multi-day settlement<br>▪ "Check" could bounce | % of transaction (1.5%–2.5% of purchase price) |

SOURCE:  Piper Jaffray

change revenues for the card issuer of somewhere between 1% to 1.5% of the transaction. This means that the average off-line purchase generates roughly between $0.50 to $0.75 a transaction, compared with the $0.15 to $0.30 generated by on-line debit. These kinds of differences add up when millions of transactions are being processed a year. Spurred on by these potential revenues, banks and card associations have been aggressively promoting off-line debit. So much so, that off-line debit has now over-taken on-line debit in terms of number of transactions.

So on one side, banks and credit card associations are pushing off-line debit while on the other side, merchants and the Regional Network Switches are pushing on-line debit. While to many people this battle seems like much ado about nothing, it in fact represents one of the open-ing skirmishes in a battle between payment systems, a battle that will intensify in the world of EC (we'll discuss this more in the "Trends" sec-tion of this chapter).

## Automated Clearing House (ACH) Payment System

The ACH payment system is a completely electronic payment system for making "pre-authorized payments." Today, the main method most con-

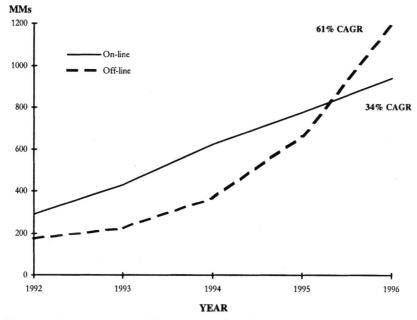

**Figure 4.6**  On-Line and Off-Line Debit Volumes 1992–1996  *Source: The Nilson Report*

sumers and businesses use to make pre-authorized payments is the lowly paper check. Each month, many companies pay their employees with a paper check. These employees in turn pay their mortgages, car payments, and other bills with their own paper checks.

The ACH system was created in an attempt to eliminate all of this paper shuffling, by enabling both businesses and consumers to make pre-authorized electronic payments. One of the most well-known uses of the ACH system is "Direct Deposit" whereby paychecks or benefits are directly deposited into an employee's bank account. The ACH system is also used by many consumers to "automatically" pay recurring monthly bills such as mortgage, insurance, and car payments.

Like paper checks, ACH payments are processed in batches, take a couple of days to clear, and can technically bounce. An ACH transaction is a pretty simple affair (see Figure 4.7). A business or consumer instructs its bank to originate an ACH transaction. The bank groups or batches all of its ACH transactions together and then sends them to an Automated Clearing House operator. The operator processes all of the ACH transactions at once and sends the results to the appropriate receiving banks.

ACH was established in the early 1970s, but did not begin to experience substantial growth until the mid 1980s. Over the last ten years, ACH vol-

**Table 4.5**   ACH Payment System Description

| Entity | Generic role | Brief description | Examples |
|---|---|---|---|
| National Automated Clearing House Association (NACHA) | Certifying authority | Sets standards for ACH message formats. Organizes committees to manage ACH aspects of the ACH "system." Promotes use of ACH transactions. | ▪ NACHA |
| Automated Clearing House Operator | Central processors | Processes batches of ACH transactions from originators and routes them to receivers. Provides net settlement services. | ▪ Federal Reserve<br>▪ New York Clearing House<br>▪ VISA |
| Originators/ receivers | End processors | Initiate and/or receive ACH transactions on behalf of their customers. | ▪ Chase<br>▪ Citibank<br>▪ NationsBank |
| Third-party processors | End processors | Process ACH transactions on behalf of financial institutions, businesses, or consumers. Cannot initiate payments. | ▪ Checkfree<br>▪ First Data |
| Software vendors | Payment support providers | Provide software that enables ACH processing. Integrate ACH processing with other payment systems. | ▪ Checkfree<br>▪ Transaction System Architects |

SOURCE: Piper Jaffray

ume has increased substantially, growing from 750 million transactions in 1986 to 3.1 billion transactions in 1996 representing a healthy rate of about 15% a year.[6] (see Figure 4.8). Measured by dollar volume, the ACH system is 10 times bigger than the credit card and EFT payment systems *combined*. The largest ACH operator is the Federal Reserve which processed 94% of all ACH volumes in 1995. The Federal Reserve does not charge for processing ACH transactions which, as one might imagine, makes it very difficult to compete against. According to the National Automated Clearing House Association (NACHA), ACH transactions cost banks an average of 5.7 cents per transaction compared to 10.5 cents per paper check.[7]

The ACH system is of particular importance to the EC industry because it is the principal electronic payment system used for both electronic bill payment and Financial Electronic Data Interchange (F-EDI) transactions. Electronic bill payment is used to pay recurring bills (see the Bill Payment

---

[6] Figures from the Federal Reserve Bank of New York. Does not include non-Federal reserve ACH payments.

[7] "Direct Payment Market Analysis," NACHA. Study completed for NACHA by Payment Systems Inc.

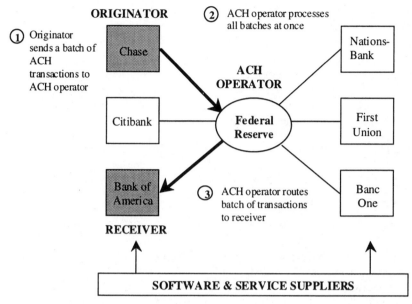

**Figure 4.7**   ACH Transaction Example   *Source: Piper Jaffray*

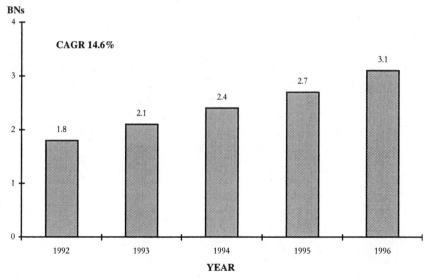

**Figure 4.8**   ACH Payment Volumes   *Note: Includes Federal Reserve ACH payments only. Source: Federal Reserve Bank of New York*

Sidebar in this chapter). F-EDI is used by businesses to transmit both payment and remittance together in one EDI transmission (see Chapter 6). In addition to these activities, the ACH system appears poised to potentially play a major role in emerging payment forms such as Electronic Checks and Electronic Bill Presentment.

Taken together, the three payment systems we just described, Credit Card, EFT, and ACH, form the backbone of the Electronic Payments Sector. This backbone does not get a lot of attention, but it is very difficult to understand what is going on in the Electronic Payments Sector without understanding how this backbone works.

### New Payment Devices

While understanding the backbone of the Electronic Payments Sector is important, understanding the new types of payments being created by the rise of EC is perhaps even more important. Smart cards, electronic cash, and electronic checks, to name a few, all have the potential to not only change the mix of payments, but perhaps even the payment systems themselves. The next part of this section steps through each of the major new types.

### Electronic Check

The electronic check is a new and much improved electronic version of that old standby, the paper check. The electronic check itself is nothing more than a specially formatted e-mail message sent over the Internet. Inside the e-mail message is all of the same information one would expect to find on a paper-based check including payee name, amount, payment date, payor's account number, and payor's financial institution. The message is sent via the Internet to either the payee or its bank. Once the electronic check is "deposited" at the payee's bank, it is processed through the ACH payment system as if it were a normal ACH transaction (see Figure 4.9).

To ensure its security as it travels over the Internet the electronic check uses many of the key security technologies outlined in Chapter 2. Electronic checks are "signed" with the digital signature of the sender and encrypted with the public key of the receiver. They also include a digital certificate from the sender's bank stating that the account number is valid and belongs to the person who signed the check.

The electronic check has several advantages over the paper-based equivalent:

1. *It's **much** more secure.* Forging paper-based checks is not a difficult process. In fact, just about anyone with a decent computer and laser

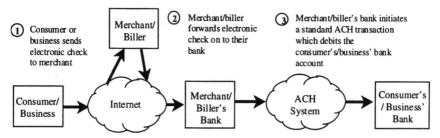

**Figure 4.9**   Electronic Check Transaction Example   *Source: Piper Jaffray*

printer can create checks that many people would have a hard time spotting as fakes. But forgery is a lot harder to accomplish with electronic checks. The digital certificate provided by the bank ensures that the account number is valid and that it belongs to a particular person. The digital signature of the account holder ensures that the check was actually "signed" by that person. In addition, the digital signature has the added advantage of ensuring that the contents of the check (payment amount and date) have not been tampered with since the check was signed. Encrypting the check with the recipient's public key guarantees that the check will remain private until it reaches its destination.

2. *It's faster.*   Whereas paper checks often take several days to reach their destination, electronic checks can be sent over the Internet and arrive at their destination in minutes. While there is still a chance that an electronic check may get "lost" on the Internet, the Internet will likely prove to be considerably more reliable than the U.S. postal service.

3. *It's easier to process.*   Paper-based checks must be handled, processed, sorted, and stored. Electronic checks require none of this manual attention. In addition, because the amount, dates, and signatures are all in electronic format, electronic checks greatly reduce the cost of processing a check and improve processing times.

Although the electronic check is still in pilot testing, with all of its inherent advantages it may not be long before many people are saying, "The check is in the *e*-mail."

## Electronic Cash

Electronic cash has probably garnered the most attention of all of the new payment types. Like paper cash, electronic cash provides final and immediate settlement at the point of sale. Like the electronic check, electronic cash is just a specially formatted e-mail message. Each message, or note, contains the same information found on regular cash: who issued it, how much it is worth, and a unique serial number. The cash is digitally signed by the entity that issued it (usually a bank) so that the amount and serial number cannot be forged. It is also encrypted so that only the recipient can use it.

Electronic cash comes in two forms: accountable and nonaccountable (see Table 4.6).

### Accountable Electronic Cash

Accountable electronic cash requires each transfer of the electronic cash to be authorized by the issuer. In an accountable system, the issuer of the cash keeps a record of all cash that has been issued and to whom it has been issued. When two parties want to complete a transaction, the recipient of the cash must contact the issuer and ask it to authorize the transaction. The issuer then checks the serial numbers on the cash to make sure that the cash has not already been spent elsewhere and that it belongs to the person who is trying to spend it. If everything checks out, the issuer cancels the old serial numbers, issues new ones, and then forwards them on to the recipient.

The advantage of using an accountable electronic cash system is that there is a complete record of who has what cash and who has paid whom.

**Table 4.6**   Different Types of Electronic Cash

| Cash type | Accountable | Nonaccountable |
|---|---|---|
| Description | Central record of all cash is kept. Transactions must be authorized by issuer in order to be completed. | No record of cash is centrally kept after it is issued. No authorization is required for transactions. |
| Advantages | ■ Can trace prior transactions<br>■ Can re-issue cash if it is lost<br>■ "Double spending" not possible | ■ Anonymous<br>■ No need for authorization<br>■ Can be used to make non-Internet transfers |
| Disadvantages | ■ Costs more to operate<br>■ Must be "on-line" to use<br>■ Issuer must be available to authorize transaction<br>■ Not anonymous, i.e. limited privacy | ■ Tougher to prevent double spending<br>■ Usually requires smart card<br>■ Easier to use for criminal activity<br>■ Could threaten Federal Reserve's control of money supply<br>■ Can lose cash |
| Examples | ■ Cybercash<br>■ Digicash | ■ Mondex<br>■ Visa Cash |

This means that the issuer can simply reissue cash if someone loses it. It also means that authorities can trace all of the electronic cash transactions.

Accountable systems have two main disadvantages. The first disadvantage is that they require authorization. This requirement adds to the cost of the system and makes it impossible to make payments if the issuer is "off-line." The second problem is privacy. Because payments can be traced, accountable systems are not anonymous.[8] These two disadvantages highlight the dirty little secret of accountable electronic cash system: it really isn't electronic cash. Because every transaction is authorized by the issuer, and the issuer keeps a record of who owns what cash, accountable electronic cash is more akin to a cross between a traveler's check and an EFT transaction than it is to real cash.

### Nonaccountable Electronic Cash

Nonaccountable electronic cash systems are about as close to the real thing as one can get. Just like paper cash, once nonaccountable cash is issued, it can be transferred to other people without the aid or knowledge of the issuer so there is therefore no central record of what payments have been made. In addition, because nonaccountable systems do not require authorization, transactions also cost less to process. While nonaccountable electronic cash is great in concept, it has a number of important risks and problems that must be addressed before it can be widely deployed.

The big risk in nonaccountable electronic cash is that someone will copy the serial numbers from their electronic cash and try to spend it twice. After all, with no central record of who owns what cash it would be impossible for someone to determine that the cash they were receiving had already been spent. To control this risk, nonaccountable systems encrypt the serial numbers. But encryption is not enough; special software must also be used to process each transaction. The software contains a set of rules that outline exactly how cash transfers can occur and acts as a "gatekeeper" making sure that every transaction conforms to the set of rules. This gatekeeping process is what prevents the cash from being copied or spent twice.

Obviously, it's pretty important to protect this gatekeeper software from alteration. The most secure way to do this is to permanently imprint the software on a computer chip. Thus, most non-accountable systems use a smart card or chip card. So, there is a solution to the double spending

---

[8] Digicash has developed an accountable cash system that still preserves privacy by using a technique called a blinded signature. Essentially this technique prevents banks from tracking their customers' individual payments.

problem, but the drawback is that it generally requires a physical card to solve. So much for purely "electronic" cash.

Another problem with nonaccountable electronic cash is that its nonaccountable nature potentially makes it easier for criminals to hide illegal activities. Today, doing a $30 million drug deal requires 300,000 $100 bills. That much paper is a major inconvenience to transport around and also provides rather conspicuous evidence that illegal activity has taken place. Theoretically, nonaccountable electronic cash could be used to effortlessly close $30 million drug deals. To prevent this from occurring, issuers generally limit the amount of cash that a chip card can have on it to a few hundred dollars.

One other problem for the authorities: nonaccountable cash can technically be issued by anyone who wants to. What if the issuer goes bankrupt or refuses to honor the cash when someone wishes to exchange it for "real" money? What if the issuer issues cash without any "real" money backed by it (i.e., they inflate their currency)? These problems all highlight the fact that issuing electronic cash is like creating a mini-monetary system. Each issuer of electronic cash could potentially become its own little central bank with the power to influence money creation and cause inflation.

While this may seem like a radical development, hundreds of private monetary systems already exist. Frequent Flyer or travel reward programs provide a classic example. These reward programs provide customers with points that are readily convertible into sources of value such as free flights and hotel stays. Users of these programs are already familiar with the perils of "private" monetary systems. Changes to these programs, such as increasing the number of points needed to obtain a reward, have the same effect as inflation—they devalue all of the points in the system. These programs have learned to be very careful about what actions they take because if they devalue their points, then people will assign a lower value to the program which may lead to decreases in customer loyalty.

The same logic goes for electronic cash: If people feel that the private cash systems are not well run, they will not value them as highly as other forms of exchange. In fact, at various points in the history of the United States there have often been multiple versions of both private and public cash, so there is no reason to suspect that anything will innately prevent multiple electronic cash systems from existing on the Internet.

That does not mean, however, that the Federal Reserve will be willing to tolerate the existence of such private cash schemes if they get large enough to start weakening the Fed's control of the short-term money supply. However, that point in time is a long way off and the Fed has bigger things to worry about in the interim (such as the bond market).

One final problem with nonaccountable electronic cash is that, just like real cash, it can be lost or destroyed. Losing the smart card with the serial numbers on it is just like losing a wallet full of cash. The solution to this problem is the same one that people use in real life; they try not to carry a lot of cash around with them.

## Stored Value Cards

Stored value cards, also known as prepaid cards, allow consumers to pre-pay for purchases by loading "value" onto a card. They can then use this card to make future purchases of specific goods and services usually by putting their card into a special card reader. The card reader reduces the notional "value" on the card by the amount of the purchase. The cards tend to look like credit cards or ATM cards, but they often come in a wide variety of sizes.

Stored value cards are essentially a stripped-down version of nonaccountable electronic cash. They are a lot like non-accountable cash in that:

1. If they are lost the value is lost.

2. They are anonymous.

3. They do not require authorization.

Where they differ from nonaccountable electronic cash is that they are typically "issuer specific" in that they are only honored by the entity that issued them. They also differ from electronic cash in that they:

1. Can be used by a person who finds (or steals) a card.

2. Can only be used for a specific type of activity or purchase.

3. Do not require a secret key to authorize transactions.

4. Do not use a computer chip or software "gatekeeper."

In the U.S., stored value cards are often found in transportation systems. In New York City, the "Metrocard" is a stored value card that can be used to pay for subway and bus trips. In Europe, most telephone companies issue stored value cards for use in pay phones, while in Japan, stored value cards are used for just about everything, from fast-food restaurants to beer vending machines.

Stored value cards' simple operation, low cost, and added convenience have made them an attractive alternative to consumers for repetitive, small value retail purchases. Businesses have partly been attracted to stored valued cards as a way to reduce cash handling costs, but the real attraction is ability to earn payment float. Because stored value cards are prepaid cards, between the time they load value onto the card and the time they make purchases, consumers are essentially making interest-free loans to companies. For businesses that invest this cash, "float" income can be quite considerable in very large stored value systems.

The major drawback of stored value cards is that their simplicity and lack of security features make them very susceptible to fraud. For example, in Japan the Japanese Mafia runs large stored value counterfeiting rings. These rings have caused huge losses to some of the biggest issuers of stored value cards.

## Smart Cards

Smart cards are plastic cards that have their own computer processor. The computer processor dramatically increases the range of functions that the card can be used for, thus making it a lot "smarter." The processor also allows the card to use encryption technologies, which in turn make the card a very secure place to store information.

Smart cards have probably gotten the most attention as potential vehicles for the use of electronic cash. It is important to note that smart cards are *not* a payment system; they are just a piece of plastic with a computer processor and some software on it. Smart cards have also gotten attention as a potential way to eliminate the authorization required of credit card and debit card transactions. Eliminating the need for these authorizations would reduce the telecommunications costs of these payment systems.

One advantage of smart cards over other payment devices is that they can potentially be used for a wide range of applications including electronic cash, loyalty programs, and computer network security (see Chapter 2). Theoretically, consumers could have one "master" card that they can use for everything from credit card purchases to starting their car.

## Electronic Benefit Transfers (EBT)

EBT involves the electronic transmission of federal and state entitlements to beneficiaries. These transfers include social security, welfare, and veterans payments. In the past, the government made these payments in the form of checks or scrip such as "food stamps."

In 1996, the government passed the "Debt Collection Improvement Act" which specifies that all federal government payments must be electronically distributed by January 1, 1999. This has set off a mad rush to figure out how to get this done.

For most of these payments the government will do little more than simply use the ACH payment system to directly deposit benefit checks into people's accounts. However, the government has a big problem in that many of its benefit recipients do not have bank accounts.

To get these benefits to consumers electronically, the government is looking into a variety of electronic payment methods including smart cards. Other schemes for distributing the benefits include providing people with special accounts at banks that can only be accessed from ATM and Point-of-Sale machines.

The important thing to note about EBT is that rather than creating new payment systems for EBT, the government is looking to leverage existing payment systems and devices.

### Financial EDI

Financial EDI (F-EDI) transactions are a special type of Electronic Data Interchange (EDI) message that contains both payment and remittance information (see Chapter 6 for more on EDI). Companies send F-EDI messages directly to their banks using a Value Added Network (VAN) or the Internet. The banks then read the payment instructions, debit the companies' accounts, and initiate a special type of ACH transaction. The receiving bank deposits the payment into its customer's account and then forwards the remittance information on to the customer via VAN or the Internet (see Figure 4.10).

F-EDI volume has increased quickly since its introduction in the late 1980s (see Figure 4.11). Even so, it still represents a small fraction of total EDI volumes. F-EDI has the potential to play an important role in EC as it allows companies to easily bundle both payment and remittance information into a message that both their EDI partners and the banks can understand.

### SIDEBAR: ELECTRONIC BILL PAYMENT

The past several years have witnessed an explosion in electronic bill payment. Electronic bill payment allows consumers and businesses to automatically pay their monthly bills. Electronic bill payment has been available for years via the telephone, but the service has proved difficult to set up and use and as a result has never achieved widespread popularity.

In the past few years, electronic bill payment has spread from the telephone to the computer. The computer appears ideally suited to electronic bill payment because, unlike the telephone, it allows for visual confirmation of actions. In addition, the popularity of so-called Personal Finance Management (PFM) programs such as Intuit's *Quicken* and Microsoft's *Money* has created a built-in audience for electronic bill payment. As a result, electronic bill payment has been growing very rapidly over the past few years.

A variety of different pieces must work together in order to complete an electronic bill payment (see Figure 4.12). The key pieces include:

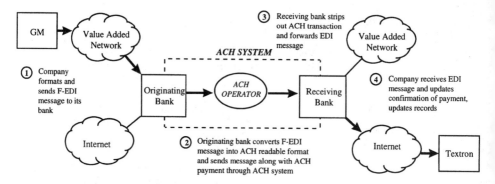

**Figure 4.10** F-EDI Transaction Example

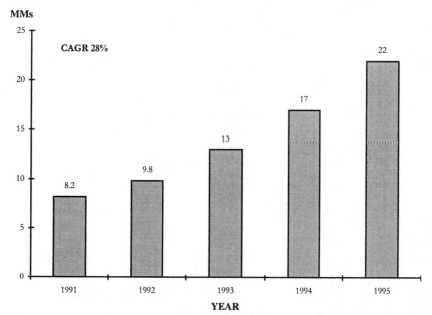

**Figure 4.11** F-EDI Volumes 1991–1995 *Source: NACHA*

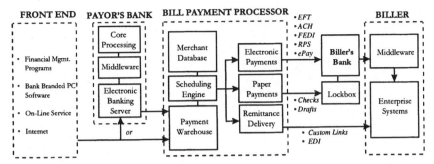

**Figure 4.12**   Electronic Bill Payment Transaction Flow   *Source: Piper Jaffray*

- *Front-End Devices:* These are the channels or devices used by consumers and businesses to access electronic bill payment services. Originally, the telephone was the only front-end device available, but now PC-based software programs (such as *Quicken* and *Money*) as well as on-line services (such as America Online) and the Internet can be used to initiate electronic bill payments. Most front-end devices are directly connected to the payor's financial institution, although some connect directly to a third-party processor.
- *Payors' Bank:* This is the financial institution (bank, brokerage, mutual fund, etc.) that holds the checking account of the bill payor.
- *Bill Payment Processor:* This is usually, but not always, a third party that processes bill payments on behalf of the payor's financial institution. Some banks, such as Citibank, act as their own bill transaction payment processor, while most other banks outsource this activity.
- *Lockbox/Concentrator:* These institutions collect and process payments on behalf of a biller. They are usually part of the biller's financial institution.
- *Biller's Bank:* This is the financial institution that maintains the deposit accounts of the biller. It receives payments from the bill payment processors and/or lockboxes and posts them to the biller's accounts. In some cases it also forwards remittance information on to the biller.
- *Biller:* While the payment stops at the biller's bank, the biller still needs to update their internal records to reflect that the payment was made to a particular account. In some cases the biller's bank forwards this "remittance" information on to the biller who uses some "middleware" to translate the information into formats its enterprise systems can understand. In other cases, remittance information is sent directly from the bill payment processor to the biller via leased lines or an EDI system.

## The Bill Payment Processor: Master of Ceremonies

The bill payment processor is the lynch pin in a bill payment transaction. The processor acts as essentially the master of ceremonies for the entire process: making sure that payments are made on time to the correct biller and in the correct format. The key functions provided by the bill payment processor include:

- *Warehousing:* Storing future payment instructions until the appropriate payment date.
- *Scheduling:* Sequencing payments to ensure that they arrive on the correct date.
- *Payment Execution:* Initiating payments on behalf of the consumer and ensuring that those payments are made at the lowest possible cost and risk to the bill payment processor.
- *Remittance Delivery:* Delivering remittance information to the biller so that it knows actually which customers paid and what bill they are paying.

Each bill payment processor also has a merchant database that contains the list of the merchants the processor can send payments to as well as specific instructions for how merchants need to receive both payment and remittance information. The merchant database is what allows the bill payment processor to automatically match payments from consumers to the appropriate merchant.

A large, robust merchant database takes years to build and requires constant maintenance and attention. The difficulty of building a merchant database currently forms a significant barrier to entry in the electronic bill payment processing business. As a result, the merchant database is often considered the "crown jewel" of a bill payment processor.

### The Process

The bill payment process starts with the consumer using a front-end device to send a bill payment instruction to the financial institution or third-party processor. If the payment goes to a financial institution, the institution simply makes a note of it and then forwards it on to the bill payment processor. The bill payment processor then sends the payment to the proper party on the proper date. There are four main ways that the bill payment is sent to the biller:

1. *Credit Card System:* Payments are grouped by the processor and sent through the credit card system in a lump sum settlement to the merchant's bank. VISA uses a system called ePay to process such transactions and MasterCard uses one called the Remittance Processing System (RPS).
2. *EFT Payment System:* Payments are authorized and settled via the ATM system. For all intents and purposes, they are treated like an ATM or on-line debit transaction.

3. *ACH System:* Payments are sent via the ACH system either together or individually.
4. *Postal System:* Payments are printed onto paper checks or drafts and then mailed to the appropriate party.

Once the payment arrives at either the merchant, its bank, or its lockbox, it is then processed and eventually posted to the merchant's account.

While this process may sound fairly simple, it is not. Unfortunately, there are a number of major problems with the electronic bill payment system, including:

- *It's not electronic.* On average, 65%–85% of all "electronic" bill payments are actually converted into paper checks by the bill payment processor before they are sent to the biller. In most cases, a paper check is sent in lieu of an electronic payment either because the bill payment processor does not know how to send an electronic payment to the merchant or because the particular merchant is not set up to receive electronic payments. In the remaining cases, the bill payment processor elects not to send an electronic payment because it has concerns that the payor may not have sufficient funds available in the account.
- *It's not integrated.* The hardest part of electronic bill payment is not paying companies, but delivering to billers the required "remittance" or account information that they need to correctly post payments to customer accounts. This process is greatly complicated by the fact that many large billers have extensively customized their billing systems. Thus, in many cases bill payment processors must build a custom connection directly to the biller's legacy systems in order to enable electronic payments.
- *It's not synchronized.* Most electronic bill payment services do not have real-time connections to a payor's checking account. This raises the risk that the consumer will schedule a payment without having sufficient funds in their account to make the payment. It also forces consumers to reconcile the balances reported to them by their financial institutions with the balances they see in their Personal Financial Management software. (These "synchronization" problems are discussed in greater detail in Chapter 5.)
- *It's not standardized.* There is no standard message format for transmitting bill payment instructions either from the consumer to the financial institution or from the financial institution to the bill payment processor. The lack of a standard locks banks and consumers into a particular bill payment processor and adds needless complexity to the process by forcing technology providers to make their systems compatible with multiple standards. While several standards have been proposed in an effort to help address this issue, there is still no agreement on which standard will be used going forward.

While serious, these problems have not been severe enough to prevent electronic bill payment from taking off. During 1996, we

$MMs

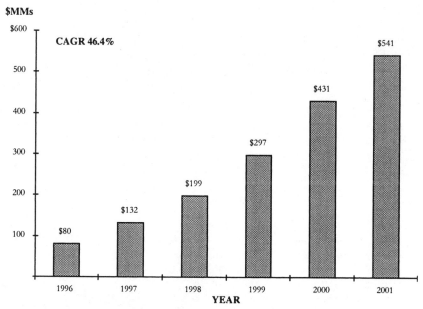

**Figure 4.13** Estimated Electronic Bill Payment Revenues—1996–2001
*Source: Piper Jaffray*

estimate that the number of consumers using electronic bill payment services more than doubled in 1996 from roughly 800,000 to 1.8 million. During 1997, the industry grew at a slightly slower, though still impressive, rate and exceeded 3.5 million customers by the end of the year. Based on our projections for the number of on-line financial services customers, the percent of customers using electronic bill payment, and the average revenue per customer per month, we estimate that electronic bill payment industry revenues should grow from $80 million in 1996 to $541 million in 2001 (see Figure 4.13). So electronic bill payment may not be pretty, but that doesn't look like it's going to hurt its popularity.

## Sub-Sectors

Despite the wide variety of payment systems and payment types, the Electronic Payments Sector actually has just four separate sub-sectors. This simple division is made possible by the fact that electronic payment processing usually requires the same set of core skills no matter what type of payment is involved.

## Card Payment Processors

This large sector encompasses the full range of non-financial services firms that help authorize, settle, and process transactions from the credit card and EFT payment systems. Firms in this sector perform all of the basic processing tasks required of payment processors, such as authorization, settlement, application, and account processing. They also conduct the full range of customer service functions such as customer service, collections, "chargeback" processing, and credit decision support.

This sub-sector is dominated by third-party processors who will perform just about any task that an issuer, acquirer, or merchant in either the credit card or debit card industries would like to outsource. The core strength of these third-party processors is in scale sensitive areas such as authorization, settlement, and account processing. Several firms in this area also own merchant acquiring operations and compete directly with financial institutions for merchants and transactions.

Credit and debit card processing is a mature, concentrated, and fiercely competitive sector. It is also the single largest sub-sector within the payment sector as well as the single largest sub-sector in the entire EC industry.

**Table 4.7**  Card Payment Processors: Selected Firms

| Company | Description |
| --- | --- |
| BA Merchant Services (BPI) | Recent spin-off from Bank of America and the 4th largest credit card merchant processor and one of the largest off-line debit processors. |
| Concord EFS (CEFT) | Designs EFT networks and transaction processing systems. Operates its own ATM network. Focused on a few key vertical markets. |
| First Data (#) (FDC) | #1 processor of credit card and debit transactions in the U.S. By far the largest player in the sector. |
| National Process Co. (NPC) | Second largest merchant processor with $74 billion in volume in 1996. National City (#) bank owns a 88% stake. |
| Nova Information Systems (NIS) | Atlanta-based card processor that has recently sold a 30% stake to First Union. |
| Paymentech (PTI) | Third largest merchant processor. Aggressive investor in EC activities. Holds a stake in First Virtual. |
| SPS Transaction Systems (PAY) | Credit card processing outsourcer. Associates First Capital announced its intent to acquire SPS in April 1998. |

## Electronic Bill Payment and Presentment

Firms in this rapidly growing sub-sector are focused on processing, settling, and remitting electronic bill payments. Electronic Bill Presentment is an emerging activity for this sector, but a complementary one to bill payment (see the Aside on Bill Presentment for more detail). The core strengths of these firms are their in-depth experience in electronic payment remittance, their proprietary merchant databases, and their remittance processing connections.

This sector is rapidly growing as electronic banking and bill payment gain increased acceptance. The sector is dominated by Checkfree which, by our estimate, processes almost 70% of all electronic bill payments.

**Table 4.8**   Bill Payment and Presentment: Selected Firms

| Company | Description |
| --- | --- |
| ATM Cardpay | Creator of a bill payment and presentment system that uses the existing EFT payment system and infrastructure as well as the Internet. |
| Blue Gill Technologies | Start-up developer of middleware that allows billers to offer Electronic Bill Presentment. |
| Checkfree (CKFR) | Dominant provider of consumer electronic bill payment services. Moving into bill presentment and business-to-business bill payments. |
| eDocs | Developer of a bill presentment system that enables billers to send HTML formatted e-mails to their customers. |
| Electronic Funds & Data Corp. | Electronic bill presentment start-up. Sells products to banks who then sign up billers. |
| Integrion | Bank owned consortium committed to entering the electronic bill payment and presentment markets. |
| Just In Time Solutions | Developer of OFX based, biller focused, bill presentment software. Worked closely with Intuit to help develop their bill presentment offerings. |
| MS-FDC | Joint venture between Microsoft and First Data Corporation. Will offer both bill presentment and bill payment services via Microsoft's MSN web site. Plans to offer service in mid-1998. |
| Online Resources | Electronic banking service bureau for small to mid-sized banks. Patent on using ATM networks for bill payment. Provides bill payment services to its service bureau customers. |
| Princeton Telecom | Electronic lockbox that is moving into Electronic Bill Presentment and Payment via a joint venture with Cybercash and Online Resources. |
| Traveler's Express | Subsidiary of Viad Corp. Second largest official check/money order player. Moving into the bill payment business. |

## Internet Payment Specialists

This sub-sector includes firms focused on developing, deploying, and processing new types of payments that have been enabled by the Internet and EC, such as electronic cash and electronic checks (see Table 4.9).

These firms rely on technological leadership, strong partnerships, and in-depth Internet and EC knowledge to secure their place in the market. This is a young, immature, and fragmented market that has yet to enter a high-growth phase similar to the Electronic Bill Payment sub-sector.

## Electronic Payment Support Providers

Includes a variety of firms that provide software, hardware, and service in support of the payment processing activities in each of the previous three sub-sectors. Primarily focused on supporting credit and debit card processing. Products provided include payment terminals, smart cards, and payment processing software.

These firms rely on manufacturing efficiency, distribution effectiveness, experience, and technical depth to effectively serve their customers. Companies in this sub-sector tend to operate in stable markets with a limited set of substantial competitors. The growth of this sub-sector is largely contingent upon the growth of the other three sub-sectors.

**Table 4.9**  Internet Payment Specialists: Selected Firms

| Company | Description |
| --- | --- |
| CyberCash (CYCH) | Provider of secure credit card payment system and an Internet-based accountable electronic cash system. Moving into electronic check and bill presentment businesses. |
| Digicash | Provider Internet-based accountable electronic cash payment system, known as eCash. Uses a special technique to enable privacy but still maintain accountability. Several major European banks are customers. |
| First Virtual (FVHI) | Provides credit card payment system that uses the Internet to transport payment messages but not credit card numbers. Refocuses business on Internet-based marketing system. |
| Mondex | Nonaccountable electronic cash system that uses smart cards. Currently owned by a consortium of banks. Multiple pilot tests underway. |
| Proton | American Express-led smart card-based nonaccountable electronic cash system. Deployed at over 60,000 points of sale in Belgium. |
| VISA Cash | Card-based non-accountable electronic cash system that can serve as both stored value and nonaccountable electronic cash. Underwhelming response to pilot test at Atlanta Olympics. |

**Table 4.10**  Electronic Payment Support Providers:
Selected Firms

| Company | Description |
| --- | --- |
| Gemplus | World's largest manufacturer of high-security magnetic stripe and smart cards. Recently sold stake to GE Capital's Consumer Finance Group. Generated an estimated $440 million in revenues in 1996. |
| Harmonic Systems | Start-up that provides a unified TCP/IP-based payment net work to retail merchants allowing them to consolidate and centrally manage their POS payment authorization and settlement requests. |
| Hypercom (HYC) | Second largest card terminal vendor behind Verifone with about 11% of the world market. Strong presence in Latin America and Asia. |
| ICVerify | Leading provider of PC-based point of sale software. Used in over 300,000 retail outlets. Market is growing rapidly. |
| Paysys | Leading provider of credit and debit card processing/management software. |
| Transaction Systems Architects (TSAI) | Provides EFT systems and software for use with credit cards, POS, and ATMs. Used by many major banks in the U.S. |
| Transaction Network Services (TNSI) | Provides a specialized communications network that has been optimized to carry payment transactions. |
| Ubiq | Start-up developer of universal issuance software for personalized smartcards. Software is front and back end agnostic giving issuers maximum flexibility to issue multiple varieties of cards, OSs, etc. |
| Verifone | Leading deployer of card terminals worldwide with just under half of the market. V-POS software allows for "virtual" terminals on the Internet. Recently acquired by Hewlett-Packard. (#) |

Like the other sectors in the EC Industry, the "soft walls" between the various sub-sectors in the Electronic Payments Sector are likely to dissolve over time. Indeed, a number of recent events point directly to this trend. First Data and First USA have both taken stakes in Internet Payment Specialist First Virtual, and First Data recently entered the electronic bill payment and presentment sub-sector through its MS-FDC joint venture with Microsoft.[9]

The only sub-sector that is likely to remain independent is the Payment Support sub-sector which will effectively act as the "arms merchant" to the other sectors.

---

[9] The MS-FDC joint venture is yet another example of Microsoft being the exception to our rule that firms will not be able to effectively play in more than one sub-sector.

# Market Size

Any way you measure it, the Electronic Payments Sector is big. In 1995, the total value of all electronic payments (credit card, EFT, and ACH) was almost $11 trillion. Between 1991–1995, the total value of electronic payments grew by roughly 50%. The vast majority of this $11 trillion was comprised of ACH volumes. ACH includes both business and consumer transactions as well as government benefit transactions such as social security and tax refund checks (see Table 4.11).

**Size of Card Payment Processing Sub-Sector.** The card payment processing sub-sector is clearly the biggest sub-sector, but the total revenues it generates are difficult to estimate because a good portion of those revenues are currently buried deep within the income statements of financial institutions. We have estimated the total size of the sub-sector using 1996 volumes and industry average revenues per transaction.

As Table 4.12 demonstrates, credit card is by far the largest revenue generator, followed by ATM transactions. Taking the midpoint between the two extremes provides an average card payment market size of about $5.5 billion in 1996. This number reflects revenues (or in the case of ACH, costs) directly associated with processing electronic payments (see Table 4.12).

**Size of the Other Sub-Sectors.** As for the other sub-sectors, we estimate that by the end of 1996 the electronic bill payment industry had about 1.8 million customers and that the average number of customers during the year was about 1.4 million. Currently, each customer generates around $4–$5 in additional monthly revenue for the sector, so we estimate that the sector generated between $76 to $84 million in revenue in 1996. Once again, several financial institutions, such as Citibank and Bank of

**Table 4.11** Number and Value of Electronic Payment Transactions—1991 vs. 1995

| | # of transactions | | | $ value of transactions | | |
|---|---|---|---|---|---|---|
| Payment type | 1991 | 1995 | CAGR | 1991 | 1995 | CAGR |
| ACH | 1,632 | 2,717 | 13.6% | $6,273 | $9,195 | 10.0% |
| General Card | 11,214 | 14,913 | 7.3% | 485 | 879 | 16.0% |
| ATM | 6,400 | 9,700 | 11.0% | 429 | 657 | 11.2% |
| "On-line" Debit | 223 | 775 | 36.6% | 6 | 19 | 33.4% |
| "Off-line" Debit | | 662 | NA | | 26 | NA |
| Total | 18,655 | 28,454 | 10.2% | $7,140 | $10,643 | 10.6% |

SOURCE: "Statistics on Payment Systems in the Group of Ten Countries." Bank of International Settlements. 1996. Nilson Report 3/96.

**Table 4.12** Estimated Revenues Generated by Card Payment
Processing Markets in 1996

| Payment types | # trans (BNS) | $ value ($BNS) | Average revenue/tran | | Estimated total revenues ($MMs) | |
|---|---|---|---|---|---|---|
| | | | Low | High | Low | High |
| ACH | 3.1 | | $0.05 | $0.06 | 155 | 186 |
| General card | | $1,006 | 0.30% | 0.60% | 3,018 | 6,036 |
| ATM | 10.7 | | $0.04 | $0.06 | 428 | 642 |
| On-line | 0.9 | | $0.04 | $0.06 | 38 | 57 |
| Off-line | | $46 | 0.30% | 0.60% | 137 | 275 |
| | | Total | | | 3,776 | 7,196 |

NOTE: Excludes card issuer processing revenues (estimated at $2 billion in 1996). Based on net revenues after interchange.

SOURCE: BIS, Bank Network News, Nilson Report, Company Annual Reports, Piper Jaffray.

America, process their electronic bill payments "in-house" so the total revenues produced by the sub-sector depend on one's perspective (we are including these firms in the total).

The Internet payment specialist industry is still largely in a developmental mode. The two most visible public firms in the area, Cybercash and First Virtual, generated a grand total of $300,000 in revenues during 1996, so the entire sub-sector would be lucky if it even broke half a million dollars in 1996.

In contrast, the payment support area is quite large. Verifone, now owned by Hewlett-Packard, alone generated $473 million in revenues in 1996. As Verifone has almost 50% of the card terminal market, that market alone looks like it generated around $1 billion in 1996. Counting the other software and hardware providers, including transaction processing software and smart card manufacturers, the total payment support industry likely generated some $2.5–$3.0 billion in 1996, making it easily the second biggest sub-sector.

Taking all of the sub-sectors together, we estimate that the entire Electronic Payment sector generated around $8.3 billion in revenues in 1996 (see Table 4.13).

## Drivers

The core driver of the Electronic Payments Sector is the shift away from paper and toward electronic payments. This shift is being inexorably propelled by the lower costs, greater convenience, and improved functionality that electronic payments offer. Behind this core driver are a series of

**Table 4.13**   Size of Electronic Payments Sector—1996

| Sub-sector | Size ($MMs) | % of total | 1996E growth % |
|---|---|---|---|
| Card payment processing | $5,500 | 66 | 20–25 |
| Electronic bill payment and presentment | $80 | 1 | 100–125 |
| Internet payment specialists | >$1 | >.01 | <500 |
| Payment support vendors | $2,750 | 33 | 20–35 |
| Total | $8,331 | 100 | 24 |

SOURCE: Piper Jaffray

supporting drivers that are accelerating the growth rate of the Electronic Payments Sector. These drivers include:

## New and Improved Payment Options

The last ten years have witnessed a flurry of electronic payment innovations, such as debit cards and electronic bill payment. As the new payment types we described earlier begin to appear (such as electronic checks and cash), the prospects for an even greater shift toward electronic payments are increasing.

In addition to increasing the electronic portion of all payments, new payment types also increase the complexity and need for specialized expertise within the Electronic Payments Sector. In this way, new payment types not only increase the growth of the sector, but broaden and deepen its structure.

## Continued Outsourcing

Payment processing is largely a fixed cost business that favors large, highly scaled firms with access to significant capital and technical expertise. Rather than attempt to compete in this highly specialized field, many financial institutions have chosen to either exit or outsource significant parts of their payment processing business. This trend toward outsourcing is in large part responsible for the 20%–25% growth experienced by firms within the Electronic Payments processing sector in recent years. While a good deal of outsourcing has already taken place in the U.S., financial institutions in Europe and Asia are only beginning to outsource their operations. As these institutions begin to confront greater competition and focus more aggressively on shareholder value, they are likely to follow their U.S. counterparts and outsource a good deal of their electronic payment processing operations.

For U.S. electronic payment firms, this continued outsourcing represents a tremendous opportunity and a powerful growth driver. The U.S. payments market is highly competitive and larger than any other electronic payment market on earth. This environment has enabled U.S. firms to build tremendous scale economies while conditioning them to be opportunistic, aggressive, and highly competitive. These traits should enable U.S. firms to successfully compete for outsourcing business around the world.

### Increasing Convenience

As electronic payment systems expand in size, functionality, and speed, they are not only becoming cheaper, but they are also becoming more convenient. They are, in effect, enjoying the effects of Metcalf's Law (see Chapter 1), becoming exponentially more attractive and useful. For example, from 1991–1995 the number of on-line debit card terminals increased 530% from 88,000 to over 554,000. At some point these payment systems will reach the "tipping" point where it becomes uneconomic for consumers and businesses not to use them.

Credit cards are a good example of a payment system that has already passed the tipping point. It is very difficult if not impossible to make hotel reservations, buy airplane tickets, or rent a car without a major credit card. While it is currently hard to imagine utilities refusing to accept a paper check or supermarkets refusing to accept cash, the laws of economics and network externalities suggest that this day will inevitably occur.

Together, the three specific drivers both support and supplement the key driver in Electronic Payments Sector: the slow, but inevitable shift away from paper and toward electronic payments.

### SIDEBAR: ELECTRONIC BILL PRESENTMENT

Ask just about anyone in the Electronic Payments Sector what the "next big thing" is going to be and they are likely to respond "electronic bill presentment."

Electronic bill presentment is similar to, but not to be confused with, electronic bill payment. Whereas electronic bill *payment* is focused on electronically transmitting *payments* from consumers to businesses, electronic bill *presentment* is focused on electronically transmitting *bills* from businesses to consumers.

### Something for Everyone

Consumers are attracted to the concept because electronic bills can't get lost in the kitchen, they don't have to be stored in old shoe boxes, and they can be paid from a personal computer with a "point, click, and pay" simplicity.

Billers are attracted to the concept for five separate but related reasons:

1. *Reduced mailing costs:* Billers currently spend $0.65 to $1.25 on printing, postage, and advertisements for each bill. Electronic bill presentment could cut this cost to just a few cents per bill.
2. *Reduced customer service costs:* Electronic bills will have more detail available which should help cut down on billing inquiries and customer service costs.
3. *Increased electronic payments:* Still more savings will be generated by a special "return address" on the electronic bill. The "return address" will ensure that the bill can also be paid electronically which will generate additional savings by reducing processing and financing costs.
4. *Increased flexibility:* Billers will have the freedom to easily modify the appearance of bills to customize their "look and feel" for each customer.
5. *Increased cross-sell revenues:* With electronic bill presentment, there is no limit to the number of "statement stuffers" that billers can send. In addition these stuffers could be much improved with multimedia pitches and instantaneous purchases.

Altogether, we estimate that these improvements could net billers $0.75 to $1.25 per bill. Given that billers send out 15 billion consumer bills a year, that is anywhere from $11 to $19 billion in total potential savings a year. For a large biller with 2 million customers, even if only 10% of the customer base elects to receive their bills electronically, that is a net benefit of anywhere from $2 to $3 million a year.

The Electronic Payments Sector is attracted to the concept because this sector anticipates processing and presenting these bills. If 10% of bills are presented electronically and the processors split the cost savings 50/50 with the billers, that would be a $560–$940 million opportunity.

Based on the level of on-line banking users, the percent likely to use electronic bill presentment, and the number of bills/customer that can be presented electronically, we expect that by 2001, almost 534 million bills will be electronically presented (see Figure 4.14). Even though this is a big number, it represents just 3.5% of estimated total bills in the year 2001.

## Four Different Ways and Counting

So, there's something for everyone to like about electronic bill presentment. However there is just one problem: no one can agree on how and where to present the bills. Indeed, there are no fewer than four competing schemes for electronic bill presentment. As Table 4.14 lays out, each alternative has its pros, cons, and assorted supporters.

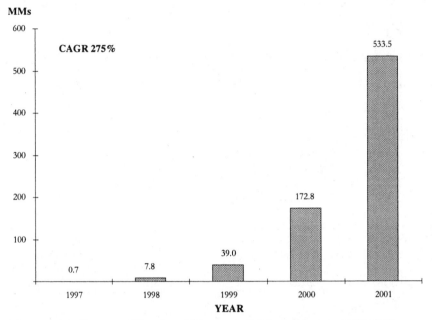

**Figure 4.14**  Estimated Number of Electronic Bill Presentments 1997–2001
*Source: Piper Jaffray*

Presentment at the biller's site has taken an early lead because it is fairly easy to do and does not require any coordination with other firms. However, presentment at a financial institution's Internet site is quickly gaining ground as it provides a way to link payment and presentment. The only problem with presenting at a financial institution's Internet site is that a biller would have to build connections to each financial institution's Internet site.

To avoid this situation, firms called "Consolidators" have entered the tray. These firms operate Internet sites that allow any biller to post bills to the site and any financial institution or customer to visit the site. The advantage for the billers is that they only have to build a single connection. However, given that the consolidator has the potential to become very powerful, none of the various parties can agree on who should become the consolidator and are unlikely to ever do so.

One solution is to have billers simply post all of their bills on an electronic bulletin board of sorts. This would allow anyone with the proper clearance to enter a biller's site and collect all of the bills they need. This way banks could simply visit the biller's site on behalf of their customer, collect the bills they needed, and then post them at their own Internet site.

Another solution is to simply send the bill directly to the consumer in the form of an e-mail formatted to look like a "web page" from an

**Table 4.14**   Competing Options for Bill Presentment

| Option | Description | Supporters | Pros | Cons |
|---|---|---|---|---|
| Present at biller's Internet site | Each biller creates a bill presentation section of their Internet site. Customers visit the site to review and pay their bill. | ▪ Billers<br>▪ Web site developers | ▪ Biller has complete control | ▪ Consumer must visit 10 to 15 sites<br>▪ No direct link between payment and presentment |
| Present at financial institution's Internet Site | Billers make monthly bills available to a third party payment provider, such as Checkfree, or a Financial Institution, such as Citibank, who then gathers all of a customer's bills into one place for review and payment. | ▪ Banks<br>▪ Third party processors | ▪ Direct link between payment and presentment<br>▪ Consumers only have to go to one Internet site | ▪ Billers lose some control to bank<br>▪ Must link biller to multiple Internet sites |
| Present via PFM software | Biller's allow consumers to download bills into Personal Financial Management (PFM) software for review and payment. | ▪ PFM software developers<br>▪ PFM users | ▪ Easily integrated into PFM software<br>▪ No need to go through intermediaries | ▪ Loss of control for billers<br>▪ No direct link between payment and presentment<br>▪ Not all consumers use PFMs |
| Present via e-mail | Billers send HTML formatted e-mails directly to consumers. Consumers review bill and send message to make payment. | ▪ Billers | ▪ Simple<br>▪ Widely available | ▪ No link between payment and presentment |

Internet site. The consumer would fill out the bill and then send it to the bank, which would then forward the payment on to the biller.

## An Interesting Side Effect

While it is not clear which scheme will become predominant, there is one very interesting side effect of bill presentment. Remember the special "return address" on each bill presentment? This address will include detailed instructions for electronically paying the bill and remitting the payment information back to the merchant.

This is potentially very bad news for electronic *bill payment* providers. Today those companies rely on detailed merchant databases and proprietary remittance connections to send their bill payments. These two assets not only make electronic bill payment possible, but they also make it very hard to enter the business because they take years to build (see the Sidebar on Electronic Bill Payment earlier in this chapter).

But in the world of electronic bill presentment, all of a sudden these two assets become pretty much worthless as the return address on the bill makes it easy for just about any payment processor to flawlessly send an electronic or paper bill payment to a merchant even if the processor has never dealt with the merchant before.

To be sure, in reality things won't be that easy. For example, before any of this can happen the industry will have to agree on a standard (which could take years). But this feature does make bill presentment a bit of a mixed blessing for electronic bill payment providers.

## Potential

The shift between electronic and paper-based payments cannot continue forever. At some point, electronic payments will either reach 100% of payments or the point at which the cost of eliminating the remaining paper payments is not worth the time or effort. Many years before this point is reached, growth in the electronic payments industry will begin to slow and will finally converge close to the overall growth rate of the economy. With many Electronic Payment stocks valued well in excess of 20 times earnings, a slowdown to single-digit growth could be very bad news for investors.

This naturally begs the question: How much more double-digit growth is left in the Electronic Payments industry? In the U.S., the answer is: quite a bit.

The main retail payment mechanism in the U.S. remains the paper check. In 1995, check volumes exceeded $73 trillion. That is almost seven times the size of all other retail electronic payments combined (credit card, debit, ATM, and ACH). However, the growth rate in paper check dollar volumes is well below that of other electronic payments and is actually falling when adjusted for inflation. This slowdown in growth rates is leading to a slow but gradual decline in checks' total share of payment volumes (see Figure 4.15).

But how much further will the checks' share of total payment volumes fall? This is a difficult question to answer and one that is probably best answered by putting the U.S. payment system into a comparative perspective. When it comes to checks, the U.S. is an international anomaly. While checks account for 77% of total noncash payments in the U.S., they account for an average of only 23% of the total in the other major industrialized countries. In some countries, such as Germany and Switzerland, almost all checks have been moved to ACH-like systems. If U.S. check volumes just decreased to the international average, the Electronic Payments Sector would be *three times* its current size.

However, payment systems traditionally evolve at glacial paces and such musings are of little import if the shift takes 100 years to occur. So the real question is: What are the prospects for dramatic shifts toward electronic payments in the short term? Once again the answer to this may best be found in looking at comparative data. Figure 4.16 shows that between 1990 and 1995, check shares in the two countries with the second and third

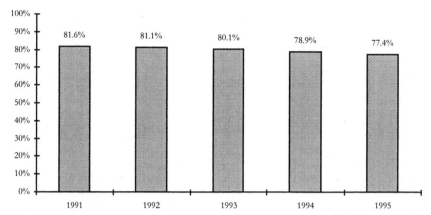

**Figure 4.15** Paper Check Share of Total U.S. Payment Volumes
*Source: "Statistics on Payment Systems in The Group of Ten Countries." Bank for International Settlement, 1996*

highest check shares, Canada and the U.K., fell at four times the rate that they did in the U.S., while card payments (credit and debit) increased at 2–3 times the rate of the U.S. These statistics indicate that there is indeed room for acceleration in the decline of U.S. check volumes and a corresponding increase in the number of electronic payments.

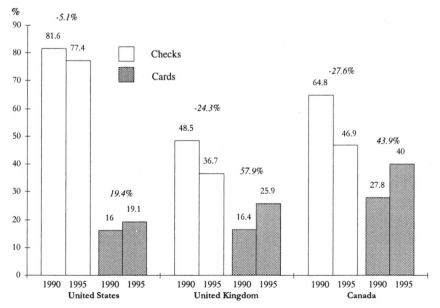

**Figure 4.16** Check vs. Card Payment Shares in Three Countries
*Source: "Statistics on Payment Systems in The Group of Ten Countries." Bank for International Settlement, 1996*

Overall there appears to be plenty of room for continued growth within the U.S. Electronic Payments Sector. This growth should particularly benefit the card payment processing sub-sector as these firms are directly involved in processing the types of electronic payments, such as credit and debit transactions, that are most likely to benefit from the continued decline of the check.

Card payment processing firms should also benefit from their increased international emphasis. The total size of the international general purpose card market (credit and charge cards) was about $1.8 trillion in 1996 with the U.S. representing only 50%, or about $870 billion, of that total.[10] This represents a substantial and largely unrealized opportunity for potential growth.

*In total, we expect the Card Payment Processing sub-sector should continue to grow at a rate of 20%–25% a year.* This growth is well above forecasted total credit card payment volume growth of around 10% (see Figure 4.17). This additional growth within the sector will be driven by continued outsourc-

[10] The Nilson Report. 4/97

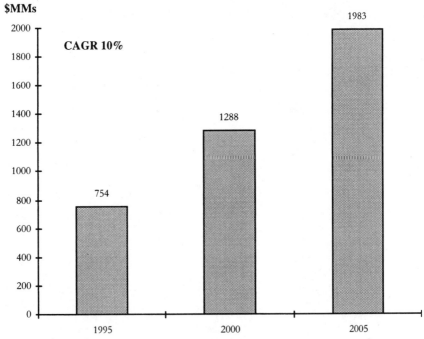

**Figure 4.17** Forecasted Credit Card Payment Volumes *Note: Includes only general purpose card volume. Source: The Nilson Report*

ing, an accelerating shift from checks to debit card transactions, increased international focus, and the continued emergence of new payment types.

Growth prospects for other parts of the sector are also promising. The electronic bill payment and presentment sub-sector appears poised for quick growth over the coming years driven primarily by the increasing use of electronic banking. At the end of 1997 there were 3–3.5 million of these customers. Various studies have projected that this number will grow to between 10 million and 15 million over the next five years (see Chapter 5). These projections imply that the sub-sector should expect transaction volumes to grow at an annual rate of 35%–50% over the next five years and should be a $500–$600 million business by 2001.

The growth prospects for the Internet payment specialists are a little less clear than they are for other areas. Demand for these products has yet to be clearly established and these products have yet to be widely deployed. We believe that these revenues will be driven by the general increase in the Internet population as well as by increases in the percent of Internet users willing to make purchases on the Internet. Based on these two trends, we estimate that Internet payment specialist revenues will grow from $0.5–$60.0 million by 2001.

Meanwhile, the payment support sub-sector's growth should closely track the card payment sector as its major customer market. Therefore, we expect that the payment support provider sub-sector will also grow at 20%–25% over the coming years.

A final stimulant to the sector's growth rate should be a U.S. government mandate that all of its payments must be made electronically by January 1, 1999. The government already makes 57% of its payments electronically, so its mandate will only add about 360 million electronic payments which should reduce check volumes by just 0.5%. However, there should be a "multiplier effect" as the government mandate forces government contractors to make investments in receiving electronic payments which would then force or encourage their own suppliers to make the required investments.[11]

Taking all of different sub-sectors and drivers together, we expect that the Electronic Payments Sector will grow from its current base of $8.3 billion to over $21.2 billion by the year 2001 (see Figure 4.18). The average annual growth rate should be about 21% and will be largely driven by growth in the card payment processing sub-sector. Electronic bill payment/presentment and Internet payments will undergo tremendous growth during this period but will still comprise just a small portion of total sector revenues.

---

[11] For a general discussion of the U.S. government's efforts to comply with the 1996 Debt Collection Act see: "EFT Progress Report, EFT Implementation Plan Update." United States Treasury. 6/4/97. or www.fms.treas.gov/eft

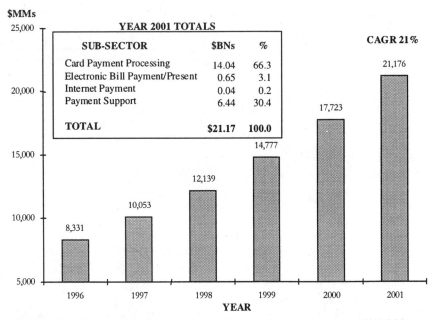

**Figure 4.18** Estimated Total Electronic Payment Sector Revenue—1996–2001
*Source: Piper Jaffray*

## Trends

### Consolidation in the U.S. Card Payment Processing Sector

Perhaps the most important trend in the Electronic Payments Sector over the past five years has been the consolidation of card payment (credit and debit) processing. For example, the market share of the Top 10 merchant acquirers has increased from 49% to 77% in just four years[12] (see Figure 4.19).

Consolidation is also happening on the issuing end of the card sector with 68% of credit card volumes being controlled by the Top 10 issuers in 1996. In the "on-line" debit market, the Top 10 switches are now responsible for 89% of the market.[13] The consolidation of these payment systems is being driven by three main factors:

*Scale Economies:* The fixed cost nature of the Electronic Payments Sector dictates that as volumes increase, unit costs decrease. The largest pay-

[12] The Nilson Report. 3/97

[13] Bank Network News 1996 Fact Book.

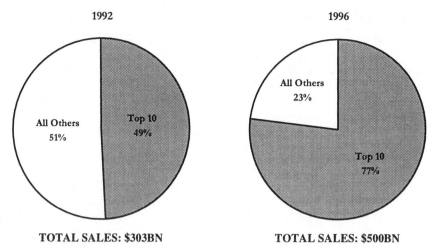

**Figure 4.19**   Top 10 Credit Card Merchant Acquirers Market Share
*Source: The Nilson Report*

ment processors therefore enjoy substantial scale economies over smaller players. This creates a situation in which the larger payment processors can lower prices to the point at which smaller processors are forced to sell. Scale economies are invariably cited as a major factor whenever there is a merger or acquisition in the sector.

*Increasing Complexity:*  New technologies and payment options create an ever more intricate and elaborate web of payment systems. This complexity is beginning to overwhelm both businesses and financial institutions. Businesses are being besieged with requests to add new payment options such as electronic bill payment and electronic cash, while financial institutions are being forced to incorporate an ever increasing number of payments into their back office systems.

Rather than attempt to keep up with this added complexity, many institutions have come to the conclusion that they would be better off outsourcing or selling their electronic payment operations. These decisions are leading to increased consolidation.

*Financial Services Consolidation:*  The same drivers prompting consolidation in the Electronic Payments Sector are also hard at work in the overall financial services industry and have prompted a series of high profile mergers between the major financial institutions, such as the Chase Manhattan/Chemical Bank merger. When financial institutions merge, they also merge their payment processing operations. Thus consolidation in the financial services industry also drives consolidation in the Electronic Payments Sector.

## A Shift in the Balance of Power

As the payment systems consolidate, the balance of power within these systems is starting to shift. Traditionally, this balance of power has been concentrated in the hands of the central processors. By definition, these processors took part in all transactions. As a result they were often far larger than any of the end processors and thus had tremendous scale and information advantages. These advantages gave central processors enough influence and sheer size that they were able to set the agenda for the payment system.

The current wave of consolidation within the Electronic Payment Sector has been taking place at the end processor level. As these end processors become larger and larger, the usefulness of the central processor begins to decrease. This happens for two reasons.

1. The end processors begin to generate an increasing number of "on-us" transactions. "On-us" transactions are not sent to the central processor because both the originator and the receiver of the transaction are customers of the same end processor. As the percentage of "on-us" transactions increases, the central processor's volumes decrease and consequently its unit costs increase. "On-us" transactions also deprive the central processor of its information advantage as it no longer has access to all transactions.

2. As the number of distinct end processors decreases, the process of "routing" transactions to the appropriate party decreases in importance and perceived value. The central processor is therefore seen as more of an unnecessary middleman than a value-added processor.

## The Death of "The Switch"

Ultimately, consolidation within the electronic payments system will create strong incentives for end processors to "jump the switch" by building direct "peer-to-peer" connections between themselves. By doing so the end processors not only avoid paying "interchange" fees to the central processor, but they also gain effective control of the payment system. Eventually these "peer-to-peer" connections deprive the central switch of enough volume such that it must "downsize" or it risks collapsing under its own weight. Even if "the switch" is successful in downsizing, it will become just a shadow of its former self, relegated to mere "peer" status with other end-processors (see Figure 4.20). It is in this way that the ultimate evolution of the electronic payment industry will mean the death of the central processor.

## Current Payment System Structure

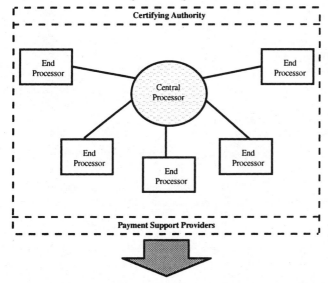

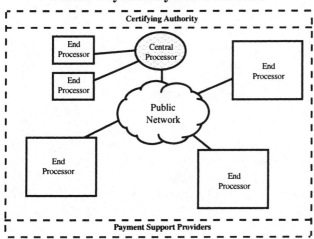

## Future Payment System Structure

**Figure 4.20**  Current vs. Future Payment System Structure
*Source: Piper Jaffray*

## Implications

What does this trend toward payment system consolidation and the death of "the switch" mean for firms within the Electronic Payments Sector? For the large firms in the card payment processing sub-sector, the trend is very positive. Not only will these firms lead the consolidation due to their scale efficiencies and operational expertise, but their increased size will put them on a more equal footing with the central processors and present them with an opportunity to "jump the switch" and thereby capture additional cost savings while increasing their market power.

For firms currently in the Electronic Bill Payment and Presentment and Internet Payment Specialist sub-sectors, payment system consolidation is a long-term negative trend. Today, these two sectors are largely independent from the card payment processing sub-sector, but as firms within the card payment processing sub-sector become increasingly powerful, there is a greater likelihood that they will migrate out of their sub-sector and into both Electronic Bill Payments/Presentment and Internet Payments, especially in light of the tremendous growth potential of these sub-sectors.

Indeed, there is evidence that this migration is already under way. For example, Paymentech has purchased a stake in Internet payment specialist First Virtual Holdings, while First Data Corporation and Microsoft have formed a joint venture called MS-FDC to enter the Electronic Bill Payment and Presentment sub-sector. Existing firms in these sub-sectors will either need to partner with these firms or find a defensible market niche. Outright competition against such large, profitable, and highly-scaled firms is not a realistic long-term option.

For Payment Support Providers, consolidation is either a negative to neutral trend. The negative effects of consolidation will be felt most acutely by providers of centralized services such as payment processing software. The more consolidation, the fewer the payment processors, the fewer the customers for software, network services, and technical support. However, for providers of point of sale products, such as card terminals, the effects of consolidation will be more than offset by the continued growth of electronic payments and the increase in the number of point-of-sale outlets associated with that growth.

## Blurring of the Lines . . .

In the long run, consolidation will help eliminate the distinctions between the different types of payment processors by creating a series of mega-processors. These firms will have tremendous resources which should allow them to easily make the required investments to enter adjacent sub-sectors. They will also have tremendous scale economies and established relationships that they can leverage to quickly become competitive in a new sub-sector.

For financial institutions and businesses struggling to manage multiple payment processing relationships, it will become increasingly attractive for them to consolidate all of their payment business at a single processor. Not only will this allow them to get the best price possible, but it will greatly reduce the amount of management attention that they have to devote to this issue.

The day of the mega-processors is still many years away and to a large extent is dependent on the progress financial institutions make in rationalizing their core processing systems (see Chapter 5), but the fundamental forces driving this vision are already hard at work. Firms that begin to position themselves to prosper in this new environment are likely to benefit the most from this natural evolution of the "payment system."

## Success Factors

So what will it take to be successful in the increasingly concentrated and contentious Electronic Payments Sector of the future? The basic formula for success appears to be pretty much as it has been in the past: focus on what can be done best and get as big as possible as fast as possible. To that end a few specific factors will be particularly important. They include:

*Size:* Size creates scale economies, which enable lower prices, which usually result in higher market share and thus greater size. Size gives firms not just market share but market power, which they can then use to influence the structure and operation of the market. Size also gives firms a strong cash flow base that they can use to enter new sub-sectors. When it comes to the Electronic Payments Sector, bigger truly is better.

*Partnerships with Financial Institutions:* Like it or not, financial institutions still have a tremendous influence over the Electronic Payments Sector. While they may not be the most technically savvy or operationally efficient firms, they do have one thing: the customers. They also happen to control (at least for now) almost all of the different payment systems. Firms with healthy relationships with financial institutions are likely to benefit from an increased share of outsourcing business and a generally less contentious operating environment.

*Payment Breadth:* As consolidation begins to blur the lines between the different payment sectors, financial institutions and businesses will increasingly look for "full service" providers that can process a full range of payments. Successful firms will position themselves to either fulfill this role or complement it.

## New Opportunities

The opportunity to form a so-called mega-processor from scratch is probably past. Instead, mega-processors will likely emerge out of the current players in the industry as time goes by. New opportunities are likely to be created in peripheral areas as a consequence of the sector's continued evolution.

> *Payment Integration:* Smart Cards, electronic cash, stored value, and electronic checks. All of these new payment devices must somehow be seamlessly incorporated into both point of sale operation and back end processing operations. Integrating these different payment devices into one easy-to-manage payment "service" will be a major challenge. Designing software and services that enable merchants and financial institutions to efficiently manage these new payment devices and incorporate them into their back office systems will no doubt prove to be an important opportunity.

> *PC-Based Payment Software:* The increasing power of personal computers, combined with more robust operating systems (such as *Windows NT 5.0*) and an increased emphasis on processing Internet originated payments, should provide strong impetus for the development of PC-based payment processing, analysis, and support software. Companies with experience designing software to process thousands of web server transactions a minute could very well combine their Internet "transaction processing" knowledge along with their PC-based software development experience to create a new class of Internet-enabled, PC server-based payment software.

## Investment Considerations

The Electronic Payments Sector is like the Chevrolet of the EC industry. It's not sexy or terribly exciting, but it is very big and dependable. The business model of the industry is well-established, firms have a good deal of control over their growth, and the key players are all well-known and established. For those investors looking to play in the EC industry, but also looking for long track records, relatively predictable growth and stable management, the Electronic Payments Sector provides a solid option.

INDEX

**Figure 4.21**   Electronic Payments Sector Index vs. EC Index and S&P 500
*Source: Piper Jaffray*

## Recent Investment Performance

With electronic payment volumes continuing to grow nicely over the past two years, it is surprising to discover that the Electronic Payments Sector has been the poorest performing sector within the EC industry since the beginning of 1997. Everything seemed all right during the first half of 1997, when the Electronic Payments Sector tracked very closely against the overall EC industry. However, the wheels started coming off the cart in the late summer/early fall when a series of firms in the sector, including industry leader First Data and Paymentech, announced that their earnings would be below analysts' estimates due largely to intense price competition in the space. This made the sector especially vulnerable to the market turmoil caused by economic problems in Asia, and, as a result, the sector promptly headed south and stayed there for the rest of 1997.

So far, 1998 hasn't proved to be any better. While the rest of the EC industry experienced sharp run-ups in stock prices, the Electronic Payments Sector was stuck in neutral as fears about price competition and growth rates prevented investors from generating any real enthusiasm for the sector. As the sector enters the second half of 1998, many investors appear to be in a "wait and see" mode as they try to determine if the sector can recover from recent bouts of price competition.

**Table 4.15**   Firms in the Electronic Payments Sector Index
(*As of July 1, 1998*)

| Company | Ticker | Mrkt cap | $Vol/ day ($MMs) | % price Δ/day | 1997 revs ($MMs) | 1997 earn ($MMs) | 1998E P/E | 1999E P/E | 1997 P/S |
|---|---|---|---|---|---|---|---|---|---|
| First Data | FDC | $14,873 | $77.2 | 1.8% | $5,235 | $357 | 20.4 | 17.8 | 2.8 |
| ConcordEFS | CEFT | 2,432 | 10.4 | 2.3 | 240 | 43 | 40.2 | 20.4 | 9.3 |
| Checkfree | CKFR | 1,630 | 14.1 | 2.7 | 176 | (162) | NM | 95.0 | 7.2 |
| Nova Corp. | NIS | 1,224 | 1.9 | 2.2 | 336 | 17 | 45.8 | 29.8 | 3.0 |
| Transaction Systems Architects | TSAI | 1,049 | 7.0 | 1.8 | 215 | 24 | 35.3 | 27.9 | 4.4 |
| SPS Transaction Services | PAY | 856 | 1.0 | 1.6 | 540 | 39 | 19.0 | 17.2 | 1.6 |
| First USA Payment Technologies | PTI | 741 | 2.3 | 2.3 | 186 | 4 | 38.8 | 29.8 | 3.6 |
| National Processing Co. | NAP | 541 | 0.3 | 2.2 | 406 | 21 | 25.4 | 19.4 | 1.2 |
| BA Merchant Services | BPI | 328 | 1.3 | 2.1 | 161 | 37 | 22.4 | 18.5 | 2.0 |
| Transaction Network Services | TNSI | 267 | 0.9 | 2.5 | 63 | 7 | 27.4 | 21.1 | 3.9 |
| Cyber Cash | CYCH | 155 | 3.0 | 3.6 | 4 | (26.2) | NM | 19.7 | 28.4 |
| First Virtual | FVHI | 36 | 0.3 | 5.6 | 1 | (15.9) | NM | NM | 27.0 |
| Total | | $24,133 | $119.6 | 1.4% | $7,564 | $345 | 26.2 | 20.3 | 3.2 |

SOURCE: Company reports, First Call, Piper Jaffray

From an investment perspective, our definition of the Electronic Payments Sector includes firms that are focused on either processing or supporting the processing of electronic payments. We have taken an admittedly subjective approach to including firms in the sector based on our appraisal of their current focus on electronic payments as well as their future focus on electronic commerce. Some notable firms that we have not included in the sector are: Deluxe Corporation (#), Total Systems, PMT Services, and National Data Corporation (#).

As of now there are twelve public firms in the Electronic Payments Sector, three of which went public in 1996. Key statistics for this group as of 7/1/98:

*Market Capitalization:* While there are only twelve firms in the Electronic Payment sector, it has a market capitalization of $24.1 billion. This capitalization is led by First Data Corporation which accounts for 62% of the sector's total. The high market capitalization reflects that fact that there are many well-established firms producing substantial revenues and growing at 20+% a year in the sector.

*Liquidity:* An average of $120 million in stock trades within the Electronic Payment sector each day. This makes it the most liquid EC sector in terms of total dollars traded. However, the pace of trading is not as high as in the other sectors with market capitalization turning over an average of only every 202 days compared to 83 days for the EC industry in general. This low turnover rate makes the Electronic Payments Sector the least active sector in the EC industry relative to its total market capitalization.

*Volatility:* Prices in the sector changed a capitalization weighted average of 1.4% a day making the Electronic Payment's sector the least volatile of the five sectors. However, this average daily price change of 1.4% was still 66% higher than the S&P's 0.8% average change.

*Revenues:* Revenues grew a comparatively tame 11% in 1997, but on a base of $6.8 billion.

*Earnings:* In a nice twist for the EC industry, this sector actually has earnings. After adjusting for a few large nonoperating losses, earnings were $345 million in 1997.

*Valuations:* At 26.2 times 1998 earnings, the sector is actually the "cheapest" in the EC industry. This P/E ratio is even below the S&P's PE of 27.6 times 1998 estimates.

## Risks

While broad indications would suggest that the sector has a fairly strong foundation, it still has a number of risks that could negatively affect the sector:

*"Backlash":* Increasingly, the financial services industry seems to be having a serious case of "seller's remorse." Many financial services executives look enviously at the 20%–25% growth rates and lofty P/Es of the Electronic Payment sector firms and openly wonder how they let such opportunity "slip" through their fingers. As financial service firms become more sensitive to this issue, there is the risk that there will be a "backlash" against non-financial institutions. This "backlash" could result in decreased outsourcing and even the re-creation of bank owned processing cartels, both of which could result in decreased growth for third-party electronic payment processors.

*Consolidation:* Consolidation in the financial services industry is continuing to take place at a steady rate. As the financial services industry consolidates, the number of potential customers for Electronic Payment firms is gradually decreasing. Firms with heavy revenue concentrations in customers that are likely takeover candidates should be carefully scrutinized. This is not as serious an issue for firms that sell primarily to merchants.

*Pricing:* While firms have gone to great lengths to build value-added products and services, they still cannot hide the fact that, at its core, payment processing is a commodity product. The pricing environment is already highly competitive and as firms get larger and larger, they are using their increasing scale economies to put continued pressure on pricing. Significant decreases in prices can put substantial pressures on margins, especially for mid-scale players. We anticipate that periodic pricing wars and scares will depress values in the industry and look forward to them as an opportunity to buy the best positioned players in the industry.

## Conclusion

The Electronic Payments Sector is a large and important part of the EC industry. The sector was processing electronic payments long before the Internet and the World Wide Web became household words and it will continue its boring yet critical role no matter what happens in the rest of the EC industry. While the sector has experienced rapid growth over the past few years, there appears to be ample market opportunity, both domestically and internationally, to sustain the sector's current growth rates for at least the next few years. The big issue for firms in the Electronic Payments Sector is positioning themselves to not just survive, but prosper in a rapidly consolidating sector. Large, highly-scaled firms with an aggressive focus on expanding their business into all aspects of electronic payments, an international growth strategy, and an intense but diplomatic drive appear best positioned to survive in this challenging environment.

# 5

# Financial Software and the Rise of the Integrator

## Introduction

U.S. consumers and businesses control some $27 trillion in financial assets. The EC industry is counting on this reservoir of wealth to provide the raw materials necessary to buy, sell, invest, and lend on the Internet. However, there is just one problem: most of these assets are locked away, deep within financial institutions. Without an easy way to electronically access, analyze, and manipulate these assets, the EC industry will be deprived of its lifeblood, unable to fuel the engines of commerce.

The Financial Software Sector is dedicated to solving this access problem by building bridges between the EC industry and the financial services industry. Currently, this sector is hard at work building the basic connections necessary to provide consumers and businesses with access to their financial accounts over the Internet. These efforts are not only opening up an important avenue for the flow of funds into the EC industry, but also increasing the general public's overall exposure to and confidence in the EC industry.

But the financial software sector's work will not stop at this level. Beyond just providing access to financial accounts, the sector is beginning to focus on how to apply new technologies to not only reengineer the process of providing financial services but to enable entirely new services that were not even possible before the rise of Electronic Commerce.

This chapter explores the current structure of the Financial Software Sector, the challenges facing it, and the growth prospects going forward.

## Structure

While the Financial Software Sector may have visions of enabling new services dancing in its head, before it can act on those visions it must first deal with the reality of the current situation. The reality is that most businesses and consumers cannot access their financial accounts electronically and that even when they can access their accounts, subtle but significant problems prevent the Financial Software Sector from fulfilling its mandate.

To understand why this is the case, it is necessary to take a look at just how the sector is currently "solving" the problem of providing customers with access to their financial accounts. We will focus our discussion on the challenges being experienced by the banking industry in its efforts to provide "on-line banking" services, but the issues covered in our discussion are generally applicable across other parts of the financial services industry including insurance and investments.

In order to provide on-line banking services, it is necessary to string together four basic components: some front-end software, a middleware system, a core processing environment, and an electronic payment processing operation (see Figure 5.1). Each of the components has a specific role:

**Front-End Software.**   Software that enables consumers and businesses to access their financial accounts. Typically, this software allows customers to not only access their accounts, but to also manipulate and analyze their account information. When most people think of on-line banking, they usually think of the front-end software. There are a number of different types of front-end software, each with its own distinctive characteristics (see Figure 5.2):

> *Voice Response Software:* This is software that runs on Voice Response Units (VRUs). VRUs are computers that allow customers to access their

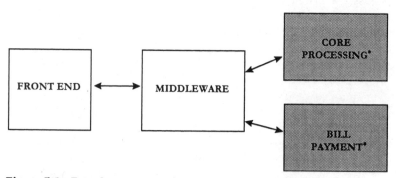

**Figure 5.1**   Four Components of the Financial Software Sector
*Bill payment area is part of payments sector. Core processing area is not part of EC industry.*

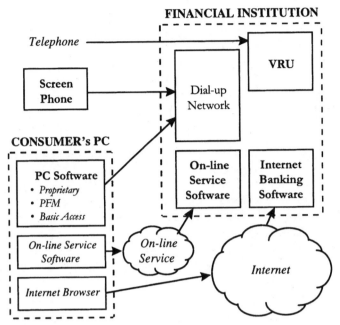

**Figure 5.2**  Front-End Software

accounts *via the telephone* by listening to spoken instructions and then typing in a series of numeric commands. Anyone who has used "voice mail" has used a VRU. VRUs are a very basic, yet effective, way for customers to electronically access their bank accounts. All of the software resides at the bank, so the consumer needs nothing more than a telephone to access the service. The Achilles heal of VRU software is that it lacks "visual confirmation" (i.e., you can't see what you're doing). This makes it very difficult for most consumers to use VRU software for anything other than just basic transactions such as checking their account balance.

*Screen Phone Software:*  This is software that enables "screen phones" to conduct banking transactions. Screen phones are specialized phones that include a small LCD screen and some custom software. Customers can use screen phones to access their bank accounts and make basic transactions. Screen phones are an attempt to overcome VRUs' problem of lack of visual confirmation while still using the well understood and universally deployed telephone. The screen phone's major drawback is it costs a lot (over $100) and there are currently very few things to do with it outside of on-line banking. Despite great anticipation, there has yet to be significant acceptance of screen phones in the market.

**PC Software.** This is software that enables bank customers to conduct on-line banking from their personal consumers. Consumers must load the programs on to their machines and then must use a modem to connect to a special "dial-up" network set up by the bank. In order to offer PC banking software, banks must set up their own "dial-up" networks. These networks allow customers to contact the bank directly without having to go through the Internet or an on-line service. There are three different types of PC software:

*Proprietary Software:* These are first-generation programs developed by individual banks. In the tradition of the banking industry, rather than contract the work out to actual software companies, the banks had their best COBOL programmers create these programs. Needless to say, the results of these efforts were a group of unattractive and painfully straightforward software programs. Most of these early efforts have already been mercifully retired. However, a few stalwarts live on, such as Citibank's venerable home banking software (although this program will be retired shortly).

*Personal Financial Management Programs (PFMs):* Programs that allow consumers to electronically manage and plan the full range of their financial affairs. Since late 1995, these programs have also had built-in "on-line banking" features which allow consumers to initiate banking transactions from directly within the PFM. Intuit's *Quicken* program was the first PFM and remains the most popular title. Microsoft's *Money* and MECA's *Managing Your Money* are the other two major PFMs in use today.

*Basic Access Software:* Stripped-down versions of PFMs that focus on account access and do not attempt to address more complex issues such as financial management and planning. The emphasis of these programs is on making the on-line banking experience as simple and as straightforward as possible.

*On-line Services Software:* This is software that allows banks to offer banking services via one of the major on-line services, such as America Online and Compuserv. This software is located "server side" at either the bank or the on-line service so customers do not need special banking software on their PC to access their account. However, customers do need a subscription to a specific on-line service and the appropriate on-line service software. Using on-line services allows banks to get out of the "dial up" network management business.

*Internet Software:* This is software used to operate an "Internet Banking" service. The software resides on the bank's Internet server. Customers need Internet access and Internet browser software (such as Netscape's *Navigator* or Microsoft's *Explorer*) to access their accounts.

The multiplicity of front-end software has presented banks with a difficult problem: which software to offer? Banks are afraid that they will spend a lot of time and effort developing their services for one type of software when it turns out that their customers actually prefer banking with another type. This fear of betting on the "losing" software has led banks to offer as many different front-end options as possible. This so-called "shotgun strategy" for picking the winning option has provided the banks with piece of mind, but it has also added a great deal of complexity to the next component of the sector.

## Middleware

Middleware serves as the nerve center and traffic cop of an on-line banking operation. The middleware component serves as a bridge from the new world technologies of PCs, on-line services, and the Internet to banks' old world legacy processing systems, which are usually large mainframe computers. This task is greatly complicated by the "shotgun" strategy described above. Most front-end software uses its own special protocols for communicating with the middleware component. Therefore, banks must build not just one bridge, but multiple bridges—one for each type of software offered. These "bridges" are actually pieces of software that translate messages between the front-end software and the legacy systems. Middleware components often have so-called "message servers" whose sole job is to translate messages from one format into another.

Middleware components also typically have a temporary account database that is used to store certain messages as well as customer account information (see Figure 5.3). This database is necessary because many bank legacy systems still process transactions in batches instead of in real-time.

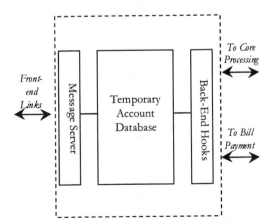

**Figure 5.3** Middleware

The middleware component must not only struggle to incorporate multiple types of front-end software, it must also connect to and communicate with multiple parties on the backend. These connections or "hooks" must be built into the bank's own legacy core processing computers as well as to third-party electronic bill payment providers.

### Core Processing

The core processing component contains a bank's legacy processing and customer information systems. These core processing systems are the engines of the modern banking system in that they store, analyze, and process almost all account transactions and information. Many small banks actually outsource their core processing activities to large data processors such as EDS, Fiserv, and Alltel much in the way they outsource their payment processing to companies such as First Data.

For those banks that have their own core processing systems (as well as for outsourcers), bridges must be built between the core processing systems and the middleware component in order to provide account access. Customers must not only be able to retrieve account information from these systems, but they must also be able to update these systems with any changes or transactions they may wish to make.

In general, most banks do not have a single core processing system but rather a collection of separate processing systems, each of which has its own databases and applications (see Figure 5.4). Many banks, especially large banks, have also extensively customized their core processing systems. This means that each separate processing system typically requires its own customized bridge to the middleware component.

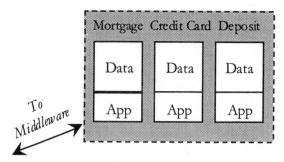

**Figure 5.4**   Core Processing

### Electronic Bill Payment

This component is actually part of the Electronic Payments Sector and is covered in detail in Chapter 4, but it is included here because it too must interface with the middleware component (see Figure 5.5). As with both the front-end and core processing components, a bridge must be built between the middleware component and the electronic payment operation in order to electronically transmit bill payment instructions. Most banks currently outsource electronic bill payment, so they must build this bridge in coordination with their third-party processor.

Stringing together these four components, along with a lot of hard work and a little bit of luck, will create an on-line banking operation that appears to work. Customers can use the system to access their accounts, pay bills, and even manage their finances.

However, poke a bit deeper and it quickly becomes apparent that the current on-line banking system is an unsustainable collection of technical compromises and quick fixes that at some point will have to be restructured. Specifically, the current structure suffers from three major problems (see Figure 5.6):

1. *Lack of Messaging Standards*
   As the previous section pointed out, one of the hardest tasks in on-line banking is incorporating messages from both the front- and back-end components into the middleware component. This task has been greatly complicated by the fact that almost every major player in the sector has their own message standards. That is not a problem for a bank if it only uses one vendor's products, but once the bank tries to mix and match products from different vendors, it can become a nightmare trying to incorporate all of the different standards into the middleware component. The lack of a single message standard is also a

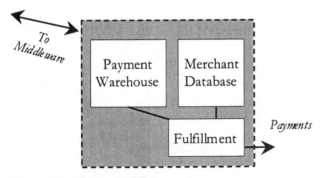

**Figure 5.5**   Electronic Bill Payment

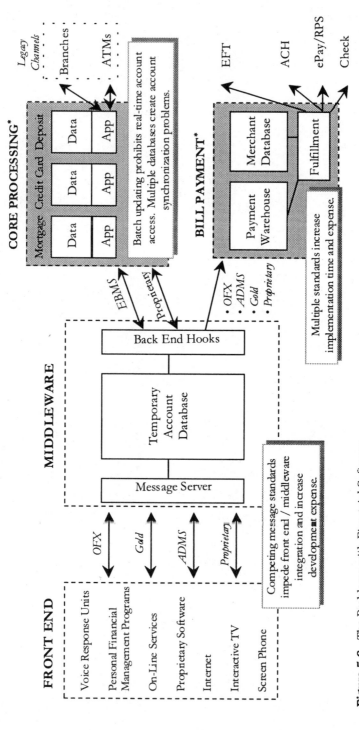

**Figure 5.6**  The Problems with Financial Software

*Bill payment area is part of payments sector. Core processing area is not part of EC industry.

*Source: Piper Jaffray*

major problem for most front-end software vendors. From the vendor's perspective, the lack of a single standard greatly increases implementation time and expense as it essentially has to build a new "bridge" for every installation.

Several companies have responded to this problem by proposing separate "single standards." Checkfree, Microsoft, and Intuit have announced that they will support a standard called Open Financial Exchange (OFX) while Integrion, a consortium owned by eighteen large U.S. banks, has proposed its own "Gold" standard. All of these firms have the right idea, yet the existence of competing "single standards" has put the industry right back to square one.

2. *Batch Updating*

As the on-line banking market began to take off in 1995 and 1996, many banks wanted to be able to offer on-line banking as soon as possible and with as little expense as possible. Unfortunately, building custom bridges between core processing systems and the middleware component was (and still is) a relatively long and expensive process.

To get around this issue, many banks used a process called "batch updating." Batch updating allowed banks to give their consumers the illusion of directly accessing their accounts without actually requiring the bank to build the necessary custom bridges to its core processing system.

In "batch updating," a bank creates copies of customer account records every night and then puts these copies into a separate database that is accessible by its on-line banking customers. When customers access their accounts they see these batch copies, not a real-time view of their account information. This illusion of having real-time account access only works as long as the customer has not performed any other transactions between the time the batch copy was created and the time the account was accessed.

If the customer has done another transaction during that time period, such as withdraw money from an ATM, then the transaction won't show up on the batch copy. This lack of synchronization can lead to situations in which customers bounce a check because the balance they saw on their batch copy was not the actual balance in the account at the time. This problem can also happen in reverse. If an on-line banking customer makes some electronic bill payments, these payments will not be reflected in the balance seen at the ATM or given by a teller at the branch.

So, batch updating may have provided banks with a quick and dirty way to enter the on-line banking market, but it has also set off a good deal of confusion with consumers who cannot understand why they are now getting two different balances from the same bank.

3. *Core Processing Fragmentation*

As we noted earlier, most banks do not have a single core processing system. Rather, banks tend to have different processing systems for different products. It's not uncommon to find a single bank with separate systems for its deposits, credit cards, mortgages, investments, etc.

The existence of separate systems gives banks a certain amount of flexibility, but it also creates a tremendous amount of headaches. First off, if the bank wants to provide both checking account and credit card information electronically, it has to build two separate middleware bridges, one to each system. Second, because the systems are separate, it is often difficult for a bank to combine information from different products. To this day most banks cannot send their customers a single printed statement of all their accounts because the bank cannot easily integrate the information from the different systems.

Together these three problems are not only increasing the time and effort it takes to implement on-line banking offerings, but they are also preventing banks from offering a true real-time, integrated on-line banking service.

## How to Solve These Problems

On paper, the solution to these problems is pretty straightforward. Theoretically, all it takes is just two simple steps:

1. Adopt a single message standard and then build it into every single piece of software on both the front, middle, and back ends.

2. Replace the fragmented core processing systems with a modern core processing system that has a single, unified customer database.

Together these two simple steps would greatly simplify the entire on-line banking process (see Figure 5.7). With a single message standard, each vendor would only have to build one message standard into its product and once the vendor did, it could almost effortlessly integrate its products into any bank's systems. The banks, meanwhile, would only need to support a single message standard which would greatly reduce their development workload and would give them the flexibility to mix and match vendors on both the front and the back-ends.

A single, advanced core processing system would eliminate the problems caused by core processing fragmentation and would enable it to offer real-time access to all of a customer's accounts.

These two steps would also have some additional bonuses. First off, they would entirely eliminate the need for a separate middleware component. After all, if every system is speaking the same language, there is hardly a need for a translator.

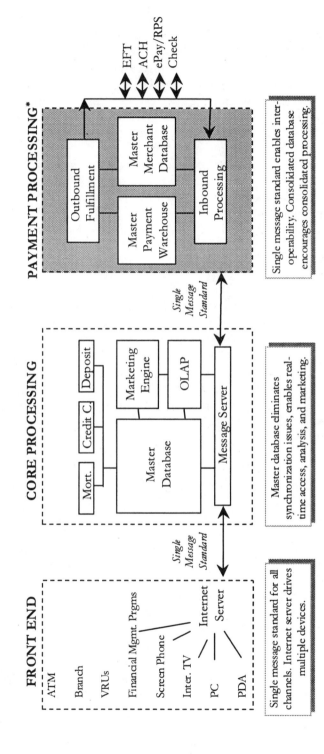

**Figure 5.7** Ideal Solution to Financial Software Problems
*Payment processing area is part of the electronic payments sector.
Source: Piper Jaffray

Second, if banks consolidated their core processing, they could very well put pressure on payment processors to do the same. Today, core processing fragmentation actually supports the fragmentation of payment processing by making it possible, if not desirable, for banks to choose a separate payment processor for each separate processing system. However, if a bank only had one core processing system, it's quite likely that it would only need one payment processing system.

Finally, with all of their customer information in one place, banks could analyze that information in real-time and send proactive marketing messages to their customers while they were connected to the bank. This kind of "one-to-one" marketing could not only help banks increase customer cross-selling, but also help them develop stronger relationships with their customers.

### Back to Reality

While these two simple steps could indeed solve almost all the problems facing the on-line banking business, the prospects for such radical changes in the structure of the on-line banking industry are fairly remote.

As far as the prospects for a single standard go, while all of the parties acknowledge that there should be a single standard, the issue is getting caught up in a much larger strategic battle between the banks and the non-banks (which we will discuss further in the Trends section of this chapter). For now, suffice it to say that in the near term the industry looks as though it will have to deal with two standards, OFX and Gold, instead of just one. That is not an ideal situation, but it is a great improvement over the current situation of no standards. Ultimately, there is a decent chance that the two standards will be merged into one, but the progress towards this vision has been difficult.

While there is at least a glimmer of hope on the standards front, prospects for solving the core processing problem look bleak. Banks are incredibly loath to risk even a slight disruption of their core processing operations. They often take years just to phase in the latest upgrade to the processing software they are using. While much of this is due to the highly customized nature of their processing environments, it also has a lot to do with the fact that replacing the core processing environment is the equivalent of performing a simultaneous heart and brain transplant operation while the patient is still awake. It might be technically possible to do, but no one wants to try it.

Still, without this surgery, banks know that they will be incapable of providing the kind of services that their customers expect. One middle-of-the-road solution to this dilemma that appears to be gaining momentum is for banks to install a separate core processing system that *only* services their on-line banking operations (see Figure 5.8). This data-

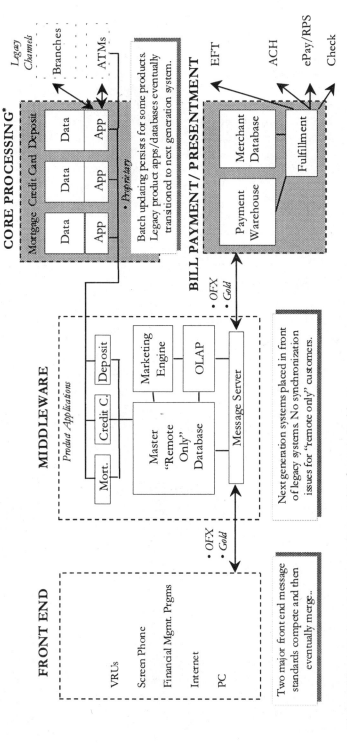

**Figure 5.8** A Realistic Solution to Financial Software's Problems
*Payment processing area is part of payments sector. Core processing area is not part of the EC industry.
Source: Piper Jaffray

base is in turn linked to the bank's old core processing environment by a series of custom bridges (yes, more bridges). This solution allows banks to avoid disrupting their core processing environments, but still enables them to enjoy some of the benefits of a unified core processing environment, such as integrated account information and real-time one-to-one marketing. Several banks starting up new "direct banking" units, such as ING in Canada, are currently experimenting with this type of solution and if it works, the practice may become much more wide-spread.

There will undoubtedly be many more twists and turns in the path to solving the various technical problems confronting the on-line financial services industry. The good news for firms focused on this sector is that the journey is bound to keep them very busy.

## Sub-Sectors

Categorizing the different firms that make up the financial software sector into meaningful groups is a fairly challenging exercise. The sector has become a sort of competitive crossroads with a motley collection of firms offering a variety of products and services.

To try and bring some clarity to the situation, we have taken a two-step approach. First, we have divided the sector into three large groups of firms according to their motives for being involved in the sector. These large groups include:

1. *Core Suppliers:* These firms provide the core software and services. They are intensely focused on the Financial Software Sector.

2. *Resellers:* These firms re-sell the software and services developed by the core suppliers. They complement the core suppliers more than they compete with them.

3. *"Ulterior Motive" Firms:* These firms also provide software and services, but they have ulterior motives for being involved in the sector in that they are actually trying to sell another product or service. Their long-term commitment to the sector is questionable.

The second step we have taken is to split the first group of firms, the core suppliers, into four separate sub-sectors. For all intents and purposes, the core suppliers make up "the sector." The other two groups of firms are not part of the sector, but their involvement (or some might say meddling) makes it important to keep an eye on them.

# Core Suppliers

## Consumer Software

The consumer software sub-sector is composed of a wide range of firms that all share one thing in common: a focus on providing front-end software to financial institutions and consumers. The keys to success in this sub-sector are a strong product offering grounded in solid technology and in-depth consumer understanding. Partnerships with financial institutions are also an important key to success in this sub-sector. This is a crowded and competitive market and to date, this is where most of the action has been in the Financial Software Sector.

## Business Software

Surprisingly, this sub-sector is far less crowded than consumer software. Firms in this sector provide small business and corporate on-line banking software, primarily in the areas of cash management, though there are a myriad of other potential areas. Whereas integration with financial management and planning is an option in the consumer software sub-sector, it is an essential requirement for the business software sector. EC Partners and Intuit are focused on providing cash management software to small businesses. FICS is focused on providing custom solutions to the large corporate market. In-house development is the largest competitor in this market, especially for the corporate banking market. Many of the consumer software providers plan to move into this market aggressively over the next year or so, mainly into the small business space.

## Middleware Vendors

Provide middleware solutions for integrating front-end devices and back-end processing software. Products are mostly message transaction systems as well as transaction processing software. Key to success in this market is an in-depth understanding of legacy system integration and hands-on experience with transaction processing environments. Integrion and Microsoft have both entered this space in the last year.

## Ancillary Applications

Developers of niche applications designed to complement other offerings in the sector by providing in-depth support for specific products or services. Potentially a much bigger sub-sector as the overall market matures and begins to look for value-added applications. Customized marketing,

**Table 5.1**   Consumer Software: Selected Firms

| Company | Description | Key product/service |
|---|---|---|
| Affinity Technology (AFFI) | Develops Internet-based loan origination and mangement software. | |
| CFI Proservices (PROI) | Solid provider of PC-based on-line banking software. Moving into Internet Banking. Provides its own bill payment processing. | ▪ Personal Branch |
| Corillian | Spin-off from Checkfree that develops multiple types of front end software, including ActiveX controls. | |
| Destiny Software | Developer focused on building custom, object oriented Internet banking applications. | ▪ Granite Credit Card System |
| Digital Insight | Rapidly growing Internet Banking software developer and site hosting service. Strength in Credit Unions. Over 60 customers on-line. | ▪ AXIS Web banking software |
| Edify (EDFY) | "Self-service" Internet applications vendor. Currently have several banks running its Internet banking software. | ▪ On-line banking system |
| Home Account | Start-up developer of Java-based Internet banking applications. | ▪ Home Account Java software |
| Home Financial Network | Founded by ex-principals of MECA Software. Main product is a stripped-down ATM-like PC software program. | ▪ Home ATM |
| InterVoice (#) (INTV) | Major VRU vendor looking to extend into Internet banking. | ▪ Visual Connect |
| Intuit (#) (INTU) | Clear leader in consumer financial services software. #1 PFM market share. Broadening out product line and integrating it. Co-sponsor of OFX standard. | ▪ Quicken, BankNOW, Quicken Financial Network |
| MECA Software | PFM software developer. Owned by Nationsbank, Bank of America, and Royal Bank. Closely aligned with Integrion. | ▪ Managing Your Money, MYMLite |
| Microsoft (MSFT) | Distant #2 PFM vendor. Moving aggressively into Internet banking arena. Single most powerful influence on the sector. | ▪ Microsoft Money, Investor, Marble, Viper |
| Q-Up | Texas-based start-up offering Internet banking and web site development services to local banks. | ▪ Internet Banking System |
| Quadravision | Canadian developer of financial services Internet sites. Recently acquired by financial printer Browne & Co. | ▪ Custom site development, "Me!" personalization software |

**Table 5.1** Consumer Software: Selected Firms (Continued)

| Company | Description | Key product/service |
|---|---|---|
| Reality On-Line | Subsidiary of Reuters. Offers turnkey Internet trading sites for brokerages. | ■ Custom site development |
| Security First (SFNB) | Pioneer in Internet Banking. Focused on large banks. Developing a server-based consolidation engine to compete with PFM products. | ■ Virtual Financial Manager, Virtual Credit Card Manager |
| Syntellect Inc. (#) (SYNL) | Integrated messaging and CTI company that is developing Internet-based customer service and account access software. | ■ Syntellect interactive services |
| Ultradata (ULTD) | Credit Union core processor that has built an impressive Internet banking system that requires its core processing environment to fully function. | ■ Ultrafis, Ultra-Access |

**Table 5.2** Business Software: Selected Firms

| Company | Description | Key products/services |
|---|---|---|
| ADP | Leading provider of private label small business account access software to banks. Has deals with most of the small business accounting software providers. | ■ Private label PC cash management software |
| Concorde | Spin-off from Bank of America that has developed an advanced, CORBA-based, object-oriented development environment suitable for both business and consumer/customer application development. | |
| Credo Group | Irish developer of Internet-base corporate cash management system that can access multiple accounts at multiple banks. | ■ Fontis |
| FICS | Belgium developer of banking software. Strong object-oriented development. Moving into US markets with a focus on corporate Internet Banking solutions. | ■ Custom-developed software |
| Harbinger (HRBC) | Largely an EDI firm, but provides a successful private label small business online banking program that is resold by banks. | ■ TrustedLink Banker |
| Intuit (#) (INTU) | Growing presence in small business accountingsoftware. Strong area of future focus. | ■ Quick Books |

**Table 5.3** Middleware: Selected Firms

| Company | Description | Key products/services |
|---|---|---|
| Applied Communications | Subsidiary of Transaction Systems Architects. Major vendor of fault tolerant EFT processing software. Recently purchased IVR/Home banking company. | ▪ Base 24 |
| Integrion | Jointly owned by 18 North American banks. Middleware and bill payment/presentment provider. IBM is a key supplier of network and products. Acquired major stake in Checkfree. | ▪ Gold, GoldRush, Integrion Financial Network |
| Intellidata (INTD) | Focused on back-end hooks. Acquired Braun Simmons 10/96. Vendor of bill payment engines and middleware bridges. Moving into OFX Servers. | ▪ Interpose Financial Engine, Unigate |
| Microsoft (MSFT) | Focused on messaging system. Offering a package of Microsoft servers designed to simplify the front-end and move Microsoft into back-end. | ▪ Marble, OFX Server, Internet Server |

**Table 5.4** Ancillary Applications: Selected Firms

| Company | Description | Key products/services |
|---|---|---|
| Brightware | Developer of artificial intelligence-based e-mail sales support system. | ▪ BrightResponse<br>▪ BrightAdvisor |
| Concerto | Leading provider of charting services to major online trading firms. Also operates BigCharts.com Internet site. | |
| Interactive Insurance Services | Subsidiary of Intuit. Runs an insurance quote service on the Internet but also provides development tools and support to insurers trying to get on to the Internet. | ▪ Insuremarket |
| Multi-logic | Licenses web-based interactive sales and service modules for complex products such as restricted stock to major brokerage firms. | |
| Neural Applications Corp. | Creates Java-based chart and quote monitoring tools for use at Internet trading sites. Has licensed technology to E*Trade. | ▪ Net Prophet |
| Quote.com | Provides real-time and delayed stock quotes as well as other information and tools for brokerages to use in setting up Internet trading sites. | ▪ Real-time quotes, new earnings forecasts, and charts |
| Vertigo | Developing Internet-based financial advisory and planning applications along with customized "push" marketing applications. | ▪ One-on-One Banking |

financial planning, and investment analysis/advice are key areas of focus. Partnerships with major business and consumer software providers are important parts of this sub-sector.

### On-Line Service Bureaus

Composed of outsourcers that are dedicated to offering a full package of on-line banking services to smaller banks which lack the required resources to develop and manage on-line financial service offerings. Major competitors are the established data processing service bureaus that are developing their own "packaged" offerings. In addition, some of the Internet banking software providers, such as Digital Insight and Security First, also offer service bureaus.

### Resellers

As noted earlier, these firms resell the core supplier's software and services to their existing customer bases. There are two significant groups of resellers in the industry:

1. *Data Processing Service Bureaus*
   These firms provide data processing services to banks and brokerages on an outsourcing basis. They have been aggressively partnering with the core suppliers in the sector in an effort to offer their service bureau customers complete financial software solutions. As a result they are really acting as resellers on behalf of the software vendors. For small software firms, partnering with these firms can be of tremendous benefit as these partnerships allow smaller firms to essentially outsource

**Table 5.5**   On-Line Service Bureaus: Selected Firms

| Company | Description | Key products/services |
|---|---|---|
| EDS | Major data processor looking to provide "turnkey" Internet banking solutions for banks. | ▪ Internet Banking, bill payment, web hosting |
| Integrion | Bank consortium plans to act as a service bureau for small- to medium-sized banks. Recently purchased VISA Interactive from VISA. | ▪ Gold, GoldRush, Integrion Network |
| On-line Resources | On-line banking service bureau offering full range of products including bill payment via ATM network. Focused on small- to medium-sized banks. | ▪ Internet banking, bill payment, screen phones |

their sales efforts. In addition, from a technical perspective once a software provider's products have been integrated into a service bureau, they can usually be offered to all customers of that service bureau with little or no additional implementation work. Selected firms in this sector include: Alltel, FiServ, Jack Henry & Associates, and M&I.

2. *Regional EFT Switches*
   As you may recall from Chapter 4, these firms are the central processors in the Electronic Funds Transfer (EFT) payment system. Like the service bureaus, these firms are primarily acting as resellers of the core supplier's software and services. The switches' interest in the sector stems largely from a desire to drive more transactions, such as bill payment and presentment, through their transaction networks. They are also looking at this sector as a way to diversify their revenue streams. Selected firms in this sector include: Cash Station, Honor, Magic Line, and NYCE.

## Ulterior Motive Firms

Everybody wants something and what these firms want generally has nothing to do with Financial software. They are only participating in the sector in an attempt to lure customers to their main products. While the lack of a true focus on the sector makes them unlikely long-term winners, their presence in the sector makes them a force that has to be dealt with. Three groups of firms comprise this category:

1. *Payment Processing Providers*
   The main business of these firms is processing electronic payments. They have been distributing financial software largely in an attempt to gain customers for their electronic bill payment offerings. There are two major divisions: bill payment firms trying to create bill payment volume and clearing firms trying to create trading volume. Their long-term commitment to the Financial Software Sector is questionable. Example firms include: Checkfree, First Data, National Financial, and Pershing.

2. *Legacy System Core Processors*
   These firms are offering Financial Software solutions largely in an effort to protect their role as legacy system processors. Their offerings are typically focused on middleware components. They are offering Financial Software in an attempt to stop the vendors of distributed computer solutions from invading the core processing area. Example firms include: IBM, Tandem, and Unisys.

3. *Distributed System Core Processors*

These companies develop modern core processing systems that are multi-tier, distributed computing-based architectures and employ either a Unix or *Windows NT* operating system. Such systems offer superior price/performance relative to legacy mainframe environments, but most financial institutions are *very* reluctant to switch their core processing systems. These firms are pitching their core processing systems to financial institutions building "green field" Internet or Direct Banking operations in an attempt to gain a foothold in the back office. Example firms include: CS Computing, Microsoft, Open Solutions, and Sanchez Computer Assoc.

## Current Size

The best (and perhaps the only) way to measure the current size of the Financial Software market is to use estimates of the total number of consumers and businesses using on-line banking and brokerage products today.

### On-Line Banking

As far as on-line banking products go, there have been a number of surveys and studies in the past year that have looked at the size of the market. They all have come out with estimates of around two million U.S. households in 1996. This is about double the number estimated during in 1995. This number is actually a bit more impressive than it first seems in that many banks either don't offer on-line banking or have yet to promote it heavily.

For those banks that *do* offer on-line banking and promote it heavily, on-line banking customers represent, on average, 5% to 7% of their customer base. In the case of huge banks like Wells Fargo, Citibank, and NationsBank, that 5% to 7% can equal hundreds of thousands of customers. These three banks alone have over a million on-line banking customers between them and all are adding customers at a healthy clip.

What's surprising is that some smaller banks have even higher penetration rates. Conventional wisdom has held that smaller banks would not attract the type of customers most likely to use on-line banking. But conventional wisdom has so far proved wrong. For example, Commerce Bank, a $3.4 billion New Jersey Bank, had 24,000 or 9% of its customers using on-line banking as of the first quarter of 1997. Indeed, the highest penetration rates of all can be found in small credit unions targeted at prime demographic groups, such as the First Technology Credit Union, which currently has 26% or 15,000 of its 57,000 members using its on-line banking services.

This higher level of penetration in banks that offer *and promote* their services suggests that while only two million households used on-line banking in 1996, there were probably another three to five million households that *would have* used on-line banking if their banks offered and/or promoted it. This hidden unmet demand can be clearly seen during the initial roll-out of on-line banking at major banks. During these rollouts banks are typically inundated with requests for the service. Such outpouring of demand has actually overwhelmed several banks, including NationsBank, which all had to pull back on their marketing efforts in order to let their back office and operations personnel catch up. Given the current supply constraints, the demand for on-line banking looks quite healthy indeed.

### On-Line Trading

There has been a similar and perhaps even more intense explosion of interest in the on-line trading market. According to *Forrester Research,* the market grew 150% during 1996 from 600,000 to 1.5 million accounts as major players such as Charles Schwab and Fidelity Investments launched significant initiatives. E*Trade, an on-line-only brokerage, saw account growth in 1997 of 130% from 113,000 to 260,000 accounts. Schwab, one of the largest and most successful discount brokers, claims over 1 million on-line trading users (but the number of exclusive on-line accounts is much lower).

The growth of the on-line trading market has been so strong and so pronounced that even full-service brokerage firms such as Merrill Lynch and Smith Barney have announced plans to offer at least account access over the Internet.

## Drivers

While growth to date in both of these markets has been pronounced, what has attracted everyone's attention is projected growth going forward. This growth is being driven forward by a number of demand and supply side drivers. Some of the most significant drivers include:

### Strong Consumer Interest

Survey after survey indicates that there is strong consumer interest in using on-line banking. About two-thirds of computer owners are at least somewhat likely to use on-line banking (see Figure 5.9). Given that home

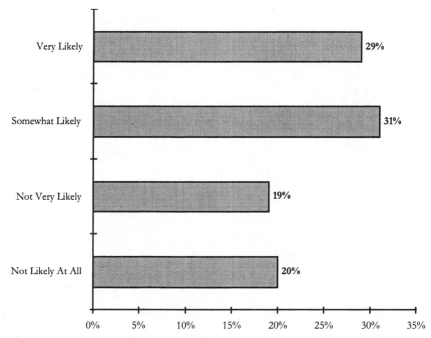

**Figure 5.9**  Consumers Likely to Use On-Line Banking
*Source: Bank Administration Institute/Gallup. 4/95*

PC ownership rates are 35% to 40% of the population, that's 20% to 25% of the U.S. population that currently not only has the necessary equipment to use on-line banking, but also the inclination to use it. These figures are backed up by *Payment System International's* annual consumer survey which indicates that in 1996 10.4% of the U.S. population would definitely use PC banking if it were available to them.[1] These figures indicate that the financial services industry will have its hands full just trying to meet pre-existing demand.

## Cost Advantages

On the supply side, large cost disparities between on-line and physical distribution channels are driving financial institutions to provide on-line offerings. In the banking industry, both PC and Internet banking channels are orders of magnitude cheaper than traditional branch transactions (see Figure 5.10). This substantial cost advantage has encouraged many banks

---

[1] See "1996 Financial Service Research Program." Payment Systems International. 3/96. Page 439.

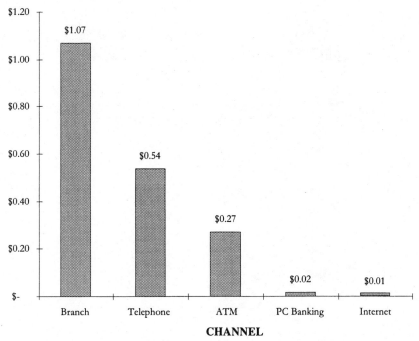

**Figure 5.10**  Cost Per Transaction by Channel  *Source: Booz, Allen & Hamilton*

to make on-line banking a cornerstone of their expense reduction efforts. Banks hope that by migrating their customer bases to these cheaper channels they will be able to reduce total distribution costs and improve the profitability of marginal customers.

The cost advantages provided by on-line trading are evident in its dramatically lower commission rates. Before on-line trading, the "discount" trading industry typically charged $50 to $100 a trade. Today, several on-line trading companies are now charging under $10 a trade. These price cuts have been made economically possible by the cost advantages of on-line trading.

## Move to Outside Development

Modern PC software development and design is now beyond the capabilities of even the largest banks. As a result, many banks are increasingly outsourcing their software design, development, and maintenance to outside firms by agreeing to use "shrink-wrapped" software developed by these dedicated software firms. This trend will only accelerate as software development becomes more complex and involved.

## Continued Innovation

Increases in available bandwidth and processing power along with new standards and technologies, such as Open Financial Exchange (OFX) and Java, will continue to fuel demand for new product development. There are still numerous technologies (such as Electronic Bill Presentment and "push" technology) as well as new access devices (such as set-top boxes and Internet Access Devices) that need to be incorporated into financial software. The development work necessary to incorporate these new technologies will create additional growth for Financial Software Sector firms.

Beyond incorporating these technical improvements, from an applications standpoint the sector is still very immature. There are numerous opportunities to expand both the scope and depth of existing applications as well as to create new applications which integrate other elements of the EC Industry more closely with the Financial Services sector.

# Potential

Together these four drivers should result in considerable growth of the sector. Projections for growth of the on-line banking market over the next few years range from 10 million to 17 million households (see Figure 5.11). While this is a fairly wide range of estimates, it is still at least five times as big as the current market.

As for on-line trading, it is projected by Forrester Research to grow to over 10 million accounts during the same time period (see Figure 5.12). These projections reflect a substantial "upward revision" from Forrester's earlier estimates.[2]

While these growth projections are enough to make a financial software executive giddy, it's important to caution that there are several factors that will limit the industry's long-term market potential.

**Computer Ownership.**    Computer ownership essentially caps the potential size of the on-line banking and brokerage markets, and the growth rate of home PC ownership is slowing (see Table 5.6). This slowdown in growth will limit growth in the size of the total potential market.

**Consumer Comfort.**    Even though many consumers may soon be capable of using on-line banking, there is still no guarantee that they will actually use it. One sobering statistic for the industry is that only 50% of consumers

---

[2] In 1995, Forrester projected that the industry would only reach 1.3 million accounts by 1998. By Forrester's own count, there were almost 1.5 million accounts in 1996.

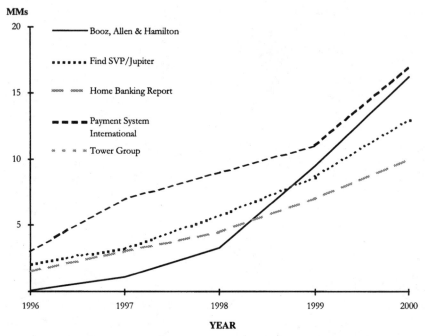

**Figure 5.11**   Various On-Line Banking User Projections
*Source: Booz, Allen & Hamilton, FInd SVP, Faulkner & Gray, PSI, Tower Group*

use ATM machines, even though these machines have been around for over 25 years and are readily available to close to 100% of the population (see Figure 5.13).

Given these limiting factors, growth is likely to slow considerably once 20%–25% of the population is using the service, a figure which should be reached sometime in the middle of the next decade.

**Table 5.6**   Computer Shipments and Household Penetration Rates

|                      | 1994   | 1995   | 1996   | 1997   | 1998   | 1999   |
|----------------------|--------|--------|--------|--------|--------|--------|
| Total Installed Base | 30,388 | 39,119 | 47,383 | 55,342 | 62,347 | 69,159 |
| Growth Rate (%)      |        | 29     | 21     | 17     | 13     | 11     |
| Penetration Rate (%) | 25.1   | 29.0   | 32.6   | 34.9   | 36.3   | 37.7   |

SOURCE: Dataquest 3/96.

**MMs**

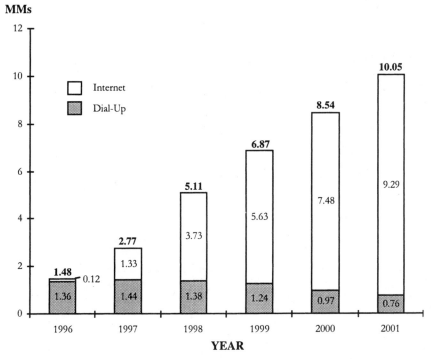

**Figure 5.12**   On-Line Trading User Projections   *Source: Forrester Research*

## Supply Side Drivers

On the supply side, banks and brokerages are furiously building on-line offerings in an attempt to meet both existing and expected demand. Worldwide, the number of banks with Internet sites grew 279% in 1996 (see Figure 5.14) and all indications are that this robust growth is likely to continue. For example, according to a survey by *Mentis Corp.*, over 38% of banks with greater than $1 billion in deposits have plans to add PC banking software, while over 53% have plans to add Internet banking software within the near future. Given that there are about 25,000 banks and thrifts within the U.S. alone, the potential for continued growth in this sector is substantial.

Of course, the growth of the overall market is only good news for the Financial Software Sector if it results in an accompanying growth in revenues and profits. Fortunately, early indications are that there will indeed be a strong correlation between the growth of the market and the growth of Financial Software Sector. For example, a survey by The Tower Group indicates that banks plan to increase their total spending on on-line bank-

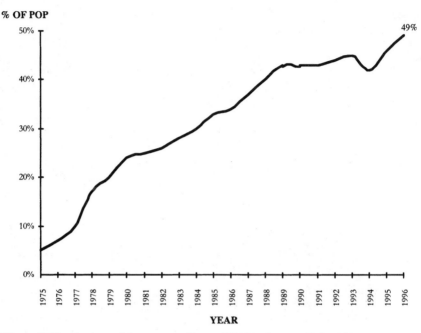

**Figure 5.13**   Percent of Consumers Using ATM Machines 1975–1996
*Source: Payment Systems International*

ing considerably from just under $200 million in 1996 to over $750 million in the year 2000 (see Figure 5.15).

Given all of these trends, we project that the total revenue base of the entire Financial Software Sector will expand from $1.2 billion today to $2.9 billion within the next five years. This equates to a compound annual growth of some 24% over the next four years. While the core drivers in the sector will actually grow faster than this rate, we believe that pricing pressures combined with the movement toward the Internet will restrain overall revenue growth somewhat.

## Trends

Amidst all of this growth, there are a number of trends currently under way which have the potential to dramatically change the Financial Software Sector. These trends are setting off a series of battles that threaten to cause a good amount of friction in the sector over the next few years as major players battle over much larger strategic issues. This situation will make it imperative for smaller players to pick and choose their spots carefully and do their best to stay out of the cross-fire.

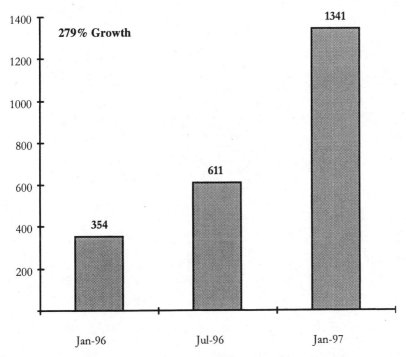

**Figure 5.14** Number of Bank Sponsored Internet Sites Worldwide
*Source: Booz, Allen & Hamilton*

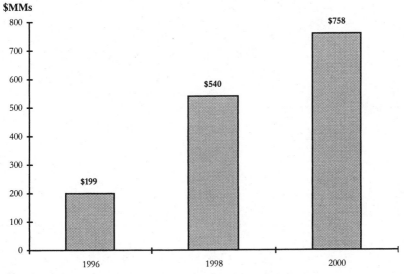

**Figure 5.15** Projected Bank Spending on On-Line Banking
*Source: The Tower Group*

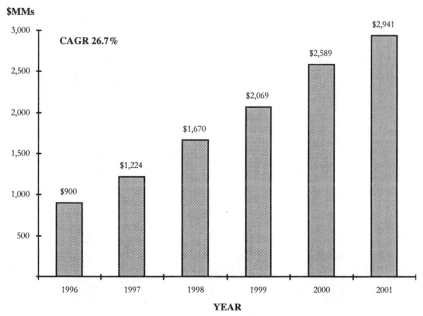

**$MMs**

**Figure 5.16**   Estimated Financial Software Sector Revenues—1996–2001
*Source: Piper Jaffray*

## Movement Toward the Internet

The most pronounced trend over the past year or so has been a distinct and accelerating movement away from proprietary "dial-up" networks and toward the Internet. This is not altogether surprising given that the Internet enjoys many practical advantages over "proprietary dial-up" services such as:

*Lower Cost.* Today, many firms must maintain large modem farms and communication networks to support their "dial-up" services. Moving to the Internet allows financial service firms to shift communication and network costs to their customers.

*Easier Administration:* When a firm wants to update PC software, it must send new software to all of its customers. This increases the expense and effort involved in administering the system. In addition, customers often inadvertently modify or erase their software which results in increased customer service inquiries. Moving to the Internet allows financial institutions to do away with PC software and its attendant headaches as all of the software sits on the host server. In addition, any updates to the software only have to be done once and they are available to all users immediately.

*Greater Flexibility:* The Internet provides firms with a much more flexible platform for delivering their services. Not only can they update their product and service offerings easily, but they can link their Internet site to other sites, thereby enabling them to offer new features and services.

The great inhibitor to this movement toward the Internet has been security concerns and it is still a major issue. However, these concerns are quickly fading as existing Internet-based banks and brokerages continue to operate without major security problems. (See Chapter 2 for a discussion of EC security.)

This trend is already evidencing itself in the development plans of the Financial Software Sector. Every major PC software vendor had either an Internet version of its existing product or a completely new Internet product out by the end of 1997. That does not mean that all PC software disappeared at the end of 1997, but it does mean that almost all of this software somehow became "Internet enabled." "Internet enabled" means that people may still use a copy of *Quicken* software to conduct their on-line banking, but they will increasingly connect to their bank via the Internet.

## Integration

There is much more to this trend toward the Internet than just simply switching the way that customers access their financial accounts. At the root of this migration is a realization that the Internet may well indeed enable the financial services industry to play a new and potentially powerful role in the world of Electronic Commerce: the "Integrator."

The role of the integrator is fairly straightforward. The integrator's job is to bring together all of a customer's financial and transaction information into a single place and then to organize and analyze that information on behalf of the customer. On a practical level, this means that the integrator uses the Internet to automatically collect account and transaction information from all of a customer's financial institutions including brokerages, insurance companies, banks, mutual funds, etc. By automatically bringing together all of this information, the integrator would take much of the drudgery and hassle out of financial management and planning and would then be in position to offer a number of value-added services such as:

1. Automatically pay monthly bills for customers based on pre-defined criteria set by the consumer.

2. Proactively provide financial planning based on observed financial patterns.

3. Recommend and assist with financial purchases.

Of course, the integrator concept is not new. Accountants, private bankers, and financial planners all play a similar role today. What is new about this integrator role is that the Internet, along with improvements in software technology, is making it possible to make such exclusive services as "private banking" and "personal accountants" widely available and at a mere fraction of the current cost.

But the attraction of the integrator role extends well beyond just improving customer service. The role of the integrator affords an institution two major advantages:

1. *Information Control:* The integrator has access to all of a customer's financial information. Theoretically, this "information advantage" should enable it to identify cross-selling opportunities and to more accurately assess both credit risk and potential profitability. This advantage should allow the integrator to proactively respond to customer needs and price more aggressively than others can.

2. *Customer Control:* Not only will it take time to set up a relationship with an integrator, but the integrator will also, much like a good assistant or travel agent, "learn" a customer's needs and behaviors over time. These two features will make it difficult for customers to switch Integrators as they would have to train their new integrator over a period of time. These increased "switching costs" should bolster customer retention and control.

Ultimately, the goal of the integrator is to generate an increasing stream of revenues from its customers by not only charging for financial management services, but also by generating fees from their customers' purchases of other companies' products, just as insurance agents or mortgage brokers do today.

All of this visionary talk might seem a bit farfetched in a world where most consumers can't even access their bank accounts electronically yet. Indeed, given the current state of affairs, it might seem as though it would be a lot more appropriate to have this discussion five years from now. But we are talking about integration today because the vision is starting to drive the market.

## The Coming Battle for Integration

One group of firms that are clearly sold on the power of integration is the Personal Financial Management (PFM) firms. Automatic checkbook balancing, integration, and analysis are all features that the PFMs have been trying to offer for years. Unfortunately for PFM firms, there has never been a way to automatically assemble and integrate this information into their programs. As a result, customers have to manually input almost all of this information. The problem is that the number of people who have the patience and discipline necessary to consistently update their PFM is limited to about 10%–15% of the population. Growth in the PFM marketplace has already slowed considerably and the PFM firms realize that unless they make their programs much easier to use, they will be permanently stuck with a total potential market size of just 10% to 15% of the population.

The Integrator role, with its ability to facilitate the *automatic* collection, input, and analysis of customer data, represents the panacea that the PFM firms have been looking for. With the requirement to manually input data eliminated, the PFMs should be able to expand their potential market to well beyond 10%–15% of the population.

By becoming an integrator, the PFMs will also cement themselves at an important crossroads, in effect becoming the gateway that consumers and businesses use to enter the world of EC. Not only will an integrator see every single transaction that a consumer or business conducts, but it will become a customer's trusted advisor and counselor, just like many real-world private bankers and accountants are today.

*Ultimately, this role should put integrators in position to collect a small advisory or brokerage fee on almost every single transaction its customers undertake.* Such a position has for some years represented the "holy grail" of the EC industry. Indeed many in the EC industry scoff at the idea of an entity collecting "tolls" on every transaction that passes through it as mere fantasy. But the PFM firms are quietly, but diligently, working to put the pieces in place to make this "fantasy" a modern day reality.

## Standards: Two Birds With One Stone

However, these firms face one critical problem in their drive to position PFMs as integrators. How do they automatically collect all of this information and assemble it into their programs? As we noted in the first part of this chapter, there are currently no standards in place for passing messages between the different components of the Financial Software Sector. This lack of standards not only creates a number of technical difficulties, but it also makes it very difficult to combine data from two different institutions. So a single standard would in fact allow the PFMs to kill two birds with one stone: first, it would resolve many of the technical problems facing the industry and second, it would also make it possible for PFMs to automatically collect data from multiple financial institutions.

To this end, the two major PFM firms, Microsoft and Intuit, along with Checkfree, proposed the Open Financial Exchange (OFX) message standard. With the OFX message standard in place, a consumer's financial statements could automatically flow into the PFM programs and the PFM companies would finally be able to fulfill their vision of becoming integrators.

The only problem with this vision is that the PFM companies are not the only ones interested in being the integrator. Financial institutions understand the power and attractiveness of the integrator role just as well as the PFM firms do. What's more, the financial institutions can clearly see that the integrator will have an important and highly valuable role in the world of Electronic Commerce. Naturally then, financial institutions also want to serve as integrators. There is only one problem, by definition *there can only be one integrator.* This simple fact has left the entire industry asking the same question: who will be the integrator?

Rather than waiting for the answer, all of the different parties have begun a series of maneuvers designed to ultimately position themselves as the integrator.

## The Bankers Strike Back

Of the financial institutions, banks have taken the most aggressive tack to date but also the most predictable. Their solution to the problem of who will be the integrator relies on two well worn tactics: shared ownership organizations and regulatory protections.

The banks' drive to establish shared ownership organizations started in 1995 when three very large banks, Bank of America, NationsBank, and Royal Bank of Canada, got together to buy the #3 PFM company, MECA Software. In buying MECA, the banks hoped to create a credible alternative to Intuit's *Quicken* and to Microsoft's *Money.* These three banks have subsequently sold portions of MECA to other financial institutions and have licensed the software to still others.

The same three lead banks who purchased MECA also started, in partnership with IBM and fourteen other banks, a company called Integrion (see the Sidebar on Integrion). Integrion was ostensibly designed to allow banks to outsource network management to a single entity, but Integrion is more properly thought of as part of a broader strategy to ensure that banks both maintain their role in the payments system as well as their potential role as integrators.

Integrion's first major act was to announce that it was going to propose its own "single message standard" called Gold. Like OFX, Gold is designed both to solve the technical problems facing banks and to enable integration of information. Unlike OFX, Gold is controlled by the banks and thus provides them with greater comfort that they will be in the driver's seat when it comes to integration.

Both of these steps, the purchase of MECA and the formation of Integrion, are classic responses by banks to external threats. Similar shared ownership organizations were formed in the credit card and EFT industries in an attempt to ensure that the Electronic Payments sector remained in bank hands.

Another classic response of banks is to lobby regulatory bodies to keep out competitors. On this front, the Banker's Roundtable, an organization of the largest banks (which, not surprisingly, includes most of the Integrion owners), has formed a subcommittee called the Banking Industry Technology Subcommittee (BITS). BITS is proposing that banks be given the right to approve any proposed message or payment standards.[3] Given their close ties to Integrion, it doesn't take a lot of imagination to guess which of the two standards—Gold or OFX—the BITS group is likely to endorse.

### Microsoft and Intuit Forge Ahead

Like the banks, the technology firms have also resorted to their own tried and true methods. Microsoft and Intuit have put the full weight of their development efforts behind the OFX standard in an attempt to establish OFX as the de facto standard simply by the sheer weight of its support within the Financial Software Sector.

Microsoft in particular has been methodically using its considerable influence and standards setting prowess to line up developers across the industry to support the OFX standard. Indeed in our conversations with financial software firms, we found only one company which was not firmly committed to supporting OFX: MECA Software.

The weight of these efforts are paying off for both Microsoft and Intuit as they both released OFX-enabled versions of their PFMs in the fall of 1997, and plan to have all of the pieces of the OFX "system" in place by early 1998. Ironically, the adoption of OFX will also be aided by the banks themselves. Currently, many bank customers use either Microsoft's *Money* or Intuit's *Quicken* to do their on-line banking. When Microsoft and Intuit switch these PFMs to the OFX standard this coming fall, the banks will have no choice but to switch to OFX as well.

In response to this situation, many banks have begun to think about cutting the PFMs off at the pass, by integrating customer information *before* the PFMs receive it. By performing this integration "server side" on their own computers, banks would eliminate the need for consumers to even use a PFM.

But alas, this strategy is almost impossible for most banks to execute because, as we saw at the beginning of this chapter, most banks lack the technical infrastructure necessary to integrate account information. Indeed most banks cannot even integrate information from different inter-

---

[3] Our conversations with members of both the executive and legislative branches indicate little if any support for the BITs initiatives. In fact, folks inside the beltway generally seemed a bit incredulous that BITs thought it could declare something a standard and then enforce it. After all, that's the government's job.

nal accounts held by the same customer, let alone integrate information from external accounts. It is highly ironic that the PFMs, with their single message standard, single database, and unified processing represent, at the PC level, what banks are so desperately trying to build into their mainframe environments. With neither the time nor the resources to adequately restructure their internal systems, many banks may very well be forced to accept the OFX standard and the triumph of distributed, multi-tier computing that it represents.

## Wildcard

One wildcard in this entire situation is that consumers may choose to do their integration elsewhere; not at their bank or on their PC, but at a third-party Internet site set up expressly for the purpose. These "Integrator" sites would be dedicated to providing integration services and, unlike banks, consumers could be sure that these third-party sites did not have a vested interest in selling them a particular financial product.

These sites could also use the Internet to assemble a vast array of educational and planning materials as well as databases that provide consumers with the ability to find the absolute best deal for their new mortgage, insurance, mutual fund, or credit card (see Figure 5.17). Ultimately, these sites could become the central focus point or crossroads for consumer and small business participation in Electronic Commerce.

Sound farfetched? There are actually several of these integrator sites already up and running on the Internet. And guess who owns the two

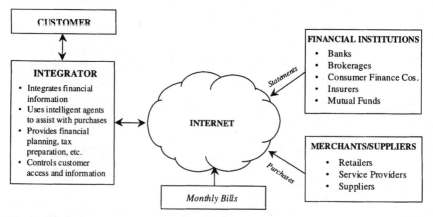

**Figure 5.17** Integrator Site: Hypothetical Role *Source: Piper Jaffray*

biggest Integrator sites? Microsoft and Intuit, the two biggest PFM firms (see Table 5.7). So these firms not only have the PFM angle covered, but if Integrator sites ever takes off, they have that angle covered too.

Although most banks don't realize it, the emergence of the integrator site has the potential to turn the tide of battle. Unlike the software world, where the PFM firms dominate the distribution channels and can leverage their installed base, the Internet presents banks with a comparatively wide-open situation. Banks can open their own integrator sites and substitute them for the centralized databases and unified processing environments that they currently lack. So, this is now where the industry stands, with the race toward integration in full swing and with many banks not realizing that the Internet has given them a second chance.

To date, much of the maneuvering in the industry has resembled an intense, but gentlemanly game of chess. As the stakes continue to rise, though, the prospect of open hostility between the banks and the PFM firms is rapidly increasing. Already, several banks including Chase Manhattan and Wells Fargo have begun to use pricing incentives as a way to direct their customers away from the PFMs and toward their own Internet sites.

**Table 5.7** Integrators: Selected Sites

| Firm | Site | Description |
| --- | --- | --- |
| America On-Line | Personal Finance Center | The Personal Finance Center is one of the busiest areas on AOL. It already offers portfolio tracking, credit card statements, on-line banking and on-line trading. OFX could provide AOL with the means to "integrate" it all together. |
| Block Financial | Conductor | Internet site owned by H&R Block, the parent of Compuserve. Partnering with community banks to offer them a way to give their customers access to large investment firms in an "integrated" fashion. Also has its own on-line credit cards and personal loans. |
| Intuit | Quicken.com | Internet site that provides Intuit customers with investment, tax, and insurance advice. Future versions of Quicken will be "integrated" with the site. Major alliances with Excite and AOL. |
| Microsoft | Investor | Officially part of the Microsoft Network Service, but accessible through the Internet. Focused on investments, but nothing prevents it from moving into other areas of financial services. Already plans to use the site to deliver OFX statements. |

## Battle for the Glass House

At first glance, Microsoft's involvement in this battle seems non-sensible. Why should Microsoft risk alienating all of those big banks? After all, these banks buy tens of thousands of copies of Microsoft's system software and applications. Surely Microsoft is more interested in that business than it is in being an Integrator.

In fact, Microsoft is indeed interested in the banks' internal business and that interest extends well beyond selling copies of *Windows* and *Word* to banks. What Microsoft is most interested in is the core processing business, otherwise known as the back-end or the glass house. According to the *Mentis Corporation*, while banks spent only $100–$200 million on on-line banking software in 1996, they spent about $2.7 billion on back-end processing, data centers, and applications. Microsoft can read a pie chart as well as the next company and there is no doubt that Microsoft recognizes that the glass house is where the money really is.

That of course begs the question: What company now dominates the glass house in most financial institutions? Why, it's IBM. And what company is the original proponent of Integrion, the banking industry's most visible response to encroachment by technology firms? IBM yet again. Who is Microsoft really after? That's right, IBM.

No doubt Bill Gates has dreams of clusters of *NT* workstations humming away where once sat monolithic IBM 3090s and no doubt Lou Gerstner has nightmares that Bill Gates' dreams will come true.

When put in this light, Microsoft's support of OFX begins to make sense. In supporting OFX, Microsoft is actually supporting a standard that will help it in its drive toward the glass house. OFX requires "OFX servers" which are essentially *Windows NT* PCs that process OFX messages as quickly as possible. Theoretically, a group of OFX servers linked or "clustered" together is capable of processing millions of OFX messages a second. After awhile, OFX servers start to sound a lot like, well, IBM mainframes.

However, unlike IBM, OFX servers are not doing the core processing chores of processing payments and updating accounts. Banks have traditionally only let the most reliable and proven vendors, such as IBM, take on these mission-critical tasks. However, if Microsoft is able to convince banks that it can do a good job of processing OFX messages, maybe banks will give them a shot at processing loan applications, or checks, or maybe, just maybe, the core processing operations themselves.

IBM is well aware of Microsoft's intentions and has done a masterful job convincing banks that Microsoft is trying to take their customers, when Microsoft is, in all likelihood, more interested in taking IBM's customers.

So how is Microsoft going to finesse the issue of OFX and its Integrator potential? Doesn't the integration issue have the potential to derail Microsoft's entire glass house initiative by antagonizing the banks? Yes, it does.

So rather than risk that possibility, Microsoft is going to great lengths to assure banks that it has no designs on their customers. They are even offering pieces of their PFM (Microsoft *Money*), called Active X controls, to the banks for free and allowing the banks to incorporate these controls into their Internet sites as they see fit.

Given that the banks will need Microsoft's *Marble*, Internet Information, and OFX servers to run the Active X Controls and that the banks' customers will need Microsoft's *Explorer* software to view them, Microsoft might just be able to get over the "loss" of giving away its second-ranked PFM product.

Will this strategy work? So far Microsoft appears to have the upper hand, but it's not clear that IBM will be outmaneuvered. This "battle of the elephants" is far from over and the outcome is still uncertain; however, one thing that is certain is that any firm which gets in the middle of this battle risks being trampled to death.

Note: Just before we went to press, Microsoft announced an agreement with IBM and Integrion to combine the Gold and OFX standards into a single standard. However, they have yet to spell out exactly what the standard will look like, and it appears as though it will look a lot more like OFX than Gold, essentially meaning that Microsoft won the battle after all.

## Success Factors

So this is where the Financial Software Sector stands: tensions rising over the integration issue and two titans of the industry fighting over control of the glass house and willing to do whatever it takes to win the battle. What does this mean for the other firms in the industry?

We believe that there are a few basic keys to success in the Financial Software Sector going forward:

1. *A healthy relationship with financial institutions.*   Like it or not, these are the industry's main customers. Failure to maintain productive relationships with these firms can only be a negative.

2. *A strong focus on the Internet.*   The migration to the Internet is fast becoming a stampede. These is no sense spending development dollars on anything else.

3. *A commitment to pragmatic neutrality.*   While the war between Microsoft and IBM may have religious undertones, the successful financial software firms will stay agnostic and work with both parties in an even-handed manner.

4. *Focus on future areas of opportunity.*   While there is a tremendous battle raging in the consumer software sub-sector today, other areas remain relatively quiet. We believe that successful firms will migrate to these greener pastures in advance of the herd.

## New Opportunities

Specifically, we see four areas of opportunity for financial software firms going forward:

*Specialized Applications:* Specialized applications offer a real opportunity in that they generally comprise too small a market for any of the big players to worry about and also require a good deal of specialized knowledge and experience to deliver. This market is likely to grow as financial service firms search for ways to competitively differentiate themselves in an increasingly crowded field. Take, for example, the Integrion banks. How are they going to differentiate themselves if all sixteen banks are using the exact same platform? Specialized applications would provide these banks with an easy way to separate themselves from the pack. Some of the most promising specialized applications include real-time and "one-to-one" marketing applications, in-depth investment planning, and specialized investment and trading tools.

*Corporate Banking:* This is a tremendous area of opportunity for the Financial Software Sector, but also one that requires in-depth product knowledge and a willingness to customize. Small business is a significant opportunity, but the middle market and large corporate areas could perhaps represent even greater opportunities.

*International:* Much as other U.S. firms have followed the Internet wave around the world, successful financial software firms in the U.S. will seek to capitalize on the leading role of the U.S. in Internet development to generate International sales. Indeed statistics would seem to indicate that many countries such as Sweden, Finland, Australia, France, and Canada represent better markets for financial software than the U.S.

*On-line Service Bureaus:* On-line service bureaus allow financial institutions to outsource their on-line financial services activities. As the Financial Software Sector grows in size and complexity, chances are that demand for the on-line service bureau industry will explode. It has happened in other areas with similar characteristics and we expect that this sector will be no exception. However, we also expect that careful positioning will be required in this sector to coexist peacefully with the major core processing service bureaus that will likely view on-line service bureaus as a natural extension of their business.

### SIDEBAR: INTEGRION

What happens when eighteen of the biggest banks in North America get together with IBM and VISA? They throw the entire Financial Software Sector into disarray, that's what.

In September of 1996, each of these institutions threw $4 million into the pot to form Integrion. What is Integrion? That's a good question. According to the company itself, Integrion is a private for-profit company that "is a provider of interactive banking and electronic commerce services to financial institutions."

Beyond this rather amorphous public pronouncement, the exact role and structure of Integrion has been purposely kept somewhat ill-defined, partly in order to give Integrion some latitude in determining what it is going to do and partly to keep potential competitors on their heels. However, it is possible to put two and two together to get a better sense of just what Integrion is and what it plans to do.

## Structure

Integrion has its own employees who have been recruited from both the banking and technology industries and is run by a veteran banking executive named Bill Fenimore. Integrion is actually composed of five major piece parts, each with its own separate purpose:

*A Network:* Integrion uses a so-called Value Added Network (VAN) to link together its financial institutions, the Internet, and local "dial-up" Points of Presence (POPs). By using the same VAN, the banks effectively get to share network and communication costs, thereby increasing scale efficiencies. The specific VAN used by Integrion is the IBM Global Network (IGN).

*Some Middleware:* Integrion is building the necessary middleware bridges to connect its owners' core processing systems to the network. This task is somewhat simplified by the fact that most of Integrion's owners use (surprise) similar IBM equipment and software in their core processing operations.

*A Group of Applications:* Integrion is developing a set of basic Internet banking applications that its owners can then use to offer Internet Banking services. These applications can be customized and "branded" by each of the member banks. Initial applications will focus on consumer banking and bill payment, but later applications will focus on small business and "electronic commerce activities."

*Some Databases:* Integrion is also building some databases. It's not entirely clear what these databases will eventually be used for, but it appears as though at the very least they will be used for "warehousing" electronic bill payments and electronic bill presentments. These databases could also possibly house other payment and customer information.

*A Message Standard:* Integrion has developed a message standard called "Gold." The Gold message standard is the glue that holds this whole collection of parts together. This standard not only links the core processing systems to the applications and the databases (via the middleware) but it also links the Integrion network with the Internet (or any other network) and any piece of software that supports the Gold standard.

## Role

What will Integrion do with all these piece parts? While the exact role of Integrion has yet to be finalized, there are several roles that it is clearly committed to fulfilling:

*On-line Banking Services:* Allows banks to offer both "dial-up" and Internet Banking services using a shared network infrastructure and shared group of applications and databases. This role effectively enables banks to outsource network management tasks and application development to Integrion, thereby reducing the total costs for everyone involved.

*Bill Payment:* Integrion is committed to offering electronic bill payment services. The only problem is that it does not have a merchant database, remittance connections to merchants, or a paper check printing operation. All of these items are critical to offering a bill payment service (see Chapter 4). To rectify these deficiencies, Integrion acquired all of USA Interactive in 1997, along with a 20% stake in Checkfree.

*Bill Presentment:* Integrion is publicly committed to also providing electronic bill presentment services. It will leverage the connections it builds to merchants for bill payment to provide this service. It has an advantage in this area in that it can use its owner's existing relationships with billers to create a completely electronic "closed loop." With the investment in Checkfree, Integrion will work closely with Checkfree to develop its bill presentment services.

*Service Bureau:* Integrion is not content being just an exclusive service provider for eighteen of the largest banks in North America; it also wants other banks to "join" its network. However, these new banks would be customers, not owners. Apparently, eighteen owners are enough.

Together these roles would put Integrion smack dab in the middle of the Financial Software Sector. It would be providing essentially all of the middleware component and almost all of the bill payment component. Internet banking applications would also put it in the front-end software component and its middleware bridges would connect its to the core processing environment. To round it all out, the service bureau will enable it to create further scale economies (see Figure 5.18).

## Future Roles?

If that wasn't enough to keep Integrion busy, there are a number of future roles that Integrion will clearly be in position to serve. While Integrion has not announced anything formally, at the end of the day it wouldn't be all that surprising to see it move into these roles:

*Certificate Authority:* It makes logical sense for Integrion to move into this area. If you remember from Chapter 2, certificate authorities provide the digital equivalents of driver's licenses

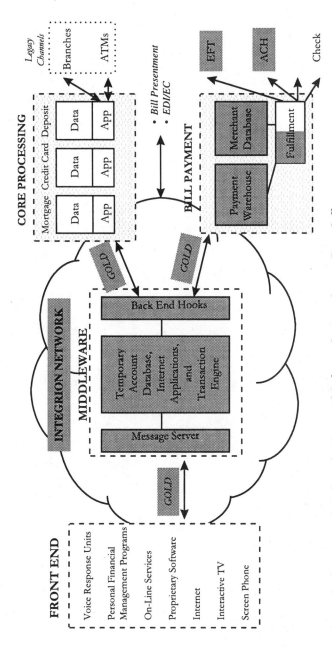

**Figure 5.18** Integrion's Role in the Financial Software Sector    *Source: Piper Jaffray*

and passports to people. Integrion will already have to issue
certificates to all network users, so its owners may just use it as ·
the "master CA" for all of its customers.

*Integration:* Integrion is in an ideal position to serve in the
integrator role. It will have connections to merchants, banks,
and consumers and it will be processing electronic bill
presentments, payments, and account information. What better
place to integrate all of its information?

*"On-us" Transaction Network:* This is perhaps the biggest stretch
for Integrion, but it's a logical out-growth of its current plans.
If you remember from Chapter 4, an "on-us" transaction is one
that does not have to pass through a central processor. As a
result, the end processor saves transaction fees and deprives
the central processor of information. With 60%–75% of the
market, it is fairly likely that a transaction initiated by one
Integrion member is destined for another Integrion member.
Rather than send these "on-us" payments through the ACH,
EFT, or Credit Card Payment systems, Integrion could simply
"jump the switch" and do its own payment switching, netting,
and settlement. And it would not just have to limit itself to
electronic bill payments, it could also process electronic cash,
credit card, and EFT payments as well.

While these are all possibilities for Integrion, none of them is a "sure
thing" yet. One certainty, though, is that Integrion was not formed to
build just a few insignificant applications and hook up a handful of
banks to the Internet. Integrion is clearly part of a "master plan" that
some in the banking industry have for solidifying banks' role in the
Electronic Commerce industry.

## Problems

For the Financial Software Sector, Integrion presents some major
problems. After all, Integrion claims to collectively represent about 60%
of the banking households in America, so if it decides to enter a
particular market or software segment, there probably won't be much
left over for anyone else. Between Integrion and Microsoft, picking a
spot where these firms won't get stepped on by a giant will become a
fine art.

That is not to say that Integrion doesn't have some problems of its
own, not the least of which is that it is owned by eighteen separate,
strong-willed, competitive banks. Managing the different development
priorities, concerns, and egos of this widely disparate group will be a
challenge in its own right that will only get tougher as these banks
begin to compete more directly with each other.

The second problem Integrion has is that its own owners aren't
exactly 100% committed to the Integrion band wagon. Many of them
are not only continuing to work with other firms, but they are signing
long-term contracts with them, as Barnett Bank (now part of
Nationsbanc) recently did with Security First. Finally, other banks
might not be all that keen on signing up as customers of Integrion

given that they would be putting their on-line livelihoods into the hands of an organization run by some of their biggest competitors.

So Integrion's future is by no means assured and it remains to be seen if it truly can become the lynch pin in the master plan to save the banking industry. But Integrion does have $70 million in up-front capital, a clear mandate, and some strong high-level support. These assets ensure that, at the very least, Integrion can cause some major trouble for anyone who tries to pick a fight with it.

## Investment Considerations

Currently, the opportunity to invest in the Financial Software Sector is limited by the small number of public firms that are in the sector. To be included in this sector from an investment perspective, a firm has to have a strong and growing presence in the Financial Software Sector as well as a strategic focus on expanding that business over the long-term and right now there are only seven public firms which meet those requirements.

### Recent Investment Performance

The Financial Software Sector has recently come back to life after underperforming the rest of the EC industry for quite some time. Indeed, for most of 1997, the sector handily underperformed the EC Index, due largely to the sluggish stock performance of sector-bellwether Intuit. However, late in 1997, Intuit suddenly became a major positive (instead of a drag on

**Figure 5.19** Financial Software Index vs. EC Index and S&P 500
*Source: Piper Jaffray*

performance), and the sector began a sustained run-up. By the latter half of 1998, the sector was handily outperforming the overall EC industry and had even surpassed the returns of the broader market in general.

Unfortunately, the sector's strong performance is due almost entirely to Intuit, which accounts for 83% of the sector's overall market capitalization. Excluding Intuit, a very different picture of 1998 emerges, as companies such as CFI Proservices, Edify, and Intellidata all had major declines in their stock prices due to disappointing earnings announcements. Unlike Intuit, these companies were not able to capitalize on investors' increasing enthusiasm for Internet stocks, and so when they stumbled, they were punished quite severely.

### Market Characteristics

We have included in the Financial Software Sector index only those public firms that are focused primarily on producing and/or servicing financial software. Notable exclusions include service bureaus (such as Alltell and M&I) as well as VRU firms (such as Intervoice and Syntellect).

As of now there are only seven public firms of the Financial Software Sector, three of which went public in 1996 (see Table 5.8). Key statistics for this group as of 7/1/98:

*Market Capitalization:* The seven firms had a total combined value of $4.3 billion at the end of 1997. Intuit dominated the market, accounting for 83% of total capitalization. This capitalization makes the Financial Software Sector the smallest sector in the EC universe, just behind Commerce Content.

**Table 5.8**  Firms in the Financial Software Sector Index

| Company | Ticker | Mrkt cap ($MMs) | $Vol/ day ($MMs) | % Price Δ/day | 1997 Revs ($MMs) | 1997 Earn ($MMs) | 1998E P/E | 1999E P/E | 19 P/ |
|---|---|---|---|---|---|---|---|---|---|
| Intuit | INTU | $3,599 | $60.6 | 2.9% | $599 | ($2.9) | 69.6 | 51.0 | 6 |
| Sanchez Computer | SCAI | 237 | 2.3 | 3.6 | 28 | 3.5 | 46.3 | 28.7 | 7 |
| Edify | EDFY | 171 | 1.8 | 3.3 | 57 | 4.0 | NM | 25.3 | 2 |
| Security First | SFNB | 157 | 1.3 | 3.9 | 5 | (28.0) | NM | NM | 30 |
| CFI Proservices, Inc. | PROI | 85 | 0.6 | 2.2 | 73 | 4.7 | 15.7 | 13.0 | 1 |
| Ultradata Corp. | ULTD | 40 | 0.1 | 4.3 | 29 | (3.5) | NM | NM | 1 |
| Intellidata | INTD | 30 | 0.2 | 4.4 | 60 | (90.1) | (2.1) | 19.4 | 0 |
| Total | | $4,320 | $66.8 | 2.3% | $851 | ($112.4) | 172.5 | 48.5 | 5 |

NOTE: All statistics are as of 7/1/98.
SOURCE: Company reports, First Call, Piper Jaffray

*Liquidity:* As with the other sectors in the EC universe, trading volumes in Financial Software Sector are fairly high. An average of $67 million a day traded hands in the sector during the second quarter of 1997. At these trading volumes, market capitalization in the sector is turning over an average of every 65 days compared to 83 days for the entire EC industry. This makes the sector the third most actively traded sector in the EC industry behind Commerce Content. However, most of this activity was due primarily to Intuit's stock which turned over at a lightening fast rate of once every 59 days.

*Volatility:* With high activity often comes high volatility. Stock prices in the sector changed a capitalization weighted average of 2.3% per day during the last 12 months, making the Financial Software Sector the second most volatile sector in the EC industry.

*Revenues:* Revenues grew an anemic 19% in 1997 from $709 million in 1996 to $846 million in 1997 due primarily to Intuit's slow growth. This made the Financial Services Software Sector the second slowest growing sector in the EC industry even though its core drivers expanded by 100%. However, excluding Intuit, revenues grew 51% or the second fastest rate in the EC industry.

*Earnings:* In total, the sector lost $112 million in 1997 thanks largely to acquisition related charges.

*Valuations:* Stocks are currently trading at 49 times their 1999 estimates compared to the EC industry's average of 29.8 times 1999. On a price-to-sales basis, the sector is actually the second cheapest in the EC industry at 5.1 times 1997 sales.

## Risks

With all of the high stakes power plays between financial institutions, Microsoft, and IBM underway, investing in the Financial Software Sector has more than a few risks associated with it:

*Slowing On-Line Banking/Brokerage Adoption:* Expectations are for 500%–700% growth in the size of both the on-line banking and brokerage populations within five years. Should actual growth rates fall below these expectations, this sector will suffer accordingly. A leading indicator of this trend would be a slowdown in PC/Internet adoption.

*Security Breaches:* Security is of particular concern to consumers and businesses conducting on-line financial service activities. A widely publicized security breach in a financial institution's on-line operations could cause a general slowdown in consumer adoption of the on-line financial services and could cause many financial institutions to reappraise their current operations. Given the varying levels of security being employed by different financial institutions on the Internet, we believe that this is a significant risk for the sector.

*Integrion:* Integrion's position as a "preferred supplier" to eighteen of the largest banks in North America makes it a powerful market force. A decision by Integrion to move into any sub-sector or area of opportunity could have a significant impact on the investment prospects for other firms in that area. In addition, Integrion's decision to endorse a specific firm's products or services could have a negative impact on the value of that firm's direct competitors.

*Consolidation:* Consolidation in the financial services industry is continuing to take place at a steady rate. Given that a few major banks can often account for the majority of a financial software firm's revenues, investors should carefully evaluate the revenue concentration of the smaller firms in this industry.

*Pricing:* Pricing in the industry is currently unstable as Microsoft is essentially giving away its front-end software to banks in an effort to get their Internet server, browser, and OFX business. Firms that compete directly with Microsoft are therefore likely to experience a challenging pricing environment, to say the least.

## Conclusion

The Financial Software Sector is still an emerging market. However, with the sector's fundamental drivers forecast to grow anywhere from five to seven times over the next five years, the market is clearly poised for significant growth. As the market grows, it will also increase in importance due to a shift from merely providing access to providing value added products, such as integration, that link financial institutions to the EC industry and bring them closer to their customers. The keys to success in this sector will be to focus on providing applications and services that enable financial institutions to competitively differentiate themselves in what will be an increasingly crowded sector. Firms that can provide these applications while avoiding the "elephants" should have a bright future.

# 6

# Business Commerce and the Rise of the Distributed Extraprise

## Introduction

In 1996, U.S. businesses had total revenues of around $15 trillion.[1] The EC industry played a role in generating less than 0.02% of that total. The task of raising this paltry share has fallen largely on the shoulders of the Business Commerce Sector.

The Business Commerce Sector provides software and services that enable businesses to efficiently conduct EC. Building these types of products and services takes more than a creative mind; it takes an in-depth understanding of business processes and priorities. The ultimate goal of this sector is to make the communication, coordination, and collaboration that accompanies commerce as seamless and efficient as possible.

## Structure

The Business Commerce Sector covers a lot of ground. It not only supports business-to-business EC, with its orders, invoices, and shipping notices,

---

[1] Estimation based on data from "Corporation Income Tax Returns: Balance Sheet, Income Statement, and Tax Items for Specified Income Years, 1980–1994," U.S. Internal Revenue Service.

but also business-to-consumer EC with its stores, malls, and catalogs. This wide range of activity within the Business Commerce Sector has generated a good deal of confusion over just how all of the different activities supported by the sector fit together.

These activities are in fact organized around three distinct business systems. The rest of this section will review each of these business systems and explain how they fit together to create the Business Commerce Sector.

## Open Commercial Exchange

If there ever was an ideal vision of EC, Open Commercial Exchange (OCE) is it. OCE involves using the Internet to spontaneously buy and sell products. With OCE, the Internet is transformed into a giant 24-hour-a-day international marketplace where consumers and businesses alike can shop to their heart's content and purchase the best products and services that their dollars, pounds, yen, or deutche marks can buy.

The defining characteristic of OCE is that it is *spontaneous*. Nothing needs to be prearranged and no special technology is needed. Consumers and businesses can just jump right in and engage in EC at a moment's notice.

In order to make this vision of spontaneous EC possible, the digital equivalents of marketplaces, storefronts, and auction houses must first be built (see Figure 6.1). This mandate requires a few critical pieces of soft-

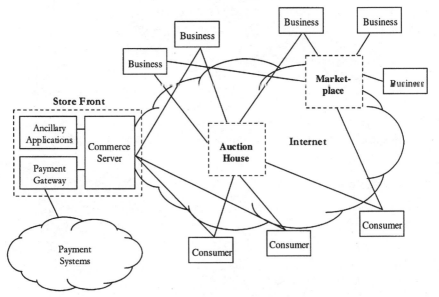

**Figure 6.1** Open Commercial Exchange Business System   *Source: Piper Jaffray*

ware that the Business Commerce industry is more than happy to provide including:

*Commerce Server:* This is the workhorse of the OCE industry. It is the equivalent of an electronic storefront and then some. Typically it includes everything that a company needs to set up shop on the Internet: a catalog application to present its wares; a database to store inventory, order, and customer information; and a "gateway" to the electronic payment system. It is important to note that many commerce servers include "hooks" that allow companies to link their commerce servers with their company's enterprise systems. It is also important to note that commerce servers aren't just for retail consumer sales; these servers are just as happy selling industrial lubricants as they are bottles of wine or the latest best-sellers. Essentially, any firm that wants a store on the Internet needs to have a commerce server. Given that a lot of firms want to have a store on the Internet, this part of the Business Commerce Sector is one of the fastest growing, but also one of the most competitive. IBM, Microsoft, Oracle, Netscape, and numerous others are all hawking commerce servers with ferocious intensity. As the market matures, a clear segmentation is developing between the high-end products that offer everything a business could possibly need (as well as a $10,000 to $100,000 price tag) and low-end products that do not have a lot of bells and whistles, but will get the job done for under $5,000.

Commerce servers are also sometimes known as "electronic catalog" servers. Most companies cringe at being called "catalog" companies because they (quite rightfully) claim that their software does quite a bit more than just present pretty pictures of merchandise. However, at the end of the day what the consumer or business sees is the pretty pictures, so the "electronic catalog" moniker is understandable and likely to stick. In fact, companies that already publish a paper catalog are some of the most likely buyers of commerce servers.

*Marketplace Server:* This is essentially a commerce server on steroids. These software systems enable a single Internet site to host multiple stores, in effect creating the digital equivalent of the suburban mall. Many high-end commerce servers are now casting themselves as marketplace servers in an attempt to fulfill the need and to escape the heat of competition in the commerce server space.

*Auction Server:* Auction servers recreate the tension, pace, and intensity of live actions by linking bidders together in real-time to auction off everything from airline tickets to computer monitors. To date, most auction servers have been custom-built, but as the OCE business system begins to take off, the appearance of shrink-wrapped "auction in a box" software is not far off.

*Payment Gateways:* Payment gateways link all of the above servers to electronic payment systems. These gateways can be built right into the commerce server. The intricacies of payment systems usually require that the payment gateways be developed by firms familiar with the ins and outs of the electronic payment system.

*Ancillary Applications:* These applications complement the commerce, marketplace, and auction servers by providing additional, in-depth functionality in specific areas such as marketing, customer service, or sales analysis. Over time, the most popular ancillary applications, such as customized marketing, will probably be subsumed by the servers.

All of this software must run on top of an Internet server. The Internet server takes care of basic functions such as presenting web pages to individual users. The biggest vendors of Internet server software include Netscape, Microsoft, and Oracle. The most popular Internet server, called Apache, is freely available.

In creating the storefronts, marketplaces, and auction houses of the Internet, the OCE business system is effectively creating a digital version of the "retailing industry" for both business-to-consumer and business-to-business transactions.

The major shortcoming of the OCE business system is that in pursuit of spontaneity it sacrifices customer intimacy and integration. OCE may be fine for the occasional purchase over the Internet, but what about when two firms want to conduct business on a regular basis? These firms are not interested in high-gloss brochures and color catalogs; they are interested in building a tightly integrated *two-way* electronic connection that enables them to efficiently conduct commerce on a regular basis.

## EDI

One solution to building these two-way connections, called Electronic Data Interchange (EDI), has actually been around since the late 1960s. Indeed, back when the Internet was still an amusing academic experiment, the EDI business system was humming away creating tightly integrated two-way electronic connections between like-minded businesses. Today, EDI is a quickly growing business system within the Business Commerce Sector.

EDI is a system for exchanging specially formatted text messages that enables businesses to electronically exchange information without human intervention. Businesses use this highly automated, efficient system to exchange e-mail messages about orders, shipments, deliveries, and payments. Unlike the OCE business system, the EDI business system is strictly a "business-to-business system." It is also a closed system that requires participants to prearrange their communications and purchase a variety of specialized software and services. Thus, companies that use the EDI business system are usually regular "trading partners." Regular enough that the added expense of the specialized EDI software and services, along with the increased hassle of coordinating their actions, is worth the expense and effort. So in comparison to OCE, EDI sacrifices spontaneity and flexibility in return for intimacy and efficiency.

The EDI business system involves a number of piece parts that all must work together in order to facilitate tightly integrated two-way connections (see Figure 6.2). These piece parts are:

*Enterprise Systems:* These computer systems form the "guts" of the modern corporation. They typically manage the company's inventory, order management, finance, accounting, and payroll systems. The fundamental goal of EDI is to link one company's enterprise systems to another one so that these systems can automatically and therefore efficiently communicate about orders, shipments, deliveries, and payments.

*Mapping Software:* Mapping software "maps" the location of specific information fields on enterprise systems to specific parts of EDI text messages. These maps form links or bridges between the EDI business system and a company's enterprise systems. Mapping software is similar to the middleware found in the Financial Software Sector. Mapping software is typically imbedded in translation software.

*Translation Software:* Translation software converts internal messages into properly formatted EDI e-mail messages. By following standard set message formats, translation software ensures that any other company with EDI software will be able to read the messages it sends. Translation software also works in reverse. It takes messages received from trading partners and translates them into messages that the company's internal systems can understand. Typically, translation software also allows companies to manage the flow of EDI messages into and out of its network and to set up connections with new trading partners.

*Scheduling Software:* This software allows companies to schedule their EDI activities. For companies that send large numbers of EDI messages, this software can help them "load balance." It can also help the company synchronize its EDI system with its internal systems.

*A Value Added Network (VAN):* VANs are private communications networks that link all of the different trading partners together and transport EDI text messages from one trading partner to another. VANs are similar to the Internet, except that unlike the Internet, access to a VAN is tightly regulated and administration of the VAN is typically centrally

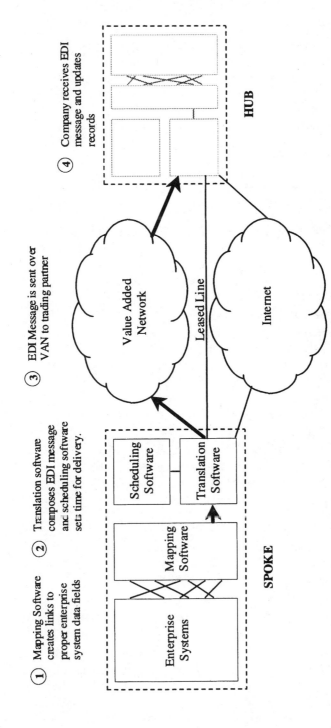

**Figure 6.2** EDI Business System and Example Transaction Flow
*Source: Piper Jaffray*

204

managed. This regulation makes VANs more secure and more reliable than the Internet. In addition, VANs also provide some "value-added" services that the Internet currently does not, including guaranteed delivery of messages, message logging, and customer support. Companies with particularly large EDI volumes will actually connect themselves to a trading partner with a dedicated leased line instead of using a VAN.

As the security technologies we outlined in Chapter 2 begin to mature and as Internet Service Providers (ISPs) begin to offer many of the same Quality of Service (QOS) guarantees that VANs do, the Internet will become an increasingly attractive alternative to VANs for many companies. The Internet has two primary advantages over VANs: it costs substantially less to use and reaches far more companies than the average VAN.

Right now a small trickle of EDI volume is spilling out on to the Internet. However, lower costs, along with the power of Metcalf's Law and the maturation of security technologies will soon help turn this trickle into a flood.

Rather than have separate companies provide each different piece of the EDI business system, the pieces are typically bundled together and sold as a single package (the enterprise systems are not part of this package). Services, such as helping with EDI "rollouts" as well as providing customer service, represent a big part of this package.

The EDI business system is focused around "trading communities" or groups of trading partners. Trading communities are typically organized around a large manufacturer (known as the "hub") and its suppliers (known as "spokes"). The Hub typically establishes the trading community and then encourages its suppliers to join. Recently, many hubs have stopped encouraging and started mandating that their suppliers join. For example, both Kmart (#) and Wal-Mart (#) have mandated that their suppliers use EDI to communicate with retailers about orders, deliveries, payments, etc.

Hubs are incredibly important customers for EDI companies because capturing the hub usually guarantees sales to its spokes. A single contract with a large hub, such as an auto or airplane manufacturer, can therefore lead to thousands of additional sales.

Over the years, the EDI business system has grown from its initial roots in the shipping and transportation industries into other industries such as manufacturing and retailing.

New types of EDI have also increased its usage and appeal. A variant of EDI developed in the mid-1980s, called Financial EDI (F-EDI), solved one of the biggest weaknesses of EDI. Before F-EDI, companies could correspond via EDI about orders and shipments, but could not actually pay for them via EDI. F-EDI solved this problem by creating a special type of EDI message that could be sent through the ACH payment system (see Chapter 4).

## Benefits of EDI

Today the EDI business system handles over a billion transactions a year and is in widespread use by Fortune 100 companies. Properly installed and configured, EDI can result in substantial benefits to companies including:

*Reduced Costs:* A "full bore" EDI implementation can dramatically streamline order, inventory, and purchase management activities, thereby resulting in substantial savings. These savings often fully offset the costs of installing and maintaining an EDI system, especially for large companies.

*Improved Asset and Liability Management:* EDI's automatic tracking of purchase orders, shipments, deliveries, and payments can enable firms to significantly improve their management of key asset and liability line items. For example, some retailers have EDI linked all the way down to the point of sale. As individual items are scanned at the checkout counter, inventory levels are adjusted in real time. EDI systems monitor these inventory levels and as soon as an item reaches a certain stock level, an EDI message is automatically sent to the retailer's supplier telling the supplier to ship more product. This practice keeps shelves full of "hot" selling products, but still reduces excess inventories. Together these two improvements boost overall sales while freeing up working capital.

*Improved Competitive Positioning:* EDI enables firms to improve its coordination and communication with its suppliers. This tighter integration reduces costs and enables firms to more quickly respond to market developments which in turn improves their competitive positioning in the marketplace.

## Problems With EDI

For all of its apparent advantages, EDI does have some important shortcomings:

*High Cost:* EDI is expensive to install and operate. Licenses for mapping, translation, and scheduling software can run from $50,000 for PC-based software up to well over $100,000 for high-volume mainframe software.

In addition, there are typically installation fees as well as annual maintenance fees. Companies also pay a per transaction fee based on the length of the messages they send. For smaller firms, especially very small suppliers, the costs to implement and run an EDI system can actually be quite prohibitive. In recognition of this cost barrier, the industry has dedicated a significant amount of effort in recent years to lowering up-front investment and operating costs for small businesses so that they can economically participate in EDI. Internet EDI should dramatically reduce the cost to access an EDI system.

*Difficult Implementation:* Getting an EDI system up and running can be a very difficult exercise. Linking together the EDI system with the enterprise system is often easier said than done. While mapping software can greatly speed this process, extensively customized enterprise systems can prove difficult to link to. This problem has been partially alleviated by the development of standard interfaces to popular enterprise systems such as SAP and PeopleSoft, but EDI implementations can still be a trying experience for many businesses, especially large businesses with custom enterprise systems. One perverse side benefit of EDI's difficult implementation is that it creates a good deal of "sunk cost" that many corporations are unwilling to walk away from.

*Non-Real-Time Design:* At its heart, EDI is still a "store and forward" e-mail system. While large hubs process and respond to EDI messages in real time, many smaller spokes only retrieve their EDI messages a few times a day. Thus EDI is not a true "real-time" system.

*Lack of Spontaneity:* EDI's detailed and involved setup process limits its appeal to only those trading partners that have a substantial commercial relationship today and anticipate maintaining that relationship going forward.

*Rigid Operation:* EDI works because it is based on a tightly defined set of standards that all parties must adhere to. While these rigid standards ensure interoperability, they also limit the flexibility that trading partners have to customize their electronic integration. So EDI's rigid nature is both a blessing and a curse.

*Non-Interactive Nature:* One of EDI's chief benefits is that it is highly automated and requires little, if any, human intervention. This high degree of automation is ideal for executing and monitoring decisions, but not for *making* them. Making decisions often requires a highly interactive phase of data collection and analysis. EDI's rigid, non-spontaneous, non-real-time nature prevents trading partners from engaging in the kind of collaborative, interactive analysis that is often required to finalize a contract, shipment schedule, or payment.

Despite these shortcomings, EDI remains very good at doing what it was designed to do: automate the tedious and expensive process of handling paper purchase orders, shipping bills, receipts, etc. Indeed, most of EDI's supposed "shortcomings" involve activities that it was never intended to do when it was first developed in the 1960s.

## Direct Data Interaction (DDI)

The solution to many of EDI's shortcomings is a new business system termed Direct Data Interaction (DDI). The EDI business system is in many ways a reflection of the world in the late 1960s in that it logically contemplates a stable, mainframe-based world, composed of large monolithic corporations and their captive suppliers. In contrast, the DDI business system is clearly a product of the mid-1990s: it is optimized for a highly dynamic business system, a distributed computing environment, and an economy composed of tightly focused corporations linked together by an ever changing series of alliances, partnerships, and joint ventures.

DDI has the same basic goal as EDI: to link one company's enterprise systems to another company's. But where DDI differs from EDI is that DDI is focused on enabling companies to cooperate and collaborate in the conduct of commerce, not just simply keep track of electronic paperwork. In this way EDI and DDI actually complement one another: EDI takes care of the necessary day-to-day automated messaging, while DDI takes care of the ad hoc, interactive queries and transactions.

It is difficult to characterize the structure of the DDI business system (see Figure 6.3) because part of its attraction is the lack of any real predefined structure, but it is possible to define a few generic pieces of the system:

*The Internet:* The Internet is at the heart of the DDI system. Not just the Internet in terms of its ubiquitous and inexpensive connections, but also in terms of its open standards, protocols, and software applications. DDI is an attempt to leverage the Internet's infrastructure to truly enable not only existing, but new forms of commerce.

*Interface Software:* This software allows a person at Company A to interface with Company B's enterprise systems via the Internet. The most popular interface software is the Internet Browser such as Netscape's *Navigator* or Microsoft's *Explorer.* In essence, interface software provides a user with a "window" into another company's systems and operations.

*Interaction Software:* Once a user has opened a "window" into another firm's enterprise systems, interaction software allows the user to then

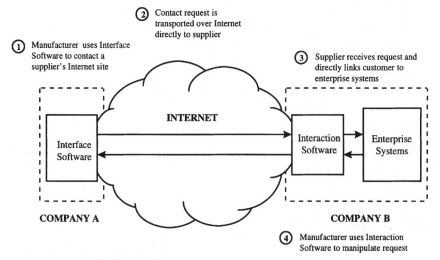

**Figure 6.3** DDI Business System and Example Transaction Flow
*Source: Piper Jaffray*

directly manipulate, analyze, and transform that firm's internal information. On the flip side, this software also limits the types of operations that can be performed by outside users as well as the specific information that they have access to.

Using interaction software, firms can gain real-time access to their trading partner's inventory and production levels, as well as their planned shipments, deliveries, payments, etc. Firms can also manipulate this data by "recutting" it or combining it with other data and they can analyze it by comparing it to their own forecasts and plans.

Interaction software is most powerful when closely married to dedicated "Analytical Applications." These applications allow users to analyze data stored in large "data warehouses" or departmental "data marts." Using analytical applications, users can extract not just "data" about shipments, payments, etc., but "knowledge" about business trends, probabilities, and customer needs.[2]

*Distributed Software Technology:* This is a set of software standards, languages, tools, objects, and architectures that allows companies to break apart their applications and databases and locate them in the most optimal places possible. It also potentially allows companies to share pieces of their applications and databases with other companies.

---

[2] See "Analytical Applications: Transferring data into knowledge to enable strategic business change," Berquist, Thomas and Kahl, Steven. Piper Jaffray Research. May 1997.

This is an emerging area of software technology, but one that eventually promises even greater integration and interaction between firms. There are several standards in this area such as Microsoft's Distributed Common Object Model (DCOM), the Open Group's Common Object Request Broker Architecture (CORBA), and the Internet Interoperable ORB Protocol (IIOP) and Java's Remote Method Invocation (RMI). Regardless of which standard becomes predominant, the effect will be the same: it will effectively blur the lines between enterprise systems as many companies will end up "sharing" pieces of software.

This technology is still generally very new, but in the coming years it should have an increasing influence on the structure of business-to-business EC by making it possible for companies to build real-time, seamless, and interactive connections to each other.

DDI's foundation on this advanced technology is what makes it such a powerful and attractive long-term option for business-to-business commerce. For example, instead of trading partners maintaining separate databases to track the same purchase orders, shipping, and payment notices, DDI will allow them to "share" a single database. Not only does this eliminate the cost of maintaining separate databases, but it eliminates the possibility of data input or translation errors and assures trading partners that they have real-time information. In a large trading community the cost savings and improvement in communication and coordination can be substantial.

## Benefits of DDI

Together these four different pieces create a business system that has several benefits for companies interested in conducting EC:

*Interactive:* DDI is designed from the ground up to allow interactivity. This ability allows firms to progress from simply coordinating their actions to collaborating with each other. This makes DDI a business tool and not just a process tool or an operational enhancement. With interaction, companies can simultaneously check the inventory, production rates, and prices of their trading partners in order to make optimal buying decisions.

The interactive emphasis is a direct result of interactivity's increasing value in the business world. As firms have become more focused and have begun to rely more heavily on partnerships, alliances, and joint ventures to produce output, the premium placed on collaboration and cooperation has increased dramatically. In many ways this makes DDI an ideal complement to the modern corporation.

*Real Time:* DDI allows real-time manipulation and analysis of data. This real-time ability eliminates the possibility of time-induced distortions and enables more informed and accurate order, purchase, and shipment decisions.

*Flexible:* Because DDI directly manipulates data, there is a greater opportunity for flexibility. Different types of interface software can be designed, modified, and updated, with no need to change the fundamental architecture, standards, or connections.

It is also easier to both "setup" and "tear down" DDI trading communities as the Internet provides universal access to all companies and, therefore, businesses need only modify the permissions they assign to their trading partners in order to expand or contract the size and extent of their trading network.

## Disadvantages

While DDI has a number of potential benefits, it also suffers from several drawbacks:

*Implementation:* Grand visions of opening "windows" into enterprise systems and directly manipulating data sound nice, but they are *very* hard to realize. Building the kind of database and application structure that allows for this kind of interaction is not a trivial undertaking. While many of the piece parts are in place, with the development tools and applications so immature, implementation of true DDI functionality can be a major undertaking. Indeed while many companies are working toward making the vision of DDI a reality, we are not aware of anyone who has yet to fully deploy what we would consider to be a fully functioning DDI "system" for the conduct of EC.

*Automation:* DDI does a very good job of complementing EDI by filling in some of its biggest gaps such as the lack of interactivity, flexibility, and a real-time interface, but the one thing that DDI currently does not do well just so happens to be EDI's strength: high-volume, autonomous messaging. Without this automated, non-interactive capability, DDI will remain only part of the solution to the business-to-business EC problem.

*Immaturity:* DDI is based on a set of standards, software tools, and applications that have only been around for a few years. As a result, DDI is still a relatively immature business system that is taking shape "on the fly." Many companies are reluctant to embrace DDI until the system becomes more mature and broad based.

Despite these drawbacks, the potential benefits of DDI are clear: it will allow firms to build the type of interactive, real-time, and flexible connections that are increasingly critical in today's fast paced, globally competitive economy. Given this important advantage, DDI should play an increasingly important role in EC.

## EDI vs. DDI

Even casual observers will have undoubtedly noticed that EDI and DDI are suspiciously similar. Besides sounding alike, they are also designed to do the same thing: to link one company's enterprise systems to another company's. If DDI is the 1990s' equivalent of EDI, and if DDI offers almost everything that EDI does, while being cheaper, more flexible, and easier to setup, isn't DDI going to steam roll EDI out of existence?

This is a highly contentious issue within the Business Commerce Sector which pits the DDI firms (which naturally claim that "EDI is dead") against the EDI firms (which claim that EDI is entering a high-growth phase and will be around forever). This public debate between the two camps can be confusing because there is little attempt made to separate the business and technology issues from one another. Right now we will address the issue from a technology perspective; later in the chapter we will address the issue from a business perspective.

### From a Technology Perspective . . .

In the short term, EDI technology is not going to be steamrolled or killed off by DDI because EDI technology has several important, but temporary, advantages over DDI:

> *It Works:* Sure it is not pretty or sophisticated, but like it or not, EDI works. Today, all most DDI firms have is a great demo, a few beta sites, and a collection of new technologies which might create something "really great." Faced with making a decision between the two systems, nine times out of ten the average systems manager is going to bet on the tried and true EDI. Sure it is dull and does not have much functionality beyond the processing clerks it replaces, but it has potential payback in less than a year and endorsements from some of the biggest companies in the U.S.

> *Sunk Costs:* Remember how hard it is to implement EDI and how much companies have to spend not only in expense but also in time and effort? These kind of sunk costs are not easy to walk away from. Indeed, walking away from an EDI investment makes a systems manager look

as if he/she made the wrong choice to begin with; "leveraging" an exist-ing EDI investment to make some incremental gains in functionality makes the manager look like a hero because it is as if the company got something for nothing.

Does this mean that EDI technology is going to be around forever? Not a chance. Remember EDI *is* 1960s' technology and it *is* relatively rigid, inflexible, and costly when compared to DDI. For the 1960s, though, it was a very ingenious technology. It was a simple, effective way to create auto-mated links between widely disparate enterprise systems. For the next century though, EDI will be more than a bit past its prime.

Today, EDI and DDI complement each other, but eventually the dis-tributed, object-oriented, software technologies and standards underlying DDI technology will become robust and widespread enough that DDI technology will also begin to offer reliable, automated, high-volume infor-mation exchange, otherwise known as EDI.

When this point is reached EDI as a technology will indeed be dead. But remember: just because EDI technology will eventually die does not mean that EDI companies will eventually die. It only means that these firms will have to transition to the new technology. We will discuss the issues around making this transition in the "Trends" section of this chapter.

## Private VANs Aren't So Lucky

While EDI may have many years before DDI becomes a major threat, the same logic does not hold for private VANs. VANs are essentially a minor league version of the Internet. Sure, they are safe and well managed, but they lack two critical things that the Internet has in abundance: scale and users. Even the largest private VAN pales in comparison to the Internet in terms of number of users and total traffic. That means that the Internet is inherently cheaper (due to its scale) and more useful (due to its vast reach) than private VANs.

So what does this imply about the fate of private VANs? Private VANs, as they are now known, are going to be absorbed by the Internet. Using technologies such as Virtual Private Networking (VPN) and improved networking hardware, Internet Service Providers (ISPs) will be able to offer secure, high-quality "Virtual" VANs over the Internet. This way the ISPs can offer the cost savings and ubiquitous reach of the Internet while still offering the security and quality of service of a VAN. Presented with this best of all possible worlds scenario, most EDI users would drop their traditional VANs in a heartbeat. Granted, this will not happen overnight, but the private VAN business, as we know it today, is on the fast track to obsolescence.

### Returning to 50,000 Feet

So, to sum up things from a comparative perspective, each of the three different business systems supported by the Business Commerce Sector currently has a defined role and purpose: OCE supports spontaneous commerce, EDI supports automated commerce, and DDI supports interactive commerce (see Table 6.1). While OCE gets most of the attention, EDI and DDI are where the majority of EC is likely to take place. Today EDI and DDI complement each other nicely, but going forward, as DDI gains more and more of EDI's automated information exchange features, it will replace EDI as the preferred business-to-business technology.

## Sub-Sectors

It should come as no surprise when one looks at the Business Commerce Sector that most of the firms currently support one of the three business

**Table 6.1**   Three Types of Business Commerce

|  | Open Commercial Exchange (OCE) | Electronic Data Interchange (EDI) | Direct Data Interaction (DDI) |
|---|---|---|---|
| Description | Digital "retailing" to businesses and through storefronts, consumers marketplaces, and auction houses | Electronic exchange of specially formatted e-mail messages between businesses without human intervention | Direct, real-time, Internet-based manipulation of data and business applications by trading partners |
| Segments Supported | ▪ Business-to-consumer ▪ Business-to-business | ▪ Business-to-business | ▪ Business-to-business |
| Key Characteristics | ▪ Spontaneous ▪ Real-time | ▪ Pre-arranged ▪ Store and forward ▪ Automated | ▪ Pre-arranged ▪ Real-time ▪ Interactive |
| Pros | ▪ Closest to vision of unfettered global EC marketplace ▪ Enables unknown buyers and sellers to meet | ▪ Automates processing of orders, shipments, payments, etc. ▪ Improves asset & liability management | ▪ Enables close collaboration between business partners ▪ Can add and change functionality easily ▪ Easy set-up and tear-down |
| Cons | ▪ Not integrated with buyer's systems | ▪ High cost ▪ Difficult to implement ▪ Rigid and inflexible | ▪ Difficult to implement ▪ Limited automation capabilities |

systems. Unlike many of the other sectors, in the Business Commerce Sector most of the firms are already 100% focused on the industry.

## OCE Sub-Sector

If two is company and three is a crowd, then the OCE sector is a stampede. Just about any Business Commerce company worth its demo model has an OCE product out on the market today that it claims is the best in the sector. Lately, the industry's big elephants (Microsoft, Netscape, IBM, and Oracle), have been wandering around in this sub-sector making it a market for only the brave and agile. Already a few industry high fliers, such as Nets.Inc, have had their wings melted. A considerably more significant shakeout is coming.

## EDI

OCE firms can have their splashy web sites and $5,000 software packages; EDI firms will be happy to take their multimillion dollar implementation deals with oil companies, trucking firms, and discount retailers instead. That is not to say that EDI firms are ignoring the OCE market, but their efforts tend to stop at electronic catalog "front-ends" to their EDI systems. It should be noted that the two biggest firms in the sector, IBM and GE Information Systems (GEIS), are part of their much larger parents. Not included on the list are the telecommunication companies (AT&T, MCI, etc.), many of whom cannot seem to make up their minds as to whether or not they want to take this market seriously.

## DDI

The Direct Data Interaction market is sparsely populated next to the OCE and EDI worlds, but should soon see a few refugees from these highly competitive arenas dropping by in search of greener pastures. Given the sector's eventual importance and the heavy interest of larger players in the DDI market, don't be surprised to see many of these early firms are acquired by industry heavyweights. Also, don't be surprised to see IBM, Netscape, Microsoft, and Oracle make explicit commitments to this market within the next year as they move on from conquering the OCE market to bigger and better things.

**Table 6.2** Selected OCE Firms

| Company | Description | Key products/services |
|---|---|---|
| Broadvision (BVSN) | High-end merchant server that allows companies to personalize customer interactions on the web site. | ▪ One-to-One |
| Commerce Wave | Low-end merchant server and Internet Catalog software developer. Also hosts its own Internet Mall. | ▪ MerchantWAVE |
| Connect, Inc. (CNKT) | Provider of high-end, scalable sales and order management software. Targeting both the business-to-business and business-to-consumer markets | ▪ OneServer<br>▪ Order Stream<br>▪ Purchase Stream |
| Elcom International (ELCO) | Provider of electronic catalog software mainly to computer resellers. Expanding the software to include consumer-to-business applications such as purchasing grocery items. | ▪ Pecos.Net |
| IBM (IBM) | Two different offerings. One is an extension to Lotus' Domino products and the other is a stand-alone software package. Aggressive pricing. | ▪ Net.Commerce (IBM), Domino Merchant (Lotus) |
| iCat | Provider of mid-tier user friendly web site catalog software including database and payment interfaces. | ▪ EC Suite |
| Inex | Provides an electronic catalog that can be used either as a business-to-consumer or business-to-business application. Targeted at the turn-key, entry level market. Also sell ISP mall-hosting software. | ▪ Commerce Court<br>▪ Dynamic NT |
| Intershop Communications | Developer of a full-range of mid-tier catalog software including stand alone and multi-store versions. Very strong in Europe. | ▪ Intershop 3 |
| Interworld | Comprehensive business-to-business and business-to-consumer EC software, including an object-oriented customer development environment. | ▪ Interworld Commerce Exchange |
| Microsoft (MSFT) | Largest PC software provider in the world. Purchased eShopsoftware and has now reintroduced its software under Microsoft brand. | ▪ Microsoft Merchant Server |
| Open Market (OMKT) | High-end provider of large-scale Internet transaction processing software. Repositioning product towards the business-to-business space. Strong sales to telecommunications firms worldwide. | ▪ OM-Transact, OM-Access |

**Table 6.2** Selected OCE Firms (Continued)

| Company | Description | Key products/services |
|---|---|---|
| Outreach | Offers low-end turn-key merchant server and mall hosting software. | • Store Manager, Mall Manager |
| Pandesic | Joint venture of Intel and SAP that provides merchants with a turn-key Internet catalog operation. | • Pandesic |
| Spaceworks | Business-to-business order management software. Allows customized pricing, order status inquires. | • Order Manager |
| The Internet Factory | Providers of a low-end, turn-key merchant server/catalog system. Includes built-in support for credit cards and cyber cash. | • Merchant Builder |
| Trade'ex | Business-to-Business developer of both "buy side" and "sell side" document and distribution software. | • Market maker, Document, Distributor |
| Viaweb | Internet mall hosting service. Merchants can set up "store" on Viaweb's site in a couple of hours. Acquired by Netscape in June 1998. | • Viaweb |

### Service Sub-Sector

Complexity breeds service organizations and there is no doubt about it, the Business Commerce Sector is complex. With all of these new technologies floating around, one can bet even money that a lot of firms will outsource their Business Commerce operations. That is where the service firms get involved. Right now there are only a few service firms that are dedicated to EC, but have no fear, they are coming.

### Potential Competitors

There is a pretty thin fence around the Business Commerce Sector and a lot of non-EC firms are eyeing the sector with increasing envy. Firms within the fragile confines of the sector better keep an eye on the following groups:

*Systems Integration Firms*

Systems integrators see a gold mine in potential EC implementation projects. They also may be tempted to start either service or software operations. While it looks as though these firms will keep their noses

**Table 6.3** Selected EDI Firms

| Company | Description | Key products |
|---------|-------------|--------------|
| Sterling Commerce (SE)(#) | Third largest EDI provider. Strong in large corporations. Spun-off from Sterling Software. | ▪ Commerce, Gentran, Connect, Vector |
| GE Information Systems (GE)(#) | Second largest EDI player. Full service provider with its own VAN. Aggressive stance on the Internet. | ▪ EDI Express, Trading Partner Network (TPN), Tradeweb |
| IBM Global Network (IBM) | Leading EDI provider. Full service provider with its own VAN. Leverages IBM's relationships with large corporations. | ▪ CommercePOINT |
| Harbinger (HRBC) | Midsized, fast growing provider of EDI services and software. Strong growth due to focus on small to medium-sized businesses. Noted for implementation expertise. | ▪ TrustedLink |
| Quick Response Services (QRSI) | Maintains the largest on-line catalog of retail products used by merchants and suppliers to order merchandise. | ▪ QR Solutions |
| Premenos (PRMO) | Provider of EDI services with a market niche on AS-400 platform. Recently acquired by Harbinger. | ▪ Templar |
| ARI Network Services (ARIS) | Vertical EDI provider with a focus on the agriculture market. Having trouble growing beyond niche. | ▪ ARIse |
| St. Paul Software | EDI software provider. Focused on simplifying EDI through application integration. Opening an Internet EDI service bureau. | ▪ spEDI |

out of the Business Commerce Sector, one never knows. Regardless of their product intentions, these firms should still be kept under close scrutiny as they will be important partners in actually making everything work. Examples of such firms include: Anderson Consulting, Price Waterhouse, and Deloitte & Touche.

*Enterprise Resource Planning (ERP) System Vendors*

The ERP vendors increasingly control many of the "enterprise systems" that the Business Commerce Sector is working so hard to hook together. We will talk a bit more about these firms later on, but for now suffice it to say that their control of the enterprise systems makes them important players that have to be taken into consideration. Examples of such firms include: Baan (#), PeopleSoft, and SAP.

**Table 6.4**   Selected DDI Firms

| Company | Description | Key products/services |
|---|---|---|
| Ariba | Developer of Java-based, buy-side focused purchasing management software that includes integrated purchase approval workflow. | |
| Calico | Develops order configuration software that can be used by sales forces or directly over the web. Software is used to run Cisco's $5 million/day web site. | ▪ Cocinity |
| Commerce One | Provider of end-to-end business to business EC catalog system. Providing both "buy" and "sell" side solutions. Comparable to Actra's solution. | ▪ C1 Buysite<br>▪ C1 Sellsite |
| CrossRoute Software | Developing a real-time, distributed, java-based system that uses the Internet to link trading partners' enterprise systems and automate business processes. | ▪ CrossRoute integrated application suite |
| Instill | Creator of an Internet-based vertical service targeted at the restaurant supplies industry. | |
| Ironside Technologies | Develops java-based Internet order entry systems. Emphasis is on real-time connections that allow direct interaction with existing data. | ▪ Fahrenheit |
| PCOrder | Spin-off from Trilogy Software that provides Web-based order configuration and pricing software. Focused on PC reseller market but expanding sales to multiple industries. | ▪ pcOrder pricing, configuration, and billing modules |

## Current Size

How big is the Business Commerce Sector market? Well, it depends on which of the three sectors one looks at.

### OCE Market

The OCE market was still quite small in 1996. The three public firms that are exclusively focused on the OCE market (Open Market, Connect, and Broadvision) generated $43 million in 1996 revenues. We estimate that Netscape sold another $30 million in Commerce Server software in 1996.[3]

[3] Netscape had $291 million in product revenues in 1996, with 27% or $93.6 million coming from sales of server products. Based on *Netcraft's* survey of web sites, just under one-third of Netscape's customers use its commerce server, so Netscape probably sold a grand total of around $30 million in Business Commerce software in 1996.

**Table 6.5**   Selected Service Firms

| Company | Description |
|---|---|
| Cybergold | Offers innovative, Internet-based "cash back" marketing programs, as well as cash-based customer loyalty programs. |
| Cybersource | Delivers digital content and processes related payment transactions on behalf of other Internet sites. |
| Digital River | Facilitates sale of software over the Internet via both individual sites, as well as its own network of web sites. |
| FreeMarkets.com | Arranges on-line supplier actions on behalf of major industrial firms. Suppliers receive training prior to bidding. Can justify cost with a single auction. |
| NetIncentives | Offers private label, Internet-based loyalty programs to major Internet sites including Yahoo! |
| Pandesic | Joint venture of Intel and SAP that allows merchants to outsource Internet catalog operations. |
| ServiceNet | Start-up founded by BBN and Anderson Consulting. Will provide basic network services along with software and service integration. |
| TechWave | Focused on developing software that enables electronic software distribution, especially volume licensing at large corporations. |

Generously adding in $5 million for Microsoft's *Merchant Server* (which was released in the fourth quarter) and another $10 million for everyone else gets us to $88 million. So, the actual number is probably somewhere between $75 to $100 million. This is up from $20 to $25 million in 1995. Not exactly a gigantic market, but definitely a quickly growing one.

**EDI Market**

Compared to the UCE market, EDI is a relatively mature and quite sizable market. *International Data Corporation* estimates that the EDI market was $664.2 million in 1996, with the IBM Global Network taking the top spot with 29.1%, or $193.3 million, of the total revenues (see Figure 6.4). However, IDC defines the market very narrowly, focusing on the VAN or network services side and generally does not include product software sales. For example, it reports Sterling Software's EDI revenues at $108 million when the firm's total revenues were $268 million and it reports Harbinger's revenues as $28 million when its total revenues were $42 million. Including software sales, we estimate that the total EDI revenues were about $1 billion in 1996.

One important area of EDI that has been slowly accelerating over the past few years has been Financial EDI. F-EDI is showing year-over-year improvements in growth rates. F-EDI is closer to true EC in that it involves

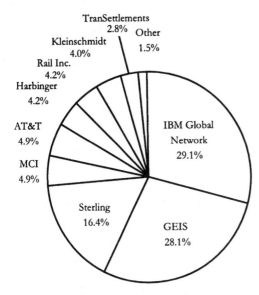

**TOTAL REVENUES: $664.2MM**

**Figure 6.4**   1996 EDI Sector VAN Revenues
*Source: IDC Research*

the actual payment for goods and services. Its improving growth rate is a sign of the expanding market for EDI.

## DDI Market

The DDI market is still in the developmental stage and, like the OCE market a couple of years ago, generated less than $25 million in total revenues in 1996.

## Drivers

So, the actual market size of the Business Commerce Sector is very small today. But for such a small sector, it surely is attracting the attention of a tremendous number of firms. This attention is due to a recognition that powerful drivers will dramatically expand the market over the next five years. While these drivers include the usual suspects of increased Internet usage and decreased communications and hardware costs, there are a few specific drivers which warrant further discussion:

*Increased Purchasing Rates*
    The big "if" for the Business Commerce Sector has always been: This sector will be huge *if* consumers and businesses feel comfortable buying

over the Internet. Initial indications were not promising with most consumers and businesses staying away from purchases due to security concerns. However, as users have become more comfortable with the Internet, they are starting to purchase more (see Figure 6.5).

While today most Internet users are still quite reluctant to use the Internet to make actual purchases, experience in other areas suggests that Internet users will eventually overcome their initial insecurities.

Just look at mail order firms. When they first started to grow, there was a widespread belief that consumers would feel "uncomfortable" and "insecure" shopping over the phone. Many years later, mail order is a $220 billion business and counting.[4]

But why rely on historical analogies, when there are already clear indications of demand. Just take the publicly released numbers from just a few firms and it quickly becomes clear that there is already significant demand for this product (see Table 6.6). Just five Internet sites did *at least* $3.5 bil-

[4] Estimation based on 1992 Data from the *US Statistical Abstract: 1996–7*. The Reference Press Inc. 785.

**% PURCHASING**

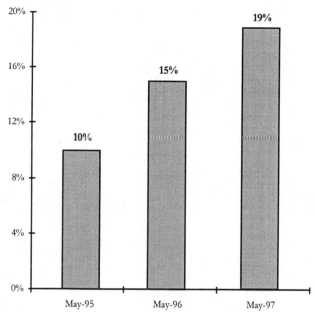

**Figure 6.5** Internet User Purchasing Rates
*Source: GVU Internet Surveys 1995–1996*

**Table 6.6**   Daily Sales of Selected Electronic Commerce Sites—1997

| Company | Line of business | Primary markets | Sales ($MMs) | As of |
|---|---|---|---|---|
| Cisco Systems | Networking Equipment | ▪ Business-to-business | $5.6/Day | 12/97 |
| GE (#) | Trading Process Network (Part of GEIS) | ▪ Business-to-business | $2.7/Day | 6/97 |
| Dell Computer | Personal Computers | ▪ Business-to-business<br>▪ Business-to-consumer | $4/Day | 12/97 |
| Amazon | Bookstore | ▪ Business-to-consumer | $0.7/Day | 12/97 |
| On-Sale | Internet Auction House | ▪ Business-to-business<br>▪ Business-to-consumer | $0.5/Day | 12/97 |

SOURCE: Company Press Releases, Published Reports

lion in direct EC over the Internet in 1997, and that is with only 15% to 20% of the 35 million consumer Internet users doing any purchasing. As aggregate demand grows by a factor of 2 to 4 over the next five years and as the percent of users buying over the Internet continues to expand, it is not a big stretch to suggest that these numbers will grow dramatically. All of this buying and selling will no doubt spur further growth of the sector.

*Productivity Pressures*

A lot of economists are marveling at the U.S. economy of late. It has managed to grow at a very healthy rate and yet price inflation has been extremely tame. Arguably, one of the main contributors to this puzzling economic situation is that firms are substituting productivity improvements for price increases. They are not doing this because they want to be good citizens but because they are operating in an increasingly competitive world where prices are becoming more transparent.

In the drive to improve productivity, many firms have exhausted all of the "low hanging fruit" and are focusing on "business process redesign" and thus fundamentally restructuring the way that they do business. It just so happens that technology plays a major role in these transformations and sooner or later a firm is going to have to consider either EDI or DDI in order to bring its productivity to the next level. This trend toward improved productivity as a source of growth and its resultant impact on EC spending should continue as trade barriers continue to fall and as capital becomes increasingly mobile.

*Forced Adoption*

Given these productivity pressures, millions of businesses are going to use EC whether they like it or not. Not content to let firms take their time to make up their own minds, many of the most powerful users of EC are forcing their suppliers and partners to adopt EC.

As we discussed earlier, the EDI sub-sector provides one of the most telling examples. For years many large firms maintained voluntary EDI programs for their suppliers or provided slight pricing incentives to encourage adoption. However, as competition has intensified in their core businesses, many of these firms have either lost patience with their suppliers or deemed it a competitive necessity to move to EDI as soon as possible.

Wal-Mart started the ball rolling with a mandated EDI conversion. Once Wal-Mart bit the bullet, other firms, notably Kmart and GE, followed with supplier mandates of their own. Not to be outdone, the U.S. Congress has mandated that all government agencies must pay suppliers electronically, most likely via F-EDI, by 1998.

So there are some powerful fundamental trends driving the growth of commerce on the Internet and therefore driving the growth of the Business Commerce Sector.

## Potential

With a robust set of fundamental drivers pushing the Business Commerce Sector forward, there is, like the rest of the EC Industry, the potential for strong growth. Today a relatively small number of large firms are using Business Commerce software. Going forward, Business Commerce software should gain widespread usage throughout the business community. Over the next few years, revenues in the sector will be largely driven by this continued expansion, first in the United States and later in Europe and Asia.

### OCE Potential

Within the United States, out of a total of 6.3 million business establishments, we estimate that as of the end of 1996, less than 50,000 businesses had commerce-oriented web sites. By segmenting the population of business enterprises into different industrial classifications and then projecting the likely penetration for each segment, we estimate that the total number of commerce-oriented web sites should grow from 49,000 in 1996 to 1.48 million in 2001 (see Figure 6.6). While this increase represents a rapid growth rate of 98% a year over the next five years, it still means that less than two in every ten businesses will have a commerce enabled Internet site five years from now.

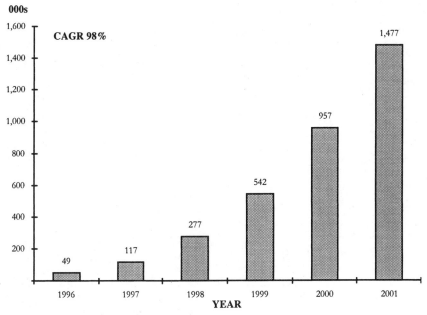

**000s**

**CAGR 98%**

**Figure 6.6** Estimated Number of Commerce-Oriented Internet Sites
*Source: Piper Jaffray*

This growth in the number of commerce-oriented web sites will occasion a corresponding growth in OCE revenues as companies purchase the software required to add real-time spontaneous commerce capabilities to their web sites. We estimate that the total size of the OCE market should therefore grow from $153 million in 1997 to $902 million in 2001 (see Figure 6.7). As time progresses, growth will slow somewhat as upgrade and maintenance of the installed base will account for an increasingly significant proportion of revenues.

**EDI Potential**

Traditional EDI revenues should continue their strong growth for the next few years. However, starting in 1999, two trends will begin to retard growth somewhat. The first will be declining VAN revenues due to an increasing shift toward the Internet and the second will be declining EDI software growth rates due to increasing DDI adoption. Therefore, we expect EDI revenues to grow from their current base of $1.3 billion to $2.8 billion by the year 2001 or about 21% a year between now and 2001 (see Figure 6.8). In 2001, we actually expect to see a drop in EDI VAN revenues;

$MMs

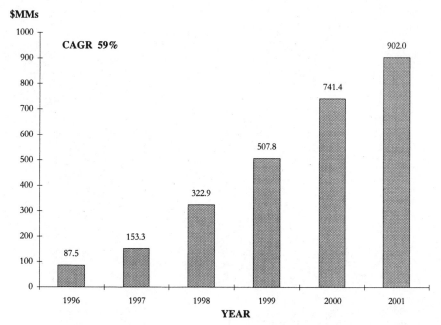

**Figure 6.7**  Estimated OCE Revenue—1996–2000   *Source: Piper Jaffray*

$BNs

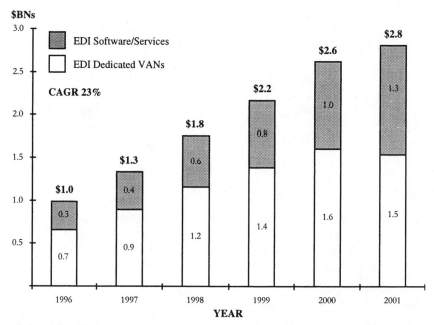

**Figure 6.8**  Estimated EDI Revenues—1996–2001   *Source: Piper Jaffray*

however, this decline could come sooner if quality of service standards are deployed more quickly by ISPs than anticipated.

## DDI Revenues

Almost nonexistent today, DDI revenues should grow quickly over the next few years as corporations seek to take advantage of DDI's interactive and collaborative capabilities. However, the longer implementation times required for DDI will mean that there will be a delayed reaction between market expansion and DDI revenue growth. We therefore expect that DDI revenue will grow from $50 million in 1997 to $814 million in 2001 with a growth rate of about 101%. This makes the DDI market the fastest growing part of the Business Commerce Sector over the next five years. While much of this growth will be additional, there will be an increasing cannibalization of EDI revenues starting in 1999.

## Overall Potential

Taken together, we expect that the three markets will grow by an average of 32% a year over the next four years and will generate almost $4.5 billion

$MMs

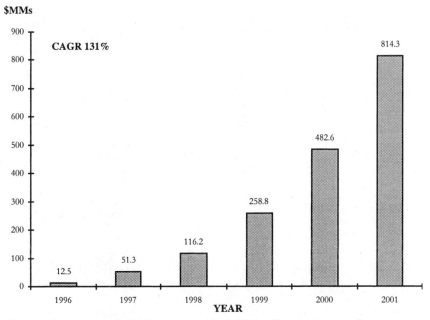

**Figure 6.9** Estimated DDI Revenues—1996–2001  *Source: Piper Jaffray*

in revenues by the year 2001 (see Figure 6.10). This represents the total revenues generated by all firms in the sector including any of the "elephants."

## Trends

### Here Comes the Shakeout

As the Internet started to explode in 1993 and 1994, a lot of people began predicting that millions of consumers would soon be spending billions of dollars over the Internet. This vision of consumers buying everything from plane tickets to lawn chairs captured the imagination of the popular press as well as the development budgets of a lot of software firms.

Now, just two years later, the fruits of these development efforts are finally reaching the market. The good news for these new software firms is that it appears as though millions of consumers are indeed spending billions of dollars over the Internet and doing so sooner than expected. The bad news for these firms is that everyone else in the software industry had the same idea two years ago and they are now just coming to market with their own "killer app" for consumer focused OCE.

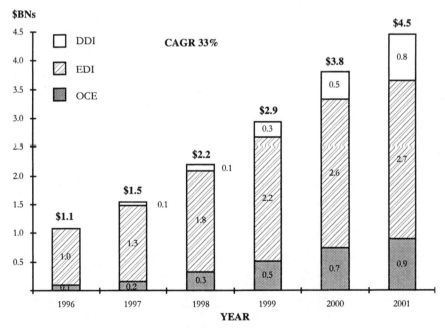

**Figure 6.10**  Estimated Business Commerce Sector Revenues-1996–2001
*Source: Piper Jaffray*

This situation has resulted in a clear oversupply of consumer-focused OCE software. Very few other software categories support more than five major titles (if that), yet there are ten to twenty firms hawking painfully similar OCE software packages. Add to this the fact that several of the most powerful firms in the entire computer industry (IBM, Microsoft, and Oracle) have entered the sector with a vengeance and what some pictured as an area of boundless opportunity now looks like a foreboding battle-field. Indeed the first shots have already been fired, as price competition has begun to intensify and with it dreams of 70% profit margins have begun to disappear.

The prospect of a brutal and battle-scarred landscape has prompted an increasing exodus from the business-to-consumer-focused OCE market toward greener pastures. The pasture of choice for these refugees is the business-to-business OCE market. Indeed, many companies have recently undergone a sudden marketing metamorphosis. Whereas they once talked incessantly about Internet malls and virtual stores, they now trip over themselves in attempting to extol the virtues of "business-to-business" EC.

The funny thing is, they can easily do this. Transforming OCE software from a "business-to-consumer" focus to a "business-to-business" focus can be as simple as changing catalog pictures from groceries to gear shafts.

Unfortunately, because it is this easy to do, almost everyone is doing it, including the major players. Because of this flight, the line between OCE business-to-consumer and business-to-business software is rapidly blur-ring. Drawing distinctions based on market focus has almost become use-less as almost all firms now claim to cover both markets with essentially the same product. This has put many of the smaller firms back where they started: small fish in a pond full of a few very large sharks. To compound the problem, even EDI firms have begun to offer their own Internet "front-ends" which essentially give them the ability to pretend that they are part of the OCE market.

With the twin pressures of the EDI firms and the industry elephants bearing down on the OCE market, the day of reckoning is fast approach-ing. Many of the smaller firms in the industry face a choice: sell out or get run over.

## EDI's Identity Crisis

At the same time the OCE market is coming to a boil, the EDI market is searching for an identity. Its forays into the OCE market are just one exam-ple of the EDI industry's increasing restlessness. As we discussed before, EDI technology in its current form will eventually fade away. But these technology issues do not necessarily mean that EDI firms will also fade away. The extent to which EDI firms survive in this new environment will be determined by how well they manage the transition from one technology to the next.

Initially, many EDI firms downplayed the Internet and its potential impact on their businesses. The sentiment was that security and quality of service concerns would discourage "serious" firms from using the Internet for business-to-business commerce. But as the Internet begins to solve its security and service problems with increasing speed and precision, many EDI firms have begun singing a different tune, called "Internet EDI." By taking the best features of the Internet (low cost, ubiquitous reach, low-entry barriers) and combining it with the best of EDI (precision, automation, interoperability), the EDI firms are attempting to create a hybrid solution partway between EDI and DDI that leverages the existing investments of their customers while slowly but surely pushing them toward the future.

The problem for the EDI firms is that while this strategy greatly appeals to their existing customers, it has much less appeal to new customers. This is not a small problem either as most EDI firms were counting on these new customers, mainly small and medium-sized businesses, to fuel their growth going forward. Without the sunk costs or elaborate enterprise systems, many of these smaller companies will be sorely tempted to jump straight into the DDI camp.

But EDI firms have an important weapon that they can use to stop this migration: capital. Unlike many of the smaller firms in the OCE or DDI markets which are living on either venture seed money or the cash reserves left over from their IPOs, most EDI firms are either making money or have access to deep pocketed parents.

In the recent past, EDI firms have largely used this capital to make acquisitions in the EDI sector. However, as these firms increasingly shift their attentions to future growth, it is a sure bet that their acquisition activity will also shift. Strategic acquisitions by EDI companies of either OCE or DDI companies should therefore be expected over the coming months. Given the likely fallout in the OCE market, there may be plenty of excellent bottom fishing opportunities at some point in the near future.

It is important to note that while the current version of EDI will gradually fade away, the need for an EDI-like functionality will not. Firms will still need high speed, integrated, automated messaging systems; they just will not use the classic form of EDI to do it.

The challenge for EDI firms then is to "go with the flow" by using their capital and cash flow to gracefully transform their current business without getting outflanked by other players.

The difficulty of making this transition should not be understated though. History is replete with examples of firms which have failed to follow their customers and make the leap from one technology to the next.

For example, the passenger railroad industry watched airplanes go from aeronautical demonstration vehicles to intercity transportation workhorses and yet not one major passenger railroad started a successful airline. Similarly, very few mainframe or minicomputer makers successfully made the transition to the PC world. The EDI firms will have to study their history lessons if they want to make the transition to the next technology.

## The Distributed Extraprise: The Corporation of the Future?

With their direct, Internet-based connections, emphasis on interaction, and flexible architectures, DDI firms appear poised to inherit the world of EC from the tired workhorses of the EDI industry. If only it were as easily done as it is said.

To be sure, the DDI business system is falling into place nicely. DDI firms are taking full advantage of developments in the other sectors of the EC industry to build secure, fully featured applications that offer greatly improved functionality. These applications may very well change the way commerce is conducted.

But the true potential for DDI can only be understood if its emergence is put into a larger perspective which looks at DDI as just one factor in a much larger change in the structure of commerce.

At a structural level, increasing specialization, accelerated product cycles, and global competition are changing the nature of commerce by making it increasingly necessary for firms to partner and ally themselves with other firms. With these partnerships come access to scarce resources, faster times to market, and greater distribution power.

This trend is creating a network of suppliers, alliances, and partners that must constantly communicate, coordinate, and collaborate in order to generate production. In essence, the corporation is being transformed from a self-contained entity into a "*Distributed Extraprise,*" or dynamic collection of specialized firms that are distributed around the world and linked together by technology.

Within the Distributed Extraprise, the process of coordinating and collaborating with "partners" and "alliances" becomes as important if not more important than managing internal operations. Maintaining these external connections, of course, is what EDI and DDI have been trying to accomplish. They have been trying to enable the "Distributed Extraprise" by connecting firms' enterprise systems.

## ERP Expansion

But what about the enterprise system vendors? Don't they realize that the world is changing? Don't they also want to participate in this new paradigm? Of course they do, and that participation could potentially be a major problem for EDI and DDI firms.

Today, enterprise systems form the heart, brain, and soul of most corporations. Over the past few years, corporations have been upgrading their enterprise systems, usually with products from the so-called Enterprise Resource Planning vendors, such as SAP, PeopleSoft, Oracle, and Baan. Implementing these new systems makes implementing EDI and DDI look like child's play, with new installations often taking years and costing literally hundreds of millions of dollars.

But the potential payoff is enormous. These ERP systems allow companies to bring a new level of coordination, discipline, and control to their internal operations that was simply not possible before.

But in the world of the "Distributed Extraprise" just having an internally coordinated system isn't good enough; now companies need to have systems that coordinate across multiple enterprises. So naturally, the ERP vendors are working on doing just that: expanding their systems to allow "enterprise-like" functionality across multiple systems.

This migration of the ERP firms into the Distributed Extraprise introduces a set of potent and formidable competitors into the Business Commerce Sector. After all, if the ERP vendors directly connect their enterprise systems to each other, who needs any of the Business Commerce vendors? Thus the ERP vendors could potentially run a good chunk of the current firms in the Business Commerce Sector out of the business.

Fortunately for the Business Commerce Sector, the ERP vendors are currently so busy selling and installing their software that they have very little time to spend constructing grandiose visions of the "Distributed Extraprise." Instead they have generally chosen to partner with firms in the Business Commerce Sector. In fact, with the cooperation of the ERP vendors, most of the EDI and DDI vendors have already built standardized interfaces to the major ERP systems. But over time the ERP vendors will inexorably find themselves building more and more of the Distributed Extraprise directly into their software as customers begin to demand increasing levels of integration with their partners and suppliers. The long-term key for the Business Commerce Sector will be to reposition itself as a partner and value-added applications provider to the ERP vendors.

## Success Factors

With intense competition in OCE, gradual obsolescence in EDI, and ERP competition in DDI, succeeding in the Business Commerce Sector is not going to be easy. But given the trends we have laid out as well as the potential opportunities available, there are a few key factors that we believe are going to be critical to the success of firms in this sector.

## Partnerships

Having the right partnerships is going to make a big difference in the Business Commerce Sector, especially for the small start-ups entering the field. We see three key groups for firms to partner with:

1. *ERP Vendors:* Given the last section this almost goes without saying, but successful partnerships with ERP vendors will prove crucial to long-term viability.
2. *Systems Integrators:* Very important to develop relationships with these firms as they are often in a position to make product recommendations.
3. *Distributors/VARs:* Especially important relationships for OCE companies as they struggle to gain competitive position in a market where distribution strength will be critical to success.

## Migration Plans

While the Business Commerce Sector is going to change slowly, it is still going to change. Successful firms will have a clear plan for navigating their eventual migration to this new environment. This does not necessitate that they will have everything mapped out in detail today, but rather a general sense of where they want to take the company and what they need to do to get there. Firms focused solely on the existing opportunity risk having the world pass them by.

## Opportunistic and Aggressive Posture

Dynamic environments present a lot of challenges, but they also present a lot of opportunities. As the different areas of this sector continue to evolve, successful firms will seize upon the uncertainties created by turmoil and friction to make opportunistic acquisitions or to take particularly aggressive actions with respect to marketing investments and/or product roll-outs.

## Management Strength

Make no mistake, successfully managing a firm in the Business Commerce Sector will be a difficult undertaking over the next few years. Firms with senior managers who are experienced in establishing partnerships, successfully integrating acquisitions, and managing business transformations will have a greater chance of success in this unstable environment.

# New Opportunities

In general, the Business Commerce Sector appears poised for rapid growth, but there are a few specific opportunities that should prove particularly attractive over the next six to twelve months.

### EDI "Leveraging"

EDI may eventually disappear, but for now EDI firms have the opportunity to leverage the sunk costs of their installed base to sell Internet "add-ons" to their existing EDI implementations. Selling their customers a series of incremental bridges to future technology will not only help EDI firms keep their customers in the fold, but it will also result in greater revenues over the life of the customer.

### Vertical Applications

With the industry elephants focused on providing the core solutions, such as Commerce Servers, smaller Business Commerce firms will likely find more opportunity creating products that enhance and complement the core solutions rather than compete with them. Both industry-specific vertical applications, as well as niche application add-on products, should prove to be attractive opportunities. The EDI industry has already proven that a vertical industry focus can sustain many smaller firms even in the face of much larger competition.

### Service Bureaus

Today many EDI firms are essentially service bureaus in that they help with implementation, offer network services, and provide customer service. The complexity, importance, and dynamic nature of Internet-based EC indicate that this service bureau approach is likely to become prevalent in the Internet world as well. Already a number of ISPs have formed separate divisions to sell and service EC "solutions." We expect that this market will grow dramatically and will support both existing players, such as the ISPs and the large integrators, as well as brand new ventures such as Service.Net.

# Investment Considerations

## Market Overview

As an investment market, the Business Commerce Sector currently provides opportunities for investing in either the OCE or EDI sub-sectors.

The EDI sector is a relatively mature sector. Several firms have multiyear operating histories and stable business models already established. OCE firms tend to be start-up providers of commerce servers with rapidly growing top line revenues, but negative cash flows. As far as the DDI sub-sector is concerned, this market has yet to emerge from the private sector, but some of the OCE firms are trying to reposition themselves into this sector.

## Recent Investment Performance

Since the beginning of 1997, the Business Commerce Sector has closely tracked the performance of the overall Electronic Commerce industry. In the beginning of 1997, the sector was caught, along with the rest of the industry, in the general weakness affecting small capitalization stocks. Like the rest of the industry, the Business Commerce Sector recovered in late April/early May of 1997, but was stuck within a fairly narrow range throughout the rest of 1997.

During the first few months of 1998 though, the sector exploded out of this range and quickly appreciated by over 33% in the space of just three months. Not only did market leader, Sterling Commerce, perform well during this rally, but the OCE stocks, such as Broadvision and Open

**Figure 6.11** Business Commerce Sector vs. EC Index and S&P 500
*Source: Piper Jaffray*

Market, also did particularly well. In fact, the Business Commerce stocks did so well that many investors became concerned that they were over valued by April 1998 and started to take some profits.

These fears quickly eased though as investors gained renewed enthusiasm for the Internet and Business-to-Business Electronic Commerce. As a result, by the middle of 1998 the sector had handily outperformed the EC industry in general and had closed much of the gap between its own performance and that of the broader market.

### Market Characteristics

We have included only those firms focused on providing Business Commerce software and services in the sector's index. These firms include companies focused on the OCE, EDI, or DDI markets. Some notable firms that we have not included: Microsoft, IBM, Oracle, Netscape.

As of now there are eight public Business Commerce firms. Four of the eight firms went public during 1996. Key statistics for this group as of 7/1/98:

*Market Capitalization:* The eight firms had a combined value of $7.1 billion as of 7/1/98. Sterling Commerce dominated the sector with over 63% of the total value.

*Liquidity:* On an average day, $50 million in stock trades hands in the sector. At current monthly trading volumes, market capitalization in this sector turns over an average of every 143 days compared to 83 days for the entire EC industry. This makes the sector the second least active sector overall.

**Table 6.7**   Firms in Business Commerce Index

| Company | Ticker | Mrkt cap ($MMs) | $Vol/day ($MMs) | % Price △/day | 1997 Revs ($MMs) | 1997 Earn ($MMs) | 1998E P/E | 1999E P/E | 1997 P/S |
|---|---|---|---|---|---|---|---|---|---|
| Sterling Commerce | SE | $4,437 | $23.5 | 1.9% | $351 | $55.4 | 38.8 | 30.3 | 10.7 |
| Harbinger | HRBC | 1,012 | 10.4 | 3.1 | 121 | (32.5) | 44.8 | 31.4 | 7.9 |
| Open Market | OMKT | 607 | 7.6 | 3.8 | 61 | (58.0) | NM | 78.6 | 9.3 |
| Broadvision | BVSN | 576 | 5.0 | 3.3 | 27 | (7.4) | 199.0 | 58.2 | 18.1 |
| Quick Response Svs | QRSI | 321 | 2.6 | 2.4 | 72 | 8.8 | 29.2 | 22.8 | 4.3 |
| Elcom International | ELCO | 101 | 0.5 | 2.9 | 760 | 10.3 | NM | NM | 0.1 |
| Connect Inc. | CNKT | 27 | 0.2 | 6.6 | 9 | (14.6) | NM | 20.6 | 2.7 |
| ARI Network Srvs | ARIS | 11 | 0.0 | 7.7 | 7 | (3.3) | NM | NM | 1.4 |
| Total | | $7,090 | $49.7 | 2.4% | $1,408 | ($41.2) | 52.2 | 33.5 | 5.0 |

NOTE: All statistics are as of 7/1/98.
SOURCE: Company reports, Factset, First Call, Piper Jaffray Research

*Volatility:* Stock prices in the sector changed a capitalization weighted average of 1.6% a day during 1997 compared to 1.3% for the EC industry and 0.8% for the S&P 500. It is hard to believe but even with this level of price volatility, the sector is the second least volatile in the industry.

*Revenues:* Total revenues for the sector (excluding Elcom's distribution revenues) grew 36% in 1997. OCE market revenues more than doubled while the much larger and more mature EDI market's revenues grew at a more leisurely rate.

*Earnings:* The sector actually lost $41 million in 1997, but these losses were due largely to acquisition charges at Harbinger as well as extensive operating losses at Open Market and Connect. On an operating basis, many of the EDI firms were solidly profitable, with market leader Sterling reporting a net margin of 16%.

*Valuations:* The industry trades at a rich 10.9 times 1997 revenues and 52.2 times 1998 estimated earnings. This makes the Business Commerce Sector the second most expensive on a price to sales basis and the third most expensive on a P/E basis.

## Risks

Investing in the EC industry entails some risk and the Business Commerce Sector is no exception. Some of the most important risks for investors to consider include:

### ERP Vendor Expansion

As mentioned, the ERP vendors will be increasingly forced to modify their systems to support the Distributed Extraprise. To date they have chosen to do this by supporting EDI and DDI vendor efforts to build bridges between enterprise applications. However, there is a high degree of risk that the ERP vendors will increasingly build these features directly into their own applications. Business Commerce firms closely allied with, or dependent on, the ERP vendors should have a detailed plan for dealing with these eventualities.

### Reluctance to Purchase Over the Internet

The sector is expecting a moderate and gradual decline in both consumer and business reluctance to purchase goods and services over the Internet. While there is clear evidence in the form of increasing purchase rates and increasing sales that this expectation is being borne out, any significant slowdown in this trend could have an adverse impact on stock valuations. A slowdown in purchasing could be precipitated by a significant security breach or continued problems with consumers and businesses obtaining timely and reliable Internet connections.

### Expansion of Industry Elephants

The smaller firms in this sector remain largely at the mercy of the large competitors. If any of these elephants decide to offer a particular product, feature, or service, they could rapidly undercut other players in the market. For example, if Microsoft announced it was going to devote substantial resources to developing targeted marketing applications that can be attached to their Commerce Servers, any other companies that were developing targeted marketing solutions could come under severe pressure. Key "herds of elephants" to watch include: ISPs, Systems Integrators, and major software providers.

A potential wild card competitor is the telecommunications industry. Both MCI (#), AT&T (#), and Sprint currently play largely transport roles in the EDI industry. While in the past they have shown a reluctance to dive deeper into the sector, with the recent mergers between Telcos and ISPs (such as MFS-WorldCom and BBN-GTE) there is an increasing likelihood that the Telcos will recommit to the sector, probably as service bureaus. This, of course, would be bad news for any existing service bureaus, but would not have a significant impact on software providers.

### Pricing Pressures

Pricing within the OCE Sector is currently unstable due to the dynamic competitive environment. Today, prices for OCE software packages range from $1,500 to $250,000. While competitive pressures have already forced significant pricing realignment and created a rough three-tier pricing structure, this structure remains fragile. Attempts by established competitors such as IBM and Microsoft to consolidate the market through predatory pricing could significantly and rapidly erode the market positions of existing players.

## Conclusion

Prospects for the growth of the Business Commerce Sector appear strong. But along with this growth, the sector will also be gradually transformed as new technologies make it possible to build even tighter integration between firms. This growing and dynamic market will prove difficult for many firms to successfully manage and will inevitably lead to major shakeouts, the first of which is likely to be in the OCE market within the next twelve months. Succeeding in the new environment will not only require a deft use of alliances and significant management acumen, but also a keen appreciation for the vision of the Distributed Extraprise. For it is the evolution toward this vision which will help transform not only this sector, but the very conduct of commerce over the coming years.

# 7

# Commerce Content: Brands Battle Intelligent Agents

## Introduction

Unlike the other four sectors, Commerce Content firms are not focused on building the EC infrastructure, but on merely using that infrastructure to offer goods and services over the Internet.

While Commerce Content firms may not be part of the EC infrastructure, that does not mean that they are unimportant. To the contrary, Commerce Content firms are where the "rubber hits the road" for the EC industry. Thus, these firms provide constant feedback on how well the EC industry is meeting the needs of its customers and how strong demand is for EC in general. In this way, the success of the Commerce Content sector is inherently linked to the success of the overall EC industry. Strong growth in this sector indicates that "all systems are go" in the EC industry; whereas, weak growth either indicates a problem within the EC infrastructure or potential slowdown in the growth of demand. Investors in the EC industry would therefore do well to keep their hands on the pulse of the Commerce Content sector as it is likely to prove to be a leading indicator for the overall health of the EC industry.

## Structure

The Commerce Content Sector has no real structure, but rather it is a heterogeneous collection of firms. Some firms, such as Amazon.com and

CDnow, are new firms that solely conduct business on the Internet, while others, such as Wal-Mart (#) and Wells Fargo, are large, established firms.

With such a wide variety of firms, it is often difficult to determine whether or not a firm truly belongs in the sector. For our purposes, those firms that generate revenues primarily from *the sale* of goods and services over the Internet qualify for inclusion in the Commerce Content sector. It is important to note that this definition excludes advertising and/or subscription supported Internet firms such as Starwave, CNET, and Wired Ventures. While all of these companies derive significant revenues from their Internet operations, these revenues are not generated by commerce-related activities, that is buying and/or selling on the Internet.

## Sub-Sectors

The firms that do qualify as true Commerce Content firms can be divided into three major groups: retailers, financial service providers, and business-to-business firms.

### Retailers

Retailers are perhaps the most obvious choice for the Commerce Content sector. While it is possible for almost any retailer to sell over the Internet, certain types of retailers are more suited to the Internet than others. Specifically, the most successful Internet retailers tend to sell products with four key characteristics:

*Well-known Content:* Products that are well-known and understood are easier to sell over the Internet because customers have a high degree of confidence that they know what they will be getting.

*Large Product Selections:* The greater the number of possible selections in a product category, the better the Internet is suited to retail those products. Unlike the physical world, Internet retailers do not have to worry about running out of shelf space or room to store inventory. This means that customers at Internet-based retailers can often be assured of tremendously wide product selection. Examples of such products include books, CDs, wine, and industrial gaskets.

*High Search Costs:* The harder it is to find a particular product, the better suited the product is to Internet retailing. Unlike the physical world, on the Internet customers can use advanced search engines to quickly locate the product they want without having to rely on uninformed store clerks or out-of-date print publications.

*Appeal to Internet Demographics:* Products that appeal to educated, well-off consumers, such as software, books, and computer equipment, are better suited to Internet-based retailing. This is becoming less prevalent as the demographic base of the Internet widens, but should remain an important factor for the foreseeable future.

Firms that retail products with these four characteristics have found that the Internet not only provides a viable distribution channel for their products, but in many ways a superior one. Some examples of early leaders in this area include:

| | |
|---|---|
| **Company:** | **Amazon.com** |
| **Address:** | www.amazon.com |
| **Date Launched:** | 7/95 |
| **Server Software:** | Netscape Commerce 1.12 |
| **Ownership:** | Became a public company in May of 1997 |
| **Security:** | SSL |
| **Payment Types:** | Major Credit Cards, Checks, Money Orders |

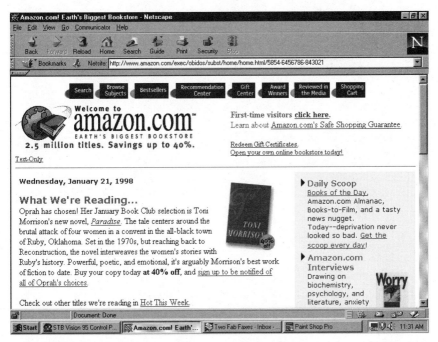

An Internet-only bookstore. It was the original Internet bookstore and has built a strong presence and a loyal group of customers. Amazon's revenues have grown from just $500,000 in 1995 to $148 million in 1997.

| Company: | Auto-by-tel |
|---|---|
| Address: | www.autobytel.com |
| Date Launched: | 3/95 |
| Server Software: | Microsoft IIS 2.0 |
| Ownership: | Private company |
| Security: | SSL |
| Payment Types: | NA |

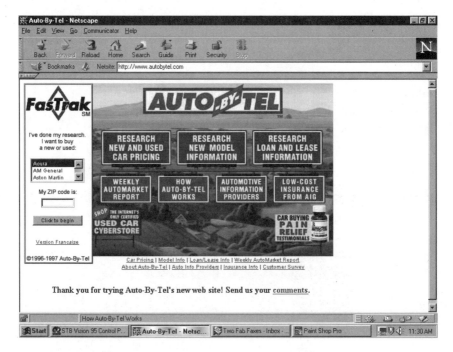

An Internet site that matches car buyers with auto dealers from around the country. Dealers pay to be a member of the network while consumers participate for free. Processes over 40,000 purchase/lease requests a month.

| | |
|---|---|
| **Company:** | **CDnow** |
| **Address:** | www.cdnow.com |
| **Date Launched:** | 9/94 |
| **Server Software:** | Apache 1.1.1 |
| **Ownership:** | Became a public company in February of 1998 |
| **Security:** | SSL, PGP (to encrypt Credit Card numbers) |
| **Payment Types:** | Major Credit Cards, Checks, ECash |

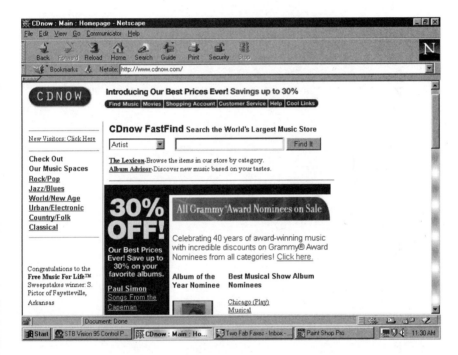

An Internet-only record store. CDnow has 250,000 record titles to chose from and recently added 35,000 video titles. CDnow was the pioneer in the CD retailing business and its success has spawned a multitude of impressive impersonators.

| Company: | **Internet Shopping Network** |
| --- | --- |
| Address: | www.isn.com |
| Date Launched: | 4/94 |
| Server Software: | Netscape Commerce 1.1 |
| Ownership: | Subsidiary of Home Shopping Network |
| Security: | SSL |
| Payment Types: | Major Credit Cards, Checks, Money Orders, Purchase Orders |

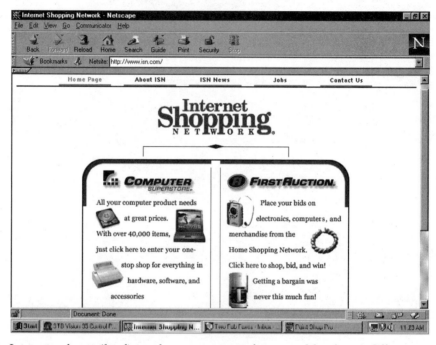

Internet-only retailer focused on computer software and hardware. Offers over 40,000 products for purchase, including 900 software titles that can be downloaded over the Internet.

| | |
|---|---|
| **Company:** | **Wal-Mart Stores, Inc.** |
| **Address:** | www.wal-mart.com |
| **Date Launched:** | 7/96 |
| **Server Software:** | Netscape Enterprise |
| **Ownership:** | Public company |
| **Security:** | SSL |
| **Payment Types:** | Major Credit Cards |

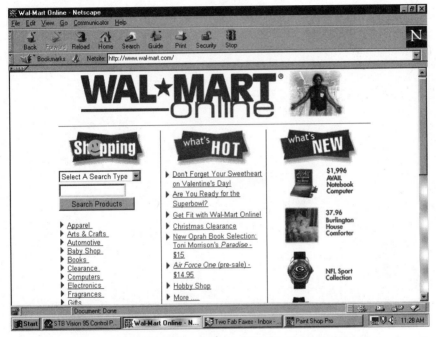

Internet site of the largest discount retailer in the U.S. Sells a wide variety of products. Recently added over 20,000 computer products to bring total store count to over 40,000 products available for purchase.

| Company: | Virtual Vineyards |
|---|---|
| Address: | www.virtualvin.com |
| Date Launched: | 4/95 |
| Server Software: | Netscape Commerce 1.1 |
| Ownership: | Private company |
| Security: | SSL |
| Payment Types: | Major Credit Cards, Cybercash |

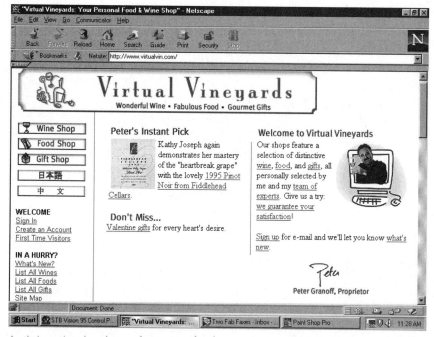

An Internet-only wine and gourmet food store. One of the first pioneers in Internet commerce. While the Company started with wine, it has recently begun to offer gourmet foods and gift assortments.

## Financial Service Providers

The Internet is an ideal channel for the distribution of Financial Services: it is cheap, it has a wide reach, and it has attractive demographics. Concerns over security have kept a large number of financial service firms on the sidelines. However, some of the early movers in the sector are beginning to experience tremendous growth and their success is attracting a tidal wave of competitors.

On-line brokerage trading has been the standout success of financial services commerce content with the number of users exploding in 1997 from 1.5 to 3 million. Internet banking has lagged somewhat but appears ready for explosive growth in 1998 as several of the Top 10 banks in the U.S. and most of the Big 6 banks in Canada launch Internet Banking services. The Insurance sector lags badly behind the rest of the Financial Services industry. Insurers are hamstrung by their fear of alienating their existing agent networks with very few insurers publicly planning on offering insurance services via the Internet.

Examples of some of the clear early leaders in this area of Commerce Content include:

| | |
|---|---|
| **Company:** | E*Trade |
| **Address:** | www.etrade.com |
| **Date Launched:** | 2/96 (Internet Site) |
| **Server Software:** | Netscape Commerce 1.12 |
| **Ownership:** | Became a public company in August of 1996 |
| **Services Offered:** | Stocks, Options |

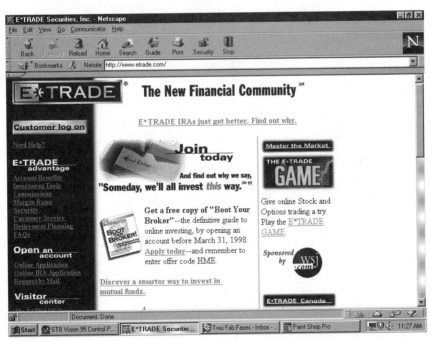

An on-line trading focused brokerage company. Aggressive pricing and advertising have enabled it to take a leading position in the crowded on-line brokerage field. Accounts grew 130% from 113,000 to 260,000 in 1997.

| Company: | Insuremarket |
|---|---|
| Address: | www.insuremarket.com |
| Date Launched: | 5/96 |
| Server Software: | Netscape Commerce 1.12 |
| Ownership: | Subsidiary of Intuit Inc. |
| Services Offered: | Annuities, Life Insurance |

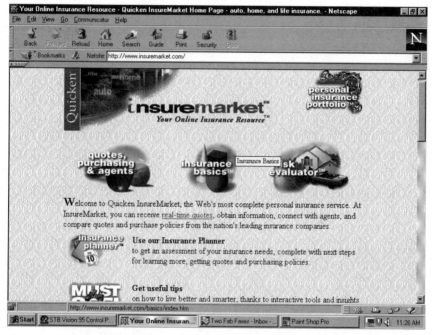

An Internet only insurance site. Allows consumers to educate themselves about insurance and then purchase it on-line. Offers life insurance, but is moving into other areas such as auto insurance. Part of Quicken.com. Purchased by Intuit in 1996.

| Company: | Quicken.com |
|---|---|
| Address: | www.quicken.com |
| Date Launched: | 6/96 (Launched as separate site) |
| Server Software: | Netscape Communications 1.1 |
| Ownership: | Part of Intuit Inc. |
| Services Offered: | Financial services information, mutual fund performance comparisons, insurance purchases |

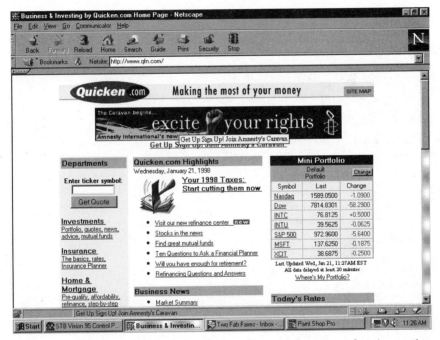

Financial services "supersite." Educates consumers about tax planning, retirement, mutual funds, insurance, and banking. Includes Net Worth, a mutual fund analysis site, and Insuremarket. Signed deals to integrate the site with the Excite search engine site and AOL personal finance areas.

| Company: | **Charles Schwab & Co.** |
|---|---|
| Address: | www.schwab.com |
| Date Launched: | 5/96 (Internet Site) |
| Server Software: | Netscape Enterprise 2.01a |
| Ownership: | Public Company |
| Services Offered: | Stocks, Options, Bonds, Mutual Funds |

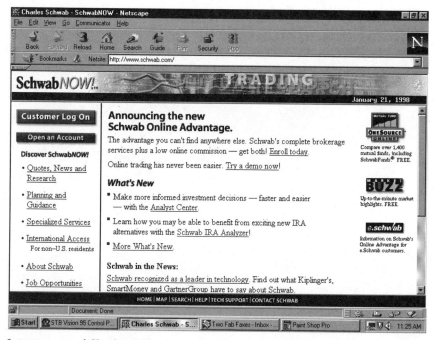

Internet arm of Charles Schwab, a major discount brokerage firm. Allows on-line trading and provides access to Schwab's wildly successful OneSource mutual fund supermarket. Schwab claims that over 1 million of its customers have used its on-line brokerage services.

| **Company:** | **Quick Quote** |
| --- | --- |
| **Address:** | www.quickquote.com |
| **Date Launched:** | 7/95 |
| **Server Software:** | Netscape Commerce 1.12 |
| **Ownership:** | Private Company |
| **Services Offered:** | Insurance quotes, software for insurers, form processing, telephone servicing |

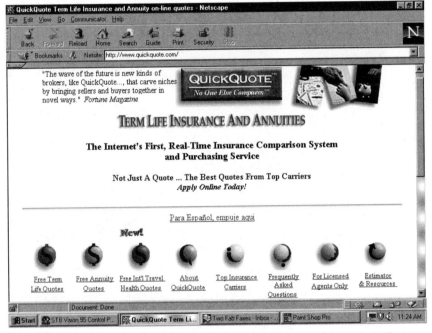

Offers quotes from major insurance agencies directly to consumers via its Internet site. Has managing general agent contracts with numerous insurers. Expanding into outsourcing and international markets.

| | |
|---|---|
| **Company:** | **Wells Fargo On-line Banking** |
| **Address:** | www.wellsfargo.com |
| **Date Launched:** | 5/95 |
| **Server Software:** | Netscape Communications 1.1 |
| **Ownership:** | Public Company |
| **Services Offered:** | Bill payments, Checking, Savings, Money Market, Credit Cards, Lines of Credit |

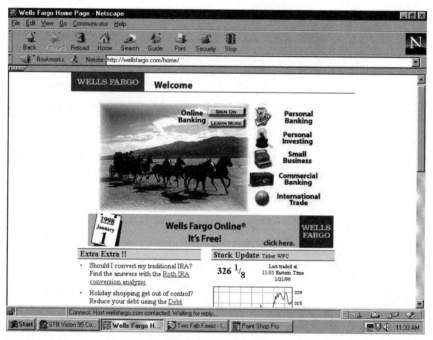

First major bank to offer Internet account access. Now offers full range of services via the Internet. Claims 180K Internet users. Moving all of its 330K on-line banking users to the Internet and plans to have two million Internet banking users by the year 2000.

## Business-to-Business

Business-to-business is the least glamorous but most significant area of Commerce Content. Firms in this area are already conducting large amounts of commerce over the Internet and have plans to rapidly increase their participation. As we outlined in Chapter 6, this should be the single biggest area of Electronic Commerce. Some of the standout companies in this area include:

| | |
|---|---|
| **Company:** | **Cisco Systems, Inc.** |
| **Address:** | www.cisco.com |
| **Date Launched:** | 7/96 |
| **Server Software:** | Proprietary Cisco software |
| **Ownership:** | Public Company |

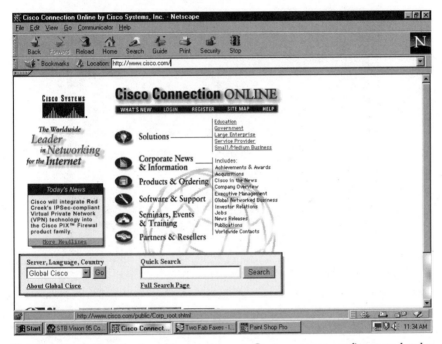

Dominant provider of networking equipment. Customers can configure and order equipment from site. Sold $2 billion via site in 1997, up from $100 million in 1996. Plans to do 30% of total revenue on site within two years.

| Company: | **Dell Computer** |
|---|---|
| Address: | www.dell.com |
| Date Launched: | 7/96 |
| Server Software: | Microsoft IIS 3.0 |
| Ownership: | Public Company |

Leading direct marketer of personal computers. Internet site allows customers to configure and buy personal computers and peripherals. Doing over $4 million a day in business through its Internet site as of the end of 1997.

| Company: | Onsale |
|---|---|
| Address: | www.onsale.com |
| Date Launched: | 5/95 |
| Server Software: | Netscape Fast track 2.0a |
| Ownership: | Became a public company in April of 1997 |

Internet-based auction house of surplus merchandise, mainly computer-related items. Sold $116 million worth of merchandise in 1997. Sells to both consumers and businesses.

| Company: | **GE Trading Process Network** |
| --- | --- |
| Address: | www.tpn.geis.com |
| Date Launched: | 1/96 |
| Server Software: | Netscape Enterprise 2.0a |
| Ownership: | Part of General Electric |

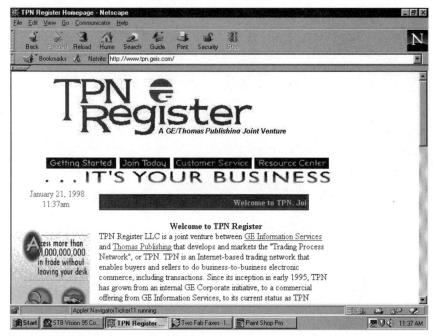

Subsidiary of GE's Information Systems (GEIS) division. Formed to allow GE suppliers to bid on upcoming GE contracts. Expanding to include non-GE companies and suppliers. Plans to do $5 billion worth of deals in 1998.

## Market Size

Estimating the current size of the Commerce Content market is an imprecise art, though it is possible to generate some rough approximations for a couple of different metrics.

### Number of Commerce Content Sites

As of January 1997, there were 828,000 separate Internet domains.[1] The number of domains roughly corresponds to the number of separate Internet

---

[1] Figure from Network Wizard's 1/97 survey of Internet hosts and domains.

sites. A survey by *O'Reilly & Associates Inc.* late last year indicated that only 1% of Internet sites had enabled Secure Sockets Layer (SSL) and digital certificate security.[2] Assuming this high level of security is an indication that the site is offering some sort of commerce service would indicate that there are at least 8,000 sites that are in some way currently conducting commerce, i.e. allowing customers to pay for purchases, over the Internet. This is likely to be a minimum number, as many major Internet commerce sites do not yet employ certificate technology. The true number is probably somewhere between 10,000 to 20,000 sites at the end of 1996. There is a second group of commerce oriented sites that do not allow customers to complete purchases over the Internet, but do allow them to do product research and product selection. We estimate that by the end of 1996 there were between 30,000 to 50,000 of these sites.

### Volume of Commerce

Estimating the total volume of commerce is even more difficult. The best that can be done is to form a minimum baseline and then estimate upward from there. In 1996, the single largest commerce content site appears to have been GE's Trading Process Network (TPN) which claims to have done over $350 million in bids. Cisco Systems claims that it did $100 million on its own site during the six months it was operational in 1996 as well. The sales figures from Amazon.com and Onsale add another $32 million in sales for a total of just $500 million. Being very generous with all of the remaining sites around the world, the total commerce conducted in 1996 was probably somewhere around $0.75 to $1.25 billion (not counting EDI traffic through VANs).

This number does not include the commerce activities associated with customers accessing their financial accounts via the Internet. The best way to measure the size of this market is to look at the number of on-line-banking and brokerage users which, as we discussed in Chapter 5, appears to have been around 3.0 to 3.5 million users in 1996.

So, a rough analysis indicates that the Commerce Content sector, like many of the Electronic Commerce sectors, was not that significant at the beginning of 1997, despite the considerable amount of attention it has received from both the media and the public.

## Drivers

The small size of the Commerce Content sector may be partially due to the fact that in the past, the growth of the sector has lagged the growth of the

[2] "State of Web Commerce." O'Reilly & Associates. 12/96.

four other EC sectors. This lag is due largely to companies' general reluctance to establish commerce sites before the infrastructure pieces were fully developed. This reluctance is fading as companies realize that the EC infrastructure is becoming increasingly robust. Going forward we will see four major drivers of the Commerce Content sector's growth:

**Cost Differences.**   The differences in distribution cost between the Internet and alternatives, such as retail outlets, are so significant that they will inexorably encourage migration to the Internet over time. For example, Internet-based banks can theoretically operate at one-fourth the expense level that traditional banks can. In the on-line trading area, similar cost savings have driven some trading commissions below $10, a level that would have been unthinkable just a few years ago. Over time, such significant cost differences will force many companies to do an increasing amount of their business through the Internet.

**Lower Barriers to Entry.**   Just a year ago, developing a Commerce Content site could easily take hundreds of thousands of dollars in custom programming and software design. Today, developing a first rate stand-alone Commerce site still takes a sizable investment (+$1 million), but turnkey software packages as well as Commerce hosting services have dramatically lowered the barriers to entry in the Commerce Content sector. Using a turnkey merchant server software package, a business can easily get its own commerce server up and running for less than $25,000. Using a hosting service, a business can open its own Internet store for as little as $100/month. These dramatically lower costs are encouraging many businesses to take their first tentative steps toward the Internet.

**Increasing Comfort with Internet Purchasing.**   As we detailed in Chapter 6, currently less than 15% of Internet users make purchases over the Internet. This number is slowly but surely expanding and will continue to do so as users become acclimated to the Internet and more confident with its security solutions. As this number expands, it will drive further growth for Commerce Content.

**Growth of Internet Usage.**   Every 1% increase in the penetration of U.S. Internet usage adds about $60 billion in disposable personal income to the potential pool of consumer Internet spending.[3] Every 1% increase in business penetration adds about $150 billion in revenues to the potential pool of business-to-business commerce.[4] With large increases forecast for both

---

[3] Author's calculation based on statistics from "National Income and Product Accounts," Bureau of Economic Analysis. 5/30/97

[4] Author's calculation based on "Corporate Income Tax Returns: Balance Sheet, Income, and Tax Items for Specified Income Years: 1980–1994," U.S. Internal Revenue Service. 9/96.

business and consumer use of the Internet, this will undoubtedly increase demand for Commerce Content services.

## Potential

Based on these trends, as well as the macro level trends in terms of Internet growth and costs, there should be a significant expansion in both the number and volume of Commerce Content sites. As we discussed in Chapter 6, we expect that the total number of commerce-oriented Internet sites should grow to 1.4 million with just under two out of every ten U.S. businesses having an Internet presence. This wide base of supply combined with the specific drivers we just outlined should spur a huge increase in Internet-based purchasing. We will explore the potential of both the consumer and the business-to-business markets separately.

A quick note before we start, though. Our estimates for the total purchases over the Internet include those goods and services that are *paid for* via the Internet. The Internet will undoubtedly be used by both businesses and consumers to help research and establish initial contact with merchants and/or suppliers for many purchases; however, our definition of "purchase" includes only those transactions that are paid for over the Internet.

### Consumer Market

Consumer purchases over the Internet are not just a function of the size of the Internet and the percentage of people willing to make purchases over it, but also of the types of goods and services that can be bought over the Internet. To account for this effect, we took disposable consumer income and removed from it those items that are not likely to be purchased over the Internet any time soon, such as rent, gasoline, or utilities. This left us with an adjusted disposable income or income that could truly be spent over the Internet. As Table 7.1 outlines, we believe that by 2001, just under one-half of Internet users will be purchasing over the Internet and on average these people will be spending $1,660 or 7.3% of their adjusted disposable income over the Internet. This should generate about $26.4 billion in total Internet-based purchases in 2001.

### Business-to-Business Market

In theory, the total size of the business opportunity is capped by total business revenues, which were around $15 trillion last year. It is safe to say that the industry will not be approaching this number anytime soon. However, the total amount of business-to-business EC *is* likely to be much more than anyone thought just two or three years ago.

**Table 7.1** Estimated Consumer Purchases Via
the Internet—1995–2001

|  | 1995 | 1996 | 1997 | 1998 | 1999 | 2000 | 2001 |
|---|---|---|---|---|---|---|---|
| U.S. Households (HH) Internet | 4.0 | 8.0 | 15.0 | 21.0 | 26.0 | 31.0 | 34.0 |
| % HHs Purchasing Over the Net | 10% | 15% | 19% | 24% | 30% | 39% | 49% |
| Total Purchasing HHs (MMs) | 0.3 | 0.9 | 2.2 | 4.3 | 7.2 | 11.0 | 15.9 |
| Adj. Disposable Income/ HH ($s) | 15,953 | 16,910 | 17,925 | 19,000 | 20,140 | 21,349 | 22,630 |
| % of Available Expend. | 0.8% | 1.9% | 2.85% | 3.61% | 4.57% | 5.79% | 7.34% |
| Total Internet HH Purchases ($MMs) | 38 | 289 | 1,116 | 2,971 | 6,598 | 13,608 | 26,391 |
| *Purchases/Purchasing HH ($s)* | *128* | *321* | *511* | *686* | *921* | *1,237* | *1,660* |

SOURCE: Piper Jaffray Research, GVU Visualization Lab Studies, U.S. Statistical Abstract

Just consider the fact that GE plans to do $5 billion in sales over its Trading Process Network in 1998 alone and the potential size of the opportunity starts to become apparent. Also, consider the fact that firms will increasingly move EDI transactions via the Internet. EDI transactions often deal with purchases worth thousands, if not millions of dollars. Those types of transactions add up quickly.

Based on these trends we estimate that total direct business-to-business sales should be roughly $200 billion within five years. (See Figure 7.1.) These may seem like fantastic numbers to many but consider the fact that GE and Cisco alone plan to account for almost 2/3 of 1998's $13.4 billion.

Taken together, we expect that total consumer and business-to-business purchases made over the Internet will amount to $225 billion by the year 2001. (See Figure 7.2.) While this is a large number and represents a tremendous increase from today's levels, it is still relatively small when compared to "macro-level" economic data. For example, $225 billion should represent only 3% of projected wholesale and retail sales, just 2.4% of nominal Gross Domestic Product, and just 1.2% of projected business revenues. When put into this perspective, we believe these numbers are not only readily achievable but fairly conservative.

## Trends

### Early Movers Set the Pace

Sometime in early 1994, the first seeds of the Commerce Content sector were planted as entrepreneurs across America began to realize the

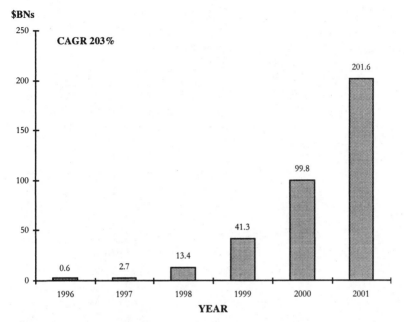

**Figure 7.1**   Estimated Business-to-Business Internet Purchases—
1996–2001   *Source: Piper Jaffray*

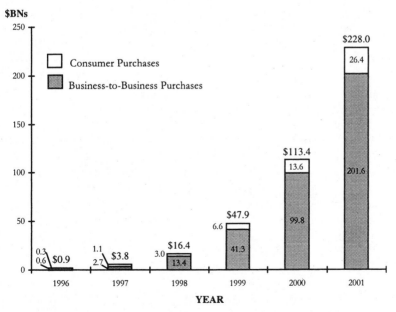

**Figure 7.2**   Estimated Total Internet-Based Purchases—1996–2001
*Source: Piper Jaffray*

tremendous potential of the Internet's World Wide Web and set to work creating the first Commerce Content sites. These entrepreneurs plunged ahead despite a lack of commercial software, poor development tools, and a generally incomplete security infrastructure.

Their efforts led to the creation of a series of firms between late 1994 and mid-1995 including many of the most well-known Commerce Content companies such as Amazon.com, CDnow, Onsale, and Virtual Vineyards. Most of these firms were the first movers in their industry segment and therefore operated with a virtual monopoly for several months. By virtue of their pioneering status and uncontested positions, these firms received a tremendous amount of publicity thereby ingraining their names into the minds of the burgeoning Internet population.

### Established Brands Fight Back

By mid- to late-1995, corporate America began to take serious notice of the Internet and even began to worry that many of these upstart companies had possibly beaten them to the punch in what might become one of the most important distribution channels of the next century.

Suitably motivated, corporations began to redeploy their investment dollars (from Interactive TV no doubt) toward the Internet. However, concerns over security prevented all but the bravest of companies from wholeheartedly embracing actual commerce. It was not until early-to-mid 1996, a full year after the initial start-ups had opened for business, that a few corporations began to open Commerce Content sites. Led by GE at the beginning of 1996, the pace picked up during the summer with the likes of Wal-Mart, Fidelity, and Schwab opening up their sites. Even computer industry stalwarts such as Cisco and Dell did not have their Commerce sites up and running until the summer of 1996. Still, these companies only represented the leading edge of adoption and even by early 1997 many major companies had yet to launch commerce-ready Internet sites.

Only now is the first sporadic combat between traditional corporations and the now established early movers beginning to take place. A classic example of this combat is the intensifying battle between Amazon.com and Barnes & Noble. Amazon reigned as the dominant bookstore on the Internet without any serious opposition for almost two years. Barnes & Noble's belated entry in the market has resulted in an intense price war as well as several lawsuits over claims the two firms were making on their web sites.

This kind of bare knuckled, no-holds barred competition between the deep pocketed, late arriving corporations and the scrappy, emerging first movers should continue to heat up over the next six to twelve months as major corporations begin to "flip the switch" on their Commerce Content sites.

Many traditional corporations, though, are still acting like a deer caught in the headlights of an oncoming train. This tendency is especially pronounced in the Financial Services industry where concerns over disintermediating established sales channels are leading to a tremendous internal struggle for many firms, especially full-service brokerage firms and insurers. These firms recognize the growth and attractive economics of the Internet but do not want to conduct actual transactions over the Internet for fear of alienating their brokers and agents. In the interim, these firms have established rather feeble and contrived informational Internet sites as they struggle through the internal conflicts set off by the Internet's arrival.

## Fog of War

As competition has intensified and as the number of competitors within each industry sector has blossomed, the Commerce Content sector has begun to resemble a gigantic battle that is now out of control and beyond the comprehension of any one person. Most affected by this situation are consumers and businesses that are now overwhelmed with the number of choices that the Internet is presenting them. Whereas simple searches for a record store might have yielded just one name a year or two ago, now those same searches produce an increasing multitude of names to choose from. In an attempt to escape this confusion, consumers have been flocking to well-known, established brands.

Most of the early entrepreneurial efforts have not been able to overcome fifty years of concerted brand management and have been quickly overshadowed by the established corporations. Only the most prominent first movers have been able to withstand this initial push.

Conventional wisdom now holds that the window of opportunity for new entrepreneurial efforts is largely closed and that the traditional corporations will slowly but surely use their purchasing power, existing brands, and deep pockets to eventually assume control of the different industry sectors from the young upstarts.

## Brand at Its Apex

To a degree, the conventional wisdom is no doubt correct. The power of the brand, especially in a crowded market, has proved itself once again. As have the same ingredients that are important in any other market: access to capital, scale, and experience. However, the balance of power is not as firmly in the hands of the established corporations as the conventional wisdom might suggest. Indeed the power of branded commerce may be at its apex on the Internet.

Just as software developers responded to the need for turnkey merchant servers and enhanced development tools, they are also beginning to respond to consumer and business complaints about information overload and the inability to find the best deals on goods and services. In fits and starts, solutions to these problems are starting to emerge.

Using techniques such as collaborative filtering, companies such as FireFly and Net.Perceptions are beginning to lay the foundation for enhanced searching capabilities that identify only those items likely to be of most concern to a customer.

Perhaps even more importantly, Intelligent Agent technology is beginning to emerge from research labs and find real-world applications in the world of Commerce Content. While Intelligent Agents may sound like science fiction, working versions of these agents already exist today.

One powerful working version of the technology, called BargainFinder (http://bf.cstar.ac.com/bf/), has already been developed by Anderson Consulting. BargainFinder allows consumers to rapidly search several different Internet record stores to determine which site has the best price for a given album. Anderson developed the technology merely to demonstrate the potential of Intelligent Agents, but the service proved so popular that several sites, fearful of intensified price competition and decreased

**Figure 7.3**  Intelligent Agent Example: BargainFinder

customer loyalty, took direct measures to block the agent from searching their record catalogs. While these sites can successfully block primitive agents such as BargainFinder today, in the future it will be almost impossible for them to discern between a human being and their duly deputized Intelligent Agent.

Intelligent Agents will thus swing the pendulum away from brand and back toward price and product selection, especially for "known" goods such as books, CDs, and industrial commodities. This swing toward price competition will make efficiency, scale, and focus more important than brand in many areas of Commerce Content.

### Trust: Brand's Backstop

That is not to say that "brand is dead" and big corporations are eventually doomed to failure on the Internet. There is no doubt that brand will continue to play an important role, especially in situations where an element of trust is required. Trust cannot be searched for by a computer, in which it must be built over time through a series of communications and interactions. So in industries in which trust is an important element of the sales process, such as financial services, brand (and the promise of trust that it represents) is likely to remain an important factor.

Beyond brands, established corporations will still have a definite advantage when it comes to scale and investment capital. However, it is clear that despite these advantages, emerging Intelligent Agent technologies may well make the battle to dominate the Commerce Content sector much less of a walkover than many are now predicting.

## Success Factors

Given this rapidly evolving environment with its competitive threats, changing technology, and uncertain future, it is difficult to pick individual winners today; however, there are a few key success factors which clearly will be important in the Commerce Content sector going forward:

*Branded:* Didn't we just get through determining brand is dead? Not really. What the last section laid out was a situation in which brand played a greatly diminished role over time in certain industries with "known" goods. However, that's in the long term and only in specific industries. In the short term, brand will continue to play a very important role as consumers do not yet have the tools they need to sort through all of the options and brand provides them with one of the easiest and most readily available options for making their decisions. Thus, in the short term, nurturing and promoting a strong brand may indeed be one of the wisest things that a Commerce Content company can do. After all, it won't hurt to have a brand in the long term; it will just be difficult to afford the advertising to support it.

*Efficient:* The increasing price transparency brought about by the Internet and eventually Intelligent Agents will make it increasingly necessary for companies to wring every last operating and financial efficiency out of their business model. In order to capture possible savings to the full extent, companies will have to intimately integrate the Internet into their fundamental business processes. They must also financially isolate their Internet operations from their other businesses so as not to burden their Internet operations with corporate overhead or pressures to cross-subsidize other less efficient parts of their business.

*Trusted:* Trust in a commercial relationship is a difficult quality to build, but once it is built, it forms a formidable obstacle to competitors. The successful firms will concentrate on building trust with their customers, more often than not with the help of technology. This trust will go a long way toward securing a competitive and profitable position for these companies in the future.

## New Opportunities

Taking these three success factors into account, along with the likely evolution of the sector, there are likely to be several areas of opportunity in the Commerce Content Sector, despite what the conventional wisdom may hold.

*Channel Conflicts:* Those industries whose Internet efforts are frozen by the conflict between the Internet and their established sales channels provide ideal opportunities for new Internet-only competitors to seize the initiative and grow quite large at the established companies' expense. Competing against these firms is like fighting against someone with one arm tied behind his back.

The brokerage and insurance industries appear particularly vulnerable in this regard, but so do the mortgage broker and industrial distributor markets. All of these industries suffer from "repricing" paralysis whereby if they reprice their entire portfolio to compete with Internet upstarts, they will suffer a massive revenue hit.

This situation is analogous to that which the major credit card issuers faced in the early 1990s as new "mono-line" competitors such as MBNA and Capital One used superior technology and cost positions to eat away at the customer bases of the major credit card issuers. Rather than bite the bullet and reprice their entire portfolio, these firms chose to cede a portion of the market to the newcomers while they reorganized themselves to compete more effectively.

The same situation now conforms firms such as full-service brokerages that have largely decided to cede a portion of the market rather than try to tackle the gut-wrenching task of restructuring their channels and/or revenue models.

*New Products and Services:* New technologies will undoubtedly create new opportunities for enterprising firms. For example, the Integrator role described in Chapter 5 is clearly a new opportunity that will be created by improved technical standards as well as the development of Intelligent Agents. Intelligent Agent services for travel and other purchases should also be a major opportunity.

## Investment Considerations

### Market Overview

The Commerce Content Sector is perhaps the most difficult of all of the EC sectors to invest in. This stems from the fact that companies in this sector share little in common beyond using the Internet to generate the majority of their revenues. Amazon.com cannot be compared in any meaningful way to E*Trade because one company is a book seller and the other is a brokerage. Obviously, these companies need to be compared against firms within their particular industry. However, the small size of the sector dictates that Commerce Content companies must often be compared to non-Internet-based firms within their industry. This approach can be dangerous as non-Internet-based firms compete in very different operating environments and have different business models, so making direct comparisons can be misleading.

### Recent Investment Performance

There is no doubt about it: From an investment perspective, the Commerce Content Sector has, hands down, been the top performing sector of the Electronic Commerce industry since the beginning of 1997. Not that there was much of a sector at the beginning of 1997. Indeed, of the nine firms currently in the sector, only E*Trade was public as of 1/1/97. E*Trade was not joined by another firm until March of 1997 when Ameritrade went public. During the remainder of 1997 and the first half of 1998 another seven Commerce Content firms went public.

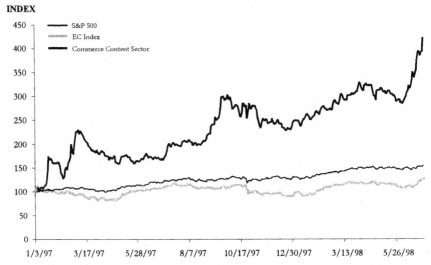

**Figure 7.4**   Commerce Content Sector vs. EC Index and S&P 500
*Source: Piper Jaffray*

Collectively the performance of these firms has been astounding. The nine firms are up an *average* of 193% since their IPO, with Amazon.com leading the pack, up an incredible 1008%. These stocks have performed so well for a number of reasons, including their high degree of visibility with retail investors, the small amount of float or shares available for purchase, the overriding enthusiasm of investors for Internet stocks and, most importantly, the very high revenue growth of the industry leaders.

As of 7/1/98 there were nine public Commerce Content Sector companies (see Table 7.2). Key statistics for this group as of 7/1/98:

*Market Capitalization:*  The nine firms had a total combined value of $8.0 billion at the end of second quarter 1997. This makes the Commerce Content Sector the third largest sector in the EC industry.

*Liquidity:*  On average, $202 million of Commerce Content stock trades hands each day. At current trading volumes, market capitalization in this sector turns over an average of every 40 days compared to 83 for the entire EC universe. This makes the Commerce Content Sector the most active in the EC industry. However, the sector should calm down a bit as the stocks move further away from their IPO dates and begin to assemble a more stable investor base.

*Volatility:*  Stock prices in the sector changed a capitalization weighted average of 2.4% a day compared to 1.3% for the EC industry and 0.8%

**Table 7.2** Firms in the Commerce Content Index

| Company | Ticker | Mrkt cap ($MMs) | $Vol/ day ($MMs) | % Price Δ/day | 1997 Revs ($MMs) | 1997 Earn ($MMs) | 1998E P/E | 1999E P/E | 1997 P/S |
|---|---|---|---|---|---|---|---|---|---|
| Amazon.com | AMNZ | $4,933 | $133.8 | 3.9% | $148 | ($27.6) | NM | NM | 22.5 |
| E*Trade | EGRP | 901 | 28.4 | 3.0 | 156 | 13.9 | 36.4 | 27.3 | 4.1 |
| Onsale | ONSL | 464 | 9.5 | 4.7 | 89 | (2.5) | NM | 225.0 | 4.0 |
| Preview Travel | PVTL | 442 | 7.5 | 4.7 | 14 | (10.2) | NM | NM | 31.3 |
| Ameritrade | AMTD | 355 | 4.2 | 3.0 | 92 | 13.8 | NM | 15.3 | 3.0 |
| CDNOW | CDNW | 322 | 7.4 | 4.3 | 17 | (10.7) | NM | NM | 13.0 |
| N2K | NTKI | 279 | 6.8 | 4.4 | 11 | (29.3) | NM | NM | 16.2 |
| NetBank | NTBK | 181 | 3.2 | 2.9 | 2 | (5.6) | 118.0 | 39.3 | 79.3 |
| Peapod | PPOD | 101 | 1.1 | 4.7 | 60 | (13.0) | NM | NM | 1.5 |
| Total | | $7,979 | $201.7 | 2.1% | $589 | ($71.1) | NM | NM | 13.5 |

NOTE: All statistics are as of 7/1/98.

SOURCE: Company reports, Factset, First Call, Piper Jaffray

for the S&P 500. This makes Commerce Content the most volatile sector in the EC industry.

*Revenues:* Total revenues for the sector grew 202% in 1997. Amazon's revenues grew from almost nothing in 1995 to $148 million in 1997. During 1998, revenue growth for the sector should stay strong as Amazon alone appears poised to grow well over 100% while strong growth from most others also appears likely.

*Earnings:* The nine firms in the sector lost a combined total of $71 million in 1997 due primarily to heavy investments in advertising by firms such as Amazon, Onsale, Preview Travel, and N2K. During 1998 most of these firms are expected to continue losing money as they forsake profits in a mad dash for market share.

*Valuations:* The industry trades at around 13.5 times 1997 revenues which makes it the most expensive sector on a price-to-sales basis. The sector does not trade on a P/E basis because it is not even expected to make money until the year 2000. While these valuations are very high, it is important to keep in mind that revenues are expected to grow by at least 100% in 1998.

# Risks

Companies in the Commerce Content sector share the unique distinction of facing two sets of risks. The first set of risks is specific to the particular industry that the firm operates within. The second set of risks is applicable to all Commerce Content firms due to their use of the EC infrastructure to generate the vast majority of their revenues. The first set of risks is best discussed elsewhere, but the second set of risks deserves treatment in this report:

## Competition from Established Players

As we mentioned earlier, many established corporations are only now beginning to open their own commerce capable sites on the Internet. As this trend accelerates, the stocks in this sector may come under increasing competitive pressure. For example, Amazon.com will soon be facing competition from not just Barnes & Noble, but also Borders Bookstores. This intensified competition could lead to slower revenue growth and decreasing margins for many firms in the sector much as it has for firms in the Business Commerce Sector.

## Acceptance of Internet Commerce

This sector's overall health is premised on the increasing acceptance of Internet-based commerce. Expectations are that there will be a gradual but substantial increase in the percent of Internet users willing to purchase over the Internet. Should these expectations not be borne out, the sector would suffer accordingly.

## Growth of the Internet

Commerce Content stocks should prove even more sensitive to the growth of the Internet because unlike other sectors such as electronic payments or security, these stocks derive the vast majority of their revenues from Internet-related activities.

## Pricing Pressures

In general, the Internet increases price competition, as economists would say, by dramatically lowering the cost of price discovery and thereby effecting greater price transparency. This simply means that the Internet makes it easier for consumers and businesses to compare prices. Intelligent Agents promise to make price comparison even easier. The combination of lower price discovery costs combined with intensified competition could lead to serious pricing pressures.

This intensified price competition has already occurred in the on-line trading area where commissions have quickly fallen from $30 to $40 a trade to $10 to $20 a trade. Continued pricing competition in this market is likely as some firms are already offering sub $10 trades. Similar pricing pressures in other areas of Commerce Content are to be expected.

When firms are forced to reprice, their net margins fall overnight. Therefore repricing has the potential to have a sudden and sharp impact on the stock values of Commerce Content firms.

### Dependence on EC Infrastructure

The Commerce Content sector is dependent on four other EC sectors for its technological and commercial foundations. Major problems in any of these areas could have an adverse impact on the Commerce Content sector. For example, long delays in the deployment of the Secure Electronic Transaction (SET) standard or major problems in deploying certificate-based security could negatively impact the industry. Investors in the Commerce Content Sector should pay careful attention to the state of the other four EC sectors.

## Conclusion

The Commerce Content Sector is still very young, but as the finishing touches are put on the initial EC infrastructure, it is rapidly beginning to take shape. Driven forward by fundamental cost advantages as well as the rapid growth of the Internet, the sector should quickly expand in the coming years. This expansion will bring with it increasing competition from established players as well as intensified price competition. Over the long term, technological improvements will create new opportunities but they will also intensify price competition and devalue brands for some product categories. Successful companies will focus on developing trusted roles that allow them to efficiently provide branded goods and services in the short term and compete based on price and service in the long term. Provided that the Internet continues its impressive growth and users gradually become more comfortable with Internet purchasing, this sector can look forward to a prosperous future.

# Appendix

# Company Profile:
## AMAZON.COM INC

## AMZN

### Stock Data

| | |
|---|---|
| Stock Price as of | 6/30/98 $99.75 |
| Shares Outstanding | 49.45 |
| Market Cap | $4,933 |
| 52 Week High | $104.75 |
| 52 Week Low | $8.88 |
| % of 52 Week High | 95% |
| 3 Month Return | 133% |
| 12 Month Return | 978% |
| Avg Daily Volume (past mo.) | 4.29 |

### Quarterly EPS Performance

| Date | IBES Est | Actual | Suprise |
|---|---|---|---|
| 3/98 | (0.24) | (0.20) | 0.04 |
| 12/97 | (0.22) | (0.20) | 0.03 |
| 9/97 | (0.21) | (0.18) | 0.03 |
| 6/97 | (0.16) | (0.14) | 0.02 |
| 3/97 | | (0.07) | |

### Annual Fundamentals

| | 12/96 | 12/97 |
|---|---|---|
| Revenue | 15.7 | 147.8 |
| Growth | | 838% |
| Gross Sales | 3.5 | 28.8 |
| Operating Income | (6.0) | (29.2) |
| Net Income | (5.8) | (27.6) |

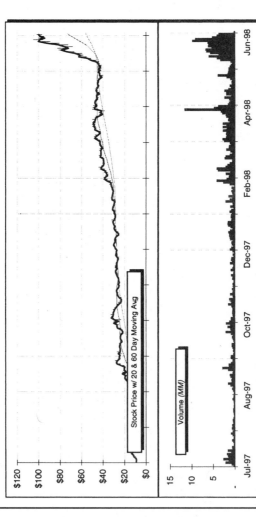

Stock Price w/ 20 & 60 Day Moving Avg

Volume *(MM)*

Jul-97   Aug-97   Oct-97   Dec-97   Feb-98   Apr-98   Jun-98

### Quarterly Fundamentals

| | 6/96 | 9/96 | 12/96 | 3/97 | 6/97 | 9/97 | 12/97 | 3/98 |
|---|---|---|---|---|---|---|---|---|
| Revenue | 2.2 | 4.2 | 8.5 | 16.0 | 27.9 | 37.9 | 66.0 | 87.4 |
| Seq'l Growth | | 87% | 103% | 89% | 74% | 36% | 74% | 32% |
| Y/Y Growth | | | | | 1149% | 808% | 680% | 446% |
| Gross Sales | 0.5 | 0.9 | 1.9 | 3.5 | 5.2 | 7.2 | 12.9 | 19.3 |
| Operating Income | (0.8) | (2.5) | (2.4) | (3.1) | (7.1) | (9.2) | (9.9) | (8.9) |
| Net Income | (0.8) | (2.4) | (2.3) | (3.0) | (6.7) | (8.5) | (9.3) | (9.3) |

| | | | | | | | | | | | |
|---|---|---|---|---|---|---|---|---|---|---|---|
| Gross Margins | 21% | 22% | 22% | 19% | 19% | 20% | 22% | | Gross Margins | 22% | 20% |
| Operating Margin | -35% | -59% | -28% | -25% | -24% | -15% | -10% | | Operating Margin | -38% | -20% |
| Net Margin | -34% | -57% | -27% | -24% | -22% | -14% | -11% | | Net Margin | -37% | -19% |
| | | | | | | | | | | | |
| Cash & S-T Invest. | NA | 6.2 | 7.2 | 56.4 | 48.2 | 125.1 | 116.8 | | Cash & S-T Invest. | 6.2 | 125.1 |
| L-T Debt | NA | NA | - | 0.2 | 0.2 | 76.7 | 76.7 | | L-T Debt | - | 76.7 |
| StkHldrs Equity | NA | 3.4 | 2.8 | 45.6 | 37.4 | 28.5 | 19.8 | | StkHldrs Equity | 3.4 | 28.5 |
| Op. Cash Flow | NA | NA | 1.2 | 1.4 | (6.4) | 7.3 | (6.6) | | Op. Cash Flow | (1.7) | 3.5 |

**Per Share Data**

| | | | | | | | | | | | |
|---|---|---|---|---|---|---|---|---|---|---|---|
| Shares Out | NA | 31.80 | 47.60 | 47.72 | 47.72 | 47.87 | 48.33 | | Shares Out | 31.80 | 47.87 |
| Net Income | NA | (0.07) | (0.06) | (0.14) | (0.18) | (0.20) | (0.19) | | Net Income | (0.18) | (0.58) |
| Cash & S-T Inv. | NA | 0.20 | 0.15 | 1.18 | 1.01 | 2.61 | 2.42 | | Cash & S-T Inv. | 0.20 | 2.61 |
| Book Value | NA | 0.11 | 0.06 | 0.95 | 0.78 | 0.60 | 0.41 | | Book Value | 0.11 | 0.60 |

**Earnings Estimates & Valuation:**

| | IBES EPS | Price Multiple |
|---|---|---|
| Current Yr Est | (1.33) | NM |
| Fwd Yr. Est. | (0.85) | NM |
| Last FY End | 97.12 | |
| # IBES Estimates | 10.00 | |

| | Growth | P/E to LT Growth |
|---|---|---|
| EPS Growth | -36.1% | NM |
| IBES L-T Growth | 64.8% | NM |

**Misc:**

| | |
|---|---|
| Employees | 614 |
| IPO Date | 5/15/97 |
| First Day Close | $11.75 |

## Company Description

AMZN is the largest seller of books on the Internet, offering a catalog of 2.5 million titles. The Company provides customers with numerous features to enhance the electronic shopping environment including, intuitive searching and browsing, email, personalized shopping, streamlined ordering, secure payment and direct shipping. The Company's has also benefited from its syndicated selling approach in which its "Associate Websites" (now numbering over 30,000) establish links to Amazon's website. Amazon recently started selling music from its site

Sources: Piper Jaffray Research, FactSet, IBES, Compustat, Company Reports
Figures in millions, except per share amounts

Piper Jaffray Equity Research
Electronic Commerce

# Company Profile:
## AMERITRADE HLDG CORP -CL A

## AMTD

**Stock Data**

| | 6/30/98 |
|---|---|
| Stock Price as of | $27.00 |
| Shares Outstanding | 13.15 |
| Market Cap | $355 |
| 52 Week High | $39.00 |
| 52 Week Low | $14.63 |
| % of 52 Week High | 69% |
| 3 Month Return | -3% |
| 12 Month Return | 71% |
| Avg Daily Volume (past mo.) | 0.11 |

**Quarterly EPS Performance**

| Date | IBES Est | Actual | Suprise |
|---|---|---|---|
| 3/98 | (0.07) | (0.02) | 0.05 |
| 12/97 | (0.70) | (0.77) | (0.07) |
| 9/97 | 0.33 | 0.40 | 0.07 |
| 6/97 | 0.33 | 0.32 | (0.01) |
| 3/97 | | 0.26 | |

**Annual Fundamentals**

| | 9/96 | 9/97 |
|---|---|---|
| Revenue | 62.0 | 92.2 |
| Growth | | 49% |
| Gross Sales | 26.1 | 36.4 |
| Operating Income | 26.1 | 36.4 |
| Net Income | 11.2 | 13.8 |

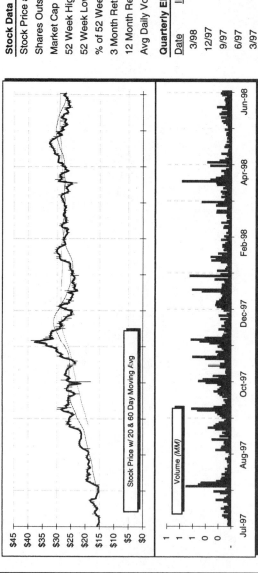

Stock Price w/ 20 & 60 Day Moving Avg

Volume (MM)

| | Jul-97 | Aug-97 | Oct-97 | Dec-97 | Feb-98 | Apr-98 | Jun-98 |

**Quarterly Fundamentals**

| | 6/96 | 9/96 | 12/96 | 3/97 | 6/97 | 9/97 | 12/97 | 3/98 |
|---|---|---|---|---|---|---|---|---|
| Revenue | 17.3 | 14.8 | 18.3 | 21.7 | 24.2 | 28.0 | 30.0 | 35.6 |
| Seq'l Growth | | -15% | 23% | 19% | 11% | 16% | 7% | 18% |
| Y/Y Growth | | | | | 40% | 89% | 65% | 64% |
| Gross Sales | 6.8 | 5.5 | 2.8 | 8.7 | 11.4 | 13.5 | (13.1) | 5.2 |
| Operating Income | 6.8 | 5.5 | 2.8 | 8.7 | 11.4 | 13.5 | (13.1) | 5.2 |
| Net Income | 2.1 | 2.3 | (0.1) | 3.5 | 4.6 | 5.8 | (11.2) | (0.3) |

Piper Jaffray Equity Research
Electronic Commerce

| | | | | | | | | |
|---|---|---|---|---|---|---|---|---|
| *Gross Margins* | | 39% | 37% | 40% | 47% | 48% | -44% | 15% |
| *Operating Margin* | | 39% | 37% | 40% | 47% | 48% | -44% | 15% |
| *Net Margin* | | 18% | 15% | 16% | 19% | 21% | -37% | -1% |
| Cash & S-T Invest. | NA | 191.4 | 258.9 | 326.0 | 381.7 | 373.3 | 323.9 | 543.2 |
| L-T Debt | NA | 2.9 | 5.7 | - | - | - | - | 10.0 |
| StkHldrs Equity | NA | 30.7 | 30.6 | 55.3 | 60.6 | 67.0 | 55.7 | 55.4 |
| Op. Cash Flow | NA | 0.5 | (4.7) | (7.9) | 39.5 | (41.8) | 14.0 | |
| **Per Share Data** | | | | | | | | |
| Shares Out | NA | 12.81 | 12.81 | 14.52 | 14.52 | 14.52 | 14.52 | 14.52 |
| Net Income | NA | 0.18 | (0.01) | 0.24 | 0.32 | 0.40 | (0.77) | (0.02) |
| Cash & S-T Inv. | NA | 14.94 | 20.20 | 22.45 | 26.29 | 25.71 | 22.31 | 37.42 |
| Book Value | NA | 2.39 | 2.39 | 3.81 | 4.17 | 4.61 | 3.84 | 3.82 |

| | | |
|---|---|---|
| *Gross Margins* | 42% | 39% |
| *Operating Margin* | 42% | 39% |
| *Net Margin* | 18% | 15% |
| Cash & S-T Invest. | 191.4 | 373.3 |
| L-T Debt | 2.9 | - |
| StkHldrs Equity | 30.7 | 67.0 |
| Op. Cash Flow | 23.8 | 27.4 |
| **Per Share Data** | | |
| Shares Out | 12.81 | 14.52 |
| Net Income | 0.87 | 0.95 |
| Cash & S-T Inv. | 14.94 | 25.71 |
| Book Value | 2.39 | 4.61 |

**Earnings Estimates & Valuation:**

| | IBES EPS | Price Multiple |
|---|---|---|
| Current Yr Est | 0.01 | NM |
| Fwd Yr. Est. | 1.77 | 15.3 |
| Last FY End | 97.09 | |
| # IBES Estimates | 4.00 | |

| | Growth | P/E to LT Growth |
|---|---|---|
| EPS Growth | NM | NM |
| IBES L-T Growth | 25.0% | 61% |

**Misc:**

| | |
|---|---|
| Employees | 415 |
| IPO Date | 3/4/97 |
| First Day Close | $19.50 |

## Company Description

AMTD provides discount brokerage services via the Internet, other electronic mediums, and human brokers. The Company also provides securities clearing to other financial institutions. The Company's online trading services provide individual investors with the electronic tools to trade stocks, options, and mutual funds, as well as portfolio management capabilities and various information resources. The Company consolidated four online trading services into two, Ameritrade and Accutrade, and with a large advertising push late 1997 was able to dramatically expand its business.

Sources: Piper Jaffray Research, FactSet, IBES, Compustat, Company Reports
Figures in millions, except per share amounts

## Company Profile:
# ARI NETWORK SERVICES

# ARIS

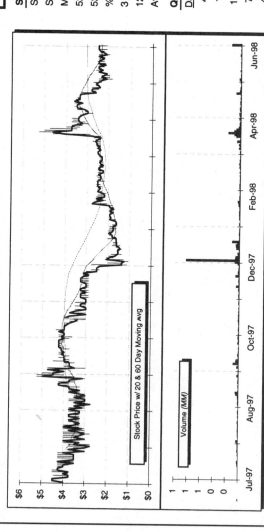

Stock Price w/ 20 & 60 Day Moving Avg

Volume (MM)

Jul-97  Aug-97  Oct-97  Dec-97  Feb-98  Apr-98  Jun-98

**Stock Data**

| | |
|---|---|
| Stock Price as of 6/30/98 | $2.50 |
| Shares Outstanding | 4.25 |
| Market Cap | $11 |
| 52 Week High | $5.25 |
| 52 Week Low | $1.06 |
| % of 52 Week High | 48% |
| 3 Month Return | 3% |
| 12 Month Return | -38% |
| Avg Daily Volume (past mo.) | 0.00 |

**Quarterly EPS Performance**

| Date | IBES Est | Actual | Surprise |
|---|---|---|---|
| 4/98 | (0.12) | (0.21) | (0.09) |
| 1/98 | (0.16) | (0.20) | (0.04) |
| 10/97 | (0.16) | (0.16) | - |
| 7/97 | (0.24) | (0.08) | 0.16 |
| 4/97 | (0.16) | (0.24) | (0.08) |

**Annual Fundamentals**

| | 7/96 | 7/97 |
|---|---|---|
| Revenue | 5.3 | 6.9 |
| Growth | | 32% |
| Gross Sales | (3.9) | (3.1) |
| Operating Income | (3.9) | (3.1) |

**Quarterly Fundamentals**

| | 7/96 | 10/96 | 1/97 | 4/97 | 7/97 | 10/97 | 1/98 | 4/98 |
|---|---|---|---|---|---|---|---|---|
| Revenue | 1.6 | 1.7 | 1.7 | 1.7 | 1.9 | 2.0 | 1.8 | 1.7 |
| Seq1 Growth | | 3% | -1% | 2% | 9% | 9% | -12% | -3% |
| Y/Y Growth | | | | | 14% | 20% | 7% | 1% |
| Gross Sales | (0.9) | (1.1) | (0.9) | (0.9) | (0.2) | (0.6) | (0.8) | (0.9) |
| Operating Income | (0.9) | (1.1) | (0.9) | (0.9) | (0.2) | (0.6) | (0.8) | (0.9) |
| Net Income | (1.0) | (1.1) | | | | | | |

| | | | | | | | | | | |
|---|---|---|---|---|---|---|---|---|---|---|
| Gross Margins | -58% | -63% | -54% | -51% | -12% | -28% | -48% | -50% | -75% | -44% |
| Operating Margin | -58% | -63% | -54% | -51% | -12% | -28% | -48% | -50% | -75% | -44% |
| Net Margin | -63% | -68% | -56% | -53% | -15% | -29% | -49% | -52% | -80% | -47% |
| | | | | | | | | | | |
| Cash & S-T Invest. | 0.4 | 0.6 | 0.1 | 0.3 | 0.1 | 1.4 | 0.1 | 0.1 | 0.4 | 0.1 |
| L-T Debt | 0.0 | 0.0 | 0.0 | 0.0 | 0.0 | 0.0 | 0.0 | 0.0 | 0.0 | 0.0 |
| StkHldrs Equity | 6.2 | 7.8 | 8.1 | 7.2 | 8.9 | 10.1 | 9.6 | 8.7 | 6.2 | 8.9 |
| Op. Cash Flow | (0.8) | (0.4) | (0.6) | (0.3) | (0.4) | (0.4) | (0.5) | (0.0) | (2.5) | (1.8) |
| **Per Share Data** | | | | | | | | | | |
| Shares Out | 3.23 | 3.58 | 3.69 | 3.69 | 3.69 | 4.14 | 4.24 | 4.25 | 3.23 | 3.69 |
| Net Income | (0.32) | (0.32) | (0.25) | (0.25) | (0.08) | (0.14) | (0.20) | (0.21) | (1.30) | (0.89) |
| Cash & S-T Inv. | 0.12 | 0.17 | 0.02 | 0.07 | 0.02 | 0.34 | 0.02 | 0.02 | 0.12 | 0.02 |
| Book Value | 1.91 | 2.19 | 2.21 | 1.96 | 2.42 | 2.44 | 2.27 | 2.06 | 1.91 | 2.42 |

## Earnings Estimates & Valuation:

| | IBES EPS | Price Multiple |
|---|---|---|
| Current Yr Est | (0.67) | NM |
| Fwd Yr. Est. | NA | NM |
| Last FY End | 97.07 | |
| # IBES Estimates | 2.00 | |

| | Growth | P/E to LT Growth |
|---|---|---|
| EPS Growth | NA | NM |
| IBES L-T Growth | 50.0% | NM |

Misc:

| | |
|---|---|
| Employees | 77 |
| IPO Date | 11/15/91 |
| First Day Close | $35.50 |

## Company Description

ARIS provides electronic data interchange (EDI) products and value added network (VAN) services to agribusiness, equipment, transportation and publishing industries. For agribusiness and equipment manufacturers, the Company's services allow trading partners to check product availability, generate sales reporting, and submit batch or individual orders. The Company also provides directories of ship-to and bill-to locations and various online catalogs. Two major customers are the Association of American Railroads and Roche Vitamins.

Sources: Piper Jaffray Research, FactSet, IBES, Compustat, Company Reports
Figures in millions, except per share amounts

Piper Jaffray Equity Research
Electronic Commerce

# Company Profile:
## AXENT TECHNOLOGIES INC

## AXNT

### Stock Data

| | | |
|---|---|---|
| Stock Price as of | 6/30/98 | $30.63 |
| Shares Outstanding | | 24.48 |
| Market Cap | | $750 |
| 52 Week High | | $32.63 |
| 52 Week Low | | $14.13 |
| % of 52 Week High | | 94% |
| 3 Month Return | | 0% |
| 12 Month Return | | 101% |
| Avg Daily Volume (past mo.) | | 0.38 |

### Quarterly EPS Performance

| Date | IBES Est | Actual | Suprise |
|---|---|---|---|
| 3/98 | 0.10 | 0.13 | 0.03 |
| 12/97 | 0.18 | 0.31 | 0.13 |
| 9/97 | 0.10 | 0.12 | 0.02 |
| 6/97 | 0.09 | 0.11 | 0.02 |
| 3/97 | 0.04 | 0.06 | 0.02 |

### Annual Fundamentals

| | 12/96 | 12/97 |
|---|---|---|
| Revenue | 25.4 | 44.6 |
| Growth | | 76% |
| Gross Sales | 23.5 | 40.4 |
| Operating Income | 3.4 | 9.7 |
| Net Income | 5.7 | (19.4) |

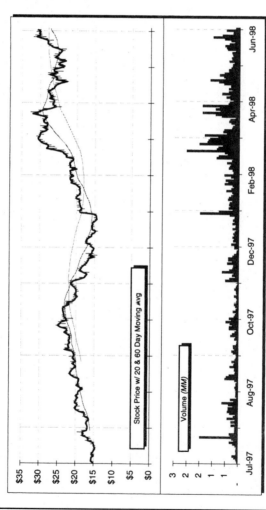

Stock Price w/ 20 & 60 Day Moving Avg

Volume (MM)

### Quarterly Fundamentals

| | 6/96 | 9/96 | 12/96 | 3/97 | 6/97 | 9/97 | 12/97 | 3/98 |
|---|---|---|---|---|---|---|---|---|
| Revenue | 6.1 | 5.7 | 8.7 | 14.5 | 10.1 | 10.5 | 15.2 | 20.9 |
| Seq'l Growth | | -6% | 51% | 67% | -30% | 3% | 45% | 37% |
| Y/Y Growth | | | | | 65% | 82% | 76% | 45% |
| Gross Sales | 5.6 | 5.3 | 8.1 | 13.2 | 9.1 | 9.5 | 13.9 | 18.8 |
| Operating Income | 0.9 | 0.5 | 1.9 | 1.5 | 1.9 | 2.2 | 4.8 | 4.2 |
| Net Income | 1.7 | 1.1 | 1.8 | (25.8) | 1.5 | 1.6 | 4.2 | (9.7) |

**Financial Data**

| | | | | | | | | | | |
|---|---|---|---|---|---|---|---|---|---|---|
| Gross Margins | 92% | 92% | 93% | 91% | 90% | 90% | 92% | 90% | 92% | 91% |
| Operating Margin | 15% | 9% | 22% | 10% | 18% | 21% | 32% | 20% | 13% | 22% |
| Net Margin | 27% | 19% | 21% | NM | 14% | 15% | 28% | -46% | 22% | -44% |
| Cash & S-T Invest. | 34.8 | 33.0 | 35.9 | 34.4 | 31.1 | 32.9 | 40.9 | 92.0 | 35.9 | 40.9 |
| L-T Debt | - | - | - | - | - | - | - | - | - | - |
| StkHldrs Equity | 31.0 | 32.0 | 34.4 | 32.3 | 33.4 | 35.5 | 43.1 | 97.1 | 34.4 | 43.1 |
| Op. Cash Flow | 2.6 | (1.7) | 4.4 | (0.7) | (2.1) | 1.2 | 8.5 | (2.1) | 6.0 | 6.8 |
| **Per Share Data** | | | | | | | | | | |
| Shares Out | 10.00 | 10.01 | 10.13 | 11.71 | 11.89 | 12.18 | 12.40 | 24.14 | 10.13 | 12.40 |
| Net Income | 0.17 | 0.11 | 0.18 | (2.21) | 0.12 | 0.13 | 0.34 | (0.40) | 0.56 | (1.57) |
| Cash & S-T Inv. | 3.48 | 3.30 | 3.54 | 2.94 | 2.61 | 2.70 | 3.30 | 3.81 | 3.54 | 3.30 |
| Book Value | 3.10 | 3.20 | 3.40 | 2.76 | 2.81 | 2.92 | 3.47 | 4.02 | 3.40 | 3.47 |

**Earnings Estimates & Valuation:**

| | IBES EPS | Price Multiple |
|---|---|---|
| Current Yr Est | 0.75 | 40.8 |
| Fwd Yr. Est. | 1.03 | 29.7 |
| Last FY End | 97.12 | |
| # IBES Estimates | 13.00 | |

| | Growth | P/E to LT Growth |
|---|---|---|
| EPS Growth | 37.3% | 108% |
| IBES L-T Growth | 37.9% | 78% |

**Misc:**

| | |
|---|---|
| Employees | |
| IPO Date | 4/24/96 |
| First Day Close | $18.75 |

## Company Description

AXNT is the developer of the OmniGuard suite of solutions that provide centralized enterprise wide security management in addition to access control, user administration, privileges management, tokens, and intrusion detection. The Company's latest offering is its virtual private network (VPN) solution that combines its token solution with a new gateway offering to enable secure remote access over public networks. In December 1997, AXNT announced the acquisition of Raptor for approximately $250MM. Raptor is best known for its Eagle firewall solution.

Sources: Piper Jaffray Research, FactSet, IBES, Compustat, Company Reports
Figures in millions, except per share amounts

Piper Jaffray Equity Research
Electronic Commerce

## Company Profile:

# BA MERCHANT SVCS INC -CL A

## BPI

### Stock Data

| | | |
|---|---|---|
| Stock Price as of | 6/30/98 | $20.19 |
| Shares Outstanding | | 16.26 |
| Market Cap | | $328 |
| 52 Week High | | $22.25 |
| 52 Week Low | | $14.13 |
| % of 52 Week High | | 91% |
| 3 Month Return | | 11% |
| 12 Month Return | | 6% |
| Avg Daily Volume (past mo.) | | 0.11 |

### Quarterly EPS Performance

| Date | IBES Est | Actual | Suprise |
|---|---|---|---|
| 3/98 | 0.18 | 0.18 | - |
| 12/97 | 0.22 | 0.22 | - |
| 9/97 | 0.21 | 0.21 | - |
| 6/97 | 0.19 | 0.19 | - |
| 3/97 | 0.15 | 0.16 | 0.01 |

### Annual Fundamentals

| | 12/96 | 12/97 |
|---|---|---|
| Revenue | 126.2 | 161.0 |
| Growth | | 28% |
| | | |
| Gross Sales | 44.9 | 55.7 |
| Operating Income | 44.9 | 55.7 |
| Net Income | 24.7 | 37.4 |

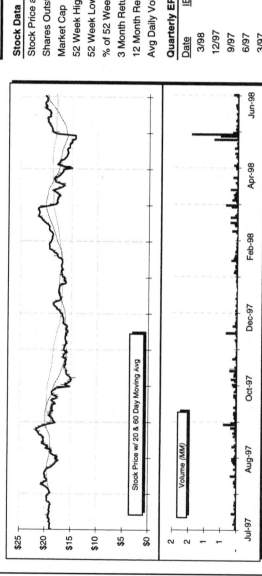

Stock Price w/ 20 & 60 Day Moving Avg

Volume (MM)

Jul-97 Aug-97 Oct-97 Dec-97 Feb-98 Apr-98 Jun-98

### Quarterly Fundamentals

| | 6/96 | 9/96 | 12/96 | 3/97 | 6/97 | 9/97 | 12/97 | 3/98 |
|---|---|---|---|---|---|---|---|---|
| Revenue | 37.0 | 35.4 | 38.1 | 36.0 | 38.9 | 41.2 | 44.9 | 41.8 |
| Seq'l Growth | | -4% | 7% | -6% | 8% | 6% | 9% | -7% |
| Y/Y Growth | | | | | 5% | 16% | 18% | 16% |
| Gross Sales | 13.6 | 11.7 | 15.4 | 11.6 | 13.3 | 15.1 | 15.7 | 12.7 |
| Operating Income | 13.6 | 11.7 | 15.4 | 11.6 | 13.3 | 15.1 | 15.7 | 12.7 |
| Net Income | 7.7 | 6.7 | 7.2 | 7.7 | 9.1 | 10.1 | 10.6 | 8.7 |

| | | | | | | | | | | |
|---|---|---|---|---|---|---|---|---|---|---|
| Gross Margins | 37% | 33% | 40% | 32% | 34% | 37% | 35% | 30% | 36% | 35% |
| Operating Margin | 37% | 33% | 40% | 32% | 34% | 37% | 35% | 30% | 36% | 35% |
| Net Margin | 21% | 19% | 19% | 21% | 23% | 24% | 23% | 21% | 20% | 23% |
| Cash & S-T Invest. | NA | 82.7 | 226.2 | 241.1 | 268.4 | 219.6 | 203.9 | 230.3 | 226.2 | 203.9 |
| L-T Debt | NA | - | - | - | - | - | - | - | - | - |
| StkHldrs Equity | NA | 103.1 | 252.1 | 259.4 | 268.5 | 280.5 | 291.3 | 300.0 | 252.1 | 291.3 |
| Op. Cash Flow | NA | NA | (0.1) | 77.3 | 30.3 | (68.8) | (19.7) | 33.3 | 23.1 | 19.0 |
| Per Share Data | | | | | | | | | | |
| Shares Out | NA | 44.20 | 46.44 | 46.44 | 46.59 | 48.65 | 48.65 | 48.66 | 46.44 | 48.65 |
| Net Income | NA | 0.15 | 0.16 | 0.17 | 0.20 | 0.21 | 0.22 | 0.18 | 0.53 | 0.77 |
| Cash & S-T Inv. | NA | 1.87 | 4.87 | 5.19 | 5.76 | 4.51 | 4.19 | 4.73 | 4.87 | 4.19 |
| Book Value | NA | 2.33 | 5.43 | 5.59 | 5.76 | 5.76 | 5.99 | 6.16 | 5.43 | 5.99 |

## Earnings Estimates & Valuation:

| | IBES EPS | Price Multiple |
|---|---|---|
| Current Yr Est | 0.90 | 22.4 |
| Fwd Yr. Est. | 1.09 | 18.5 |
| Last FY End | 97.12 | |
| # IBES Estimates | 3.00 | |

| | Growth | P/E to LT Growth |
|---|---|---|
| EPS Growth | 21.1% | 118% |
| IBES L-T Growth | 19.0% | 97% |

### Misc:

| | |
|---|---|
| Employees | 806 |
| IPO Date | 12/19/96 |
| First Day Close | $17.38 |

## Company Description

BPI is a merchant processor serving over 160,000 locations with a focus on large, multi-regional chains, middle-market merchants, and small merchants. The Company's customers include general retailers, restaurants, and supermarkets. The Company is the fourth largest processor of credit card transactions and the largest processor of debit card transactions. The Company was spun-off by Bank of America in 1996, which still retains 65% ownership and provides some marketing assistance through its branch network.

Sources: Piper Jaffray Research, FactSet, IBES, Compustat, Company Reports

Figures in millions, except per share amounts

Piper Jaffray Equity Research
Electronic Commerce

## Company Profile:

# BROADVISION INC

# BVSN

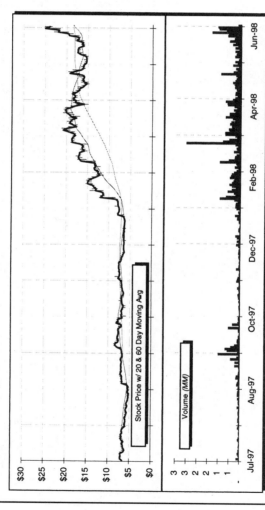

Stock Price w/ 20 & 60 Day Moving Avg

Volume (MM)

### Quarterly Fundamentals

| | 6/96 | 9/96 | 12/96 | 3/97 | 6/97 | 9/97 | 12/97 | 3/98 |
| --- | --- | --- | --- | --- | --- | --- | --- | --- |
| Revenue | 2.3 | 3.1 | 4.1 | 5.3 | 6.0 | 7.2 | 8.6 | 10.1 |
| Seq'l Growth | | 35% | 32% | 30% | 14% | 19% | 21% | 17% |
| Y/Y Growth | | | | | 162% | 131% | 111% | 90% |
| Gross Sales | 1.9 | 2.5 | 2.9 | 3.9 | 4.6 | 5.7 | 6.9 | 8.3 |
| Operating Income | (2.2) | (3.0) | (3.8) | (2.7) | (2.2) | (1.8) | (1.0) | (0.4) |
| Net Income | (2.2) | (2.7) | (3.6) | (2.5) | (2.1) | (1.7) | (1.1) | (0.5) |

| Gross Margins | 82% | 81% | 70% | 74% | 76% | 79% | 80% | 82% | | Gross Margins | 77% | 78% |
| Operating Margin | -96% | -96% | -93% | -51% | -36% | -25% | -11% | -4% | | Operating Margin | -98% | -28% |
| Net Margin | -95% | -86% | -88% | -47% | -35% | -24% | -13% | -5% | | Net Margin | -93% | -27% |
| | | | | | | | | | | | | |
| Cash & S-T Invest. | 24.6 | 23.6 | 19.7 | 15.4 | 12.4 | 9.0 | 10.5 | 57.1 | | Cash & S-T Invest. | 19.7 | 10.5 |
| L-T Debt | 0.5 | 0.6 | 0.5 | 0.6 | 0.5 | 0.6 | 3.0 | 4.0 | | L-T Debt | 0.5 | 3.0 |
| StkHldrs Equity | 24.8 | 24.1 | 21.0 | 18.9 | 17.1 | 15.8 | 15.1 | 62.0 | | StkHldrs Equity | 21.0 | 15.1 |
| Op. Cash Flow | (1.4) | (2.1) | (3.4) | (4.0) | (2.6) | (2.8) | 0.7 | (0.2) | | Op. Cash Flow | (8.4) | (8.7) |

**Per Share Data**

| Shares Out | 19.99 | 20.00 | 19.91 | 20.23 | 20.28 | 20.34 | 20.34 | 24.12 | | Shares Out | 19.91 | 20.34 |
| Net Income | (0.11) | (0.13) | (0.18) | (0.12) | (0.10) | (0.08) | (0.05) | (0.02) | | Net Income | (0.51) | (0.36) |
| Cash & S-T Inv. | 1.23 | 1.18 | 0.99 | 0.76 | 0.61 | 0.44 | 0.51 | 2.37 | | Cash & S-T Inv. | 0.99 | 0.51 |
| Book Value | 1.24 | 1.20 | 1.06 | 0.93 | 0.84 | 0.78 | 0.74 | 2.57 | | Book Value | 1.06 | 0.74 |

## Earnings Estimates & Valuation:

| | IBES EPS | Price Multiple |
| --- | --- | --- |
| Current Yr Est | 0.12 | 199.0 |
| Fwd Yr. Est. | 0.41 | 58.2 |
| Last FY End | 97.12 | |
| # IBES Estimates | 6.00 | |

| | Growth | P/E to LT Growth |
| --- | --- | --- |
| EPS Growth | 241.7% | 373% |
| IBES L-T Growth | 53.3% | 109% |

Misc:

| | |
| --- | --- |
| Employees | 188 |
| IPO Date | 6/21/96 |
| First Day Close | $7.13 |

## Company Description

BVSN's One-To-One software solution is used by companies to design websites for business-business and business-consumer electronic commerce. Distinguishing the Company's solution from other such offerings is its intense focus on personalization which entails the matching of viewer profile information to deliver targeted content and offers. The Company's solution also supports the more standard business commerce functions such as cataloging, ordering, secure payment processing, fulfillment, billing, and customer service.

Sources: Piper Jaffray Research, FactSet, IBES, Compustat, Company Reports
Figures in millions, except per share amounts

Piper Jaffray Equity Research
Electronic Commerce

# Company Profile:
# CDNOW INC

## CDNW

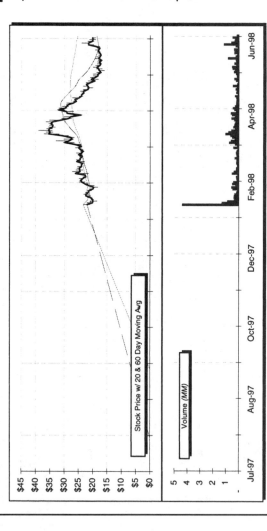

### Stock Data

| | |
|---|---|
| Stock Price as of | **6/30/98** $20.13 |
| Shares Outstanding | 16.01 |
| Market Cap | $322 |
| 52 Week High | $39.00 |
| 52 Week Low | $16.00 |
| % of 52 Week High | 52% |
| 3 Month Return | -16% |
| 12 Month Return | 0% |
| Avg Daily Volume (past mo.) | 0.35 |

### Quarterly EPS Performance

| Date | IBES Est | Actual | Suprise |
|---|---|---|---|
| 3/98 | (0.67) | (0.78) | **(0.11)** |
| 12/97 | | (0.90) | |

### Annual Fundamentals

| | 12/96 | 12/97 |
|---|---|---|
| Revenue | 6.3 | 17.4 |
| Growth | | 176% |
| Gross Sales | 0.9 | 2.8 |
| Operating Income | (0.8) | (10.6) |
| Net Income | (1.8) | (10.7) |

### Quarterly Fundamentals

| | 6/96 | 9/96 | 12/96 | 3/97 | 6/97 | 9/97 | 12/97 | 3/98 |
|---|---|---|---|---|---|---|---|---|
| Revenue | 1.4 | 1.6 | 2.2 | 2.6 | 3.0 | 3.9 | 7.9 | 10.0 |
| Seq'l Growth | | 20% | 34% | 18% | 15% | 32% | 103% | 26% |
| Y/Y Growth | | | | 119% | 140% | 261% | 288% |
| Gross Sales | 0.2 | 0.2 | 0.4 | 0.5 | 0.6 | 0.7 | 1.1 | 1.5 |
| Operating Income | (0.2) | (0.3) | (0.3) | (0.5) | (1.0) | (2.6) | (6.4) | (9.3) |

| | | | | | | | | | |
|---|---|---|---|---|---|---|---|---|---|
| **Gross Margins** | 14% | 13% | 17% | 21% | 19% | 18% | 14% | 15% | 15% | 16% |
| **Operating Margin** | -12% | -16% | -12% | -21% | -34% | -68% | -81% | -92% | -12% | -61% |
| **Net Margin** | -12% | -16% | -59% | -21% | -34% | -66% | -84% | -92% | -29% | -62% |
| Cash & S-T Invest. | NA | NA | 1.0 | NA | NA | NA | 11.7 | 60.5 | 1.0 | 11.7 |
| L-T Debt | NA | NA | 0.1 | NA | NA | NA | 1.0 | 1.0 | 0.1 | 1.0 |
| StkHldrs Equity | NA | NA | 0.5 | NA | NA | NA | (0.3) | 57.7 | 0.5 | (0.3) |
| Op. Cash Flow | NA | NA | NA | NA | NA | NA | NA | (11.7) | (0.1) | (3.2) |
| **Per Share Data** | | | | | | | | | | |
| Shares Out | NA | NA | 7.85 | NA | NA | NA | 7.85 | 16.01 | 7.85 | 7.85 |
| Net Income | NA | NA | (0.16) | NA | NA | NA | (0.84) | (0.57) | (0.23) | (1.37) |
| Cash & S-T Inv. | NA | NA | 0.13 | NA | NA | NA | 1.49 | 3.78 | 0.13 | 1.49 |
| Book Value | NA | NA | 0.07 | NA | NA | NA | (0.03) | 3.60 | 0.07 | (0.03) |

**Earnings Estimates & Valuation:**

| | IBES EPS | Price Multiple |
|---|---|---|
| Current Yr Est | (2.96) | NM |
| Fwd Yr. Est. | (2.99) | NM |
| Last FY End | 97.12 | |
| # IBES Estimates | 4.00 | |

| | Growth | P/E to LT Growth |
|---|---|---|
| EPS Growth | 1.0% | NM |
| IBES L-T Growth | 86.5% | NM |

**Misc:**

| | |
|---|---|
| Employees | 111 |
| IPO Date | 2/10/98 |
| First Day Close | $22.00 |

### Company Description

CDNW was the Internet's first major retailer of music CDs, cassettes, and related products. The Company provides a complete music catalog and allows customers to order and purchase items on its Internet site online. Visitors to its website can also listen to samples of music, order advance copies of upcoming releases, and read reviews/articles. The Company also sells a wide selection of VHS videos.

Sources: Piper Jaffray Research, FactSet, IBES, Compustat, Company Reports
Figures in millions, except per share amounts

Piper Jaffray Equity Research
Electronic Commerce

## Company Profile:
# CFI PROSERVICES INC

## PROI

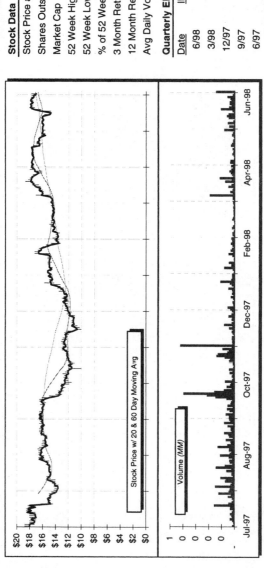

Stock Price w/ 20 & 60 Day Moving Avg

Volume *(MM)*

### Stock Data

|  |  |
|---|---|
| Stock Price as of | 6/30/98 |
| Stock Price as of | $17.00 |
| Shares Outstanding | 5.00 |
| Market Cap | $85 |
| 52 Week High | $18.75 |
| 52 Week Low | $10.00 |
| % of 52 Week High | 91% |
| 3 Month Return | 15% |
| 12 Month Return | -6% |
| Avg Daily Volume (past mo.) | 0.03 |

### Quarterly EPS Performance

| Date | IBES Est | Actual | Suprise |
|---|---|---|---|
| 6/98 | 0.21 | 0.18 | (0.03) |
| 3/98 | 0.17 | 0.19 | 0.02 |
| 12/97 | 0.28 | 0.29 | 0.01 |
| 9/97 | 0.18 | 0.12 | (0.06) |
| 6/97 | 0.27 | 0.28 | 0.01 |

### Annual Fundamentals

|  | 12/96 | 12/97 |
|---|---|---|
| Revenue | 59.9 | 72.6 |
| Growth |  | 21% |
| Gross Sales | 38.1 | 44.3 |
| Operating Income | 9.3 | 8.8 |
| Net Income | 0.1 | 4.7 |

### Quarterly Fundamentals

|  | 9/96 | 12/96 | 3/97 | 6/97 | 9/97 | 12/97 | 3/98 | 6/98 |
|---|---|---|---|---|---|---|---|---|
| Revenue | 16.3 | 17.3 | 16.0 | 17.9 | 17.9 | 20.9 | 19.1 | 19.0 |
| Seq'l Growth |  | 6% | -7% | 12% | 0% | 17% | -9% | 0% |
| Y/Y Growth |  |  |  | 10% | 10% | 21% | 19% | 6% |
| Gross Sales | 10.3 | 10.6 | 10.1 | 11.6 | 10.6 | 12.1 | 12.0 | 11.5 |
| Operating Income | 2.7 | 3.2 | 1.9 | 2.7 | 1.1 | 3.1 | 1.9 | 1.8 |
| Net Income | 1.5 | 1.8 | 0.8 | 1.4 | 0.9 | 1.5 | 1.0 | 1.0 |

| | | | | | | | | | | |
|---|---|---|---|---|---|---|---|---|---|---|
| **Gross Margins** | | | | 65% | 59% | 58% | 63% | 61% | 63% | 61% |
| *Operating Margin* | 16% | 18% | 12% | 15% | 6% | 15% | 10% | 10% | 16% | 12% |
| *Net Margin* | 9% | 10% | 5% | 8% | 5% | 7% | 5% | 5% | 0% | 6% |
| Cash & S-T Invest. | 0.2 | | | 0.1 | 0.0 | 0.7 | | NA | - | 0.0 |
| L-T Debt | 2.8 | 2.7 | 2.6 | 2.3 | 2.2 | 6.1 | | NA | 2.8 | 2.2 |
| StkHldrs Equity | 18.8 | 21.0 | 22.4 | 24.0 | 25.2 | 26.7 | 28.2 | NA | 21.0 | 26.7 |
| Op. Cash Flow | 2.1 | 1.2 | 2.4 | 0.2 | 1.5 | 2.6 | | NA | 10.2 | 5.4 |
| **Per Share Data** | | | | | | | | | | |
| Shares Out | 4.82 | 4.83 | 4.86 | 4.90 | 4.92 | 4.93 | 5.00 | NA | 4.83 | 4.93 |
| Net Income | 0.31 | 0.37 | 0.16 | 0.30 | 0.19 | 0.31 | 0.20 | NA | 0.02 | 0.95 |
| Cash & S-T Inv. | 0.04 | | | 0.02 | 0.00 | 0.14 | | NA | - | 0.00 |
| Book Value | 3.89 | 4.35 | 4.61 | 4.89 | 5.12 | 5.42 | 5.64 | NA | 4.35 | 5.42 |

## Earnings Estimates & Valuation:

| | IBES EPS | Price Multiple |
|---|---|---|
| Current Yr Est | 1.08 | 15.7 |
| Fwd Yr. Est. | 1.31 | 13.0 |
| Last FY End | 97.12 | |
| # IBES Estimates | 3.00 | |

| | Growth | P/E to LT Growth |
|---|---|---|
| EPS Growth | 21.3% | 79% |
| IBES L-T Growth | 20.0% | 65% |

**Misc:**

| | |
|---|---|
| Employees | 530 |
| IPO Date | 8/18/93 |
| First Day Close | $9.50 |

## Company Description

PROI designs and markets software to automate consumer transactions for financial institutions. Its main products simplifies the lending process for loan officers (LaserPro) and helps bank employees and customers access account information online (Encore). Other services include administrative offerings such as remittance processing. The Company has sizeable internal development efforts, but has also acquired ten software companies since it went public in 1993. It now has around 5,000 financial institution customers

Sources: Piper Jaffray Research, FactSet, IBES, Compustat, Company Reports

Figures in millions, except per share amounts

Piper Jaffray Equity Research
Electronic Commerce

## Company Profile:
# CHECKFREE HOLDINGS CORP

## CKFR

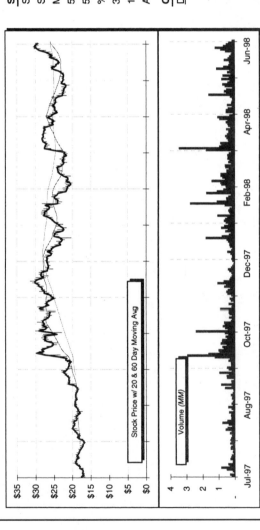

Stock Price w/ 20 & 60 Day Moving Avg

Volume (MM)

**Stock Data**

| | 6/30/98 |
|---|---|
| Stock Price as of | $29.44 |
| Shares Outstanding | 55.36 |
| Market Cap | $1,630 |
| 52 Week High | $31.44 |
| 52 Week Low | $16.50 |
| % of 52 Week High | 94% |
| 3 Month Return | 33% |
| 12 Month Return | 67% |
| Avg Daily Volume (past mo.) | 0.51 |

**Quarterly EPS Performance**

| Date | IBES Est | Actual | Suprise |
|---|---|---|---|
| 3/98 | | | - |
| 12/97 | (0.05) | (0.03) | 0.02 |
| 9/97 | (0.07) | (0.06) | 0.01 |
| 6/97 | (0.09) | (0.11) | (0.02) |
| 3/97 | (0.13) | (0.10) | 0.03 |

**Annual Fundamentals**

| | 6/96 | 6/97 |
|---|---|---|
| Revenue | 76.8 | 176.4 |
| Growth | | 130% |
| Gross Sales | 19.6 | 50.5 |
| Operating Income | (27.4) | (41.4) |
| Net Income | (138.9) | (161.8) |

**Quarterly Fundamentals**

| | 6/96 | 9/96 | 12/96 | 3/97 | 6/97 | 9/97 | 12/97 | 3/98 |
|---|---|---|---|---|---|---|---|---|
| Revenue | 29.4 | 32.7 | 38.5 | 50.2 | 55.1 | 52.1 | 56.5 | 61.8 |
| Seq'l Growth | | 11% | 18% | 30% | 10% | -5% | 9% | 9% |
| Y/Y Growth | | | | | 88% | 59% | 47% | 23% |
| Gross Sales | 1.2 | 5.3 | 9.1 | 10.1 | 18.3 | 12.8 | 19.7 | 21.3 |
| Operating Income | (18.3) | (12.3) | (8.7) | (11.2) | (9.2) | (8.2) | (2.1) | 0.0 |
| Net Income | | | | | | | | (17.5) |

| | | | | | | | | | |
|---|---|---|---|---|---|---|---|---|---|
| Gross Margins | 4% | 16% | 24% | 33% | 24% | 35% | 34% | 26% | 29% |
| Operating Margin | -62% | -38% | -23% | -17% | -16% | -4% | 0% | -36% | -29% |
| Net Margin | NM | -24% | -14% | -11% | 19% | -3% | -28% | NM | -92% |
| | | | | | | | | | |
| Cash & S-T Invest. | 39.1 | 28.0 | 40.3 | 36.5 | 64.0 | 61.3 | 64.0 | 39.1 | 36.5 |
| L-T Debt | 8.3 | 7.8 | 8.2 | 8.4 | 8.2 | 8.0 | 6.7 | 8.3 | 8.4 |
| Stk-Hldrs Equity | 137.7 | 130.1 | 119.6 | 148.6 | 161.2 | 160.9 | 177.3 | 137.7 | 148.6 |
| Op. Cash Flow | NA | (8.6) | 2.6 | (3.7) | (3.3) | 4.0 | 8.2 | NA | (7.8) |
| **Per Share Data** | | | | | | | | | |
| Shares Out | 41.52 | 41.71 | 41.51 | 54.51 | 54.77 | 55.06 | 55.36 | 41.52 | 54.51 |
| Net Income | (0.99) | (0.19) | (0.13) | (0.11) | 0.18 | (0.03) | (0.32) | (3.34) | (2.97) |
| Cash & S-T Inv. | 0.94 | 0.67 | 0.97 | 0.67 | 1.17 | 1.11 | 0.94 | 0.94 | 0.67 |
| Book Value | 3.32 | 3.12 | 2.88 | 2.73 | 2.94 | 2.92 | 3.20 | 3.32 | 2.73 |

## Earnings Estimates & Valuation:

| | IBES EPS | Price Multiple |
|---|---|---|
| Current Yr Est | (0.05) | NM |
| Fwd Yr. Est. | 0.31 | 95.0 |
| Last FY End | 97.06 | |
| # IBES Estimates | 13.00 | |

| | Growth | P/E to LT Growth |
|---|---|---|
| EPS Growth | -720.0% | NM |
| IBES L-T Growth | 43.3% | 219% |

**Misc:**

| | |
|---|---|
| Employees | 1,444 |
| IPO Date | 9/28/95 |
| First Day Close | $21.50 |

## Company Description

CKFR provides solutions that allow consumers and businesses to electronically manage regular payments and collections. It is best known as the leading provider of bill payment and presentment services to consumers on behalf of banks. The Company claims over 2 million consumers, 1,000 businesses, and 850 financial institutions as customers.

Sources: Piper Jaffray Equity Research, FactSet, IBES, Compustat, Company Reports
Figures in millions, except per share amounts

Piper Jaffray Equity Research
Electronic Commerce

# Company Profile:
# CHECK POINT SOFTWARE TECHN

## CHKPF

### Stock Data

| | |
|---|---|
| Stock Price as of | **6/30/98** | $32.75 |
| Shares Outstanding | | 33.16 |
| Market Cap | | $1,086 |
| 52 Week High | | $50.50 |
| 52 Week Low | | $21.75 |
| % of 52 Week High | | 65% |
| 3 Month Return | | -28% |
| 12 Month Return | | 40% |
| Avg Daily Volume (past mo.) | | 0.87 |

### Quarterly EPS Performance

| Date | IBES Est | Actual | Suprise |
|---|---|---|---|
| 6/98 | 0.36 | 0.43 | **0.07** |
| 3/98 | 0.32 | 0.41 | **0.09** |
| 12/97 | 0.30 | 0.37 | **0.07** |
| 9/97 | 0.19 | 0.32 | **0.13** |
| 6/97 | 0.17 | 0.21 | **0.04** |

### Annual Fundamentals

| | 12/95 | 12/96 |
|---|---|---|
| Revenue | 9.5 | 31.9 |
| Growth | | 234% |
| Gross Sales | 9.0 | 29.9 |
| Operating Income | 4.9 | 14.1 |
| Net Income | 4.8 | 15.2 |

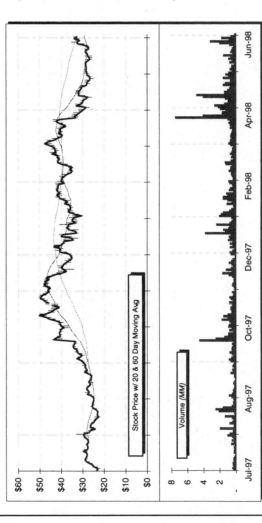

Stock Price w/ 20 & 60 Day Moving Avg

Volume (MM)

### Quarterly Fundamentals

| | 6/96 | 9/96 | 12/96 | 3/97 | 6/97 | 9/97 | 12/97 | 3/98 |
|---|---|---|---|---|---|---|---|---|
| Revenue | 7.4 | 8.0 | 11.6 | 13.7 | 17.3 | 22.4 | 29.6 | 30.9 |
| Seq'l Growth | | 9% | 45% | 18% | 26% | 30% | 32% | 4% |
| Y/Y Growth | | | | 134% | 134% | 179% | 155% | 125% |
| Gross Sales | 7.0 | 7.4 | 10.9 | 12.7 | 16.0 | 20.7 | 27.5 | 28.3 |
| Operating Income | 3.2 | 3.3 | 4.9 | 6.1 | 7.6 | 11.4 | 13.6 | 15.2 |
| Net Income | | | | | 7.7 | 12.0 | 14.1 | 15.5 |

| | | | | | | | | | | |
|---|---|---|---|---|---|---|---|---|---|---|
| **Gross Margins** | 94% | 92% | 94% | 93% | 92% | 92% | 93% | 92% | **Gross Margins** 94% | 94% |
| **Operating Margin** | 43% | 41% | 42% | 45% | 44% | 51% | 46% | 49% | **Operating Margin** 51% | 44% |
| **Net Margin** | 44% | 47% | 47% | 47% | 45% | 53% | 48% | 50% | **Net Margin** 51% | 48% |
| Cash & S-T Invest. | 8.3 | 49.7 | 54.5 | 62.7 | 71.9 | 67.4 | 65.2 | 70.6 | Cash & S-T Invest. 3.6 | 54.5 |
| L-T Debt | - | - | - | - | - | - | - | - | L-T Debt - | - |
| StkHldrs Equity | 11.1 | 52.1 | 57.6 | 64.1 | 72.3 | 84.9 | 100.2 | 117.1 | StkHldrs Equity 5.0 | 57.6 |
| Op. Cash Flow | NA | NA | NA | NA | NA | NA | NA | NA | Op. Cash Flow 4.3 | 14.8 |
| **Per Share Data** | | | | | | | | | **Per Share Data** | |
| Shares Out | NA | NA | 32.74 | NA | NA | NA | NA | NA | Shares Out 29.70 | 32.74 |
| Net Income | NA | NA | 0.17 | NA | NA | NA | NA | NA | Net Income 0.16 | 0.47 |
| Cash & S-T Inv. | NA | NA | 1.66 | NA | NA | NA | NA | NA | Cash & S-T Inv. 0.12 | 1.66 |
| Book Value | NA | NA | 1.76 | NA | NA | NA | NA | NA | Book Value 0.17 | 1.76 |

## Earnings Estimates & Valuation:

| | IBES EPS | Price Multiple |
|---|---|---|
| Current Yr Est | 1.07 | **30.6** |
| Fwd Yr. Est. | 1.58 | **20.7** |
| Last FY End | 96.12 | |
| # IBES Estimates | NA | |

| | Growth | P/E to LT Growth |
|---|---|---|
| EPS Growth | 47.7% | **78%** |
| IBES L-T Growth | 39.1% | **53%** |

Misc:

| | |
|---|---|
| Employees | 46 |
| IPO Date | 6/28/96 |
| First Day Close | $24.00 |

## Company Description

CHKPF is an Israeli based developer of FireWall-1, the #1 firewall on the market which is available for Unix and NT platforms. The Company's other enterprise security solutions include encryption software for servers and clients, which enable virtual private networks (VPNs). The Company also provides security management software as well as tools to manage bandwith and provide load balancing on networks. The Company also founded the OPSEC alliance in an attempt to encourage interoperability with other vendors.

Sources: Piper Jaffray Research, FactSet, IBES, Compustat, Company Reports
Figures in millions, except per share amounts

Piper Jaffray Equity Research
Electronic Commerce

# Company Profile:
# CONCORD EFS INC

## CEFT

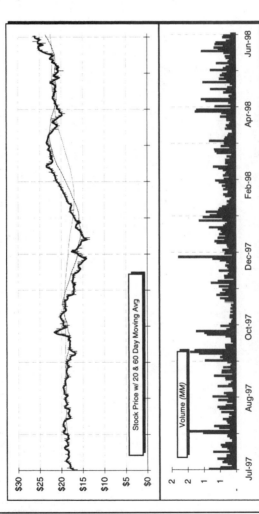

Stock Price w/ 20 & 60 Day Moving Avg

Volume (MM)

**Stock Data**

| | |
|---|---|
| Stock Price as of | **6/30/98** $26.13 |
| Shares Outstanding | 93.11 |
| Market Cap | $2,432 |
| 52 Week High | $26.50 |
| 52 Week Low | $13.33 |
| % of 52 Week High | 99% |
| 3 Month Return | 13% |
| 12 Month Return | 51% |
| Avg Daily Volume (past mo.) | 0.42 |

**Quarterly EPS Performance**

| Date | IBES Est | Actual | Suprise |
|---|---|---|---|
| 3/98 | 0.12 | 0.12 | - |
| 12/97 | 0.14 | 0.14 | - |
| 9/97 | 0.12 | 0.12 | - |
| 6/97 | 0.11 | 0.11 | - |
| 3/97 | 0.08 | 0.09 | **0.01** |

**Annual Fundamentals**

| | 12/96 | 12/97 |
|---|---|---|
| Revenue | 166.7 | 240.0 |
| Growth | | 44% |
| Gross Sales | 47.0 | 64.0 |
| Operating Income | 37.3 | 55.6 |
| Net Income | 26.8 | 42.7 |

**Quarterly Fundamentals**

| | 6/96 | 9/96 | 12/96 | 3/97 | 6/97 | 9/97 | 12/97 | 3/98 |
|---|---|---|---|---|---|---|---|---|
| Revenue | 40.9 | 44.1 | 47.9 | 47.0 | 56.8 | 64.7 | 71.5 | 69.6 |
| Seq'l Growth | | 8% | 9% | -2% | 21% | 14% | 10% | -3% |
| Y/Y Growth | | | | | 39% | 47% | 49% | 48% |
| Gross Sales | 12.4 | 12.3 | 13.0 | 12.1 | 15.2 | 16.9 | 19.8 | 16.7 |
| Operating Income | 9.1 | 10.2 | 11.4 | 10.1 | 13.3 | 14.7 | 17.5 | 14.1 |
| Net Income | 6.3 | 7.1 | 8.7 | 7.9 | 10.1 | 11.4 | 13.3 | 11.4 |

## Financial Summary

| | | | | | | | | | | |
|---|---|---|---|---|---|---|---|---|---|---|
| Gross Margins | | 24% | 28% | 20% | 26% | 26% | 28% | 24% | **28%** | **27%** |
| Operating Margin | 22% | 23% | 24% | 21% | 23% | 23% | 24% | 20% | **22%** | **23%** |
| Net Margin | 15% | 16% | 18% | 17% | 18% | 18% | 19% | 16% | **16%** | **18%** |
| | | | | | | | | | | |
| Cash & S-T Invest. | 60.6 | 98.3 | 159.5 | 186.2 | 199.7 | 176.4 | 198.7 | 220.3 | **159.5** | **198.7** |
| L-T Debt | 0.8 | 0.7 | 0.6 | 0.5 | 18.3 | 18.2 | 28.3 | 54.3 | **0.6** | **28.3** |
| StkHldrs Equity | 106.1 | 117.1 | 215.1 | 222.8 | 237.8 | 256.0 | 271.1 | 284.8 | **215.1** | **271.1** |
| Op. Cash Flow | 1.2 | 48.1 | 21.5 | 31.0 | (2.4) | (18.3) | 17.5 | 8.9 | **80.0** | **27.8** |
| **Per Share Data** | | | | | | | | | | |
| Shares Out | 84.97 | 85.88 | 91.23 | 91.25 | 91.88 | 92.56 | 92.97 | 93.11 | **91.23** | **92.97** |
| Net Income | 0.07 | 0.08 | 0.10 | 0.09 | 0.11 | 0.12 | 0.14 | 0.12 | **0.29** | **0.46** |
| Cash & S-T Inv. | 0.71 | 1.14 | 1.75 | 2.04 | 2.17 | 1.91 | 2.14 | 2.37 | **1.75** | **2.14** |
| Book Value | 1.25 | 1.36 | 2.36 | 2.44 | 2.59 | 2.77 | 2.92 | 3.06 | **2.36** | **2.92** |

## Earnings Estimates & Valuation:

| | IBES EPS | Price Multiple |
|---|---|---|
| Current Yr Est | 0.65 | **40.2** |
| Fwd Yr. Est. | 0.86 | **30.4** |
| Last FY End | 97.12 | |
| # IBES Estimates | 6.00 | |

| | Growth | P/E to LT Growth |
|---|---|---|
| EPS Growth | 32.3% | **126%** |
| IBES L-T Growth | 31.8% | **96%** |

**Misc:**

| | |
|---|---|
| Employees | 592 |
| IPO Date | 11/5/84 |
| First Day Close | $0.17 |

## Company Description

CEFT's main business is processing credit, debit, and benefit card transactions primarily for small retail merchants such as grocery stores and convenience stores. CEFT has its own ATM network and provides payment services to trucking companies and drivers including fuel purchase cards, cash advances, and payroll processing. The company also makes hardware devices such as ATMs, electronic payment and verification terminals. A unique characteristic of this third party processor is that it owns a bank, which offers no traditional banking services, but instead acts as a central transaction hub for its processing activities.

Sources: Piper Jaffray Research, FactSet, IBES, Compustat, Company Reports

Figures in millions, except per share amounts

Piper Jaffray Equity Research
Electronic Commerce

# Company Profile:
## CONNECT INC

## CNKT

### Stock Data

| | | |
|---|---|---|
| Stock Price as of | 6/30/98 | $2.06 |
| Shares Outstanding | | 12.87 |
| Market Cap | | $27 |
| 52 Week High | | $15.00 |
| 52 Week Low | | $0.88 |
| % of 52 Week High | | 14% |
| 3 Month Return | | 32% |
| 12 Month Return | | -85% |
| Avg Daily Volume (past mo.) | | 0.20 |

### Quarterly EPS Performance

| Date | IBES Est | Actual | Suprise |
|---|---|---|---|
| 6/98 | (0.17) | (0.15) | 0.02 |
| 3/98 | (0.80) | (0.73) | 0.07 |
| 12/97 | (0.55) | (0.80) | (0.25) |
| 9/97 | (0.65) | (0.85) | (0.20) |
| 6/97 | (0.95) | (0.85) | 0.10 |

### Annual Fundamentals

| | 12/96 | 12/97 |
|---|---|---|
| Revenue | 10.2 | 9.4 |
| Growth | | -8% |
| Gross Sales | 1.1 | 0.3 |
| Operating Income | (16.4) | (14.5) |
| Net Income | (16.1) | (14.6) |

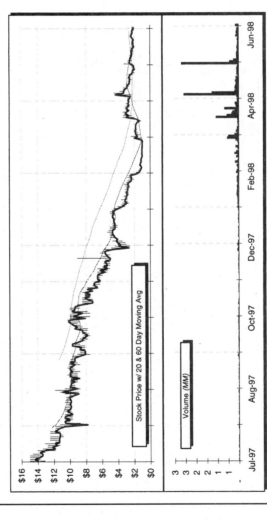

Stock Price w/ 20 & 60 Day Moving Avg

Volume (MM)

Jul-97  Aug-97  Oct-97  Dec-97  Feb-98  Apr-98  Jun-98

### Quarterly Fundamentals

| | 9/96 | 12/96 | 3/97 | 6/97 | 9/97 | 12/97 | 3/98 | 6/98 |
|---|---|---|---|---|---|---|---|---|
| Revenue | 2.9 | 3.3 | 1.9 | 3.2 | 2.0 | 2.3 | 2.3 | 1.7 |
| Seq'l Growth | | 11% | -42% | 69% | -36% | 12% | -1% | -25% |
| Y/Y Growth | | | | | -31% | -30% | 19% | -47% |
| Gross Sales | 0.6 | 1.1 | (1.0) | 0.8 | 0.1 | 0.3 | 0.7 | 0.5 |
| Operating Income | (4.1) | (3.1) | (5.2) | (3.2) | (3.1) | (2.9) | (2.8) | (2.0) |

## Margins

| | | | | | | | | | | |
|---|---|---|---|---|---|---|---|---|---|---|
| Gross Margins | | | | | | | | | 11% | 3% |
| Operating Margin | NM | -97% | NM | NM | NM | NM | NM | NM | NM | NM |
| Net Margin | NM | -94% | NM | -99% | NM | NM | NM | NM | NM | NM |

| | | | | | | | | | | |
|---|---|---|---|---|---|---|---|---|---|---|
| Cash & S-T Invest. | 17.0 | 12.2 | 8.9 | 5.6 | 2.9 | 9.6 | 7.6 | NA | 12.2 | 9.6 |
| L-T Debt | 1.0 | 0.8 | 1.6 | 1.5 | 1.3 | 10.6 | 0.7 | NA | 0.8 | 10.6 |
| StkHldrs Equity | 16.6 | 13.4 | 8.5 | 5.4 | 2.4 | (0.6) | 6.0 | NA | 13.4 | (0.6) |
| Op. Cash Flow | (3.2) | (3.9) | (4.6) | (3.3) | (2.6) | (2.5) | (1.5) | NA | (14.0) | (12.9) |

**Per Share Data**

| | | | | | | | | | | |
|---|---|---|---|---|---|---|---|---|---|---|
| Shares Out | 3.71 | 3.71 | 3.75 | 3.79 | 3.81 | 3.83 | 4.77 | NA | 3.71 | 3.83 |
| Net Income | (1.07) | (0.82) | (1.39) | (0.83) | (0.83) | (0.80) | (0.62) | NA | (4.36) | (3.81) |
| Cash & S-T Inv. | 4.59 | 3.30 | 2.39 | 1.47 | 0.75 | 2.52 | 1.59 | NA | 3.30 | 2.52 |
| Book Value | 4.48 | 3.60 | 2.26 | 1.43 | 0.63 | (0.17) | 1.26 | NA | 3.60 | (0.17) |

## Earnings Estimates & Valuation:

| | IBES EPS | Price Multiple |
|---|---|---|
| Current Yr Est | (0.57) | NM |
| Fwd Yr. Est. | 0.10 | 20.6 |
| Last FY End | 97.12 | |
| # IBES Estimates | 1.00 | |

| | Growth | P/E to LT Growth |
|---|---|---|
| EPS Growth | -117.5% | NM |
| IBES L-T Growth | NA | NM |

**Misc:**

| | |
|---|---|
| Employees | 93 |
| IPO Date | 8/15/96 |
| First Day Close | $30.00 |

## Company Description

CNKT is a developer of systems that enable the sale of products and services over the Internet. Its core product, OneServer, is software that allows businesses to establish web storefronts with the ability to deliver an interactive catalog, establish customer specific promotions, manage pricing and product information, and securely capture order information. CNKT's OrderStream is a business-to-business version of OneServer for selected vertical markets with additional flexibility in cataloging, searching, and sales and order management.

Sources: Piper Jaffray Research, FactSet, IBES, Compustat, Company Reports
Figures in millions, except per share amounts

Piper Jaffray Equity Research
Electronic Commerce

## Company Profile:
# CYBERGUARD CORP

# CYBG

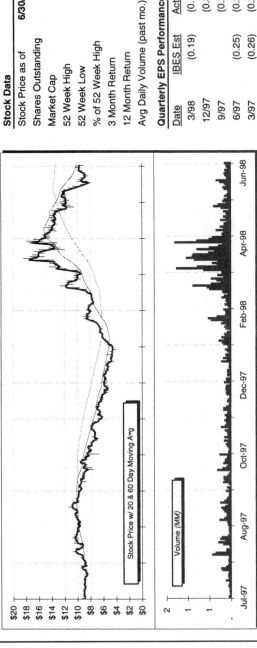

Stock Price w/ 20 & 60 Day Moving Avg

Volume (MM)

| | Jul-97 | Aug-97 | Oct-97 | Dec-97 | Feb-98 | Apr-98 | Jun-98 |

### Stock Data

| | | |
|---|---|---|
| Stock Price as of | 6/30/98 | $9.63 |
| Shares Outstanding | | 8.78 |
| Market Cap | | $84 |
| 52 Week High | | $18.38 |
| 52 Week Low | | $4.00 |
| % of 52 Week High | | 52% |
| 3 Month Return | | 1% |
| 12 Month Return | | 8% |
| Avg Daily Volume (past mo.) | | 0.13 |

### Quarterly EPS Performance

| Date | IBES Est | Actual | Suprise |
|---|---|---|---|
| 3/98 | (0.19) | (0.19) | - |
| 12/97 | | (0.32) | |
| 9/97 | | (0.22) | |
| 6/97 | (0.25) | (0.26) | (0.01) |
| 3/97 | (0.26) | (0.23) | 0.03 |

### Annual Fundamentals

| | 6/96 | 6/97 |
|---|---|---|
| Revenue | 37.4 | 15.6 |
| Growth | | -58% |
| Gross Sales | 16.4 | 8.4 |
| Operating Income | (7.0) | (7.8) |
| Net Income | (26.1) | (12.5) |

### Quarterly Fundamentals

| | 6/96 | 9/96 | 12/96 | 3/97 | 6/97 | 9/97 | 12/97 | 3/98 |
|---|---|---|---|---|---|---|---|---|
| Revenue | 11.8 | 3.1 | 3.0 | 4.1 | 5.4 | 5.1 | 4.9 | 5.2 |
| Seq'l Growth | | -74% | -1% | 35% | 32% | -6% | -4% | 6% |
| Y/Y Growth | | | | | -54% | 65% | 59% | 26% |
| Gross Sales | 4.9 | 1.2 | 1.5 | 2.2 | 3.4 | 3.3 | 3.0 | 3.4 |
| Operating Income | 4.9 | (2.2) | (2.0) | (1.6) | (1.9) | (2.2) | (2.8) | (1.7) |
| Net Income | (7.0) | (2.2) | (0.8) | (0.9) | (2.5) | (1.7) | (2.6) | (1.6) |

| | | | | | | | | |
|---|---|---|---|---|---|---|---|---|
| *Operating Margin* | 41% | -72% | -66% | -40% | -35% | -43% | -57% | -32% |
| *Net Margin* | NM | NM | -27% | -22% | -47% | -34% | -54% | -32% |
| Cash & S-T Invest. | 17.2 | 10.0 | 9.4 | 7.8 | 4.2 | 6.3 | 4.9 | 4.4 |
| L-T Debt | - | - | - | - | - | - | 0.7 | 0.7 |
| StkHldrs Equity | 18.2 | 11.8 | 12.2 | 11.9 | 9.9 | 12.2 | 10.9 | 11.8 |
| Op. Cash Flow | NA | (1.8) | (2.6) | (2.9) | (3.1) | (2.0) | (3.3) | (2.8) |
| **Per Share Data** | | | | | | | | |
| Shares Out | 6.71 | 7.00 | 7.39 | 7.38 | 7.45 | 8.03 | 8.23 | 8.76 |
| Net Income | (4.14) | (1.18) | (0.11) | (0.12) | (0.34) | (0.21) | (0.32) | (0.19) |
| Cash & S-T Inv. | 2.57 | 1.42 | 1.28 | 1.05 | 0.57 | 0.79 | 0.60 | 0.50 |
| Book Value | 2.72 | 1.69 | 1.65 | 1.61 | 1.33 | 1.52 | 1.32 | 1.35 |

| | | |
|---|---|---|
| *Operating Margin* | -19% | -50% |
| *Net Margin* | -70% | -80% |
| Cash & S-T Invest. | 17.2 | 4.2 |
| L-T Debt | - | - |
| StkHldrs Equity | 18.2 | 9.9 |
| Op. Cash Flow | (5.5) | (10.3) |
| **Per Share Data** | | |
| Shares Out | 6.71 | 7.45 |
| Net Income | (3.89) | (1.68) |
| Cash & S-T Inv. | 2.57 | 0.57 |
| Book Value | 2.72 | 1.33 |

**Earnings Estimates & Valuation:**

| | IBES EPS | Price Multiple |
|---|---|---|
| Current Yr Est | (0.75) | NM |
| Fwd Yr. Est. | 0.70 | 13.8 |
| Last FY End | 97.06 | |
| # IBES Estimates | 1.00 | |

| | Growth | P/E to LT Growth |
|---|---|---|
| EPS Growth | -193.3% | NM |
| IBES L-T Growth | NA | NM |

Misc:
| | |
|---|---|
| Employees | 97 |
| IPO Date | 10/6/94 |
| First Day Close | $2.46 |

## Company Description

CYBG is principally a developer of traditional firewall solutions that have been expanded to include functionality such as central management, user authentication, and secure remote management. In April 1997, the Company acquired TradeWave. TradeWave developed both certificate authority services and virtual private network (VPN) solutions. Over 50% CYBG's revenues are generated outside the U.S. The Company's future is somewhat uncertain as it hired an advisor to examine strategic options late in 1997.

Sources: Piper Jaffray Research, FactSet, IBES, Compustat, Company Reports
Figures in millions, except per share amounts

Piper Jaffray Equity Research
Electronic Commerce

# Company Profile:
# CYBERCASH INC

## CYCH

### Stock Data

| | | |
|---|---|---|
| Stock Price as of | 6/30/98 | $12.19 |
| Shares Outstanding | | 12.75 |
| Market Cap | | $155 |
| 52 Week High | | $27.75 |
| 52 Week Low | | $10.13 |
| % of 52 Week High | | 44% |
| 3 Month Return | | -25% |
| 12 Month Return | | 8% |
| Avg Daily Volume (past mo.) | | 0.26 |

### Quarterly EPS Performance

| Date | IBES Est | Actual | Suprise |
|---|---|---|---|
| 3/98 | (0.49) | (0.53) | **(0.04)** |
| 12/97 | (0.48) | (0.49) | **(0.01)** |
| 9/97 | (0.52) | (0.51) | **0.01** |
| 6/97 | (0.63) | (0.58) | **0.05** |
| 3/97 | | (0.83) | |

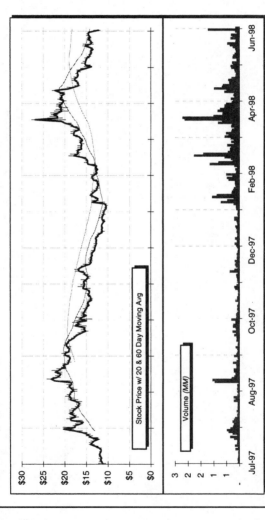

### Annual Fundamentals

| | 12/96 | 12/97 |
|---|---|---|
| Revenue | 0.1 | 4.5 |
| *Growth* | | *NA* |
| Gross Sales | (2.1) | 0.8 |
| Operating Income | (28.8) | (24.3) |
| Net Income | (26.6) | (26.2) |

### Quarterly Fundamentals

| | 6/96 | 9/96 | 12/96 | 3/97 | 6/97 | 9/97 | 12/97 | 3/98 |
|---|---|---|---|---|---|---|---|---|
| Revenue | 0.0 | 0.0 | 0.1 | 0.2 | 0.8 | 1.5 | 2.0 | 1.1 |
| *Seq'l Growth* | | *144%* | *28%* | *210%* | *425%* | *86%* | *32%* | *-43%* |
| *Y/Y Growth* | | | | | *4981%* | *3782%* | *3910%* | *637%* |
| Gross Sales | (6.9) | (8.3) | (8.6) | (7.1) | (6.6) | (6.0) | (4.6) | 0.0 |
| Operating Income | (6.9) | (8.3) | (8.6) | (7.1) | (6.6) | (6.0) | (4.6) | (6.3) |

| | Operating Margin | | | | | | | | Operating Margin | |
| | Net Margin | | | | | | | | Net Margin | |
| | NM | NM | NM | NM | NM | NM | NM | NM | NM | NM |
| | NM | NM | NM | NM | NM | NM | NM | NM | NM | NM |
| Cash & S-T Invest. | 51.5 | 43.0 | 33.9 | 26.6 | 19.8 | 29.6 | 22.3 | 31.6 | 33.9 | 22.3 |
| L-T Debt | - | - | - | - | - | - | - | - | - | - |
| StkHldrs Equity | 52.6 | 45.4 | 38.1 | 31.3 | 25.4 | 34.5 | 29.6 | 38.7 | 38.1 | 29.6 |
| Op. Cash Flow | (5.8) | (7.9) | (8.6) | (6.9) | (7.0) | (4.7) | (5.6) | (3.6) | (25.4) | (24.2) |
| **Per Share Data** | | | | | | | | | | |
| Shares Out | 10.63 | 10.66 | 10.69 | 10.84 | 10.90 | 11.03 | 11.06 | 12.22 | 10.71 | 11.06 |
| Net Income | (0.59) | (0.72) | (0.75) | (0.85) | (0.58) | (0.50) | (0.46) | (0.46) | (2.48) | (2.37) |
| Cash & S-T Inv. | 4.84 | 4.03 | 3.17 | 2.46 | 1.82 | 2.68 | 2.01 | 2.59 | 3.17 | 2.01 |
| Book Value | 4.95 | 4.26 | 3.56 | 2.89 | 2.33 | 3.13 | 2.68 | 3.17 | 3.56 | 2.68 |

**Earnings Estimates & Valuation:**

| | IBES EPS | Price Multiple |
|---|---|---|
| Current Yr Est | (1.54) | NM |
| Fwd Yr. Est. | (0.66) | NM |
| Last FY End | 97.12 | |
| # IBES Estimates | 5.00 | |

| | Growth | P/E to LT Growth |
|---|---|---|
| EPS Growth | -57.1% | NM |
| IBES L-T Growth | 100.0% | NM |

Misc:

| | |
|---|---|
| Employees | 227 |
| IPO Date | 2/15/96 |
| First Day Close | $28.25 |

## Company Description

CYCH is a leading provider of secure Internet payment services. It provides solutions that support credit card, micro-payment, and electronic checks as forms of payment. More recently it has developed a solution to allow billers to present bills on their own websites and electronically receive payment. CYCH recently merged with PC software payment provider IC Verify.

Sources: Piper Jaffray Research, FactSet, IBES, Compustat, Company Reports
Figures in millions, except per share amounts

Piper Jaffray Equity Research
Electronic Commerce

# Company Profile:
# CYLINK CORP

## CYLK

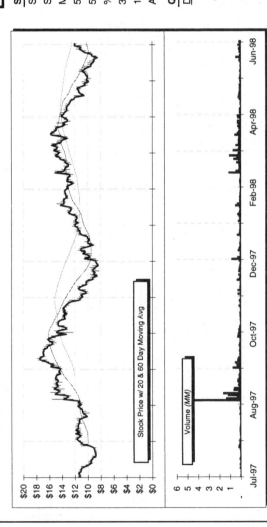

Stock Price w/ 20 & 60 Day Moving Avg

Volume (MM)

### Stock Data

| | |
|---|---|
| Stock Price as of | 6/30/98 | $12.00 |
| Shares Outstanding | | 28.98 |
| Market Cap | | $348 |
| 52 Week High | | $17.88 |
| 52 Week Low | | $8.25 |
| % of 52 Week High | | 67% |
| 3 Month Return | | -17% |
| 12 Month Return | | 5% |
| Avg Daily Volume (past mo.) | | 0.12 |

### Quarterly EPS Performance

| Date | IBES Est | Actual | Suprise |
|---|---|---|---|
| 3/98 | 0.05 | 0.04 | (0.01) |
| 12/97 | 0.05 | 0.05 | - |
| 9/97 | 0.06 | 0.04 | (0.02) |
| 6/97 | 0.05 | 0.05 | - |
| 3/97 | 0.05 | 0.04 | (0.01) |

### Annual Fundamentals

| | 12/96 | 12/97 |
|---|---|---|
| Revenue | 52.0 | 49.3 |
| Growth | | -5% |
| Gross Sales | 30.2 | 34.5 |
| Operating Income | (1.1) | (2.4) |
| Net Income | 1.2 | (58.8) |

### Quarterly Fundamentals

| | 6/96 | 9/96 | 12/96 | 3/97 | 6/97 | 9/97 | 12/97 | 3/98 |
|---|---|---|---|---|---|---|---|---|
| Revenue | 5.6 | 7.5 | 8.5 | 9.4 | 11.6 | 13.1 | 15.3 | 15.8 |
| Seq'l Growth | | 33% | 13% | 11% | 24% | 13% | 16% | 4% |
| Y/Y Growth | | | | | 106% | 75% | 81% | 69% |
| Gross Sales | 5.2 | 7.2 | 8.1 | 9.0 | 11.6 | 13.1 | 15.3 | 14.8 |
| Operating Income | 5.2 | 7.2 | 8.1 | 9.0 | 11.6 | 13.1 | 15.3 | 14.8 |
| | (.6) | (0.4) | (1.2) | (0.1) | 0.3 | (63.7) | 0.2 | 1.7 |

| | | | | | | | | | | |
|---|---|---|---|---|---|---|---|---|---|---|
| Gross Margins | 92% | 96% | 96% | 96% | 100% | 100% | 100% | 94% | 58% | 70% |
| Operating Margin | -28% | -6% | -15% | -1% | 2% | NM | 1% | 11% | -2% | -5% |
| Net Margin | | | | | | | | | 2% | NM |
| Cash & S-T Invest. | 81.9 | 79.4 | 78.8 | 73.4 | 69.0 | 25.1 | 23.0 | 58.1 | 78.8 | 23.0 |
| L-T Debt | 0.3 | 0.3 | 0.2 | 0.2 | 0.2 | 0.3 | 0.3 | 0.2 | 0.2 | 0.3 |
| StkHldrs Equity | 93.1 | 95.4 | 97.2 | 98.7 | 100.4 | 67.2 | 69.1 | 94.3 | 97.2 | 69.1 |
| Op. Cash Flow | (1.3) | (2.6) | (0.4) | (1.3) | (3.8) | 1.1 | (0.7) | (7.1) | (4.3) | (4.6) |

**Per Share Data**

| | | | | | | | | | | |
|---|---|---|---|---|---|---|---|---|---|---|
| Shares Out | 24.90 | 25.45 | 25.60 | 25.82 | 25.95 | 28.63 | 28.70 | 28.89 | 25.60 | 28.70 |
| Net Income | (0.06) | (0.02) | (0.05) | (0.00) | 0.01 | (2.22) | 0.01 | 0.06 | 0.05 | (2.05) |
| Cash & S-T Inv. | 3.29 | 3.12 | 3.08 | 2.84 | 2.66 | 0.88 | 0.80 | 2.01 | 3.08 | 0.80 |
| Book Value | 3.74 | 3.75 | 3.80 | 3.82 | 3.87 | 2.35 | 2.41 | 3.27 | 3.80 | 2.41 |

## Earnings Estimates & Valuation:

| | IBES EPS | Price Multiple |
|---|---|---|
| Current Yr Est | 0.33 | 36.4 |
| Fwd Yr. Est. | 0.64 | 18.8 |
| Last FY End | 97.12 | |
| # IBES Estimates | 7.00 | |

| | Growth | P/E to LT Growth |
|---|---|---|
| EPS Growth | 93.9% | 83% |
| IBES L-T Growth | 44.0% | 43% |

### Misc:

| | |
|---|---|
| Employees | 432 |
| IPO Date | 2/16/96 |
| First Day Close | $22.50 |

## Company Description

CYLK has been traditionally strong in link encryption products, though it is expanding its offerings to include security management and virtual private networks (VPNs). In 9/97 it acquired Israel based Algorithmic Research, which develops cryptographic solutions for data encryption and authentication, as well as certificate authority solutions. This union resulted in the successful launch of PrivateWire, a smart card based remote access solution. CYLK's primary customers are large financial institutions, telcos, and government agencies.

Sources: Piper Jaffray Research, FactSet, IBES, Compustat, Company Reports
Figures in millions, except per share amounts

Piper Jaffray Equity Research
Electronic Commerce

# Company Profile:

## EDIFY CORP

## EDFY

### Stock Data

| | |
|---|---|
| Stock Price as of 6/30/98 | $10.13 |
| Shares Outstanding | 16.93 |
| Market Cap | $171 |
| 52 Week High | $22.13 |
| 52 Week Low | $8.06 |
| % of 52 Week High | 46% |
| 3 Month Return | -50% |
| 12 Month Return | -31% |
| Avg Daily Volume (past mo.) | 0.16 |

### Quarterly EPS Performance

| Date | IBES Est | Actual | Suprise |
|---|---|---|---|
| 3/98 | (0.10) | (0.09) | 0.01 |
| 12/97 | 0.05 | 0.08 | 0.03 |
| 9/97 | 0.04 | 0.06 | 0.02 |
| 6/97 | 0.02 | 0.05 | 0.03 |
| 3/97 | - | 0.03 | 0.03 |

### Annual Fundamentals

| | 12/96 | 12/97 |
|---|---|---|
| Revenue | 33.0 | 57.1 |
| Growth | | 73% |
| Gross Sales | 21.9 | 38.6 |
| Operating Income | (2.2) | 2.3 |
| Net Income | (0.8) | 4.0 |

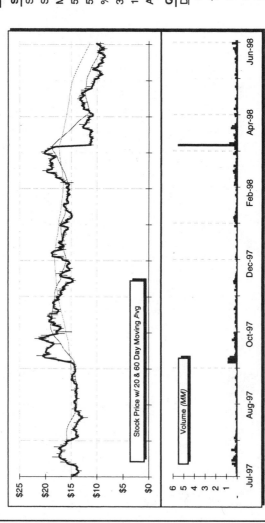

Stock Price w/ 20 & 60 Day Moving Avg

Volume (MM)

Jul-97  Aug-97  Oct-97  Dec-97  Feb-98  Apr-98  Jun-98

### Quarterly Fundamentals

| | 6/96 | 9/96 | 12/96 | 3/97 | 6/97 | 9/97 | 12/97 | 3/98 |
|---|---|---|---|---|---|---|---|---|
| Revenue | 6.9 | 9.1 | 11.2 | 12.3 | 13.5 | 14.2 | 17.0 | 13.8 |
| Seq'l Growth | | 31% | 24% | 10% | 10% | 5% | 19% | -19% |
| Y/Y Growth | | | | | 96% | 57% | 51% | 12% |
| Gross Sales | 4.6 | 5.9 | 7.4 | 7.8 | 9.1 | 9.9 | 11.8 | 8.6 |
| Operating Income | (0.8) | (0.5) | (0.2) | 0.2 | 0.4 | 0.7 | 1.0 | (2.0) |
| Net Income | | | | | | | | (1.5) |

| | | | | | | | | | |
|---|---|---|---|---|---|---|---|---|---|
| Gross Margins | | | | | | | | | |
| Operating Margin | -12% | -5% | -2% | 1% | 3% | 5% | 6% | -7% | 4% |
| Net Margin | -7% | 0% | 2% | 5% | 6% | 8% | 8% | -2% | 7% |
| | -15% | | | | | | | | |
| | -11% | | | | | | | | |
| Cash & S-T Invest. | 44.3 | 43.8 | 44.8 | 42.9 | 43.7 | 43.2 | 44.5 | 44.8 | 43.2 |
| L-T Debt | 0.6 | 0.7 | 0.7 | 0.6 | 0.4 | 0.3 | 0.3 | 0.7 | 0.3 |
| StkHldrs Equity | 48.8 | 48.8 | 49.2 | 52.1 | 54.2 | 55.8 | 55.7 | 49.2 | 55.8 |
| Op. Cash Flow | (0.1) | 0.9 | 2.6 | (1.7) | 1.0 | 0.4 | 1.1 | 3.9 | 0.6 |
| **Per Share Data** | | | | | | | | | |
| Shares Out | 16.07 | 16.08 | 16.10 | 16.36 | 16.53 | 16.61 | 16.93 | 16.10 | 16.61 |
| Net Income | (0.03) | 0.00 | 0.02 | 0.05 | 0.07 | 0.08 | (0.09) | (0.05) | 0.24 |
| Cash & S-T Inv. | 2.76 | 2.72 | 2.78 | 2.62 | 2.64 | 2.60 | 2.63 | 2.78 | 2.60 |
| Book Value | 3.04 | 3.03 | 3.05 | 3.19 | 3.28 | 3.36 | 3.29 | 3.05 | 3.36 |

## Earnings Estimates & Valuation:

| | IBES EPS | Price Multiple |
|---|---|---|
| Current Yr Est | (0.01) | NM |
| Fwd Yr. Est. | 0.40 | 25.3 |
| Last FY End | 97.12 | |
| # IBES Estimates | 4.00 | |

| | Growth | P/E to LT Growth |
|---|---|---|
| EPS Growth | NM | NM |
| IBES L-T Growth | 43.3% | 58% |

**Misc:**

| | |
|---|---|
| Employees | 349 |
| IPO Date | 5/3/96 |
| First Day Close | $33.75 |

## Company Description

EDFY develops software that allows companies to provide automated services to employees and customers via the Internet, intranet, or telephone. Its main offering, Electronic Workforce is sold as a broad "self-service" tool, but the Company offers vertically specific solutions for human resources organizations and financial institutions. Financial institutions link EDFY solutions to their core banking systems and apply the software to deliver home banking services to customers.

Sources: Piper Jaffray Research, FactSet, IBES, Compustat, Company Reports

Figures in millions, except per share amounts

Piper Jaffray Equity Research
Electronic Commerce

# Company Profile:
# ELCOM INTERNATIONAL INC

## ELCO

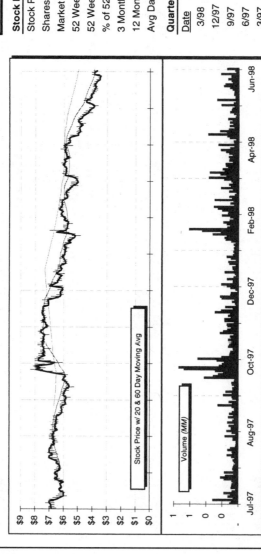

**Stock Data**

| | | |
|---|---|---|
| Stock Price as of | **6/30/98** | $3.69 |
| Shares Outstanding | | 27.39 |
| Market Cap | | $101 |
| 52 Week High | | $8.31 |
| 52 Week Low | | $3.38 |
| % of 52 Week High | | 44% |
| 3 Month Return | | -27% |
| 12 Month Return | | -46% |
| Avg Daily Volume (past mo.) | | 0.10 |

**Quarterly EPS Performance**

| Date | IBES Est | Actual | Suprise |
|---|---|---|---|
| 3/98 | | 0.05 | |
| 12/97 | 0.12 | 0.10 | (0.02) |
| 9/97 | 0.07 | 0.11 | 0.04 |
| 6/97 | 0.07 | 0.07 | - |
| 3/97 | 0.07 | 0.07 | - |

**Annual Fundamentals**

| | 12/96 | 12/97 |
|---|---|---|
| Revenue | 620.1 | 760.1 |
| Growth | | 23% |
| Gross Sales | 67.8 | 90.4 |
| Operating Income | 11.3 | 18.9 |
| Net Income | 5.6 | 10.3 |

**Quarterly Fundamentals**

| | 6/96 | 9/96 | 12/96 | 3/97 | 6/97 | 9/97 | 12/97 | 3/98 |
|---|---|---|---|---|---|---|---|---|
| Revenue | 146.3 | 156.9 | 175.5 | 176.3 | 198.2 | 198.4 | 187.3 | 190.0 |
| Seq'l Growth | | 7% | 12% | 0% | 12% | 0% | -6% | 1% |
| Y/Y Growth | | | | | 35% | 26% | 7% | 8% |
| Gross Sales | 17.0 | 17.3 | 19.3 | 20.2 | 22.7 | 24.0 | 23.5 | 22.2 |
| Operating Income | 2.5 | 2.7 | 3.8 | 3.6 | 4.1 | 5.8 | 5.5 | 4.0 |
| Net Income | 1.2 | 1.2 | 2.0 | 2.0 | 2.1 | 3.1 | 2.9 | 1.4 |

| Gross Margins | 12% | 11% | 11% | 11% | 11% | 12% | 12% | 13% | 12% | 11% | 12% |
|---|---|---|---|---|---|---|---|---|---|---|---|
| Operating Margin | 2% | 2% | 2% | 2% | 2% | 3% | 3% | 3% | 2% | 2% | 2% |
| Net Margin | 1% | 1% | 1% | 1% | 1% | 2% | 2% | 2% | 1% | 1% | 1% |
| | | | | | | | | | | | |
| Cash & S-T Invest. | 24.3 | 45.0 | 23.3 | 21.1 | 32.2 | 31.4 | 33.2 | 36.8 | | 23.3 | 33.2 |
| L-T Debt | 0.0 | 0.0 | 1.0 | 1.7 | 1.6 | 1.5 | 1.3 | 1.1 | | 1.0 | 1.3 |
| StkHldrs Equity | 93.9 | 84.9 | 98.6 | 100.2 | 103.1 | 106.1 | 110.3 | 112.5 | | 98.6 | 110.3 |
| Op. Cash Flow | (11.5) | (3.8) | (12.1) | 7.2 | (1.5) | (3.5) | (46.4) | 16.0 | | (56.3) | (44.2) |

**Per Share Data**

| | | | | | | | | | | | |
|---|---|---|---|---|---|---|---|---|---|---|---|
| Shares Out | 26.45 | 25.51 | 26.63 | 26.74 | 26.96 | 27.07 | 27.16 | 27.35 | | 26.63 | 27.16 |
| Net Income | 0.04 | 0.05 | 0.07 | 0.07 | 0.08 | 0.13 | 0.11 | 0.05 | | 0.21 | 0.38 |
| Cash & S-T Inv. | 0.92 | 1.76 | 0.87 | 0.79 | 1.20 | 1.16 | 1.22 | 1.35 | | 0.87 | 1.22 |
| Book Value | 3.55 | 3.33 | 3.70 | 3.75 | 3.82 | 3.92 | 4.06 | 4.11 | | 3.70 | 4.06 |

**Earnings Estimates & Valuation:**

| | IBES EPS | Price Multiple |
|---|---|---|
| Current Yr Est | NA | NM |
| Fwd Yr. Est. | NA | NM |
| Last FY End | 97.12 | |
| # IBES Estimates | NA | |

| | Growth | P/E to LT Growth |
|---|---|---|
| EPS Growth | NA | NM |
| IBES L-T Growth | NA | NM |

Misc:
| | |
|---|---|
| Employees | 996 |
| IPO Date | 12/20/95 |
| First Day Close | $14.25 |

## Company Description

ELCO develops electronic cataloging and ordering software (PECOS). PECOS is a client/server system that can be used over private networks with PC clients and CD-ROM for richer catalogs, as well over the Internet with browser software. PECOS is designed to be an integral part of the purchasing process and facilitate product searching analysis, ordering, fulfillment and delivery. The system can also be linked electronically with a supplier's order entry and warehouse management system. The Company's subsidiary Catalink Direct, uses PECOS to market and sell PC-related products and generated over 99% of net sales in 1996.

Sources: Piper Jaffray Research, FactSet, IBES, Compustat, Company Reports
Figures in millions, except per share amounts

Piper Jaffray Equity Research
Electronic Commerce

## Company Profile:
# E TRADE GROUP INC

# EGRP

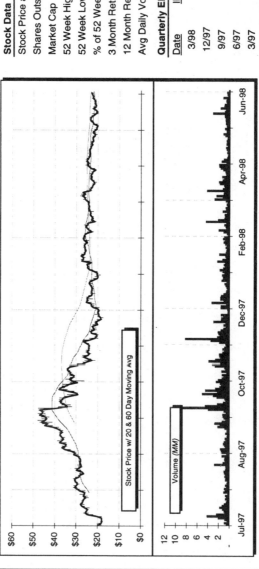

Stock Price w/ 20 & 60 Day Moving avg

Volume (MM)

**Stock Data**

| | |
|---|---|
| Stock Price as of 6/30/98 | $22.94 |
| Shares Outstanding | 39.29 |
| Market Cap | $901 |
| 52 Week High | $47.88 |
| 52 Week Low | $17.38 |
| % of 52 Week High | 48% |
| 3 Month Return | -8% |
| 12 Month Return | 17% |
| Avg Daily Volume (past mo.) | 0.83 |

**Quarterly EPS Performance**

| Date | IBES Est | Actual | Suprise |
|---|---|---|---|
| 3/98 | 0.15 | 0.15 | - |
| 12/97 | 0.14 | 0.16 | 0.02 |
| 9/97 | 0.12 | 0.15 | 0.03 |
| 6/97 | 0.09 | 0.16 | 0.07 |
| 3/97 | 0.09 | 0.09 | - |

**Annual Fundamentals**

| | 9/96 | 9/97 |
|---|---|---|
| Revenue | 53.6 | 155.9 |
| Growth | | 191% |
| Gross Sales | 22.9 | 89.4 |
| Operating Income | 2.9 | 40.8 |
| Net Income | (0.8) | 13.9 |

**Quarterly Fundamentals**

| | 6/96 | 9/96 | 12/96 | 3/97 | 6/97 | 9/97 | 12/97 | 3/98 |
|---|---|---|---|---|---|---|---|---|
| Revenue | 15.6 | 19.3 | 27.3 | 34.7 | 40.3 | 55.3 | 59.8 | 61.9 |
| Seq'l Growth | | 24% | 41% | 27% | 16% | 37% | 8% | 3% |
| Y/Y Growth | | | | | 159% | 186% | 119% | 78% |
| Gross Sales | 2.1 | 9.1 | 14.9 | 21.5 | 22.3 | 34.1 | 37.1 | 37.6 |
| Operating Income | (2.7) | 3.4 | 6.2 | 7.6 | 12.7 | 16.0 | 19.2 | 18.0 |
| Net Income | (2.4) | 0.5 | 2.3 | 3.1 | 3.1 | 5.5 | 4.9 | 6.1 |

| | | | | | | | | | | |
|---|---|---|---|---|---|---|---|---|---|---|
| Operating Margin | -18% | 18% | 23% | 22% | 32% | 29% | 32% | 29% | | |
| Net Margin | -15% | 3% | 8% | 9% | 8% | 10% | 8% | 10% | | |

| | | | | | | | | | Gross Margins | 43% | 57% |
|---|---|---|---|---|---|---|---|---|---|---|---|
| | | | | | | | | | Operating Margin | 5% | 26% |
| | | | | | | | | | Net Margin | -2% | 9% |
| Cash & S-T Invest. | 15.4 | 85.1 | 91.9 | 72.5 | 226.8 | 228.2 | 259.3 | 248.8 | Cash & S-T Invest. | 85.1 | 228.2 |
| L-T Debt | 1.9 | 0.0 | 0.0 | 0.0 | 0.0 | - | - | - | L-T Debt | 0.0 | - |
| StkHldrs Equity | 22.4 | 69.3 | 71.5 | 75.4 | 83.1 | 281.3 | 286.8 | 294.6 | StkHldrs Equity | 69.3 | 281.3 |
| Op. Cash Flow | NA | (4.1) | (0.6) | 10.3 | (53.8) | 35.2 | (7.6) | 51.4 | Op. Cash Flow | (7.8) | (8.9) |
| **Per Share Data** | | | | | | | | | **Per Share Data** | | |
| Shares Out | 29.39 | 29.54 | 29.55 | 30.44 | 30.96 | 38.66 | 38.81 | 39.23 | Shares Out | 29.54 | 38.66 |
| Net Income | (0.08) | 0.02 | 0.08 | 0.10 | 0.10 | 0.14 | 0.13 | 0.16 | Net Income | (0.03) | 0.36 |
| Cash & S-T Inv. | 0.52 | 2.88 | 3.11 | 2.38 | 7.33 | 5.90 | 6.68 | 6.34 | Cash & S-T Inv. | 2.88 | 5.90 |
| Book Value | 0.76 | 2.35 | 2.42 | 2.48 | 2.68 | 7.28 | 7.39 | 7.51 | Book Value | 2.35 | 7.28 |

### Earnings Estimates & Valuation:

| | IBES EPS | Price Multiple |
|---|---|---|
| Current Yr Est | 0.63 | 36.4 |
| Fwd Yr. Est. | 0.83 | 27.6 |
| Last FY End | 97.09 | |
| # IBES Estimates | 7.00 | |

| | Growth | P/E to LT Growth |
|---|---|---|
| EPS Growth | 31.7% | 80% |
| IBES L-T Growth | 45.3% | 61% |

**Misc:**

| | |
|---|---|
| Employees | 499 |
| IPO Date | 8/16/96 |
| First Day Close | $11.25 |

### Company Description

EGRP is the second largest provider of online discount brokerage services. The Company provides self-directed investors with automated tools for trading stocks, options, and mutual funds. The Company also delivers services that can be individualized such as portfolio tracking, Java based charting, stock quotes, real-time market commentary, analysis and other information. Through the acquisitions of OptionsLink and Sharedata, the Company provides employees of client corporations the ability to manage their stock options. The Company has agreements to open versions of E*Trade's core Internet site in over 32 countries

Sources: Piper Jaffray Research, FactSet, IBES, Compustat, Company Reports
Figures in millions, except per share amounts

Piper Jaffray Equity Research
Electronic Commerce

## Company Profile:

# FIRST DATA CORP

# FDC

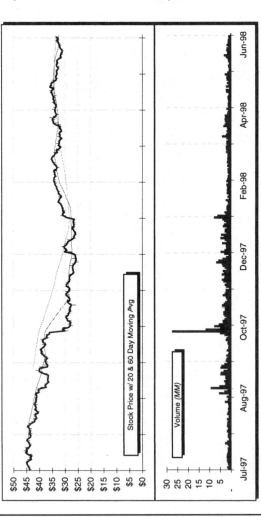

Stock Price w/ 20 & 60 Day Moving Avg

Volume (MM)

**Stock Data**

| | 6/30/98 | |
|---|---|---|
| Stock Price as of | | $33.31 |
| Shares Outstanding | | 446.48 |
| Market Cap | | $14,873 |
| 52 Week High | | $46.13 |
| 52 Week Low | | $25.00 |
| % of 52 Week High | | 72% |
| 3 Month Return | | 3% |
| 12 Month Return | | -24% |
| Avg Daily Volume (past mo.) | | 1.47 |

**Quarterly EPS Performance**

| Date | IBES Est | Actual | Suprise |
|---|---|---|---|
| 3/98 | 0.30 | 0.29 | (0.01) |
| 12/97 | 0.47 | 0.45 | (0.02) |
| 9/97 | 0.42 | 0.40 | (0.02) |
| 6/97 | 0.35 | 0.35 | - |
| 3/97 | 0.30 | 0.29 | (0.01) |

**Annual Fundamentals**

| | 12/96 | 12/97 |
|---|---|---|
| Revenue | 4,934.1 | 5,234.5 |
| Growth | | 6% |
| | | |
| Gross Sales | 1,849.3 | 1,938.1 |
| Operating Income | 1,124.6 | 1,192.2 |
| Net Income | 636.5 | 356.7 |

**Quarterly Fundamentals**

| | 6/96 | 9/96 | 12/96 | 3/97 | 6/97 | 9/97 | 12/97 | 3/98 |
|---|---|---|---|---|---|---|---|---|
| Revenue | 1200.4 | 1254.4 | 1349.6 | 1243.3 | 1318.2 | 1293.3 | 1379.7 | 1232.3 |
| Seq'l Growth | | 4% | 8% | -8% | 6% | -2% | 7% | -11% |
| Y/Y Growth | | | | | 10% | 3% | 2% | -1% |
| Gross Sales | 431.4 | 476.3 | 539.9 | 429.4 | 465.3 | 518.2 | 525.2 | 420.7 |
| Operating Income | 253.0 | 296.1 | 360.9 | 234.0 | 282.7 | 332.9 | 342.6 | 222.3 |

Piper Jaffray Equity Research
Electronic Commerce

| | | | | | | | | | |
|---|---|---|---|---|---|---|---|---|---|
| Gross Margins | | | | | | | | 37% | 37% |
| Operating Margin | 21% | 24% | 27% | 19% | 21% | 26% | 25% | 18% | 23% | 23% |
| Net Margin | 12% | 13% | 17% | 11% | -2% | 15% | 4% | 11% | 13% | 7% |
| Cash & S-T Invest. | NA | NA | 2,387.5 | NA | NA | NA | 2,586.2 | NA | 2,387.5 | 2,586.2 |
| L-T Debt | 1,768.8 | 2,012.8 | 1,198.7 | 1,879.3 | 2,157.0 | 2,135.6 | 979.5 | 1,737.8 | 1,198.7 | 979.5 |
| StkHldrs Equity | 3,322.2 | 3,504.1 | 3,709.8 | 3,803.1 | 3,569.4 | 3,412.8 | 3,657.3 | 3,758.4 | 3,709.8 | 3,657.3 |
| Op. Cash Flow | 256.2 | 287.1 | 344.9 | 199.6 | 310.4 | 432.3 | 229.2 | 281.3 | 1,053.8 | 1,171.5 |
| **Per Share Data** | | | | | | | | | | |
| Shares Out | 447.60 | 447.80 | 448.00 | 448.30 | 443.10 | 434.50 | 446.90 | 446.50 | 448.00 | 446.90 |
| Net Income | NA | NA | 0.50 | NA | NA | NA | 0.12 | NA | 1.42 | 0.80 |
| Cash & S-T Inv. | NA | NA | 5.33 | NA | NA | NA | 5.79 | NA | 5.33 | 5.79 |
| Book Value | 7.42 | 7.83 | 8.28 | 8.48 | 8.06 | 7.85 | 8.18 | 8.42 | 8.28 | 8.18 |

## Earnings Estimates & Valuation:

| | IBES EPS | Price Multiple |
|---|---|---|
| Current Yr Est | 1.63 | 20.4 |
| Fwd Yr. Est. | 1.87 | 17.8 |
| Last FY End | 97.12 | |
| # IBES Estimates | 19.00 | |

| | Growth | P/E to LT Growth |
|---|---|---|
| EPS Growth | 14.7% | 130% |
| IBES L-T Growth | 15.7% | 113% |

### Misc:

| | |
|---|---|
| Employees | 36,000 |
| IPO Date | 4/9/92 |
| First Day Close | $11.13 |

## Company Description

FDC is the dominant provider of third party payment processing services. The Company is the market leader in processing credit card transactions and authorizing checks for merchants. FDC is also dominates the money transfer services business under the banner of its well-known Western Union subsidiary. Many of the Company's ancillary businesses were sold in 1997, including First Health, Nationwide Credit, and First Image. Most of these non-core units were acquired when FDC merged with leading competitor, First Financial Management, a $6.7 billion deal in 1995.

Sources: Piper Jaffray Research, FactSet, IBES, Compustat, Company Reports
Figures in millions, except per share amounts

## Company Profile:
# FIRST VIRTUAL HLDGS INC

# FVHI

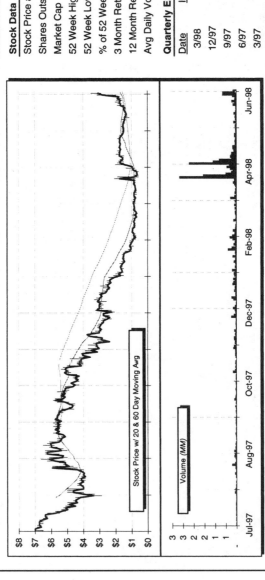

Stock Price w/ 20 & 60 Day Moving Avg

Volume (MM)

Jul-97 Aug-97 Oct-97 Dec-97 Feb-98 Apr-98 Jun-98

### Stock Data

| | |
|---|---|
| Stock Price as of | 6/30/98 | $3.06 |
| Shares Outstanding | | 11.79 |
| Market Cap | | $36 |
| 52 Week High | | $7.00 |
| 52 Week Low | | $0.56 |
| % of 52 Week High | | 44% |
| 3 Month Return | | 238% |
| 12 Month Return | | -56% |
| Avg Daily Volume (past mo.) | | 0.11 |

### Quarterly EPS Performance

| Date | IBES Est | Actual | Suprise |
|---|---|---|---|
| 3/98 | (0.27) | (0.38) | **(0.11)** |
| 12/97 | (0.40) | (0.59) | **(0.19)** |
| 9/97 | (0.36) | (0.51) | **(0.15)** |
| 6/97 | (0.42) | (0.45) | **(0.03)** |
| 3/97 | (0.38) | (0.39) | **(0.01)** |

### Annual Fundamentals

| | 12/96 | 12/97 |
|---|---|---|
| Revenue | 0.7 | 1.5 |
| Growth | | 108% |
| Gross Sales | (9.8) | 0.1 |
| Operating Income | (9.8) | (16.4) |
| Net Income | (10.7) | (15.9) |

### Quarterly Fundamentals

| | 6/96 | 9/96 | 12/96 | 3/97 | 6/97 | 9/97 | 12/97 | 3/98 |
|---|---|---|---|---|---|---|---|---|
| Revenue | 0.2 | 0.1 | 0.2 | 0.4 | 0.4 | 0.3 | 0.3 | 0.3 |
| Seq'l Growth | | -38% | 104% | 96% | 0% | -17% | 4% | -17% |
| Y/Y Growth | | | | | 150% | 236% | 71% | -28% |
| Gross Sales | (0.0) | (0.1) | (0.1) | 0.0 | 0.0 | 0.0 | 0.0 | (0.1) |
| Operating Income | (1.7) | (2.5) | (4.8) | (3.6) | (4.1) | (4.6) | (4.1) | (3.6) |

| | | | | | | | |
|---|---|---|---|---|---|---|---|
| | 1.0 | NM | | 11% | 2% | 3% | -49% |
| Operating Margin | NM | NM | NM | NM | NM | NM | NM |
| Net Margin | NM | NM | NM | NM | NM | NM | NM |
| | | | | | | | |
| Cash & S-T Invest. | 6.1 | 17.3 | 13.1 | 9.1 | 5.3 | 6.3 | 2.3 |
| L-T Debt | 1.2 | 1.2 | 1.2 | 1.2 | - | - | - |
| StkHldrs Equity | 4.7 | 14.9 | 11.5 | 7.6 | 3.1 | 4.1 | 0.7 |
| Op. Cash Flow | NA | (3.0) | (4.0) | (3.8) | (3.8) | (3.6) | (3.9) |

**Per Share Data**

| | | | | | | | |
|---|---|---|---|---|---|---|---|
| Shares Out | 10.10 | 8.80 | 8.80 | 8.87 | 8.88 | 8.90 | 10.89 |
| Net Income | (0.34) | (0.54) | (0.39) | (0.45) | (0.51) | (0.45) | (0.33) |
| Cash & S-T Inv. | 0.60 | 1.97 | 1.49 | 1.03 | 0.60 | 0.71 | 0.21 |
| Book Value | 0.46 | 1.70 | 1.30 | 0.86 | 0.35 | 0.46 | 0.06 |

(Left-most column NA for each row: Cash & S-T Invest. NA, L-T Debt NA, StkHldrs Equity NA, Op. Cash Flow NA, Shares Out NA, Net Income NA, Cash & S-T Inv. NA, Book Value NA)

Right-side summary columns:

| | 6% | NM | NM |
|---|---|---|---|
| Gross Margins | 6% | NM | NM |
| Operating Margin | NM | NM | NM |
| Net Margin | NM | NM | NM |
| Cash & S-T Invest. | 17.3 | 17.3 | 6.3 |
| L-T Debt | 1.2 | 1.2 | - |
| StkHldrs Equity | 14.9 | 14.9 | 4.1 |
| Op. Cash Flow | (7.4) | (7.4) | (15.1) |

**Per Share Data**

| | | |
|---|---|---|
| Shares Out | 8.80 | 8.90 |
| Net Income | (1.22) | (1.79) |
| Cash & S-T Inv. | 1.97 | 0.71 |
| Book Value | 1.70 | 0.46 |

## Earnings Estimates & Valuation:

| | IBES EPS | Price Multiple |
|---|---|---|
| Current Yr Est | (1.00) | NM |
| Fwd Yr. Est. | NA | NM |
| Last FY End | 97.12 | |
| # IBES Estimates | 1.00 | |

| | Growth | P/E to LT Growth |
|---|---|---|
| EPS Growth | NA | NM |
| IBES L-T Growth | NA | NM |

**Misc:**

| | |
|---|---|
| Employees | 77 |
| IPO Date | 12/13/96 |
| First Day Close | $9.00 |

### Company Description

FVHI has been through a lot change lately. Originally it was one of the early providers of payment services over the Internet with its VirtualPIN secure payment system. However recently the Company has been focusing on interactive advertising systems which create roaming storefronts that allow consumers to purchase directly from the ad banner instead of going to the vendor's website.

Sources: Piper Jaffray Research, FactSet, IBES, Compustat, Company Reports
Figures in millions, except per share amounts

Piper Jaffray Equity Research
Electronic Commerce

# Company Profile:
## HARBINGER CORP

## HRBC

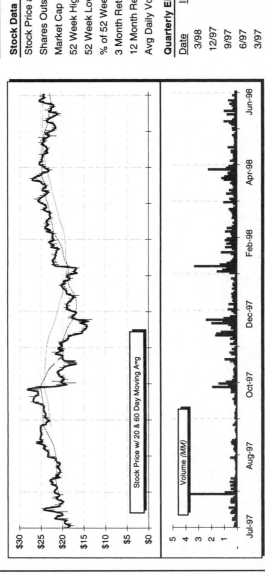

**Stock Price w/ 20 & 60 Day Moving Avg**

**Volume *(MM)***

### Stock Data

| | |
|---|---|
| Stock Price as of 6/30/98 | $24.19 |
| Shares Outstanding | 41.84 |
| Market Cap | $1,012 |
| 52 Week High | $28.33 |
| 52 Week Low | $13.04 |
| % of 52 Week High | 85% |
| 3 Month Return | -4% |
| 12 Month Return | 30% |
| Avg Daily Volume (past mo.) | 0.38 |

### Quarterly EPS Performance

| Date | IBES Est | Actual | Suprise |
|---|---|---|---|
| 3/98 | 0.09 | 0.10 | **0.01** |
| 12/97 | 0.13 | 0.14 | **0.01** |
| 9/97 | 0.10 | 0.10 | **0.00** |
| 6/97 | 0.07 | 0.07 | **0.01** |
| 3/97 | 0.05 | 0.06 | **0.01** |

### Annual Fundamentals

| | 12/96 | 12/97 |
|---|---|---|
| Revenue | 41.7 | 120.7 |
| *Growth* | | *189%* |
| Gross Sales | 28.9 | 82.2 |
| Operating Income | 7.6 | 18.6 |
| Net Income | (8.2) | (39.0) |

### Quarterly Fundamentals

| | 6/96 | 9/96 | 12/96 | 3/97 | 6/97 | 9/97 | 12/97 | 3/98 |
|---|---|---|---|---|---|---|---|---|
| Revenue | 14.8 | 15.7 | 47.3 | 24.3 | 19.7 | 21.5 | 55.2 | 31.1 |
| *Seq'l Growth* | | *7%* | *200%* | *-49%* | *-19%* | *9%* | *156%* | *-44%* |
| *Y/Y Growth* | | | | | *33%* | *37%* | *17%* | *28%* |
| Gross Sales | 9.8 | 10.8 | 32.9 | 16.0 | 13.5 | 14.7 | 37.9 | 20.4 |
| Operating Income | 0.3 | 0.8 | 1.2 | 1.3 | 3.7 | 4.9 | 8.8 | 5.5 |

| | | | | | | | | | | | Cash & S-T invest. | | 8.4 | 102.1 |
|---|---|---|---|---|---|---|---|---|---|---|---|---|---|---|
| **Gross Margins** | | | | | | | | | | | **65%** | | **66%** | **68%** |
| **Operating Margin** | 2% | 5% | 3% | | 5% | 19% | 23% | 16% | 18% | | | 18% | 15% |
| **Net Margin** | -10% | -8% | -9% | | -67% | 11% | -45% | -28% | -4% | | | -20% | -32% |

| | | | | | | | | | Cash & S-T Invest. | | 8.4 | 102.1 |
|---|---|---|---|---|---|---|---|---|---|---|---|---|
| Cash & S-T Invest. | 5.3 | 4.1 | 8.4 | 5.7 | 2.1 | 48.1 | 102.1 | 106.3 | L-T Debt | | - | - |
| L-T Debt | - | - | - | 1.3 | 1.2 | - | - | - | StkHldrs Equity | | 31.3 | 130.0 |
| StkHldrs Equity | 30.4 | 30.8 | 31.3 | 18.7 | 23.0 | 74.2 | 130.0 | 135.4 | Op. Cash Flow | | 7.8 | 1.6 |
| Op. Cash Flow | (1.5) | 1.0 | 5.8 | (1.0) | (1.1) | 0.4 | 3.3 | 1.2 | | | | |

**Per Share Data**

| | | | | | | | | | | | Per Share Data | | |
|---|---|---|---|---|---|---|---|---|---|---|---|---|---|
| Shares Out | 22.99 | 23.74 | 24.44 | 28.51 | 28.94 | 32.25 | 40.83 | 41.70 | | Shares Out | | 24.44 | 40.83 |
| Net Income | (0.06) | (0.05) | (0.18) | (0.57) | 0.08 | (0.30) | (0.37) | (0.03) | | Net Income | | (0.34) | (0.96) |
| Cash & S-T Inv. | 0.23 | 0.17 | 0.34 | 0.20 | 0.07 | 1.49 | 2.50 | 2.55 | | Cash & S-T Inv. | | 0.34 | 2.50 |
| Book Value | 1.32 | 1.30 | 1.28 | 0.66 | 0.80 | 2.30 | 3.18 | 3.25 | | Book Value | | 1.28 | 3.18 |

## Earnings Estimates & Valuation:

| | IBES EPS | Price Multiple |
|---|---|---|
| Current Yr Est | 0.52 | 46.5 |
| Fwd Yr. Est. | 0.74 | 32.7 |
| Last FY End | 97.12 | |
| # IBES Estimates | 15.00 | |

| | Growth | P/E to LT Growth |
|---|---|---|
| EPS Growth | 42.3% | 122% |
| IBES L-T Growth | 38.1% | 86% |

**Misc:**

| | |
|---|---|
| Employees | 1,032 |
| IPO Date | 8/22/95 |
| First Day Close | $6.72 |

## Company Description

HRBC provides electronic data interchange (EDI) and electronic commerce (EC) software as well as value-added network (VAN) services to support business-to-business commerce. Its VAN services are especially strong in the utility and energy industries. Its EDI/EC software solutions for mapping, translation and scheduling are very strong on the PC platform, but it also gained credibility on the AS/400 platform with the acquisition of Premenos in 12/97. The Company also has solutions that enable business commerce on the Internet. HRBC's most successful market has traditionally been small-medium sized businesses.

Sources: Piper Jaffray Research, FactSet, IBES, Compustat, Company Reports

Figures in millions, except per share amounts

Piper Jaffray Equity Research
Electronic Commerce

# Company Profile:
## INFORMATION RES ENGR INC

# IREG

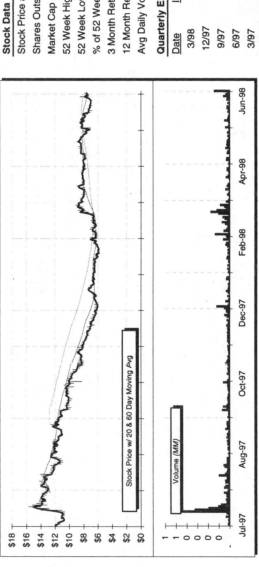

Stock Price w/ 20 & 60 Day Moving Avg

Volume (MM)

**Stock Data**

| | |
|---|---|
| Stock Price as of 6/30/98 | $7.56 |
| Shares Outstanding | 5.46 |
| Market Cap | $41 |
| 52 Week High | $15.75 |
| 52 Week Low | $5.75 |
| % of 52 Week High | 48% |
| 3 Month Return | -8% |
| 12 Month Return | -37% |
| Avg Daily Volume (past mo.) | 0.02 |

**Quarterly EPS Performance**

| Date | IBES Est | Actual | Suprise |
|---|---|---|---|
| 3/98 | (0.07) | (0.09) | (0.02) |
| 12/97 | 0.01 | (0.09) | (0.10) |
| 9/97 | 0.01 | (0.14) | (0.15) |
| 6/97 | (0.05) | (0.17) | (0.12) |
| 3/97 | | (0.26) | |

**Annual Fundamentals**

| | 12/96 | 12/97 |
|---|---|---|
| Revenue | 14.3 | 16.0 |
| Growth | | 12% |
| Gross Sales | 5.9 | 8.9 |
| Operating Income | (5.6) | (4.1) |
| Net Income | (7.1) | (3.6) |

**Quarterly Fundamentals**

| | 6/96 | 9/96 | 12/96 | 3/97 | 6/97 | 9/97 | 12/97 | 3/98 |
|---|---|---|---|---|---|---|---|---|
| Revenue | 5.1 | 2.7 | 3.2 | 3.2 | 3.7 | 4.0 | 5.1 | 4.9 |
| Seq'l Growth | | -47% | 21% | -3% | 19% | 8% | 26% | -4% |
| Y/Y Growth | | | | | -26% | 51% | 56% | 55% |
| Gross Sales | 2.0 | 1.3 | 1.4 | 1.7 | 2.1 | 2.3 | 2.8 | 2.6 |
| Operating Income | (0.5) | (1.8) | (2.3) | (1.6) | (1.1) | (0.9) | (0.6) | (0.6) |

| Operating Margin | -9% | -67% | -71% | -50% | -28% | -22% | -12% | -12% | -39% | -26% |
| Net Margin | -4% | -59% | NM | -45% | -25% | -20% | -10% | -10% | -49% | -23% |
| | | | | | | | | | | |
| Cash & S-T Invest. | 18.7 | 16.9 | 14.2 | 11.1 | 9.8 | 9.1 | 9.6 | 8.9 | 14.2 | 9.6 |
| L-T Debt | 0.0 | 0.0 | 0.0 | 0.0 | 0.0 | - | - | - | 0.0 | - |
| StkHldrs Equity | 27.9 | 26.3 | 21.9 | 20.2 | 19.3 | 18.5 | 18.0 | 17.3 | 21.9 | 18.0 |
| Op. Cash Flow | (1.6) | (0.2) | (2.0) | (2.8) | (1.1) | (0.3) | 0.6 | (0.4) | (2.6) | (3.5) |

**Per Share Data**

| Shares Out | 5.42 | 5.45 | 5.46 | 5.46 | 5.46 | 5.46 | 5.46 | 5.46 | 5.46 | 5.46 |
|---|---|---|---|---|---|---|---|---|---|---|
| Net Income | (0.04) | (0.29) | (0.80) | (0.26) | (0.17) | (0.14) | (0.09) | (0.09) | (1.30) | (0.67) |
| Cash & S-T Inv. | 3.45 | 3.10 | 2.61 | 2.03 | 1.79 | 1.66 | 1.75 | 1.63 | 2.61 | 1.75 |
| Book Value | 5.14 | 4.83 | 4.01 | 3.70 | 3.53 | 3.39 | 3.29 | 3.17 | 4.01 | 3.29 |

## Earnings Estimates & Valuation:

| | IBES EPS | Price Multiple |
|---|---|---|
| Current Yr Est | - | NM |
| Fwd Yr. Est. | 0.41 | 18.4 |
| Last FY End | 97.12 | |
| # IBES Estimates | 2.00 | |

| | Growth | P/E to LT Growth |
|---|---|---|
| EPS Growth | NM | NM |
| IBES L-T Growth | 40.0% | 46% |

Misc:

| Employees | 129 |
|---|---|
| IPO Date | 8/24/90 |
| First Day Close | $0.31 |

## Company Description

Traditionally a provider of link encryption and token products, IREG has recently developed a heavy focus on enabling virtual private networking (VPN) through its SafeNet product group. The Company claims that it delivered the first commercial VPN in 1995, well before their popular emergence in 1997. The SafeNet product family consists of a firewall, security management software and remote authentication and encryption through hard and soft tokens. The company also offers smart cards as an alternative to provide additional authentication strength.

Sources: Piper Jaffray Research, FactSet, IBES, Compustat, Company Reports
Figures in millions, except per share amounts

Piper Jaffray Equity Research
Electronic Commerce

# Company Profile:
## INTELIDATA TECHNOLOGIES CORP

## INTD

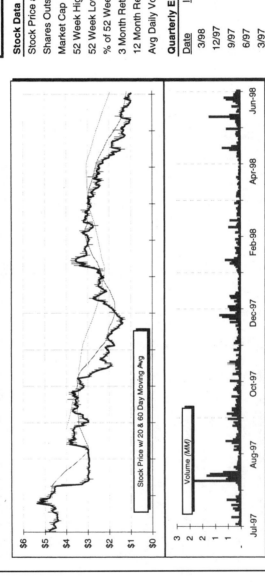

### Stock Data

| | |
|---|---|
| Stock Price as of | 6/30/98 | $0.97 |
| Shares Outstanding | | 31.17 |
| Market Cap | | $30 |
| 52 Week High | | $5.38 |
| 52 Week Low | | $0.94 |
| % of 52 Week High | | 18% |
| 3 Month Return | | -68% |
| 12 Month Return | | -80% |
| Avg Daily Volume (past mo.) | | 0.28 |

### Quarterly EPS Performance

| Date | IBES Est | Actual | Suprise |
|---|---|---|---|
| 3/98 | (0.16) | (0.15) | 0.01 |
| 12/97 | (0.21) | (0.22) | (0.01) |
| 9/97 | (0.14) | (0.31) | (0.17) |
| 6/97 | 0.03 | (0.04) | (0.07) |
| 3/97 | 0.02 | 0.04 | 0.02 |

### Annual Fundamentals

| | 12/96 | 12/97 |
|---|---|---|
| Revenue | 13.9 | 60.3 |
| Growth | | 334% |
| | | |
| Gross Sales | 3.5 | 16.8 |
| Operating Income | (20.1) | (21.6) |

### Quarterly Fundamentals

| | 6/96 | 9/96 | 12/96 | 3/97 | 6/97 | 9/97 | 12/97 | 3/98 |
|---|---|---|---|---|---|---|---|---|
| Revenue | 0.5 | 1.1 | 11.0 | 21.6 | 16.9 | 11.7 | 10.2 | 17.3 |
| Seq'l Growth | | 94% | 930% | 97% | -22% | -31% | -13% | 70% |
| Y/Y Growth | | | | | 2977% | 1000% | -7% | -20% |
| Gross Sales | 0.2 | 0.4 | 2.5 | 7.7 | 4.5 | 2.2 | 2.4 | 2.3 |
| Operating Income | (3.1) | (3.5) | (11.5) | (0.3) | (4.6) | (9.7) | (7.1) | (5.0) |

| | | | | | | | | | | | |
|---|---|---|---|---|---|---|---|---|---|---|---|
| Gross Margins | | | | | | | | | | 25% | 28% |
| Operating Margin | NM | NM | NM | -1% | | | NM | NM | NM | NM | -36% |
| Net Margin | NM | NM | NM | 1% | | | NM | NM | NM | NM | NM |

| | | | | | | | | | | | |
|---|---|---|---|---|---|---|---|---|---|---|---|
| Cash & S-T Invest. | NA | 17.5 | 39.1 | 28.5 | 24.3 | 11.1 | 11.4 | 9.2 | | 39.1 | 11.4 |
| L-T Debt | NA | 0.1 | - | - | - | - | - | | | - | - |
| StkHldrs Equity | NA | 29.0 | 124.3 | 124.5 | 121.8 | 43.0 | 37.1 | 32.3 | | 124.3 | 37.1 |
| Op. Cash Flow | NA | NA | (1.4) | (8.4) | (4.2) | (11.7) | 0.5 | (0.6) | | (8.8) | (23.8) |

**Per Share Data**

| | | | | | | | | | | | |
|---|---|---|---|---|---|---|---|---|---|---|---|
| Shares Out | NA | 16.63 | 31.82 | 31.82 | 31.85 | 31.16 | 31.18 | 31.17 | | 31.82 | 31.18 |
| Net Income | NA | (0.51) | (2.58) | 0.01 | (0.09) | (2.54) | (0.26) | (0.15) | | (3.01) | (2.89) |
| Cash & S-T Inv. | NA | 1.05 | 1.23 | 0.90 | 0.76 | 0.36 | 0.36 | 0.29 | | 1.23 | 0.36 |
| Book Value | NA | 1.75 | 3.91 | 3.91 | 3.82 | 1.38 | 1.19 | 1.04 | | 3.91 | 1.19 |

**Earnings Estimates & Valuation:**

| | IBES EPS | Price Multiple |
|---|---|---|
| Current Yr Est | (0.47) | NM |
| Fwd Yr. Est. | 0.05 | 19.4 |
| Last FY End | 97.12 | |
| # IBES Estimates | 3.00 | |

| | Growth | P/E to LT Growth |
|---|---|---|
| EPS Growth | -110.6% | NM |
| IBES L-T Growth | 35.0% | 55% |

**Misc:**

| | |
|---|---|
| Employees | 280 |
| IPO Date | 6/2/95 |
| First Day Close | $16.75 |

## Company Description

INTD is split into two distinct divisions, one that is focused on telecommunications equipment and one that develops electronic commerce offerings for financial institutions. The bulk of the Company's revenues come from designing and developing caller-ID and other telecom devices such as a smart telephones. The Company's electronic commerce division develops home banking systems for financial institutions as well as solutions that connect banks with data processors and billers. The Company has recently announced its intention to spin-off the telecommunications group.

Sources: Piper Jaffray Research, FactSet, IBES, Compustat, Company Reports
Figures in millions, except per share amounts

Piper Jaffray Equity Research
Electronic Commerce

# Company Profile:
## INTUIT INC

# INTU

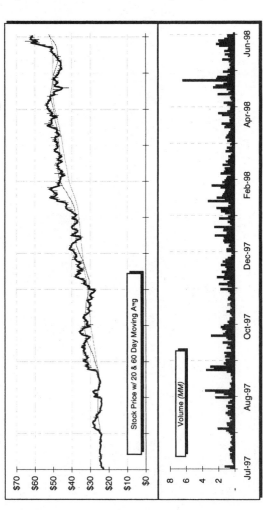

Stock Price w/ 20 & 60 Day Moving A"g

Volume (MM)

Jul-97   Aug-97   Oct-97   Dec-97   Feb-98   Apr-98   Jun-98

## Stock Data

| | |
|---|---|
| Stock Price as of | **6/30/98** |
| | $61.25 |
| Shares Outstanding | 58.76 |
| Market Cap | $3,599 |
| 52 Week High | $65.25 |
| 52 Week Low | $22.75 |
| % of 52 Week High | 94% |
| 3 Month Return | 27% |
| 12 Month Return | 167% |
| Avg Daily Volume (past mo.) | 1.03 |

## Quarterly EPS Performance

| Date | IBES Est | Actual | Suprise |
|---|---|---|---|
| 4/98 | 0.16 | 0.20 | **0.04** |
| 1/98 | 0.94 | 0.95 | **0.01** |
| 10/97 | (0.27) | (0.26) | **0.01** |
| 7/97 | (0.18) | (0.17) | **0.01** |
| 4/97 | 0.16 | 0.16 | - |

## Annual Fundamentals

| | 7/96 | 7/97 |
|---|---|---|
| Revenue | 538.6 | 598.9 |
| Growth | | 11% |
| Gross Sales | 360.9 | 433.6 |
| Operating Income | 3.0 | 21.3 |

## Quarterly Fundamentals

| | 7/96 | 10/96 | 1/97 | 4/97 | 7/97 | 10/97 | 1/98 | 4/98 |
|---|---|---|---|---|---|---|---|---|
| Revenue | 85.3 | 102.5 | 266.0 | 136.3 | 94.1 | 96.0 | 237.5 | 142.0 |
| Seq'l Growth | | 20% | 159% | -49% | -31% | 2% | 148% | -40% |
| Y/Y Growth | | | | | 10% | -6% | -11% | 4% |
| Gross Sales | 50.4 | 65.1 | 201.1 | 102.6 | 64.8 | 68.9 | 186.5 | 108.7 |
| Operating Income | (24.2) | (34.2) | 73.6 | 4.2 | (22.4) | (25.6) | 65.6 | (7.3) |

322

| | | | | | | | | | |
|---|---|---|---|---|---|---|---|---|---|
| Operating Margin | -28% | 28% | -33% | 3% | -24% | -27% | 28% | -5% | |
| Net Margin | -26% | 44% | -28% | 0% | -21% | -13% | 18% | -2% | |
| Cash & S-T Invest. | 198.0 | 455.4 | 170.8 | 472.9 | 395.9 | 461.6 | 642.8 | 726.5 | |
| L-T Debt | 5.6 | 5.1 | 5.3 | 34.4 | 36.4 | 36.5 | 31.3 | 39.2 | |
| StkHldrs Equity | 299.2 | 413.5 | 283.7 | 413.2 | 415.1 | 468.3 | 561.4 | 636.8 | |
| Op. Cash Flow | (14.6) | 110.3 | (16.0) | 25.4 | (38.6) | (52.9) | 72.5 | 54.4 | |

**Per Share Data**

| | | | | | | | | | |
|---|---|---|---|---|---|---|---|---|---|
| Shares Out | 45.81 | 46.49 | 46.26 | 46.56 | 46.94 | 47.30 | 47.83 | 48.68 | |
| Net Income | (0.48) | 2.49 | (0.61) | 0.01 | (0.42) | (0.27) | 0.87 | (0.05) | |
| Cash & S-T Inv. | 4.32 | 9.80 | 3.69 | 10.16 | 8.43 | 9.76 | 13.44 | 14.92 | |
| Book Value | 6.53 | 8.90 | 6.13 | 8.87 | 8.84 | 9.90 | 11.74 | 13.08 | |

| | | |
|---|---|---|
| Operating Margin | 1% | 4% |
| Net Margin | -4% | 11% |
| Cash & S-T Invest. | 198.0 | 395.9 |
| L-T Debt | 5.6 | 36.4 |
| StkHldrs Equity | 299.2 | 415.1 |
| Op. Cash Flow | 61.5 | 81.1 |

**Per Share Data**

| | | |
|---|---|---|
| Shares Out | 45.81 | 46.94 |
| Net Income | (0.45) | 1.46 |
| Cash & S-T Inv. | 4.32 | 8.43 |
| Book Value | 6.53 | 8.84 |

**Earnings Estimates & Valuation:**

| | IBES EPS | Price Multiple |
|---|---|---|
| Current Yr Est | 0.88 | 69.6 |
| Fwd Yr. Est. | 1.20 | 51.0 |
| Last FY End | 97.07 | |
| # IBES Estimates | 11.00 | |

| | Growth | P/E to LT Growth |
|---|---|---|
| EPS Growth | 36.4% | 282% |
| IBES L-T Growth | 24.7% | 207% |

Misc:

| | |
|---|---|
| Employees | 3,000 |
| IPO Date | 3/12/93 |
| First Day Close | $15.88 |

### Company Description

INTU is the dominant provider of software solutions to help manage personal finances (Quicken), small business accounting (Quickbooks), and tax preparation (TurboTax). The Company holds over 80% of the market for off-the-shelf finance software. INTU's latest venture is Quicken.com, a website that provides a wide breadth of personal finance information to help potential consumers of retail financial services. The Company intends to generate traffic to its site and profit from it by directing these viewers to providers of insurance, banking, brokerage, lending and other services in return for a fee. To help generate traffic, the Company made a 19% investment in Excite and struck agreements with Yahoo, CNNfn, and AOL.

Sources: Piper Jaffray Research, FactSet, IBES, Compustat, Company Reports

Figures in millions, except per share amounts

Piper Jaffray Equity Research
Electronic Commerce

# Company Profile:
## ISS GROUP INC

## ISSX

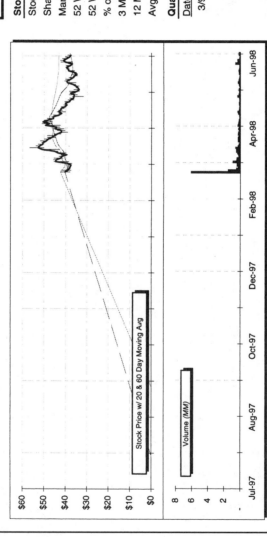

Stock Price w/ 20 & 60 Day Moving Avg

Volume (MM)

**Stock Data**

| | |
|---|---|
| Stock Price as of | 6/30/98 | $37.63 |
| Shares Outstanding | | 16.86 |
| Market Cap | | $634 |
| 52 Week High | | $56.63 |
| 52 Week Low | | $31.63 |
| % of 52 Week High | | 66% |
| 3 Month Return | | -3% |
| 12 Month Return | | 0% |
| Avg Daily Volume (past mo.) | | 0.15 |

**Quarterly EPS Performance**

| Date | IBES Est | Actual | Suprise |
|---|---|---|---|
| 3/98 | (0.14) | (0.12) | **0.02** |

**Annual Fundamentals**

| | 12/96 | 12/97 |
|---|---|---|
| Revenue | 4.5 | 13.5 |
| Growth | | 202% |
| Gross Sales | (1.2) | 12.8 |
| Operating Income | (1.2) | (4.1) |
| Net Income | (1.1) | (3.9) |

**Quarterly Fundamentals**

| | 6/96 | 9/96 | 12/96 | 3/97 | 6/97 | 9/97 | 12/97 | 3/98 |
|---|---|---|---|---|---|---|---|---|
| Revenue | NA | NA | NA | NA | NA | NA | NA | 6.1 |
| Seq'l Growth | NA | NA | NA | NA | NA | NA | NA | NA |
| Y/Y Growth | NA | NA | NA | NA | NA | NA | NA | NA |
| Gross Sales | 0.0 | 0.0 | 0.0 | 0.0 | 0.0 | 0.0 | 0.0 | 5.6 |
| Operating Income | 0.0 | 0.0 | 0.0 | 0.0 | 0.0 | 0.0 | 0.0 | (1.6) |
| Net Income | 0.0 | 0.0 | 0.0 | 0.0 | 0.0 | 0.0 | 0.0 | (1.6) |

| | | | | | | | | | |
|---|---|---|---|---|---|---|---|---|---|
| Gross Margins | NA | NA | NA | NA | NA | NA | 92% | -27% | 95% |
| Operating Margin | NA | NA | NA | NA | NA | NA | -26% | -27% | -31% |
| Net Margin | NA | NA | NA | NA | NA | NA | -27% | -25% | -29% |
| | | | | | | | | | |
| Cash & S-T Invest. | - | - | NA | NA | NA | 3.9 | 64.2 | 2.0 | 3.9 |
| L-T Debt | - | - | NA | NA | NA | 0.1 | 0.0 | 0.1 | 0.1 |
| StkHldrs Equity | - | - | NA | NA | NA | 3.8 | 63.9 | 2.5 | 3.8 |
| Op. Cash Flow | | | NA | NA | NA | NA | (0.9) | (1.5) | (1.6) |
| | | | | | | | | | |
| **Per Share Data** | | | | | | | | | |
| Shares Out | NA | NA | NA | NA | NA | 16.34 | 16.86 | 7.90 | 7.92 |
| Net Income | NA | NA | NA | NA | NA | - | (0.10) | (0.14) | (0.49) |
| Cash & S-T Inv. | NA | NA | NA | NA | NA | 0.24 | 3.81 | 0.25 | 0.50 |
| Book Value | NA | NA | NA | NA | NA | 0.23 | 3.79 | 0.31 | 0.48 |

**Earnings Estimates & Valuation:**

| | IBES EPS | Price Multiple |
|---|---|---|
| Current Yr Est | (0.22) | NM |
| Fwd Yr. Est. | 0.15 | 250.8 |
| Last FY End | 97.12 | |
| # IBES Estimates | 3.00 | |

| | Growth | P/E to LT Growth |
|---|---|---|
| EPS Growth | -168.2% | NM |
| IBES L-T Growth | 75.3% | 333% |

**Misc:**

| | |
|---|---|
| Employees | 141 |
| IPO Date | 3/24/98 |
| First Day Close | $40.38 |

### Company Description

ISSX is a leading developer of Intrusion detection and monitoring software. ISSX's RealSecure software is the leading Intrusion detection package on the market. In an attempt to broaden its product offerings, ISS is developing a SAFESuite family of products that provides a enterprise-wide Intrusion Detection and monitoring system. ISS went public in March of 1998.

Sources: Piper Jaffray Research, FactSet, IBES, Compustat, Company Reports
Figures in millions, except per share amounts

Piper Jaffray Equity Research
Electronic Commerce

# Company Profile:
## N2K INC

# NTKI

## Stock Data

| | |
|---|---|
| Stock Price as of | 6/30/98 $19.63 |
| Shares Outstanding | 14.19 |
| Market Cap | $278 |
| 52 Week High | $34.63 |
| 52 Week Low | $12.25 |
| % of 52 Week High | 57% |
| 3 Month Return | -34% |
| 12 Month Return | 0% |
| Avg Daily Volume (past mo.) | 0.57 |

## Quarterly EPS Performance

| Date | IBES Est | Actual | Suprise |
|---|---|---|---|
| 3/98 | (1.03) | (1.13) | **(0.10)** |
| 12/97 | (0.94) | (1.20) | **(0.26)** |

## Annual Fundamentals

| | 12/96 | 12/97 |
|---|---|---|
| Revenue | 1.7 | 11.3 |
| Growth | | 580% |
| | | |
| Gross Sales | 0.0 | 1.9 |
| Operating Income | (13.0) | (29.3) |
| Net Income | (18.9) | (28.7) |

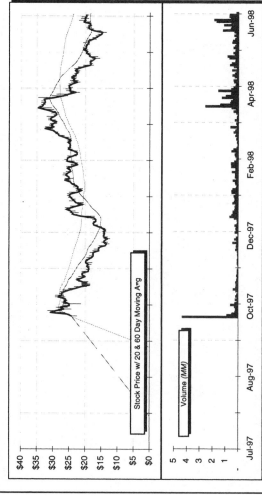

Stock Price w/ 20 & 60 Day Moving Avg

Volume (MM)

## Quarterly Fundamentals

| | 6/96 | 9/96 | 12/96 | 3/97 | 6/97 | 9/97 | 12/97 | 3/98 |
|---|---|---|---|---|---|---|---|---|
| Revenue | 0.3 | 0.4 | 0.7 | 1.1 | 1.8 | 3.6 | 4.8 | 7.0 |
| *Seq'l Growth* | | 42% | 52% | 64% | 63% | 96% | 33% | 46% |
| *Y/Y Growth* | | | | | 482% | 700% | 599% | 530% |
| Gross Sales | (0.2) | 0.1 | 0.1 | 0.2 | 1.8 | 0.9 | 0.4 | 1.1 |
| Operating Income | (2.7) | (3.3) | (5.8) | (4.4) | (6.6) | (6.6) | (12.9) | (14.2) |
| Net Income | (3.5) | (3.6) | (6.5) | (4.5) | (5.6) | (5.4) | (13.2) | (13.7) |

| | -63% | 20% | 8% | 20% | 100% | 25% | 9% | 16% | 1% | 17% |
|---|---|---|---|---|---|---|---|---|---|---|
| Gross Margins | -63% | 20% | 8% | 20% | 100% | 25% | 9% | 16% | 1% | 17% |
| Operating Margin | NM | NM | NM | NM | 100% | NM | NM | NM | NM | NM |
| Net Margin | NM | NM | NM | NM | NM | NM | NM | NM | NM | NM |
| Cash & S-T Invest. | NA | NA | 4.5 | NA | 0.7 | 0.5 | 36.8 | 27.8 | 4.5 | 36.8 |
| L-T Debt | NA | NA | 0.2 | NA | 0.3 | 0.2 | 0.7 | 0.6 | 0.2 | 0.7 |
| StkHldrs Equity | NA | NA | 5.4 | NA | 2.6 | (1.9) | 56.1 | 42.6 | 5.4 | 56.1 |
| Op. Cash Flow | NA | NA | NA | NA | NA | (9.7) | (23.5) | (7.4) | (10.7) | (43.7) |
| **Per Share Data** | | | | | | | | | | |
| Shares Out | NA | NA | 2.92 | NA | 3.08 | 3.08 | 12.12 | 14.16 | 2.92 | 12.12 |
| Net Income | NA | NA | (2.21) | NA | (1.83) | (1.74) | (1.09) | (0.97) | (6.47) | (2.37) |
| Cash & S-T Inv. | NA | NA | 1.53 | NA | 0.22 | 0.16 | 3.04 | 1.96 | 1.53 | 3.04 |
| Book Value | NA | NA | 1.86 | NA | 0.83 | (0.60) | 4.63 | 3.01 | 1.86 | 4.63 |

## Earnings Estimates & Valuation:

| | IBES EPS | Price Multiple |
|---|---|---|
| Current Yr Est | (4.18) | NM |
| Fwd Yr. Est. | (2.60) | NM |
| Last FY End | 97.12 | |
| # IBES Estimates | 5.00 | |

| | Growth | P/E to LT Growth |
|---|---|---|
| EPS Growth | -37.8% | NM |
| IBES L-T Growth | 50.0% | NM |

Misc:

| | |
|---|---|
| Employees | 267 |
| IPO Date | 10/17/97 |
| First Day Close | $24.25 |

## Company Description

NTKI sells music CDs, cassettes and related products through a number of different websites. The Company operates one general online superstore, Music Boulevard with 200,000 titles, and several more content specific "channels" such as JazzCentralStation.com, Rocktropolis.com, and ClassicalInsites.com. The Company's own e_mod system is at the core of its service and supports secure and commercially viable digital online music delivery. Visitors to its websites can buy and download singles in addition to read reviews and articles, and view MTV video clips. The Company also owns its own recording label N2K Encoded Music.

Sources: Piper Jaffray Research, FactSet, IBES, Compustat, Company Reports
Figures in millions, except per share amounts

Piper Jaffray Equity Research
Electronic Commerce

Company Profile:
# NATIONAL PROCESSING INC

## NAP

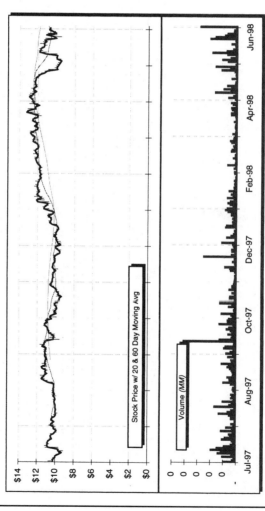

Stock Price w/20 & 60 Day Moving Avg

Volume (MM)

| | Jul-97 | Aug-97 | Oct-97 | Dec-97 | Feb-98 | Apr-98 | Jun-98 |
|---|---|---|---|---|---|---|---|

### Stock Data

| | |
|---|---|
| Stock Price as of | 6/30/98 | $10.69 |
| Shares Outstanding | | 50.58 |
| Market Cap | | $541 |
| 52 Week High | | $13.25 |
| 52 Week Low | | $9.13 |
| % of 52 Week High | | 81% |
| 3 Month Return | | -14% |
| 12 Month Return | | 4% |
| Avg Daily Volume (past mo.) | | 0.03 |

### Quarterly EPS Performance

| Date | IBES Est | Actual | Suprise |
|---|---|---|---|
| 6/98 | 0.06 | 0.06 | - |
| 3/98 | 0.12 | 0.10 | (0.02) |
| 12/97 | 0.17 | 0.12 | (0.05) |
| 9/97 | 0.16 | 0.15 | (0.01) |
| 6/97 | 0.12 | 0.14 | 0.02 |

### Annual Fundamentals

| | 12/96 | 12/97 |
|---|---|---|
| Revenue | 377.6 | 405.7 |
| Growth | | 7% |
| | | |
| Gross Sales | 99.2 | 92.9 |
| Operating Income | 50.2 | 42.2 |
| Net Income | 31.4 | 21.1 |

### Quarterly Fundamentals

| | 6/96 | 9/96 | 12/96 | 3/97 | 6/97 | 9/97 | 12/97 | 3/98 |
|---|---|---|---|---|---|---|---|---|
| Revenue | 91.8 | 97.1 | 104.8 | 88.4 | 95.0 | 100.8 | 121.5 | 114.0 |
| Seq'l Growth | | 6% | 8% | -16% | 7% | 6% | 21% | -6% |
| Y/Y Growth | | | | | 4% | 4% | 16% | 29% |
| Gross Sales | 23.5 | 25.7 | 28.5 | 18.7 | 22.2 | 23.7 | 28.4 | 23.3 |
| Operating Income | 12.7 | 12.0 | 15.7 | 5.4 | 9.7 | 11.1 | 16.0 | 8.6 |
| Net Income | 7.4 | 7.6 | 10.5 | 0.4 | 7.2 | 7.6 | 6.0 | 4.9 |

## Earnings Estimates & Valuation:

| | IBES EPS | Price Multiple |
|---|---|---|
| Current Yr Est | 0.42 | 25.4 |
| Fwd Yr. Est. | 0.55 | 19.4 |
| Last FY End | 97.12 | |
| # IBES Estimates | 2.00 | |

| | Growth | P/E to LT Growth |
|---|---|---|
| EPS Growth | 31.0% | 170% |
| IBES L-T Growth | 15.0% | 130% |

**Misc:**

| | |
|---|---|
| Employees | 10,640 |
| IPO Date | 8/9/96 |
| First Day Close | $19.00 |

| | | | | | | | | |
|---|---|---|---|---|---|---|---|---|
| Gross Margins | 26% | 27% | 27% | 21% | 23% | 23% | 23% | 20% |
| Operating Margin | 14% | 12% | 15% | 6% | 10% | 11% | 13% | 8% |
| Net Margin | 8% | 8% | 10% | 0% | 8% | 8% | 5% | 4% |
| Cash & S-T Invest. | 34.0 | 146.8 | 175.8 | 196.7 | 230.5 | 241.5 | 123.3 | 139.8 |
| L-T Debt | 2.6 | 2.6 | 2.5 | 6.5 | 6.5 | 6.4 | 2.6 | 2.5 |
| StkHldrs Equity | 187.2 | 306.1 | 315.7 | 316.1 | 323.2 | 330.9 | 336.8 | 341.7 |
| Op. Cash Flow | 3.3 | 13.9 | 0.6 | 20.0 | 10.6 | 20.0 | (16.0) | 32.1 |
| **Per Share Data** | | | | | | | | |
| Shares Out | 49.60 | 50.58 | 50.58 | 50.58 | 50.58 | 50.58 | 50.58 | 50.58 |
| Net Income | 0.15 | 0.15 | 0.21 | 0.01 | 0.14 | 0.15 | 0.12 | 0.10 |
| Cash & S-T Inv. | 0.69 | 2.90 | 3.48 | 3.89 | 4.56 | 4.77 | 2.44 | 2.76 |
| Book Value | 3.77 | 6.05 | 6.24 | 6.25 | 6.39 | 6.54 | 6.66 | 6.76 |

| | | |
|---|---|---|
| Gross Margins | 26% | 23% |
| Operating Margin | 13% | 10% |
| Net Margin | 8% | 5% |
| Cash & S-T invest. | 175.8 | 123.3 |
| L-T Debt | 2.5 | 2.6 |
| StkHldrs Equity | 315.7 | 336.8 |
| Op. Cash Flow | 34.8 | 34.6 |
| **Per Share Data** | | |
| Shares Out | 50.58 | 50.58 |
| Net Income | 0.62 | 0.42 |
| Cash & S-T Inv. | 3.48 | 2.44 |
| Book Value | 6.24 | 6.66 |

## Company Description

NAP processes card and check transactions for merchants as well as administrative and financial functions for corporations. Its corporate services include accounts payable and remittance processing. Its ticket processing division is the exclusive processor and clearinghouse for all airline tickets issues by travel agents in the US and for US government. The Company was spun off in 1996 by then parent, National City Corp. a Cleveland, OH bank, which still owns is 85% of the Company.

Sources: Piper Jaffray Research, FactSet, IBES, Compustat, Company Reports
Figures in millions, except per share amounts

Piper Jaffray Equity Research
Electronic Commerce

# Company Profile:
# NETBANK INC

## NTBK

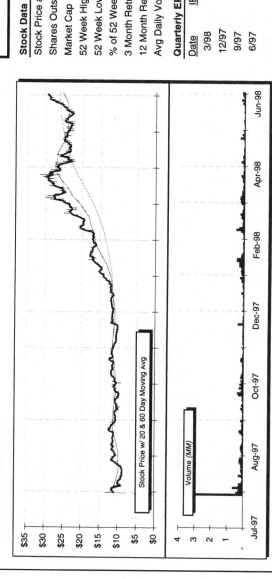

Stock Price w/ 20 & 60 Day Moving Avg

Volume (MM)

Jul-97 Aug-97 Oct-97 Dec-97 Feb-98 Apr-98 Jun-98

### Stock Data

| | 6/30/98 |
|---|---|
| Stock Price as of | $29.50 |
| Shares Outstanding | 6.15 |
| Market Cap | $181 |
| 52 Week High | $31.63 |
| 52 Week Low | $8.63 |
| % of 52 Week High | 93% |
| 3 Month Return | 19% |
| 12 Month Return | 0% |
| Avg Daily Volume (past mo.) | 0.05 |

### Quarterly EPS Performance

| Date | IBES Est | Actual | Suprise |
|---|---|---|---|
| 3/98 | (0.02) | (0.02) | - |
| 12/97 | (0.14) | (0.14) | - |
| 9/97 | (0.29) | (0.33) | (0.04) |
| 6/97 | | | |

### Annual Fundamentals

| | 12/96 | 12/97 |
|---|---|---|
| Revenue | NA | 2.3 |
| Growth | | NA |
| Gross Sales | NA | 0.3 |
| Operating Income | NA | (2.6) |
| Net Income | NA | (5.6) |

### Quarterly Fundamentals

| | 6/96 | 9/96 | 12/96 | 3/97 | 6/97 | 9/97 | 12/97 | 3/98 |
|---|---|---|---|---|---|---|---|---|
| Revenue | NA | NA | NA | NA | NA | NA | 2.3 | 2.3 |
| Seq'l Growth | NA | NA | NA | NA | NA | NA | NA | 2% |
| Y/Y Growth | | NA | NA | NA | NA | NA | NA | NA |
| Gross Sales | 0.0 | 0.0 | 0.0 | 0.0 | 0.0 | 0.0 | 0.3 | 0.1 |
| Operating Income | 0.0 | 0.0 | 0.0 | 0.0 | 0.0 | 0.0 | (2.6) | (0.4) |
| Net Income | 0.0 | 0.0 | 0.0 | 0.0 | 0.0 | 0.0 | (5.6) | (0.2) |

| | | | | | | | | Gross Margins | NA | NA |
|---|---|---|---|---|---|---|---|---|---|---|
| Gross Margins | NA | NA | NA | NA | NA | 15% | 4% | Operating Margin | NA | NA |
| Operating Margin | NA | NA | NA | NA | NM | -18% | | Net Margin | NA | NA |
| Net Margin | NA | NA | NA | NA | NM | -6% | | | | |
| | | | | | | | | Cash & S-T Invest. | NA | 29.1 |
| Cash & S-T Invest. | NA | NA | 35.1 | 29.1 | 10.1 | | | L-T Debt | NA | - |
| L-T Debt | NA | NA | - | - | - | | | StkHldrs Equity | NA | 34.1 |
| StkHldrs Equity | NA | NA | 35.0 | 34.1 | 34.1 | | | Op. Cash Flow | NA | NA |
| Op. Cash Flow | NA | NA | NA | NA | NA | | | | | |
| **Per Share Data** | | | | | | | | **Per Share Data** | | |
| Shares Out | NA | NA | 6.15 | 6.15 | 6.15 | | | Shares Out | NA | 6.15 |
| Net Income | NA | NA | - | (0.91) | (0.02) | | | Net Income | NA | (0.91) |
| Cash & S-T Inv. | NA | NA | 5.71 | 4.74 | 1.64 | | | Cash & S-T Inv. | NA | 4.74 |
| Book Value | NA | NA | 5.69 | 5.55 | 5.55 | | | Book Value | NA | 5.55 |

## Earnings Estimates & Valuation:

| | IBES EPS | Price Multiple |
|---|---|---|
| Current Yr Est | 0.25 | 118.0 |
| Fwd Yr. Est. | 0.75 | 39.3 |
| Last FY End | 97.12 | |
| # IBES Estimates | 2.00 | |
| | Growth | P/E to LT Growth |
| EPS Growth | 200.0% | 429% |
| IBES L-T Growth | 27.5% | 143% |

**Misc:**

| | |
|---|---|
| Employees | |
| IPO Date | 7/29/97 |
| First Day Close | $11.00 |

## Company Description

NTBK is Atlanta Internet Bank, an Internet-based federal savings bank that also provides its services via the phone, mail, and ATMs. The Company provides a number of online banking functions including account activity review, online account registers, electronic bill payment, interest checking certificates of deposit, and money market accounts. The bank's Internet presence allows it to provide service 7 days a week, 24 hours a day.

Sources: Piper Jaffray Research, FactSet, IBES, Compustat, Company Reports
Figures in millions, except per share amounts

Piper Jaffray Equity Research
Electronic Commerce

# Company Profile:
# NETWORKS ASSOCIATES INC

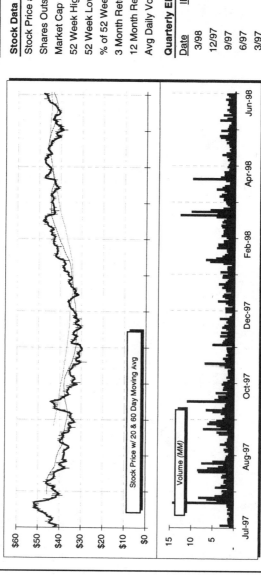

## NETA

### Stock Data

| | | |
|---|---|---|
| Stock Price as of | 6/30/98 | $47.88 |
| Shares Outstanding | | 114.73 |
| Market Cap | | $5,493 |
| 52 Week High | | $52.33 |
| 52 Week Low | | $27.42 |
| % of 52 Week High | | 91% |
| 3 Month Return | | 8% |
| 12 Month Return | | 14% |
| Avg Daily Volume (past mo.) | | 1.79 |

### Quarterly EPS Performance

| Date | IBES Est | Actual | Suprise |
|---|---|---|---|
| 3/98 | 0.36 | 0.37 | 0.01 |
| 12/97 | 0.32 | 0.33 | 0.01 |
| 9/97 | 0.29 | 0.30 | 0.01 |
| 6/97 | 0.27 | 0.29 | 0.02 |
| 3/97 | 0.22 | 0.25 | 0.03 |

### Annual Fundamentals

| | 12/96 | 12/97 |
|---|---|---|
| Revenue | 181.1 | 612.2 |
| Growth | | 238% |
| Gross Sales | 166.9 | 503.1 |
| Operating Income | 78.4 | 194.0 |
| Net Income | 39.0 | (28.4) |

Stock Price w/ 20 & 60 Day Moving Avg

Volume (MM)

### Quarterly Fundamentals

| | 6/96 | 9/96 | 12/96 | 3/97 | 6/97 | 9/97 | 12/97 | 3/98 |
|---|---|---|---|---|---|---|---|---|
| Revenue | 40.8 | 47.3 | 59.2 | 141.4 | 86.3 | 211.3 | 173.3 | 188.4 |
| Seq'l Growth | | 16% | 25% | 139% | -39% | 145% | -18% | 9% |
| Y/Y Growth | | | | | 112% | 347% | 193% | 33% |
| Gross Sales | 37.2 | 43.9 | 54.5 | 115.7 | 79.6 | 211.3 | 96.5 | 153.5 |
| Operating Income | 17.9 | 20.6 | 24.8 | 47.7 | 36.2 | 211.3 | (101.1) | 60.2 |
| Net Income | 9.4 | 12.9 | 15.6 | 13.3 | 23.7 | 15.6 | (80.9) | 41.6 |

| Gross Margins | 91% | 93% | 92% | 82% | 92% | 100% | 56% | 81% |
|---|---|---|---|---|---|---|---|---|
| Operating Margin | 44% | 44% | 42% | 34% | 42% | 100% | -58% | 32% |
| Net Margin | 23% | 27% | 26% | 9% | 27% | 7% | -47% | 22% |
| | | | | | | | | |
| Cash & S-T Invest. | 90.6 | 113.8 | 126.7 | 144.8 | 158.3 | 169.6 | 247.4 | 627.5 |
| L-T Debt | - | - | - | - | - | - | - | NA |
| StkHldrs Equity | 89.6 | 119.3 | 149.5 | 188.5 | 232.4 | 274.1 | 359.8 | 464.8 |
| Op. Cash Flow | 14.0 | 10.2 | 15.0 | 15.7 | 11.7 | 29.7 | 33.5 | 28.9 |

**Per Share Data**

| Shares Out | 71.02 | 72.11 | 72.99 | 74.77 | 76.01 | 76.89 | 104.88 | 107.50 |
|---|---|---|---|---|---|---|---|---|
| Net Income | 0.13 | 0.18 | 0.21 | 0.18 | 0.31 | 0.20 | (0.77) | 0.39 |
| Cash & S-T Inv. | 1.28 | 1.58 | 1.74 | 1.94 | 2.08 | 2.21 | 2.36 | 5.84 |
| Book Value | 1.26 | 1.65 | 2.05 | 2.52 | 3.06 | 3.56 | 3.43 | 4.32 |

| Gross Margins | 92% | 82% |
|---|---|---|
| Operating Margin | 43% | 32% |
| Net Margin | 22% | -5% |
| | | |
| Cash & S-T Invest. | 126.7 | 247.4 |
| L-T Debt | - | NA |
| StkHldrs Equity | 149.5 | 359.8 |
| Op. Cash Flow | 46.5 | 90.7 |

**Per Share Data**

| Shares Out | 72.99 | 104.88 |
|---|---|---|
| Net Income | 0.53 | (0.27) |
| Cash & S-T Inv. | 1.74 | 2.36 |
| Book Value | 2.05 | 3.43 |

## Earnings Estimates & Valuation:

| | IBES EPS | | Price Multiple |
|---|---|---|---|
| Current Yr Est | 1.63 | | 29.4 |
| Fwd Yr. Est. | 2.11 | | 22.7 |
| Last FY End | 97.12 | | |
| # IBES Estimates | 15.00 | | |

| | Growth | P/E to LT Growth |
|---|---|---|
| EPS Growth | 29.4% | 87% |
| IBES L-T Growth | 33.6% | 68% |

**Misc:**

| Employees | 1,600 |
|---|---|
| IPO Date | 10/6/92 |
| First Day Close | $4.00 |

## *Company Description*

NETA is a diversified network security provider that was created towards the end of 1997 by the merger of McAfee Associates, the leader in desktop virus protection products, with Network General, a provider of network diagnostic and management tools. NETA subsequently increased its product breadth by acquiring both Pretty Good Privacy (PGP), a leader in message encryption software, and Trusted Infromation systems, a leading firewall provider. With these acquisitions, the Company is clearly set on a course to expand beyond the market for PC-based security products into the broader market for network and enterprise security solutions.

Sources: Piper Jaffray Research, FactSet, IBES, Compustat, Company Reports
Figures in millions, except per share amounts

Piper Jaffray Equity Research
Electronic Commerce

# Company Profile:
## NOVA CORP/GA

## NIS

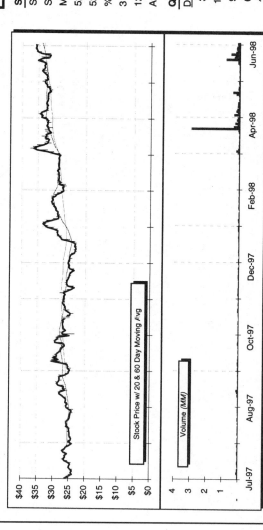

**Stock Data**

| | 6/30/98 |
|---|---|
| Stock Price as of | $35.75 |
| Shares Outstanding | 34.23 |
| Market Cap | $1,224 |
| 52 Week High | $37.44 |
| 52 Week Low | $22.75 |
| % of 52 Week High | 95% |
| 3 Month Return | 19% |
| 12 Month Return | 38% |
| Avg Daily Volume (past mo.) | 0.15 |

**Quarterly EPS Performance**

| Date | IBES Est | Actual | Suprise |
|---|---|---|---|
| 3/98 | 0.14 | 0.10 | (0.04) |
| 12/97 | 0.17 | 0.17 | - |
| 9/97 | 0.15 | 0.16 | 0.01 |
| 6/97 | 0.13 | 0.15 | 0.02 |
| 3/97 | 0.10 | 0.11 | 0.01 |

**Annual Fundamentals**

| | 12/96 | 12/97 |
|---|---|---|
| Revenue | 265.8 | 335.6 |
| Growth | | 26% |
| Gross Sales | 44.9 | 62.3 |
| Operating Income | 11.9 | 28.4 |
| Net Income | 7.3 | 17.4 |

**Quarterly Fundamentals**

| | 6/96 | 9/96 | 12/96 | 3/97 | 6/97 | 9/97 | 12/97 | 3/98 |
|---|---|---|---|---|---|---|---|---|
| Revenue | 67.6 | 70.5 | 67.6 | 66.5 | 78.0 | 87.5 | 103.6 | 133.3 |
| Seq'l Growth | | 4% | -4% | -2% | 17% | 12% | 18% | 29% |
| Y/Y Growth | | | | | 15% | 24% | 53% | 100% |
| Gross Sales | 11.2 | 11.7 | 11.6 | 12.1 | 15.6 | 16.4 | 18.2 | 19.9 |
| Operating Income | 2.5 | 3.6 | 3.6 | 4.7 | 7.0 | 7.7 | 9.0 | 8.7 |
| Net Income | 1.4 | 2.4 | 2.3 | 3.1 | 4.4 | 4.8 | 5.1 | 2.9 |

| | | | | | | | | | | |
|---|---|---|---|---|---|---|---|---|---|---|
| Gross Margins | 17% | 17% | 17% | 18% | 20% | 19% | 18% | 15% | 17% | 19% |
| Operating Margin | 4% | 5% | 5% | 7% | 9% | 9% | 9% | 7% | 4% | 8% |
| Net Margin | 2% | 3% | 3% | 5% | 6% | 5% | 5% | 2% | 3% | 5% |
| Cash & S-T Invest. | 36.4 | 35.0 | 40.3 | 43.7 | 20.3 | 20.4 | 0.7 | 1.1 | 40.3 | 0.7 |
| L-T Debt | 1.1 | 1.2 | 0.9 | 0.8 | 0.8 | 0.7 | 33.3 | 70.0 | 0.9 | 33.3 |
| StkHldrs Equity | 78.9 | 81.3 | 84.9 | 88.2 | 92.7 | 97.6 | 102.9 | 106.1 | 84.9 | 102.9 |
| Op. Cash Flow | 6.9 | 1.7 | 10.2 | 5.5 | 2.3 | 9.3 | 0.9 | 10.6 | 20.7 | 18.0 |
| **Per Share Data** | | | | | | | | | | |
| Shares Out | 28.69 | 28.69 | 28.72 | 28.82 | 28.88 | 28.89 | 29.03 | 29.13 | 28.72 | 29.03 |
| Net Income | 0.05 | 0.08 | 0.08 | 0.11 | 0.15 | 0.16 | 0.17 | 0.10 | 0.25 | 0.60 |
| Cash & S-T Inv. | 1.27 | 1.22 | 1.40 | 1.52 | 0.70 | 0.71 | 0.03 | 0.04 | 1.40 | 0.03 |
| Book Value | 2.75 | 2.83 | 2.96 | 3.06 | 3.21 | 3.38 | 3.55 | 3.64 | 2.96 | 3.55 |

## Earnings Estimates & Valuation:

| | IBES EPS | | Price Multiple |
|---|---|---|---|
| Current Yr Est | 0.78 | | **45.8** |
| Fwd Yr. Est. | 1.20 | | **29.8** |
| Last FY End | 97.12 | | |
| # IBES Estimates | 5.00 | | |

| | Growth | | P/E to LT Growth |
|---|---|---|---|
| EPS Growth | 53.8% | | **158%** |
| IBES L-T Growth | 29.0% | | **103%** |

**Misc:**

| | |
|---|---|
| Employees | 614 |
| IPO Date | 5/8/96 |
| First Day Close | $29.13 |

### Company Description

NIS is a card processor that focuses on small-to-medium sized merchants. In addition to supporting all major credit and charge cards, the Company provides access to debit card processing check verification services. The Company has developed several software applications that can be delivered to customers and updated via a proprietary telecom network.

Sources: Piper Jaffray Research, FactSet, IBES, Compustat, Company Reports
Figures in millions, except per share amounts

Piper Jaffray Equity Research
Electronic Commerce

# Company Profile:
## ONSALE INC

## ONSL

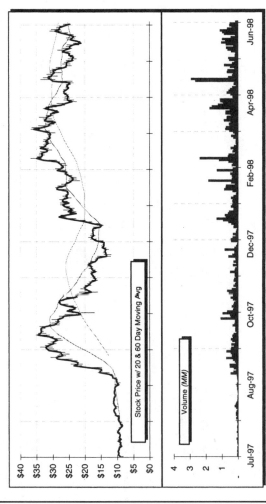

Stock Price w/ 20 & 60 Day Moving Avg

Volume (MM)

### Stock Data

| | | |
|---|---|---|
| Stock Price as of | 6/30/98 | $24.75 |
| Shares Outstanding | | 18.76 |
| Market Cap | | $464 |
| 52 Week High | | $36.81 |
| 52 Week Low | | $8.25 |
| % of 52 Week High | | 67% |
| 3 Month Return | | -20% |
| 12 Month Return | | 168% |
| Avg Daily Volume (past mo.) | | 0.56 |

### Quarterly EPS Performance

| Date | IBES Est | Actual | Suprise |
|---|---|---|---|
| 3/98 | (0.18) | (0.16) | 0.02 |
| 12/97 | (0.09) | (0.09) | - |
| 9/97 | (0.05) | (0.03) | 0.02 |
| 6/97 | (0.02) | 0.01 | 0.03 |
| 3/97 | | - | |

### Annual Fundamentals

| | 12/96 | 12/97 |
|---|---|---|
| Revenue | 14.3 | 89.0 |
| Growth | | 524% |
| Gross Sales | 2.9 | 11.3 |
| Operating Income | 0.5 | (3.4) |
| Net Income | 0.4 | (2.5) |

### Quarterly Fundamentals

| | 6/96 | 9/96 | 12/96 | 3/97 | 6/97 | 9/97 | 12/97 | 3/98 |
|---|---|---|---|---|---|---|---|---|
| Revenue | 1.8 | 3.6 | 8.3 | 12.3 | 18.6 | 25.1 | 33.0 | 40.2 |
| Seq'l Growth | | 98% | 132% | 48% | 51% | 35% | 32% | 22% |
| Y/Y Growth | | | | | 926% | 601% | 298% | 226% |
| Gross Sales | 0.4 | 0.9 | 1.2 | 1.8 | 2.4 | 3.3 | 3.7 | 4.3 |
| Operating Income | 0.1 | 0.1 | 0.1 | 0.0 | (0.4) | (0.8) | (2.3) | (4.1) |
| Net Income | 0.1 | 0.1 | 0.1 | 0.1 | (0.2) | (0.6) | (1.7) | (4.2) |

**Earnings Estimates & Valuation:**

| | IBES EPS | Price Multiple |
|---|---|---|
| Current Yr Est | (0.68) | NM |
| Fwd Yr. Est. | 0.11 | 225.0 |
| Last FY End | 97.12 | |
| # IBES Estimates | 10.00 | |

| | Growth | P/E to LT Growth |
|---|---|---|
| EPS Growth | -116.2% | NM |
| IBES L-T Growth | 58.0% | 388% |

**Misc:**

| | |
|---|---|
| Employees | 129 |
| IPO Date | 4/17/97 |
| First Day Close | $5.88 |

| | | | | | | | | |
|---|---|---|---|---|---|---|---|---|
| Gross Margins | 24% | 25% | 15% | 15% | 13% | 13% | 11% | 11% |
| Operating Margin | 6% | 3% | 1% | 0% | -2% | -3% | -7% | -10% |
| Net Margin | 6% | 3% | 2% | 0% | -1% | -2% | -5% | -10% |
| Cash & S-T Invest. | NA | NA | 2.7 | 2.7 | 12.7 | 11.2 | 56.6 | 52.0 |
| L-T Debt | NA | NA | - | - | - | - | - | - |
| StkHldrs Equity | NA | NA | 2.3 | 4.4 | 19.0 | 18.5 | 62.3 | 58.5 |
| Op. Cash Flow | NA | NA | NA | (1.7) | (4.4) | (1.4) | 0.5 | (3.4) |
| **Per Share Data** | | | | | | | | |
| Shares Out | NA | 12.18 | 12.18 | 12.18 | 16.76 | 16.80 | 18.64 | 18.75 |
| Net Income | NA | 0.01 | 0.00 | 0.01 | (0.01) | (0.03) | (0.09) | (0.22) |
| Cash & S-T Inv. | NA | 0.22 | 0.22 | 0.22 | 0.76 | 0.67 | 3.03 | 2.78 |
| Book Value | NA | 0.19 | 0.36 | 0.19 | 1.13 | 1.10 | 3.34 | 3.12 |

| | | |
|---|---|---|
| Gross Margins | 20% | 13% |
| Operating Margin | 3% | -4% |
| Net Margin | 3% | -3% |
| Cash & S-T Invest. | 2.7 | 56.6 |
| L-T Debt | - | - |
| StkHldrs Equity | 2.3 | 62.3 |
| Op. Cash Flow | 1.1 | (7.0) |
| **Per Share Data** | | |
| Shares Out | 12.18 | 18.64 |
| Net Income | 0.03 | (0.13) |
| Cash & S-T Inv. | 0.22 | 3.03 |
| Book Value | 0.19 | 3.34 |

## Company Description

ONSL operates the Internet's auction service in which it sells excess name brand merchandise consisting mainly of computer equipment, consumer electronics, fitness equipment, sports memorabilia, and specialty foods. From its website, the Company conducts thousands of auctions each week. Customers can monitor auctions and submit bids on the website, then receive notification via email. The Company's BidWatch application allows customers to monitor auctions real-time on their desktops in a more passive mode. Through its Exchange service, the Company also offers person-to-person auctions, similar to classified ads, but with the added benefit of interactive auctions.

Sources: Piper Jaffray Research, FactSet, IBES, Compustat, Company Reports
Figures in millions, except per share amounts

Piper Jaffray Equity Research
Electronic Commerce

# Company Profile:
## OPEN MARKET INC

## OMKT

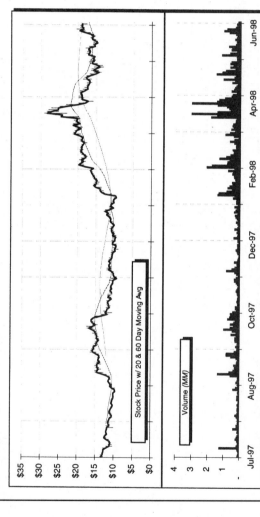

### Stock Data

| | |
|---|---|
| Stock Price as of | **6/30/98** $18.88 |
| Shares Outstanding | 32.14 |
| Market Cap | $607 |
| 52 Week High | $29.13 |
| 52 Week Low | $8.88 |
| % of 52 Week High | 65% |
| 3 Month Return | -8% |
| 12 Month Return | 42% |
| Avg Daily Volume (past mo.) | 0.44 |

### Quarterly EPS Performance

| Date | IBES Est | Actual | Suprise |
|---|---|---|---|
| 3/98 | (0.14) | (0.18) | **(0.04)** |
| 12/97 | (0.13) | (0.09) | **0.04** |
| 9/97 | (0.22) | (0.20) | **0.02** |
| 6/97 | (0.28) | (0.24) | **0.04** |
| 3/97 | (0.25) | (0.23) | **0.02** |

### Annual Fundamentals

| | 12/96 | 12/97 |
|---|---|---|
| Revenue | 22.5 | 61.3 |
| Growth | | 172% |
| Gross Sales | 17.0 | 49.6 |
| Operating Income | (29.1) | (25.0) |

### Quarterly Fundamentals

| | 6/96 | 9/96 | 12/96 | 3/97 | 6/97 | 9/97 | 12/97 | 3/98 |
|---|---|---|---|---|---|---|---|---|
| Revenue | 4.7 | 6.7 | 8.4 | 11.4 | 15.5 | 15.7 | 18.6 | 15.2 |
| Seq'l Growth | | 42% | 25% | 35% | 37% | 1% | 18% | -18% |
| Y/Y Growth | | | | | 230% | 135% | 122% | 34% |
| Gross Sales | 3.4 | 5.3 | 6.1 | 8.4 | 12.5 | 13.0 | 15.8 | 11.7 |
| Operating Income | (7.2) | (7.0) | (7.9) | (7.4) | (7.8) | (6.6) | (3.2) | (5.9) |

| Gross Margins | 73% | 78% | 72% | 74% | 80% | 82% | 85% | 77% | 76% | 81% |
|---|---|---|---|---|---|---|---|---|---|---|
| Operating Margin | NM | NM | -94% | -65% | -50% | -42% | -17% | -39% | NM | NM |
| Net Margin | NM | -88% | -85% | NM | -48% | -41% | -16% | -38% | NM | -95% |
| Cash & S-T Invest. | 89.7 | 79.3 | 72.0 | 51.9 | 46.9 | 41.8 | 30.6 | 27.7 | 72.0 | 30.6 |
| L-T Debt | 0.1 | 0.1 | 0.1 | 0.1 | 0.1 | 0.1 | 0.1 | 0.1 | 0.1 | 0.1 |
| StkHldrs Equity | 84.8 | 79.2 | 72.4 | 59.7 | 52.3 | 46.4 | 43.5 | 42.1 | 72.4 | 43.5 |
| Op. Cash Flow | (6.3) | (9.0) | (5.5) | (8.3) | (2.8) | (8.7) | (9.0) | (8.3) | (27.1) | (28.8) |
| **Per Share Data** | | | | | | | | | | |
| Shares Out | 28.14 | 28.23 | 28.57 | 31.55 | 31.64 | 31.80 | 30.97 | 32.08 | 28.57 | 30.97 |
| Net Income | (0.24) | (0.21) | (0.25) | (1.30) | (0.24) | (0.20) | (0.10) | (0.18) | (0.93) | (1.87) |
| Cash & S-T Inv. | 3.19 | 2.81 | 2.52 | 1.64 | 1.48 | 1.31 | 0.99 | 0.86 | 2.52 | 0.99 |
| Book Value | 3.01 | 2.80 | 2.53 | 1.89 | 1.65 | 1.46 | 1.40 | 1.31 | 2.53 | 1.40 |

## Earnings Estimates & Valuation:

| | IBES EPS | | Price Multiple |
|---|---|---|---|
| Current Yr Est | (0.21) | | NM |
| Fwd Yr. Est. | 0.24 | | 78.6 |
| Last FY End | 97.12 | | |
| # IBES Estimates | 5.00 | | |

| | Growth | | P/E to LT Growth |
|---|---|---|---|
| EPS Growth | -214.3% | | NM |
| IBES L-T Growth | 43.0% | | 183% |

Misc:
Employees
IPO Date 5/23/96
First Day Close $39.88

## Company Description

OMKT develops software that facilitates business-business and business-consumer transactions over the Internet. The Company's software is a client/server system that provides back office functions such as order taking, authorization, payment processing, security and customer service. The Transact product provides order management, Axcess manages user authentication and authorization and SecureLink links content with industry standard web servers. The Company also acquired the Folio Corp. in 1997, which provides electronic publishing software for the management of content over networks.

Sources: Piper Jaffray Research, FactSet, IBES, Compustat, Company Reports
Figures in millions, except per share amounts

Piper Jaffray Equity Research
Electronic Commerce

## Company Profile:
# PAYMENTECH INC

## PTI

### Stock Data

| | |
|---|---|
| Stock Price as of | **6/30/98** $20.56 |
| Shares Outstanding | 36.02 |
| Market Cap | $741 |
| 52 Week High | $32.38 |
| 52 Week Low | $11.81 |
| % of 52 Week High | 64% |
| 3 Month Return | 6% |
| 12 Month Return | -29% |
| Avg Daily Volume (past mo.) | 0.05 |

### Quarterly EPS Performance

| Date | IBES Est | Actual | Suprise |
|---|---|---|---|
| 3/98 | 0.12 | 0.12 | - |
| 12/97 | 0.18 | 0.15 | (0.03) |
| 9/97 | 0.14 | 0.12 | (0.02) |
| 6/97 | 0.22 | 0.22 | - |
| 3/97 | 0.21 | 0.21 | - |

### Annual Fundamentals

| | 6/96 | 6/97 |
|---|---|---|
| Revenue | 121.2 | 186.1 |
| Growth | | 54% |
| Gross Sales | 21.0 | 40.4 |
| Operating Income | 21.0 | 40.4 |
| Net Income | 14.3 | 3.7 |

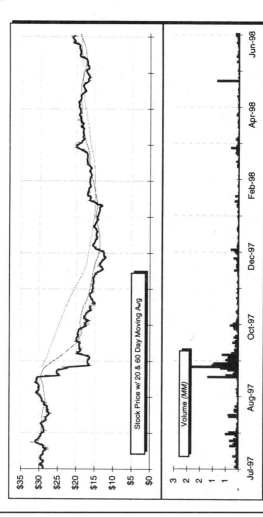

Stock Price w/ 20 & 60 Day Moving Avg

Volume (MM)

| | Jul-97 | Aug-97 | Oct-97 | Dec-97 | Feb-98 | Apr-98 | Jun-98 |

### Quarterly Fundamentals

| | 6/96 | 9/96 | 12/96 | 3/97 | 6/97 | 9/97 | 12/97 | 3/98 |
|---|---|---|---|---|---|---|---|---|
| Revenue | 34.8 | 41.1 | 48.3 | 47.0 | 49.8 | 50.3 | 55.5 | 52.4 |
| Seq'l Growth | | 18% | 17% | -3% | 6% | 1% | 10% | -6% |
| Y/Y Growth | | | | | 43% | 22% | 15% | 12% |
| Gross Sales | 7.9 | 9.7 | 13.2 | 9.1 | 8.4 | 7.9 | 3.7 | 9.0 |
| Operating Income | 7.9 | 9.7 | 13.2 | 9.1 | 8.4 | 7.9 | 3.7 | 9.0 |

Operating Margin | 23% | 24% | 27% |  | 19% | 16% | 7% | 17% |  | 17% | 17% | 22%
Net Margin | 16% | -8% | 17% |  | 16% | 12% | 12% | 8% |  | 12% | 12% | 2%

| | | | | | | | | | Gross Margins | | |
| --- | --- | --- | --- | --- | --- | --- | --- | --- | --- | --- | --- |
| | | | | | | | | | Operating Margin | 17% | 22% |
| | | | | | | | | | Net Margin | 12% | 2% |
| Cash & S-T Invest. | 105.8 | 72.8 | 69.9 | 99.8 | 108.9 | 142.0 | 151.5 | 119.5 | Cash & S-T Invest. | 105.8 | 119.5 |
| L-T Debt | - | 25.0 | 25.0 | 75.2 | 75.1 | 75.1 | 55.1 | 75.1 | L-T Debt | - | 75.1 |
| StkHldrs Equity | 231.1 | 227.8 | 333.6 | 349.8 | 366.8 | 378.3 | 391.8 | 359.4 | StkHldrs Equity | 231.1 | 359.4 |
| Op. Cash Flow | NA | 55.9 | 4.7 | 21.1 | (14.0) | 7.7 | 29.5 | 30.1 | Op. Cash Flow | 20.7 | 111.8 |
| **Per Share Data** | | | | | | | | | **Per Share Data** | | |
| Shares Out | 31.70 | 31.70 | 34.72 | 34.95 | 35.33 | 35.35 | 35.99 | 35.09 | Shares Out | 31.70 | 35.09 |
| Net Income | 0.17 | (0.10) | 0.24 | 0.21 | 0.12 | 0.19 | 0.12 | (0.25) | Net Income | 0.45 | 0.11 |
| Cash & S-T Inv. | 3.34 | 2.30 | 2.01 | 2.86 | 3.08 | 4.02 | 4.21 | 3.40 | Cash & S-T Inv. | 3.34 | 3.40 |
| Book Value | 7.29 | 7.19 | 9.61 | 10.01 | 10.38 | 10.70 | 10.89 | 10.24 | Book Value | 7.29 | 10.24 |

## Earnings Estimates & Valuation:

| | IBES EPS | Price Multiple |
| --- | --- | --- |
| Current Yr Est | 0.53 | 38.8 |
| Fwd Yr. Est. | 0.69 | 29.8 |
| Last FY End | 97.06 | |
| # IBES Estimates | 7.00 | |

| | Growth | P/E to LT Growth |
| --- | --- | --- |
| EPS Growth | 30.2% | 194% |
| IBES L-T Growth | 20.0% | 149% |

Misc:

| | |
| --- | --- |
| Employees | 1,200 |
| IPO Date | 3/22/96 |
| First Day Close | $30.63 |

## Company Description

Paymentech (PTI) is a merchant processor, primarily of credit and debit card transactions. It is the third largest payment processor of bankcard transactions in the US according to industry sources. The Company also provides third party credit and debit authorization services in addition to marketing and issuing procurement cards to corporations. PTI is a 57% owned subsidiary of First USA Financial, a wholly owned subsidiary of Bank One Corporation.

Sources: Piper Jaffray Research, FactSet, IBES, Compustat, Company Reports
Figures in millions, except per share amounts

Piper Jaffray Equity Research
Electronic Commerce

# Company Profile:
# PEAPOD INC

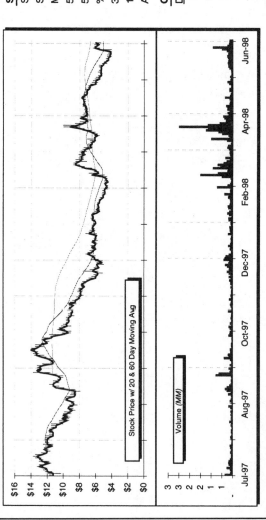

## PPOD

### Stock Data

| | |
|---|---|
| Stock Price as of | 6/30/98 |
| | $6.00 |
| Shares Outstanding | 16.89 |
| Market Cap | $101 |
| 52 Week High | $14.00 |
| 52 Week Low | $4.06 |
| % of 52 Week High | 43% |
| 3 Month Return | -19% |
| 12 Month Return | -47% |
| Avg Daily Volume (past mo.) | 0.21 |

### Quarterly EPS Performance

| Date | IBES Est | Actual | Suprise |
|---|---|---|---|
| 3/98 | (0.23) | (0.24) | (0.01) |
| 12/97 | (0.23) | (0.25) | (0.02) |
| 9/97 | (0.18) | (0.17) | 0.01 |
| 6/97 | (0.25) | (0.22) | 0.03 |
| 3/97 | | (0.23) | |

### Annual Fundamentals

| | 12/96 | 12/97 |
|---|---|---|
| Revenue | 29.2 | 59.6 |
| Growth | | 104% |
| Gross Sales | (1.6) | (2.6) |
| Operating Income | (10.0) | (14.9) |

Stock Price w/ 20 & 60 Day Moving Avg

Volume (MM)

| | Jul-97 | Aug-97 | Oct-97 | Dec-97 | Feb-98 | Apr-98 | Jun-98 |

### Quarterly Fundamentals

| | 6/96 | 9/96 | 12/96 | 3/97 | 6/97 | 9/97 | 12/97 | 3/98 |
|---|---|---|---|---|---|---|---|---|
| Revenue | 6.4 | 6.9 | 9.5 | 12.1 | 14.7 | 14.2 | 18.0 | 18.9 |
| Seq'l Growth | | 8% | 38% | 27% | 21% | -3% | 27% | 5% |
| Y/Y Growth | | | | | 128% | 106% | 90% | 56% |
| Gross Sales | (0.4) | (0.1) | (0.8) | (0.6) | (0.2) | (0.5) | (1.3) | (1.4) |
| Operating Income | (2.2) | (2.5) | (3.6) | (3.1) | (3.2) | (3.7) | (5.0) | (4.7) |

| | | | | | | | | | Operating Margin | -34% | -25% |
|---|---|---|---|---|---|---|---|---|---|---|---|
| Operating Margin | -35% | -36% | -37% | -25% | -22% | -26% | -28% | -25% | Net Margin | -33% | -22% |
| Net Margin | -33% | -33% | -36% | -24% | -21% | -20% | -23% | -21% | | | |
| Cash & S-T Invest. | NA | NA | 13.0 | 9.3 | 65.8 | 62.9 | 62.9 | 53.1 | Cash & S-T Invest. | 13.0 | 62.9 |
| L-T Debt | NA | NA | 0.3 | 0.4 | 0.5 | 0.6 | 0.7 | 0.6 | L-T Debt | 0.3 | 0.7 |
| StkHldrs Equity | NA | NA | 8.4 | 6.0 | 61.5 | 58.5 | 54.8 | 50.9 | StkHldrs Equity | 8.4 | 54.8 |
| Op. Cash Flow | NA | NA | NA | (3.4) | (1.2) | (1.8) | 0.1 | (8.8) | Op. Cash Flow | (4.5) | (6.3) |
| **Per Share Data** | | | | | | | | | **Per Share Data** | | |
| Shares Out | NA | NA | 12.53 | 16.63 | 16.67 | 16.68 | 16.85 | 16.88 | Shares Out | 12.53 | 16.85 |
| Net Income | NA | NA | (0.27) | (0.18) | (0.18) | (0.17) | (0.25) | (0.24) | Net Income | (0.76) | (0.77) |
| Cash & S-T Inv. | NA | NA | 1.04 | 0.56 | 3.95 | 3.77 | 3.73 | 3.14 | Cash & S-T Inv. | 1.04 | 3.73 |
| Book Value | NA | NA | 0.67 | 0.36 | 3.69 | 3.51 | 3.25 | 3.01 | Book Value | 0.67 | 3.25 |

### Earnings Estimates & Valuation:

| | IBES EPS | Price Multiple |
|---|---|---|
| Current Yr Est | (1.06) | NM |
| Fwd Yr. Est. | (0.57) | NM |
| Last FY End | 97.12 | |
| # IBES Estimates | 3.00 | |

| | Growth | P/E to LT Growth |
|---|---|---|
| EPS Growth | -46.2% | NM |
| IBES L-T Growth | 50.0% | NM |

**Misc:**

| | |
|---|---|
| Employees | 1,420 |
| IPO Date | 6/11/97 |
| First Day Close | $16.00 |

### *Company Description*

PPOD offers an online grocery shopping service that offers personalized shopping and delivery in several major cities across the U.S. Its members pay monthly dues and per-order fees. Members have access to an online catalog with product and pricing information, and can then place orders electronically via email, fax or phone. The Company has partnered with local supermarket chains to provide order fulfillment. In 1997, the Company had 71,500 members and processed 201,100 orders. The Company also generates a small, but growing portion of its revenues by selling advertising and market research information to consumer goods companies.

Sources: Piper Jaffray Research, FactSet, IBES, Compustat, Company Reports

Figures in millions, except per share amounts

Piper Jaffray Equity Research

Electronic Commerce

Company Profile:
# PREVIEW TRAVEL INC

## PTVL

### Stock Data

| | |
|---|---|
| Stock Price as of **6/30/98** | $34.38 |
| Shares Outstanding | 12.86 |
| Market Cap | $442 |
| 52 Week High | $38.13 |
| 52 Week Low | $6.88 |
| % of 52 Week High | 90% |
| 3 Month Return | 6% |
| 12 Month Return | 0% |
| Avg Daily Volume (past mo.) | 0.20 |

### Quarterly EPS Performance

| Date | IBES Est | Actual | Suprise |
|---|---|---|---|
| 3/98 | (0.43) | (0.41) | **0.02** |
| 12/97 | (0.50) | (0.63) | **(0.13)** |
| 9/97 | | (0.50) | |

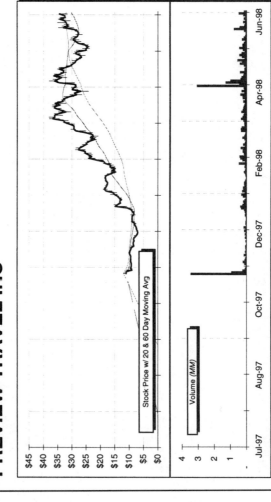

Stock Price w/ 20 & 60 Day Moving Avg

Volume (MM)

| | Jul-97 | Aug-97 | Oct-97 | Dec-97 | Feb-98 | Apr-98 | Jun-98 |

### Annual Fundamentals

| | 12/96 | 12/97 |
|---|---|---|
| Revenue | 12.4 | 13.6 |
| Growth | | 10% |
| Gross Sales | 3.1 | 4.2 |
| Operating Income | (5.5) | (10.4) |

### Quarterly Fundamentals

| | 6/96 | 9/96 | 12/96 | 3/97 | 6/97 | 9/97 | 12/97 | 3/98 |
|---|---|---|---|---|---|---|---|---|
| Revenue | 3.3 | 3.6 | 3.0 | 3.5 | 3.2 | 3.4 | 3.5 | 4.0 |
| Seq'l Growth | | 8% | -16% | 19% | -9% | 6% | 3% | 14% |
| Y/Y Growth | | | | | -3% | -4% | 18% | 14% |
| Gross Sales | 1.1 | 1.1 | 0.3 | 1.2 | 0.9 | 1.0 | 1.1 | 1.6 |
| Operating Income | (0.6) | (1.2) | (2.5) | (1.5) | (1.5) | (2.5) | (4.9) | (5.0) |

| | | | | | | | | | | Operating Margin | | |
|---|---|---|---|---|---|---|---|---|---|---|---|---|
| Operating Margin | -17% | -33% | -85% | -43% | -48% | -74% | NM | NM | | Operating Margin | -44% | -76% |
| Net Margin | -20% | -33% | -84% | -43% | -48% | -74% | NM | NM | | Net Margin | -45% | -75% |
| Cash & S-T Invest. | NA | NA | 6.0 | NA | NA | 13.6 | 28.7 | 23.9 | | Cash & S-T Invest. | 6.0 | 28.7 |
| L-T Debt | NA | NA | 1.0 | NA | NA | 1.3 | 1.6 | 1.9 | | L-T Debt | 1.0 | 1.6 |
| Stk-Hldrs Equity | NA | NA | 4.4 | NA | NA | 14.3 | 35.4 | 30.7 | | Stk-Hldrs Equity | 4.4 | 35.4 |
| Op. Cash Flow | NA | NA | NA | NA | NA | NA | (8.6) | (4.1) | | Op. Cash Flow | (1.3) | (12.8) |
| **Per Share Data** | | | | | | | | | | **Per Share Data** | | |
| Shares Out | NA | NA | 1.70 | NA | NA | 11.65 | 11.34 | 11.36 | | Shares Out | 1.70 | 11.34 |
| Net Income | NA | NA | (1.46) | NA | NA | (0.22) | (0.40) | (0.41) | | Net Income | (3.29) | (0.90) |
| Cash & S-T Inv. | NA | NA | 3.53 | NA | NA | 1.17 | 2.53 | 2.10 | | Cash & S-T Inv. | 3.53 | 2.53 |
| Book Value | NA | NA | 2.59 | NA | NA | 1.22 | 3.12 | 2.70 | | Book Value | 2.59 | 3.12 |

**Earnings Estimates & Valuation:**

| | IBES EPS | Price Multiple |
|---|---|---|
| Current Yr Est | (1.59) | NM |
| Fwd Yr. Est. | (1.20) | NM |
| Last FY End | 97.12 | |
| # IBES Estimates | 4.00 | |

| | Growth | P/E to LT Growth |
|---|---|---|
| EPS Growth | -24.5% | NM |
| IBES L-T Growth | 53.3% | NM |

Misc:

| | |
|---|---|
| Employees | 181 |
| IPO Date | 11/20/97 |
| First Day Close | $11.00 |

## Company Description

PTVL is a leading Internet travel service. The Company operates three websites, PreviewTravel.com, reservations.com, and vacations.com. Additionally, the Company provides America Online's main travel service and a cobranded travel service with Excite on the City.Net service. Customers can use PTVL's services to research destinations (including viewing photos), design custom travel plans, track the best fares, and book travel plans. While most of its services are geared towards leisure travelers, the Company also provides a specific content area for its small business travelers, which account for nearly 30% of its customers. The Company currently has 3.8 million monthly visitors to its sites.

Sources: Piper Jaffray Research, FactSet, IBES, Compustat, Company Reports
Figures in millions, except per share amounts

Piper Jaffray Equity Research
Electronic Commerce

# Company Profile:
## QRS CORP

### QRSI

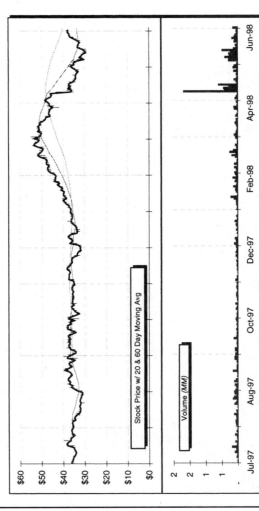

Stock Price w/ 20 & 60 Day Moving Avg

Volume (MM)

| | Jul-97 | Aug-97 | Oct-97 | Dec-97 | Feb-98 | Apr-98 | Jun-98 |

**Stock Data**

| | |
|---|---|
| Stock Price as of | **6/30/98** |
| | $37.63 |
| Shares Outstanding | 8.54 |
| Market Cap | $321 |
| 52 Week High | $54.88 |
| 52 Week Low | $29.00 |
| % of 52 Week High | 69% |
| 3 Month Return | -30% |
| 12 Month Return | 4% |
| Avg Daily Volume (past mo.) | 0.15 |

**Quarterly EPS Performance**

| Date | IBES Est | Actual | Suprise |
|---|---|---|---|
| 3/98 | 0.28 | 0.28 | - |
| 12/97 | 0.29 | 0.29 | - |
| 9/97 | 0.26 | 0.26 | - |
| 6/97 | 0.23 | 0.24 | 0.01 |
| 3/97 | 0.21 | 0.22 | 0.01 |

**Annual Fundamentals**

| | 12/96 | 12/97 |
|---|---|---|
| Revenue | 56.7 | 71.6 |
| *Growth* | | *26%* |
| Gross Sales | 22.9 | 31.2 |
| Operating Income | 9.4 | 12.6 |
| Net Income | 6.6 | 8.8 |

**Quarterly Fundamentals**

| | 6/96 | 9/96 | 12/96 | 3/97 | 6/97 | 9/97 | 12/97 | 3/98 |
|---|---|---|---|---|---|---|---|---|
| Revenue | 13.6 | 14.7 | 15.8 | 16.4 | 17.0 | 18.3 | 20.0 | 20.0 |
| *Seq'l Growth* | | *8%* | *8%* | *4%* | *4%* | *7%* | *10%* | *0%* |
| *Y/Y Growth* | | | | | *25%* | *25%* | *27%* | *23%* |
| Gross Sales | 5.3 | 5.9 | 6.8 | 7.2 | 7.4 | 7.8 | 8.8 | 8.8 |
| Operating Income | 2.2 | 2.4 | 2.9 | 2.8 | 3.0 | 3.2 | 3.7 | 3.6 |
| Net Income | 1.5 | 1.7 | 2.0 | 1.9 | 2.1 | 2.3 | 2.5 | 3.4 |

| Gross Margins | 39% | 40% | 43% | 44% | 43% | 43% | 44% | 44% | | Gross Margins | 40% | 44% |
|---|---|---|---|---|---|---|---|---|---|---|---|---|
| Operating Margin | 16% | 17% | 18% | 17% | 18% | 18% | 18% | 18% | | Operating Margin | 17% | 18% |
| Net Margin | 11% | 12% | 13% | 12% | 12% | 12% | 12% | 17% | | Net Margin | 12% | 12% |
| | | | | | | | | | | | | |
| Cash & S-T Invest. | 27.7 | 22.4 | 24.6 | 20.8 | 23.9 | 32.5 | 33.8 | 40.8 | | Cash & S-T Invest. | 24.6 | 33.8 |
| L-T Debt | | | | | | | | | | L-T Debt | - | - |
| StkHldrs Equity | 38.9 | 40.9 | 43.6 | 45.6 | 48.9 | 51.3 | 54.7 | 58.6 | | StkHldrs Equity | 43.6 | 54.7 |
| Op. Cash Flow | 1.9 | 5.0 | 3.7 | (0.4) | 4.5 | 0.1 | 3.0 | 8.0 | | Op. Cash Flow | 12.4 | 7.2 |

**Per Share Data**

| Shares Out | 8.35 | 8.37 | 8.41 | 8.42 | 8.48 | 8.49 | 8.53 | 8.54 | | Shares Out | 8.41 | 8.53 |
|---|---|---|---|---|---|---|---|---|---|---|---|---|
| Net Income | 0.18 | 0.20 | 0.24 | 0.23 | 0.25 | 0.27 | 0.29 | 0.39 | | Net Income | 0.79 | 1.03 |
| Cash & S-T Inv. | 3.32 | 2.68 | 2.93 | 2.47 | 2.82 | 3.82 | 3.96 | 4.78 | | Cash & S-T Inv. | 2.93 | 3.96 |
| Book Value | 4.66 | 4.89 | 5.18 | 5.42 | 5.76 | 6.04 | 6.42 | 6.86 | | Book Value | 5.18 | 6.42 |

**Earnings Estimates & Valuation:**

| | IBES EPS | Price Multiple |
|---|---|---|
| Current Yr Est | 1.29 | 29.2 |
| Fwd Yr. Est. | 1.65 | 22.8 |
| Last FY End | 97.12 | |
| # IBES Estimates | 9.00 | |

| | Growth | P/E to LT Growth |
|---|---|---|
| EPS Growth | 27.9% | 102% |
| IBES L-T Growth | 28.7% | 79% |

**Misc:**

| | |
|---|---|
| Employees | 216 |
| IPO Date | 8/5/93 |
| First Day Close | $16.13 |

## Company Description

QRSI has developed the world's largest UPC-based electronic catalog service. This service provides retailers with full-time, on demand access to updated information on products available from manufacturers and includes listings on more than 60 million products. With the catalog service at the core, the Company also offers replenishment, sales analysis, forecasting, logistics, and transportation solutions for retailers, manufacturers and related parties.

Sources: Piper Jaffray Research, FactSet, IBES, Compustat, Company Reports
Figures in millions, except per share amounts

Piper Jaffray Equity Research
Electronic Commerce

Company Profile:
# SANCHEZ COMPUTER ASSOCS INC

## SCAI

### Stock Data

| | |
|---|---:|
| Stock Price as of | **6/30/98** |
| | $20.38 |
| Shares Outstanding | 11.62 |
| Market Cap | $237 |
| 52 Week High | $34.63 |
| 52 Week Low | $9.00 |
| % of 52 Week High | 59% |
| 3 Month Return | -1% |
| 12 Month Return | 117% |
| Avg Daily Volume (past mo.) | 0.09 |

### Quarterly EPS Performance

| Date | IBES Est | Actual | Suprise |
|---|---|---|---|
| 3/98 | 0.06 | 0.07 | **0.01** |
| 12/97 | 0.10 | 0.11 | **0.01** |
| 9/97 | 0.07 | 0.10 | **0.03** |
| 6/97 | 0.04 | 0.05 | **0.01** |
| 3/97 | 0.01 | 0.03 | **0.02** |

### Annual Fundamentals

| | 12/96 | 12/97 |
|---|---|---|
| Revenue | 17.7 | 28.3 |
| Growth | | 60% |
| Gross Sales | 1.2 | 4.1 |
| Operating Income | 1.2 | 4.1 |
| Net Income | 1.1 | 3.5 |

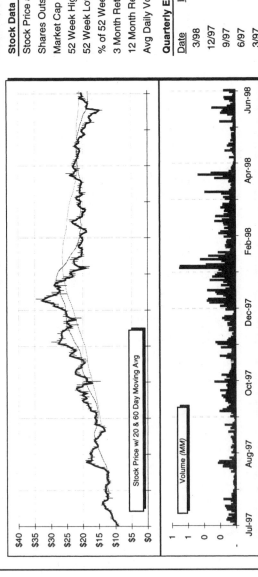

Stock Price w/ 20 & 60 Day Moving Avg

Volume *(MM)*

### Quarterly Fundamentals

| | 6/96 | 9/96 | 12/96 | 3/97 | 6/97 | 9/97 | 12/97 | 3/98 |
|---|---|---|---|---|---|---|---|---|
| Revenue | 4.8 | 4.5 | 4.9 | 5.4 | 6.2 | 8.2 | 8.7 | 8.6 |
| Seq'l Growth | | -5% | 8% | 9% | 15% | 33% | 6% | -1% |
| Y/Y Growth | | | | | 30% | 81% | 77% | 60% |
| Gross Sales | 0.5 | 0.4 | 0.4 | 0.5 | 0.6 | 1.6 | 1.6 | 1.0 |
| Operating Income | 0.5 | 0.4 | 0.4 | 0.5 | 0.6 | 1.6 | 1.6 | 1.0 |
| Net Income | 0.4 | 0.3 | 0.4 | 0.5 | 0.6 | 1.2 | 1.3 | 0.8 |

| | | | | | | | | | | |
|---|---|---|---|---|---|---|---|---|---|---|
| Gross Margins | 11% | 8% | 10% | 10% | 19% | 19% | 12% | | Gross Margins | 7% | 15% |
| Operating Margin | 11% | 8% | 10% | 10% | 19% | 19% | 12% | | Operating Margin | 7% | 15% |
| Net Margin | 8% | 7% | 9% | 9% | 15% | 15% | 10% | | Net Margin | 6% | 12% |
| Cash & S-T Invest. | 15.4 | 6.3 | 17.6 | 15.9 | 14.0 | 12.8 | 14.4 | | Cash & S-T Invest. | 15.4 | 12.8 |
| L-T Debt | NA | 0.2 | 0.2 | 0.2 | 0.1 | 0.1 | 0.1 | | L-T Debt | 0.2 | 0.1 |
| StkHldrs Equity | 18.9 | 6.6 | 19.4 | 20.1 | 21.6 | 23.2 | 24.3 | | StkHldrs Equity | 18.9 | 23.2 |
| Op. Cash Flow | (2.4) | NA | 2.3 | (1.3) | (1.8) | 0.5 | 1.9 | | Op. Cash Flow | (1.3) | (0.3) |
| **Per Share Data** | | | | | | | | | **Per Share Data** | | |
| Shares Out | 10.87 | 10.71 | 10.89 | 10.92 | 11.04 | 11.07 | 11.26 | | Shares Out | 10.87 | 11.07 |
| Net Income | 0.04 | 0.03 | 0.05 | 0.05 | 0.11 | 0.12 | 0.07 | | Net Income | 0.10 | 0.31 |
| Cash & S-T Inv. | 1.42 | 0.58 | 1.62 | 1.46 | 1.27 | 1.16 | 1.28 | | Cash & S-T Inv. | 1.42 | 1.16 |
| Book Value | 1.74 | 0.62 | 1.78 | 1.84 | 1.96 | 2.10 | 2.16 | | Book Value | 1.74 | 2.10 |

## Earnings Estimates & Valuation:

| | IBES EPS | Price Multiple |
|---|---|---|
| Current Yr Est | 0.44 | 46.3 |
| Fwd Yr. Est. | 0.71 | 28.7 |
| Last FY End | 97.12 | |
| # IBES Estimates | 3.00 | |

| | Growth | P/E to LT Growth |
|---|---|---|
| EPS Growth | 61.4% | 93% |
| IBES L-T Growth | 50.0% | 57% |

**Misc:**

| | |
|---|---|
| Employees | 241 |
| IPO Date | 11/14/96 |
| First Day Close | $18.00 |

## Company Description

SCAI develops core-banking systems for financial institutions worldwide. The Company's Profile product family is a client-server solution that supports all bank products in addition to multiple currencies and multiple distribution channels, including the Internet. The product's key benefits are its scalability and its flexibility to support the development and delivery of new products. The product is currently in strong demand internationally where financial institutions are looking to completely replace and modernize their systems, hence international sales, especially Central Europe, make up the bulk of revenues.

Sources: Piper Jaffray Research, FactSet, IBES, Compustat, Company Reports
Figures in millions, except per share amounts

Piper Jaffray Equity Research
Electronic Commerce

## Company Profile:
# SECURE COMPUTING CORP

# SCUR

**Stock Data**

| | |
|---|---|
| Stock Price as of | **6/30/98** | **$9.88** |
| Shares Outstanding | | 16.03 |
| Market Cap | | $158 |
| 52 Week High | | $15.25 |
| 52 Week Low | | $5.50 |
| % of 52 Week High | | 65% |
| 3 Month Return | | -26% |
| 12 Month Return | | 68% |
| Avg Daily Volume (past mo.) | | 0.12 |

**Quarterly EPS Performance**

| Date | IBES Est | Actual | Suprise |
|---|---|---|---|
| 3/98 | 0.02 | 0.03 | **0.01** |
| 12/97 | 0.01 | 0.02 | **0.01** |
| 9/97 | (0.05) | (0.02) | **0.03** |
| 6/97 | (0.12) | (0.08) | **0.04** |
| 3/97 | | (0.19) | |

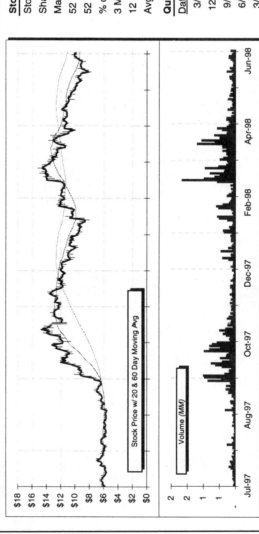

Stock Price w/ 20 & 60 Day Moving Avg

Volume *(MM)*

**Annual Fundamentals**

| | 12/96 | 12/97 |
|---|---|---|
| Revenue | 40.3 | 47.0 |
| *Growth* | | *17%* |
| Gross Sales | 21.5 | 28.2 |
| Operating Income | (13.4) | (4.8) |
| Net Income | (25.1) | (4.3) |

**Quarterly Fundamentals**

| | 6/96 | 9/96 | 12/96 | 3/97 | 6/97 | 9/97 | 12/97 | 3/98 |
|---|---|---|---|---|---|---|---|---|
| Revenue | 9.3 | 10.8 | 9.0 | 10.6 | 11.3 | 12.2 | 12.8 | 12.8 |
| *Seq'l Growth* | | *16%* | *-17%* | *18%* | *7%* | *8%* | *5%* | *0%* |
| *Y/Y Growth* | | | | | *21%* | *13%* | *42%* | *20%* |
| Gross Sales | 4.9 | 5.9 | 4.6 | 5.5 | 6.5 | 7.7 | 8.5 | 8.5 |
| Operating Income | (4.2) | (3.2) | (6.0) | (3.1) | (1.4) | (0.5) | 0.2 | 0.0 |
| Net Income | (5.7) | (2.0) | (5.7) | (3.0) | (1.2) | (0.4) | 0.3 | (7.4) |

| | | | | | | | | | | |
|---|---|---|---|---|---|---|---|---|---|---|
| Gross Margins | 52% | 55% | 51% | 52% | 58% | 63% | 66% | 67% | Gross Margins | 53% | 60% |
| Operating Margin | -45% | -29% | -66% | -29% | -12% | -4% | 1% | 0% | Operating Margin | -33% | -10% |
| Net Margin | NM | -26% | -63% | -28% | -11% | -3% | 2% | -58% | Net Margin | -62% | -9% |
| Cash & S-T Invest. | 27.5 | 21.3 | 18.1 | 13.9 | 12.0 | 8.7 | 4.9 | 4.2 | Cash & S-T Invest. | 18.1 | 4.9 |
| L-T Debt | - | - | - | - | - | - | - | - | L-T Debt | - | - |
| StkHldrs Equity | 30.9 | 31.2 | 26.2 | 24.2 | 23.0 | 23.0 | 24.8 | 18.4 | StkHldrs Equity | 26.2 | 24.8 |
| Op. Cash Flow | (1.8) | (12.9) | (2.2) | (4.1) | (1.5) | (2.7) | (3.2) | (1.4) | Op. Cash Flow | (17.5) | (11.6) |
| Per Share Data | | | | | | | | | Per Share Data | | |
| Shares Out | 6.77 | 14.87 | 15.10 | 15.41 | 15.50 | 15.62 | 15.76 | 16.00 | Shares Out | 15.10 | 15.76 |
| Net Income | (2.46) | (0.19) | (0.38) | (0.19) | (0.08) | (0.02) | 0.02 | (0.46) | Net Income | (1.66) | (0.27) |
| Cash & S-T Inv. | 4.07 | 1.43 | 1.20 | 0.90 | 0.77 | 0.56 | 0.31 | 0.26 | Cash & S-T Inv. | 1.20 | 0.31 |
| Book Value | 4.56 | 2.10 | 1.74 | 1.57 | 1.48 | 1.47 | 1.57 | 1.15 | Book Value | 1.74 | 1.57 |

## Earnings Estimates & Valuation:

| | IBES EPS | Price Multiple |
|---|---|---|
| Current Yr Est | 0.31 | 31.9 |
| Fwd Yr. Est. | 0.62 | 15.9 |
| Last FY End | 97.12 | |
| # IBES Estimates | 6.00 | |

| | Growth | P/E to LT Growth |
|---|---|---|
| EPS Growth | 100.0% | 94% |
| IBES L-T Growth | 33.8% | 47% |

### Misc:

| | |
|---|---|
| Employees | 360 |
| IPO Date | 11/17/95 |
| First Day Close | $48.25 |

## Company Description

SCUR began as a firewall provider, but like many security providers has branched out, mainly through acquisition, and now also provides tokens (both software and hardward), web filtering. access control solutions, and consulting services. Its products operate on most major platforms including Unix and Windows NT. The Company claims over 4,000 customers and generates a significant, but declining portion of its revenues from government contracts. The Company acquired token vendor Enigma Logic and firewall provider Borderware in 1996.

Sources: Piper Jaffray Research, FactSet, IBES, Compustat, Company Reports
Figures in millions, except per share amounts

Piper Jaffray Equity Research
Electronic Commerce

# Company Profile:
# SECURITY DYNAMICS TECH INC

## SDTI

### Stock Data

| | 6/30/98 | |
|---|---|---|
| Stock Price as of | 6/30/98 | $18.50 |
| Shares Outstanding | | 40.88 |
| Market Cap | | $756 |
| 52 Week High | | $44.38 |
| 52 Week Low | | $15.13 |
| % of 52 Week High | | 42% |
| 3 Month Return | | -55% |
| 12 Month Return | | -50% |
| Avg Daily Volume (past mo.) | | 0.71 |

### Quarterly EPS Performance

| Date | IBES Est | Actual | Suprise |
|---|---|---|---|
| 6/98 | 0.15 | 0.15 | - |
| 3/98 | 0.14 | 0.14 | - |
| 12/97 | 0.16 | 0.17 | 0.01 |
| 9/97 | 0.14 | 0.15 | 0.01 |
| 6/97 | 0.14 | 0.15 | 0.01 |

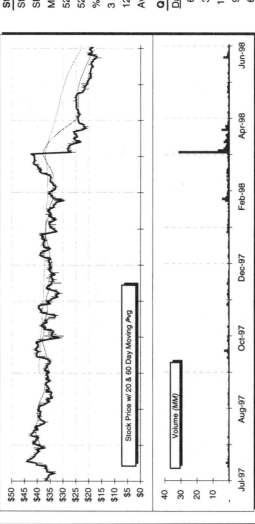

Stock Price w/ 20 & 60 Day Moving Avg

Volume (MM)

| | Jul-97 | Aug-97 | Oct-97 | Dec-97 | Feb-98 | Apr-98 | Jun-98 |

### Annual Fundamentals

| | 12/96 | 12/97 |
|---|---|---|
| Revenue | 76.1 | 135.9 |
| Growth | | 79% |
| Gross Sales | 58.6 | 107.4 |
| Operating Income | 14.0 | 24.9 |
| Net Income | 13.0 | 16.4 |

### Quarterly Fundamentals

| | 9/96 | 12/96 | 3/97 | 6/97 | 9/97 | 12/97 | 3/98 | 6/98 |
|---|---|---|---|---|---|---|---|---|
| Revenue | 21.1 | 26.6 | 29.3 | 34.9 | 34.8 | 39.7 | 40.2 | 43.4 |
| Seq'l Growth | | 26% | 10% | 19% | 0% | 14% | 1% | 8% |
| Y/Y Growth | | | | | 65% | 50% | 37% | 24% |
| Gross Sales | 15.9 | 21.1 | 22.9 | 27.8 | 28.0 | 31.2 | 31.6 | 31.5 |
| Operating Income | 3.5 | 4.6 | 6.5 | 6.9 | 5.1 | 6.5 | 6.1 | 4.2 |
| Net Income | | 7.9 | 4.9 | 5.2 | 2.3 | 4.0 | 3.0 | 10.7 |

## (Financial data table — left portion)

| | | | | | | | | | | |
|---|---|---|---|---|---|---|---|---|---|---|
| Operating Margin | 17% | 17% | 22% | 20% | 15% | 16% | 15% | 13% | 10% | |
| Net Margin | -1% | 30% | 17% | 15% | 7% | 10% | 7% | 25% | | |
| | | | | | | | | | | |
| Cash & S-T Invest. | 103.4 | 104.8 | 103.5 | 108.3 | 107.8 | 163.8 | 165.1 | NA | | |
| L-T Debt | - | - | - | - | - | - | - | NA | | |
| StkHldrs Equity | 112.1 | 121.4 | 126.1 | 132.5 | 130.4 | 199.3 | 205.3 | NA | | |
| Op. Cash Flow | (1.7) | (1.2) | (0.0) | 5.2 | 5.9 | (5.1) | 2.8 | NA | | |
| **Per Share Data** | | | | | | | | | | |
| Shares Out | 34.15 | 34.39 | 35.02 | 35.06 | 37.87 | 39.68 | 40.86 | NA | | |
| Net Income | (0.01) | 0.23 | 0.14 | 0.15 | 0.06 | 0.10 | 0.07 | NA | | |
| Cash & S-T Inv. | 3.03 | 3.05 | 2.96 | 3.09 | 2.85 | 4.13 | 4.04 | NA | | |
| Book Value | 3.28 | 3.53 | 3.60 | 3.78 | 3.44 | 5.02 | 5.03 | NA | | |

## (Financial data table — right portion)

| | | |
|---|---|---|
| Gross Margins | 77% | 79% |
| Operating Margin | 18% | 18% |
| Net Margin | 17% | 12% |
| | | |
| Cash & S-T Invest. | 104.8 | 163.8 |
| L-T Debt | - | - |
| StkHldrs Equity | 121.4 | 199.3 |
| Op. Cash Flow | (0.8) | 6.0 |
| **Per Share Data** | | |
| Shares Out | 34.39 | 39.68 |
| Net Income | 0.38 | 0.41 |
| Cash & S-T Inv. | 3.05 | 4.13 |
| Book Value | 3.53 | 5.02 |

## Earnings Estimates & Valuation:

| | IBES EPS | Price Multiple |
|---|---|---|
| Current Yr Est | 0.61 | 30.3 |
| Fwd Yr. Est. | 0.92 | 20.1 |
| Last FY End | 97.12 | |
| # IBES Estimates | 13.00 | |

| | Growth | P/E to LT Growth |
|---|---|---|
| EPS Growth | 50.8% | 75% |
| IBES L-T Growth | 40.5% | 50% |

**Misc:**

| | |
|---|---|
| Employees | 610 |
| IPO Date | 12/14/94 |
| First Day Close | $4.09 |

## Company Description

SDTI is a leading token and encryption provider. Its SecureID product is the largest selling token in the market with over 2 million in use. Through its acquisition of RSA Data Security in 1996, SDTI gained access to RSA's leading cryptography solutions. The Company licenses its cryptographic toolkit, Bsafe, to developers who then embed RSA's encryption technology into products ranging from Microsoft Windows to Quicken. Over 300MM of RSA's encryption and authentication products have been installed worldwide to date.

Sources: Piper Jaffray Research, FactSet, IBES, Compustat, Company Reports
Figures in millions, except per share amounts

Piper Jaffray Equity Research
Electronic Commerce

## Company Profile:
# SECURITY FIRST NETWORK BANK

# SFNB

**Stock Data**

| | |
|---|---|
| Stock Price as of | 6/30/98 $14.94 |
| Shares Outstanding | 10.50 |
| Market Cap | $157 |
| 52 Week High | $15.75 |
| 52 Week Low | $5.63 |
| % of 52 Week High | 95% |
| 3 Month Return | 73% |
| 12 Month Return | 117% |
| Avg Daily Volume (past mo.) | 0.09 |

**Quarterly EPS Performance**

| Date | IBES Est | Actual | Suprise |
|---|---|---|---|
| 3/98 | (0.74) | (0.57) | 0.17 |
| 12/97 | (0.62) | (0.59) | 0.03 |
| 9/97 | (0.68) | (0.61) | 0.07 |
| 6/97 | (0.72) | (0.77) | (0.05) |
| 3/97 | (0.66) | (0.89) | (0.23) |

**Annual Fundamentals**

| | 12/95 | 12/96 |
|---|---|---|
| Revenue | 4.5 | 5.2 |
| Growth | | 15% |
| Gross Sales | 2.0 | 1.1 |
| Operating Income | 0.4 | (7.6) |
| Net Income | (1.5) | (22.1) |

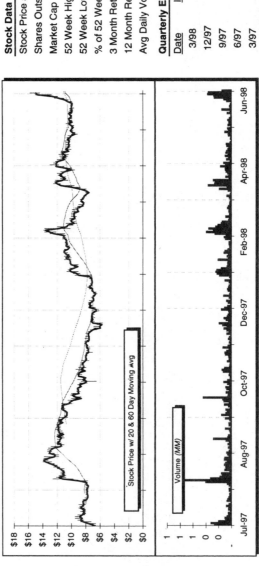

Stock Price w/ 20 & 60 Day Moving avg

Volume (MM)

Jul-97  Aug-97  Oct-97  Dec-97  Feb-98  Apr-98  Jun-98

**Quarterly Fundamentals**

| | 9/95 | 12/95 | 3/96 | 6/96 | 9/96 | 12/96 | 3/97 | 6/97 |
|---|---|---|---|---|---|---|---|---|
| Revenue | NA | 4.5 | 0.7 | 1.1 | 1.7 | 1.7 | 1.7 | 1.1 |
| Seq'l Growth | | NA | -84% | 55% | 49% | -1% | 0% | -34% |
| Y/Y Growth | | | | NA | NA | -63% | 127% | -3% |
| Gross Sales | 0.0 | 2.0 | 0.0 | (3.3) | 0.5 | 0.4 | (0.0) | (0.5) |
| Operating Income | 0.0 | 0.4 | (0.7) | (5.1) | (2.1) | (3.2) | (4.3) | (4.8) |

| | | | | | | | | | | | |
|---|---|---|---|---|---|---|---|---|---|---|---|
| Gross Margins | NA | 45% | 5% | NM | 28% | 22% | -1% | -47% | Gross Margins | 45% | 21% |
| Operating Margin | NA | 8% | -98% | NM | NM | NM | NM | NM | Operating Margin | 8% | NM |
| Net Margin | NA | -33% | -94% | NM | NM | NM | NM | NM | Net Margin | -33% | NM |
| | | | | | | | | | | | |
| Cash & S-T Invest. | NA | 5.8 | 3.8 | 27.8 | 8.8 | 5.6 | 2.3 | 5.2 | Cash & S-T Invest. | 5.8 | 5.6 |
| L-T Debt | NA | 1.3 | 1.3 | 1.2 | 1.2 | 1.2 | 1.1 | 1.1 | L-T Debt | 1.3 | 1.2 |
| StkHldrs Equity | NA | 3.5 | 2.7 | 55.3 | 50.5 | 40.1 | 33.8 | 27.7 | StkHldrs Equity | 3.5 | 40.1 |
| Op. Cash Flow | NA | NA | NA | NA | NA | NA | NA | NA | Op. Cash Flow | NA | NA |
| **Per Share Data** | | | | | | | | | **Per Share Data** | | |
| Shares Out | 2.40 | 2.40 | 2.40 | 8.09 | 8.11 | 8.26 | 8.43 | 8.62 | Shares Out | 2.40 | 8.26 |
| Net Income | NA | (0.62) | (0.28) | (0.67) | (0.60) | (1.35) | (0.70) | (0.76) | Net Income | (0.62) | (2.67) |
| Cash & S-T Inv. | NA | 2.43 | 1.57 | 3.43 | 1.09 | 0.68 | 0.27 | 0.60 | Cash & S-T Inv. | 2.43 | 0.68 |
| Book Value | NA | 1.44 | 1.14 | 6.83 | 6.23 | 4.85 | 4.01 | 3.21 | Book Value | 1.44 | 4.85 |

### Earnings Estimates & Valuation:

| | IBES EPS | Price Multiple |
|---|---|---|
| Current Yr Est | (2.86) | NM |
| Fwd Yr. Est. | (2.13) | NM |
| Last FY End | 96.12 | |
| # IBES Estimates | NA | |

| | Growth | P/E to LT Growth |
|---|---|---|
| EPS Growth | -25.5% | NM |
| IBES L-T Growth | 40.0% | NM |

**Misc:**

| | |
|---|---|
| Employees | |
| IPO Date | 5/23/96 |
| First Day Close | $41.00 |

### Company Description

S1 Technologies (S1) was the world's first dedicated developer of internet banking software and up until recently owned the world's first Internet bank. The company's Virtual Financial Manager software solution allows banking customers to access checking, electronic bill paying, money market accounts and certificates of deposit via the Internet. The Company has 66 customers including 15 of the top 100 financial institutions. In March 1998, the Company sold its banking operations to Royal Bank of Canada for a total consideration of $20 million.

Sources: Piper Jaffray Research, FactSet, IBES, Compustat, Company Reports
Figures in millions, except per share amounts

Piper Jaffray Equity Research
Electronic Commerce

# Company Profile:
## SPS TRANSACTION SERVICES INC

## PAY

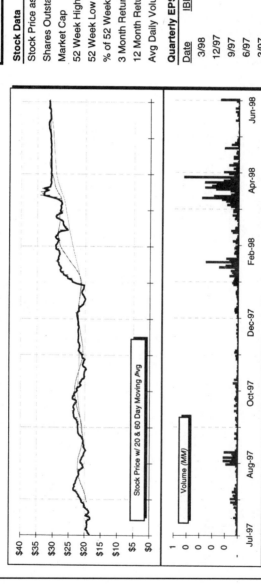

Stock Price w/ 20 & 60 Day Moving Avg

Volume (MM)

**Stock Data**

| | 6/30/98 | |
|---|---|---|
| Stock Price as of | | $31.38 |
| Shares Outstanding | | 27.28 |
| Market Cap | | $856 |
| 52 Week High | | $34.13 |
| 52 Week Low | | $18.13 |
| % of 52 Week High | | 92% |
| 3 Month Return | | 13% |
| 12 Month Return | | 70% |
| Avg Daily Volume (past mo.) | | 0.01 |

**Quarterly EPS Performance**

| Date | IBES Est | Actual | Suprise |
|---|---|---|---|
| 3/98 | 0.32 | 0.36 | 0.04 |
| 12/97 | 0.33 | 0.45 | 0.12 |
| 9/97 | 0.34 | 0.36 | 0.02 |
| 6/97 | 0.27 | 0.33 | 0.06 |
| 3/97 | 0.23 | 0.27 | 0.04 |

**Annual Fundamentals**

| | 12/96 | 12/97 |
|---|---|---|
| Revenue | 537.2 | 540.0 |
| Growth | | 1% |
| Gross Sales | 37.5 | 62.3 |
| Operating Income | 37.5 | 62.3 |
| Net Income | 23.2 | 38.5 |

## Quarterly Fundamentals

| | 6/96 | 9/96 | 12/96 | 3/97 | 6/97 | 9/97 | 12/97 | 3/98 |
|---|---|---|---|---|---|---|---|---|
| Revenue | 128.3 | 129.8 | 140.9 | 142.5 | 133.3 | 128.5 | 135.6 | 126.3 |
| Seq'l Growth | | 1% | 8% | 1% | -6% | -4% | 6% | -7% |
| Y/Y Growth | | | | | 4% | -1% | -4% | -11% |
| Gross Sales | 10.6 | 9.0 | 0.0 | 12.0 | 14.6 | 16.0 | 19.6 | 15.7 |
| Operating Income | 10.6 | 9.0 | 0.0 | 12.0 | 14.6 | 16.0 | 19.6 | 15.7 |
| Net Income | 6.6 | 5.6 | 0.0 | 7.4 | 9.0 | 9.8 | 12.3 | 9.9 |

| | | | | | | | | | | | |
|---|---|---|---|---|---|---|---|---|---|---|---|
| Gross Margins | 8% | 7% | 0% | 8% | 11% | 12% | 14% | 12% | | | |
| Operating Margin | 8% | 7% | 0% | 8% | 11% | 12% | 14% | 12% | | Operating Margin | 7% | 12% |
| Net Margin | 5% | 4% | 0% | 5% | 7% | 8% | 9% | 8% | | Net Margin | 4% | 7% |
| Cash & S-T Invest. | 61.8 | 62.3 | 56.9 | 75.3 | 74.6 | 56.7 | 51.3 | 52.3 | | Cash & S-T Invest. | 56.9 | 51.3 |
| L-T Debt | | | | | | | | | | L-T Debt | - | - |
| StkHldrs Equity | 218.7 | 224.5 | 224.4 | 232.0 | 241.1 | 251.1 | 263.0 | 274.1 | | StkHldrs Equity | 224.4 | 263.0 |
| Op. Cash Flow | 32.5 | 56.9 | 36.2 | 57.5 | (19.3) | 41.2 | 17.5 | 42.9 | | Op. Cash Flow | 195.2 | 96.9 |

Per Share Data

| | | | | | | | | | | | |
|---|---|---|---|---|---|---|---|---|---|---|---|
| Shares Out | 27.19 | 27.20 | 27.19 | 27.20 | 27.21 | 27.22 | 27.21 | 27.28 | | Shares Out | 27.19 | 27.21 |
| Net Income | 0.24 | 0.21 | 0.00 | 0.27 | 0.33 | 0.36 | 0.45 | 0.36 | | Net Income | 0.86 | 1.42 |
| Cash & S-T Inv. | 2.27 | 2.29 | 2.09 | 2.77 | 2.74 | 2.08 | 1.89 | 1.92 | | Cash & S-T Inv. | 2.09 | 1.89 |
| Book Value | 8.04 | 8.25 | 8.25 | 8.53 | 8.86 | 9.22 | 9.67 | 10.05 | | Book Value | 8.25 | 9.67 |

## Earnings Estimates & Valuation:

| | IBES EPS | Price Multiple |
|---|---|---|
| Current Yr Est | 1.65 | 19.0 |
| Fwd Yr. Est. | 1.82 | 17.2 |
| Last FY End | 97.12 | |
| # IBES Estimates | 1.00 | |

| | Growth | P/E to LT Growth |
|---|---|---|
| EPS Growth | 10.3% | 158% |
| IBES L-T Growth | 12.0% | 144% |

Misc:

| | |
|---|---|
| Employees | 3,740 |
| IPO Date | 2/26/92 |
| First Day Close | $8.69 |

## Company Description

SPS Transaction Systems (PAY) processes check, credit and debit card transactions for merchants, administers private label credit card programs for merchant issuers, processes commercial accounts receivables, and outsources call center operations for catalog order entry or customer support. In some cases the Company actually acts as an issuer for its merchant clients and owns the credit card loans outstanding. Associates First Capital announced its intention to acquire PAY in June of 1998.

Sources: Piper Jaffray Research, FactSet, IBES, Compustat, Company Reports
Figures in millions, except per share amounts

Piper Jaffray Equity Research
Electronic Commerce

# Company Profile:
# STERLING COMMERCE INC

## SE

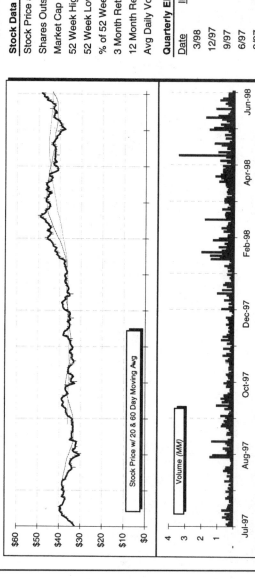

Stock Price w/ 20 & 60 Day Moving Avg

Volume (MM)

**Stock Data**

| | 6/30/98 | |
|---|---|---|
| Stock Price as of | 6/30/98 | $48.50 |
| Shares Outstanding | | 91.48 |
| Market Cap | | $4,437 |
| 52 Week High | | $50.25 |
| 52 Week Low | | $29.50 |
| % of 52 Week High | | 97% |
| 3 Month Return | | 5% |
| 12 Month Return | | 48% |
| Avg Daily Volume (past mo.) | | 0.68 |

**Quarterly EPS Performance**

| Date | IBES Est | Actual | Suprise |
|---|---|---|---|
| 3/98 | 0.29 | 0.29 | - |
| 12/97 | 0.26 | 0.26 | - |
| 9/97 | 0.29 | 0.30 | 0.01 |
| 6/97 | 0.25 | 0.25 | - |
| 3/97 | 0.23 | 0.23 | - |

**Annual Fundamentals**

| | 9/96 | 9/97 |
|---|---|---|
| Revenue | 267.8 | 350.6 |
| Growth | | 31% |
| Gross Sales | 213.4 | 280.0 |
| Operating Income | 95.2 | 120.3 |
| Net Income | 58.4 | 55.4 |

**Quarterly Fundamentals**

| | 6/96 | 9/96 | 12/96 | 3/97 | 6/97 | 9/97 | 12/97 | 3/98 |
|---|---|---|---|---|---|---|---|---|
| Revenue | 69.2 | 80.3 | 74.8 | 79.5 | 87.8 | 108.5 | 106.3 | 111.1 |
| Seq'l Growth | | 16% | -7% | 6% | 10% | 24% | -2% | 5% |
| Y/Y Growth | | | | | 27% | 35% | 42% | 40% |
| Gross Sales | 55.5 | 64.9 | 59.0 | 63.1 | 69.7 | 88.1 | 85.8 | 87.0 |
| Operating Income | 23.7 | 28.8 | 25.0 | 27.6 | 30.1 | 37.6 | 32.6 | 35.9 |
| Net Income | 14.8 | 18.1 | 16.1 | 18.8 | (7.5) | 28.0 | 24.2 | 27.0 |

| | Col 1 | Col 2 | Col 3 | Col 4 | Col 5 | Col 6 | Col 7 | Col 8 | | |
|---|---|---|---|---|---|---|---|---|---|---|
| Gross Margins | 80% | 81% | 79% | 79% | 79% | 81% | 81% | 78% | 80% | 80% |
| Operating Margin | 34% | 36% | 33% | 35% | 34% | 35% | 31% | 32% | 36% | 34% |
| Net Margin | 21% | 23% | 21% | 24% | -9% | 26% | 23% | 24% | 22% | 16% |
| | | | | | | | | | | |
| Cash & S-T Invest. | 43.1 | 44.7 | 90.3 | 495.9 | 488.1 | 484.7 | 510.3 | 542.2 | 44.7 | 484.7 |
| L-T Debt | - | - | - | - | - | - | - | - | - | - |
| StkHldrs Equity | 115.8 | 138.2 | 153.9 | 572.7 | 570.1 | 600.9 | 630.8 | 691.6 | 138.2 | 600.9 |
| Op. Cash Flow | 14.2 | 8.2 | 57.0 | 18.5 | 30.0 | 16.6 | 34.2 | 24.4 | 57.3 | 122.1 |
| | | | | | | | | | | |
| **Per Share Data** | | | | | | | | | | |
| Shares Out | 75.00 | 75.00 | 75.00 | 89.38 | 89.57 | 89.64 | 89.86 | 90.99 | 75.00 | 89.64 |
| Net Income | 0.20 | 0.24 | 0.21 | 0.21 | (0.08) | 0.31 | 0.27 | 0.30 | 0.78 | 0.62 |
| Cash & S-T Inv. | 0.58 | 0.60 | 1.20 | 5.55 | 5.45 | 5.41 | 5.68 | 5.96 | 0.60 | 5.41 |
| Book Value | 1.54 | 1.84 | 2.05 | 6.41 | 6.36 | 6.70 | 7.02 | 7.60 | 1.84 | 6.70 |

## Earnings Estimates & Valuation:

| | IBES EPS | Price Multiple |
|---|---|---|
| Current Yr Est | 1.25 | **38.8** |
| Fwd Yr. Est. | 1.60 | **30.3** |
| Last FY End | 97.09 | |
| # IBES Estimates | 21.00 | |

| | Growth | P/E to LT Growth |
|---|---|---|
| EPS Growth | 28.0% | **129%** |
| IBES L-T Growth | 30.1% | **101%** |

**Misc:**

| | |
|---|---|
| Employees | 1,700 |
| IPO Date | 3/8/96 |
| First Day Close | $29.00 |

## Company Description

SE develops electronic data interchange (EDI) and other electronic commerce solutions. Its EDI software is used to translate, map and schedule data for transmission between businesses (Gentran), and to automate and secure file transfers (Connect). The Company is a major provider of value-added-network (VAN) services (Commerce), which consist of managing message and file traffic as well as providing additional services such as catalogs and payment processing. The Company has developed web-based electronic commerce solutions for less frequent trading partners. The Company's customers are typically large companies and it is particularly strong in banking.

Sources: Piper Jaffray Research, FactSet, IBES, Compustat, Company Reports
Figures in millions, except per share amounts

Piper Jaffray Equity Research
Electronic Commerce

# Company Profile:
# TRANSACTION NETWORK SVCS INC

# TNSI

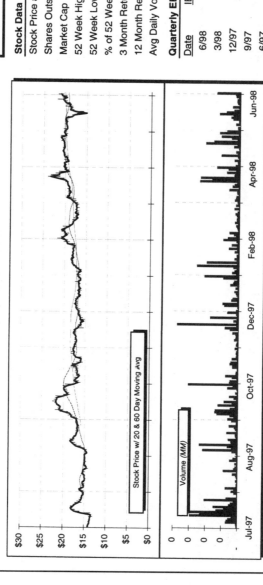

Stock Price w/ 20 & 60 Day Moving avg

Volume (MM)

| | Jul-97 | Aug-97 | Oct-97 | Dec-97 | Feb-98 | Apr-98 | Jun-98 |

## Stock Data

| | |
|---|---|
| Stock Price as of | 6/30/98 $21.06 |
| Shares Outstanding | 12.66 |
| Market Cap | $267 |
| 52 Week High | $24.00 |
| 52 Week Low | $13.00 |
| % of 52 Week High | 88% |
| 3 Month Return | 19% |
| 12 Month Return | 49% |
| Avg Daily Volume (past mo.) | 0.04 |

## Quarterly EPS Performance

| Date | IBES Est | Actual | Suprise |
|---|---|---|---|
| 6/98 | 0.17 | 0.17 | - |
| 3/98 | 0.14 | 0.12 | (0.02) |
| 12/97 | 0.20 | 0.20 | - |
| 9/97 | 0.18 | 0.18 | - |
| 6/97 | | 0.13 | |

## Annual Fundamentals

| | 12/96 | 12/97 |
|---|---|---|
| Revenue | 52.3 | 63.3 |
| Growth | | 21% |
| Gross Sales | 18.0 | 21.7 |
| Operating Income | 7.8 | 10.3 |
| Net Income | 5.8 | 7.4 |

## Quarterly Fundamentals

| | 6/96 | 9/96 | 12/96 | 3/97 | 6/97 | 9/97 | 12/97 | 3/98 |
|---|---|---|---|---|---|---|---|---|
| Revenue | 13.2 | 14.8 | 13.4 | 13.1 | 15.4 | 17.2 | 17.6 | 18.1 |
| Seq'l Growth | | 13% | -10% | -2% | 18% | 11% | 3% | 3% |
| Y/Y Growth | | | | | 17% | 16% | 32% | 38% |
| Gross Sales | 4.6 | 5.2 | 4.6 | 4.2 | 5.3 | 6.0 | 6.1 | 5.5 |
| Operating Income | 1.9 | 2.7 | 2.1 | 1.4 | 2.3 | 3.1 | 3.5 | 2.0 |
| Net Income | 1.5 | 1.9 | 1.6 | 1.0 | 1.6 | 2.3 | 2.5 | 1.5 |

| | | | | | | | | | | | | |
|---|---|---|---|---|---|---|---|---|---|---|---|---|
| Gross Margins | 35% | 35% | 35% | 34% | 32% | 35% | 35% | 35% | 31% | 34% | 34% | 34% |
| Operating Margin | 15% | 18% | 16% | 15% | 10% | 18% | 20% | 16% | 11% | 15% | 15% | 16% |
| Net Margin | 11% | 13% | 12% | 10% | 8% | 13% | 14% | 12% | 8% | 11% | 11% | 12% |
| Cash & S-T Invest. | 22.3 | 27.4 | 30.4 | 29.4 | 34.7 | 27.7 | 28.4 | | 15.2 | 30.4 | 28.4 | |
| L-T Debt | - | - | - | - | - | - | - | | - | - | - | |
| StkHldrs Equity | 57.6 | 59.6 | 62.2 | 62.6 | 63.2 | 65.3 | 68.5 | | 75.5 | 62.2 | 68.5 | |
| Op. Cash Flow | 0.2 | 2.5 | 3.0 | 1.8 | 3.9 | 4.3 | 2.3 | | 3.2 | 10.0 | 12.3 | |
| **Per Share Data** | | | | | | | | | | | | |
| Shares Out | 12.30 | 12.30 | 12.33 | 12.17 | 12.30 | 12.40 | 12.27 | | 12.60 | 12.33 | 12.27 | |
| Net Income | 0.12 | 0.15 | 0.13 | 0.13 | 0.08 | 0.18 | 0.21 | | 0.12 | 0.47 | 0.60 | |
| Cash & S-T Inv. | 1.81 | 2.23 | 2.47 | 2.42 | 2.82 | 2.23 | 2.32 | | 1.21 | 2.47 | 2.32 | |
| Book Value | 4.68 | 4.84 | 5.04 | 5.14 | 5.14 | 5.26 | 5.58 | | 5.99 | 5.04 | 5.58 | |

## Earnings Estimates & Valuation:

| | IBES EPS | Price Multiple |
|---|---|---|
| Current Yr Est | 0.77 | 27.4 |
| Fwd Yr. Est. | 1.00 | 21.1 |
| Last FY End | 97.12 | |
| # IBES Estimates | 4.00 | |

| | Growth | P/E to LT Growth |
|---|---|---|
| EPS Growth | 29.9% | 99% |
| IBES L-T Growth | 27.5% | 77% |

**Misc:**

| | |
|---|---|
| Employees | 134 |
| IPO Date | 4/22/94 |
| First Day Close | $6.67 |

## Company Description

TNSI is a communications network company specializing in transaction-oriented data services using proprietary call routing technology to provide high-speed, low-cost, and accessible network services for third party transaction processors who then offer the services on a private label basis. The majority of the Company's revenues are generated from the transmission of credit and debit card transactions at the point-of-sale (POS). Of the eight leading third party POS transaction processors five, including First Data, EDS, PTI use the Company's services.

Sources: Piper Jaffray Research, FactSet, IBES, Compustat, Company Reports
Figures in millions, except per share amounts

Piper Jaffray Equity Research
Electronic Commerce

## Company Profile:

# TRNSACTN SYS ARCHTCTS -CL A

# TSAI

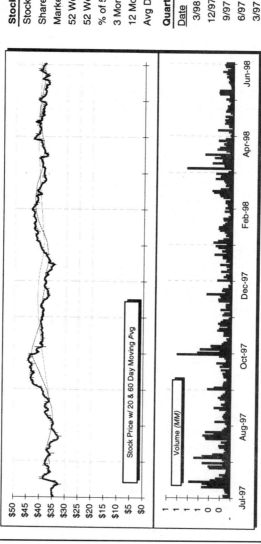

Stock Price w/ 20 & 60 Day Moving Avg

Volume (MM)

| | Jul-97 | Aug-97 | Oct-97 | Dec-97 | Feb-98 | Apr-98 | Jun-98 |

### Stock Data

| | 6/30/98 |
|---|---|
| Stock Price as of | $38.50 |
| Shares Outstanding | 27.27 |
| Market Cap | $1,050 |
| 52 Week High | $45.00 |
| 52 Week Low | $31.25 |
| % of 52 Week High | 86% |
| 3 Month Return | -1% |
| 12 Month Return | 12% |
| Avg Daily Volume (past mo.) | 0.12 |

### Quarterly EPS Performance

| Date | IBES Est | Actual | Suprise |
|---|---|---|---|
| 3/98 | 0.26 | 0.27 | **0.01** |
| 12/97 | 0.25 | 0.25 | - |
| 9/97 | 0.23 | 0.24 | **0.01** |
| 6/97 | 0.20 | 0.22 | **0.02** |
| 3/97 | 0.18 | 0.19 | **0.01** |

### Annual Fundamentals

| | 9/96 | 9/97 |
|---|---|---|
| Revenue | 159.8 | 215.5 |
| Growth | | 35% |
| Gross Sales | 95.8 | 137.6 |
| Operating Income | 20.7 | 36.7 |
| Net Income | 12.6 | 23.6 |

### Quarterly Fundamentals

| | 6/96 | 9/96 | 12/96 | 3/97 | 6/97 | 9/97 | 12/97 | 3/98 |
|---|---|---|---|---|---|---|---|---|
| Revenue | 42.9 | 47.6 | 49.8 | 53.5 | 55.2 | 57.0 | 61.1 | 64.2 |
| Seq'l Growth | | 11% | 5% | 7% | 3% | 3% | 7% | 5% |
| Y/Y Growth | | | | | 29% | 20% | 23% | 20% |
| Gross Sales | 25.7 | 29.0 | 30.6 | 34.5 | 35.5 | 37.0 | 40.1 | 42.1 |
| Operating Income | 6.0 | 7.3 | 7.6 | 9.1 | 9.7 | 10.3 | 11.2 | 11.9 |
| Net Income | 3.9 | 4.3 | 4.3 | 5.5 | 6.3 | 6.9 | 7.2 | 7.9 |

| | | | | | | | | | |
|---|---|---|---|---|---|---|---|---|---|
| Gross Margins | 60% | 61% | 61% | 60% | 65% | 64% | 65% | 66% | 66% |
| Operating Margin | 14% | 15% | 15% | 14% | 17% | 18% | 18% | 18% | 19% |
| Net Margin | 9% | 9% | 9% | 9% | 10% | 11% | 12% | 12% | 12% |
| Cash & S-T Invest. | 22.9 | 31.5 | 31.0 | 38.2 | 42.6 | 46.6 | 47.0 | 49.4 | |
| L-T Debt | 1.5 | 1.7 | 1.9 | 1.8 | 1.8 | 2.4 | 2.6 | 2.3 | |
| StkHldrs Equity | 69.9 | 76.5 | 81.4 | 89.8 | 96.1 | 104.0 | 111.8 | 123.0 | |
| Op. Cash Flow | (0.6) | 11.8 | 3.1 | 8.0 | 9.8 | 9.7 | 5.7 | 6.3 | |
| **Per Share Data** | | | | | | | | | |
| Shares Out | 25.45 | 25.91 | 26.18 | 26.25 | 27.98 | 28.05 | 28.14 | 28.44 | |
| Net Income | 0.15 | 0.16 | 0.16 | 0.21 | 0.23 | 0.25 | 0.26 | 0.28 | |
| Cash & S-T Inv. | 0.90 | 1.22 | 1.18 | 1.45 | 1.52 | 1.66 | 1.67 | 1.74 | |
| Book Value | 2.75 | 2.95 | 3.11 | 3.42 | 3.43 | 3.71 | 3.98 | 4.32 | |

| | | |
|---|---|---|
| Gross Margins | 60% | 64% |
| Operating Margin | 13% | 17% |
| Net Margin | 8% | 11% |
| Cash & S-T Invest. | 31.5 | 46.6 |
| L-T Debt | 1.7 | 2.4 |
| StkHldrs Equity | 76.5 | 104.0 |
| Op. Cash Flow | 17.8 | 30.6 |
| **Per Share Data** | | |
| Shares Out | 25.91 | 28.05 |
| Net Income | 0.49 | 0.84 |
| Cash & S-T Inv. | 1.22 | 1.66 |
| Book Value | 2.95 | 3.71 |

## Earnings Estimates & Valuation:

| | IBES EPS | Price Multiple |
|---|---|---|
| Current Yr Est | 1.09 | 35.3 |
| Fwd. Yr. Est. | 1.38 | 27.9 |
| Last FY End | 97.09 | |
| # IBES Estimates | 6.00 | |

| | Growth | P/E to LT Growth |
|---|---|---|
| EPS Growth | 26.6% | 124% |
| IBES L-T Growth | 28.6% | 98% |

Misc:

| | |
|---|---|
| Employees | 1,372 |
| IPO Date | 2/24/95 |
| First Day Close | $8.94 |

## Company Description

TSAI develops products and services primarily focused on electronic payment processing. Its software solutions help financial institutions manage large, complex payment networks, performing such functions as credit card management, transaction settlement, and reporting. The Company's software processes a variety of transactions including credit, debit, and smart cards, checks, and ACH payments. TSAI has 1,664 total customers, including over 20% of the largest 500 banks in the world. Its international operations generate 58% of revenues.

Sources: Piper Jaffray Research, FactSet, IBES, Compustat, Company Reports
Figures in millions, except per share amounts

Piper Jaffray Equity Research
Electronic Commerce

# Company Profile:
## ULTRADATA CORP

## ULTD

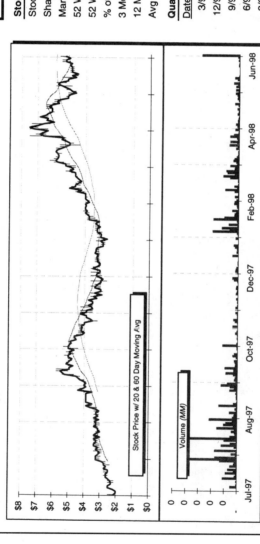

Stock Price w/ 20 & 60 Day Moving Avg

Volume (MM)

### Stock Data

| | |
|---|---|
| Stock Price as of | **6/30/98** |
| Stock Price as of | $5.25 |
| Shares Outstanding | 7.68 |
| Market Cap | $40 |
| 52 Week High | $7.50 |
| 52 Week Low | $2.00 |
| % of 52 Week High | 70% |
| 3 Month Return | 0% |
| 12 Month Return | 147% |
| Avg Daily Volume (past mo.) | 0.01 |

### Quarterly EPS Performance

| Date | IBES Est | Actual | Suprise |
|---|---|---|---|
| 3/98 | - | - | - |
| 12/97 | - | - | - |
| 9/97 | - | - | - |
| 6/97 | - | - | - |
| 3/97 | - | - | - |

### Annual Fundamentals

| | 12/96 | 12/97 |
|---|---|---|
| Revenue | 40.4 | 29.1 |
| Growth | | -28% |
| Gross Sales | 14.4 | 12.2 |
| Operating Income | (7.3) | (4.4) |
| Net Income | (7.0) | (3.5) |

### Quarterly Fundamentals

| | 6/96 | 9/96 | 12/96 | 3/97 | 6/97 | 9/97 | 12/97 | 3/98 |
|---|---|---|---|---|---|---|---|---|
| Revenue | 12.9 | 7.8 | 7.6 | 6.5 | 8.7 | 6.7 | 7.1 | 7.3 |
| Seq'l Growth | | -39% | -4% | -14% | 34% | -23% | 6% | 2% |
| Y/Y Growth | | | | | -33% | -14% | -5% | 12% |
| Gross Sales | 5.9 | 2.5 | 0.9 | 2.2 | 3.7 | 3.1 | 3.2 | 3.5 |
| Operating Income | 1.0 | (2.6) | (6.2) | (3.0) | (0.7) | (0.3) | (0.4) | 0.0 |
| Net Income | 0.7 | (1.6) | (6.5) | (3.0) | (0.4) | 0.3 | (0.3) | 0.0 |

| Gross Margins | 45% | 32% | 11% | 34% | 42% | 46% | 45% | 49% | | Gross Margins | 36% | 42% |
|---|---|---|---|---|---|---|---|---|---|---|---|---|
| Operating Margin | 7% | -33% | -82% | -46% | -8% | -5% | -6% | 0% | | Operating Margin | -18% | -15% |
| Net Margin | 5% | -20% | -85% | -46% | -5% | 4% | -4% | 1% | | Net Margin | -17% | -12% |
| | | | | | | | | | | | | |
| Cash & S-T Invest. | 7.0 | 3.7 | 3.0 | 2.0 | 2.2 | 2.1 | 1.3 | 1.6 | | Cash & S-T Invest. | 3.0 | 1.3 |
| L-T Debt | 0.0 | 0.0 | 0.3 | - | - | - | 0.1 | 0.1 | | L-T Debt | 0.3 | 0.1 |
| StkHldrs Equity | 16.9 | 15.8 | 9.5 | 6.7 | 6.3 | 6.6 | 6.3 | 6.4 | | StkHldrs Equity | 9.5 | 6.3 |
| Op. Cash Flow | (3.8) | (3.3) | (1.3) | (0.5) | 0.7 | (0.0) | (0.5) | 0.5 | | Op. Cash Flow | (11.9) | (0.4) |
| **Per Share Data** | | | | | | | | | | **Per Share Data** | | |
| Shares Out | 7.81 | 7.48 | 7.53 | 7.53 | 7.58 | 7.61 | 7.61 | 7.65 | | Shares Out | 7.53 | 7.61 |
| Net Income | 0.09 | (0.21) | (0.86) | (0.40) | (0.06) | 0.03 | (0.04) | 0.01 | | Net Income | (0.92) | (0.45) |
| Cash & S-T Inv. | 0.90 | 0.50 | 0.40 | 0.26 | 0.29 | 0.28 | 0.17 | 0.21 | | Cash & S-T Inv. | 0.40 | 0.17 |
| Book Value | 2.16 | 2.11 | 1.26 | 0.89 | 0.83 | 0.87 | 0.83 | 0.84 | | Book Value | 1.26 | 0.83 |

## Earnings Estimates & Valuation:

| | IBES EPS | Price Multiple |
|---|---|---|
| Current Yr Est | NA | NM |
| Fwd Yr. Est. | NA | NM |
| Last FY End | 97.12 | |
| # IBES Estimates | NA | |

| | Growth | P/E to LT Growth |
|---|---|---|
| EPS Growth | NA | NM |
| IBES L-T Growth | NA | NM |

**Misc:**

| | |
|---|---|
| Employees | 184 |
| IPO Date | 2/16/96 |
| First Day Close | $9.13 |

## Company Description

ULTD develops core processing systems primarily for the credit unions and other small financial institutions. Financial institutions use the Company's solutions to provide checking, savings, investment accounts, credit and debit cards, ATM access and consumer lending. The Company targets large and mid-sized credit unions directly, but its products are also used by six service organizations serving the credit union market. In total, the Company's products are used by over 400 credit unions, which serve over 6 million members.

Sources: Piper Jaffray Research, FactSet, IBES, Compustat, Company Reports
Figures in millions, except per share amounts

Piper Jaffray Equity Research
Electronic Commerce

# Company Profile:
# WAVE SYSTEMS CORP -CL A

## WAVX

**Stock Data**

| | |
|---|---|
| Stock Price as of | 6/30/98 | $3.94 |
| Shares Outstanding | | 23.07 |
| Market Cap | | $91 |
| 52 Week High | | $5.47 |
| 52 Week Low | | $0.50 |
| % of 52 Week High | | 72% |
| 3 Month Return | | 154% |
| 12 Month Return | | 142% |
| Avg Daily Volume (past mo.) | | 0.36 |

**Quarterly EPS Performance**

| Date | IBES Est | Actual | Suprise |
|---|---|---|---|

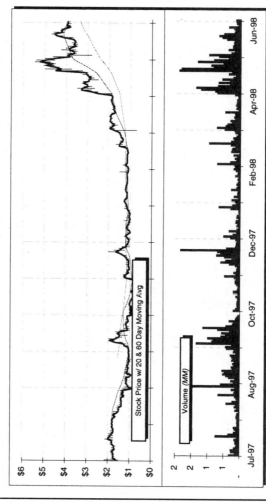

Stock Price w/ 20 & 60 Day Moving Avg

Volume (MM)

**Annual Fundamentals**

| | 12/96 | 12/97 |
|---|---|---|
| Revenue | 0.0 | 0.0 |
| Growth | | NA |
| Gross Sales | (8.9) | (10.1) |
| Operating Income | (8.9) | (10.1) |
| Net Income | (8.7) | (13.9) |

**Quarterly Fundamentals**

| | 6/96 | 9/96 | 12/96 | 3/97 | 6/97 | 9/97 | 12/97 | 3/98 |
|---|---|---|---|---|---|---|---|---|
| Revenue | NA | NA | NA | NA | 0.0 | 0.0 | 0.0 | 0.0 |
| Seq'l Growth | NA | NA | NA | NA | NA | 33% | 0% | 125% |
| Y/Y Growth | NA | NA | NA | NA | NA | NA | NA | NA |
| Gross Sales | (2.5) | (1.9) | (2.6) | (2.6) | (2.6) | (2.4) | (2.5) | (2.0) |
| Operating Income | (2.5) | (1.9) | (2.6) | (2.6) | (2.6) | (2.4) | (2.5) | (2.0) |
| Net Income | (2.4) | (1.9) | (2.6) | (2.6) | (2.6) | (7.1) | (1.7) | (2.0) |

| | | | | | | | | | Gross Margins | |
|---|---|---|---|---|---|---|---|---|---|---|
| Gross Margins | NA | NA | NA | NA | NM | NM | NM | NM | Operating Margin | NM | NM |
| Operating Margin | NA | NA | NA | NA | NM | NM | NM | NM | Net Margin | NM | NM |
| Net Margin | NA | NA | NA | NA | NM | NM | NM | NM | | NM | NM |
| Cash & S-T Invest. | 5.1 | 3.3 | 4.1 | 1.7 | 0.9 | 0.3 | 0.8 | 2.3 | Cash & S-T Invest. | 4.1 | 0.8 |
| L-T Debt | - | - | 0.5 | 0.5 | 0.5 | 0.5 | - | - | L-T Debt | 0.5 | - |
| StkHldrs Equity | 5.8 | 4.0 | 4.8 | 2.5 | 1.4 | (1.0) | (0.3) | 0.6 | StkHldrs Equity | 4.8 | (0.3) |
| Op. Cash Flow | (1.9) | (1.6) | (1.7) | (2.3) | (2.2) | (2.2) | (1.8) | (1.2) | Op. Cash Flow | (7.5) | (8.5) |
| **Per Share Data** | | | | | | | | | **Per Share Data** | | |
| Shares Out | 14.36 | 15.07 | 17.79 | 18.02 | 20.38 | 23.15 | 27.30 | 27.31 | Shares Out | 17.79 | 27.30 |
| Net Income | (0.17) | (0.12) | (0.15) | (0.14) | (0.13) | (0.31) | (0.06) | (0.07) | Net Income | (0.49) | (0.51) |
| Cash & S-T Inv. | 0.36 | 0.22 | 0.23 | 0.09 | 0.04 | 0.01 | 0.03 | 0.08 | Cash & S-T Inv. | 0.23 | 0.03 |
| Book Value | 0.41 | 0.27 | 0.27 | 0.14 | 0.07 | (0.04) | (0.01) | 0.02 | Book Value | 0.27 | (0.01) |

## Earnings Estimates & Valuation:

| | IBES EPS | | Price Multiple |
|---|---|---|---|
| Current Yr Est | NA | | NM |
| Fwd Yr. Est. | NA | | NM |
| Last FY End | 97.12 | | |
| # IBES Estimates | NA | | |

| | Growth | | P/E to LT Growth |
|---|---|---|---|
| EPS Growth | NA | | NM |
| IBES L-T Growth | NA | | NM |

**Misc:**

| | |
|---|---|
| Employees | 41 |
| IPO Date | 8/31/94 |
| First Day Close | $5.00 |

## *Company Description*

WAVX is focused on enabling secure distribution of digital content. It has created WaveMeter, a cryptographic engine and an electronic content metering system integrated in a single chip which holds consumers' account balances, transaction logs and software execution licenses. WaveMeter is complemented by WaveNet, the Company's data processing operation that facilitates payment and provides all usage tracking and related reporting. The Company's solutions are directed at publishers and content developers to manage product registration, pricing, usage monitoring and payment processing.

Sources: Piper Jaffray Research, FactSet, IBES, Compustat, Company Reports

*Figures in millions, except per share amounts*

Piper Jaffray Equity Research
Electronic Commerce

# Company Profile:
## VERISIGN INC

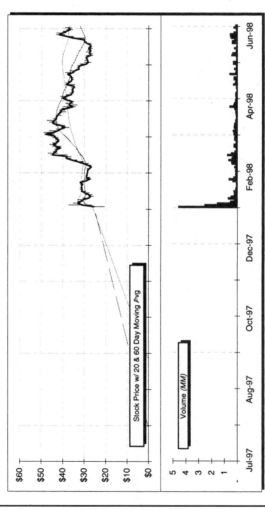

Stock Price w/ 20 & 60 Day Moving Avg

Volume (MM)

| | Jul-97 | Aug-97 | Oct-97 | Dec-97 | Feb-98 | Apr-98 | Jun-98 |

## VRSN

### Stock Data

| | |
|---|---|
| Stock Price as of | 6/30/98 $37.38 |
| Shares Outstanding | 20.74 |
| Market Cap | $775 |
| 52 Week High | $49.00 |
| 52 Week Low | $20.50 |
| % of 52 Week High | 76% |
| 3 Month Return | -15% |
| 12 Month Return | 0% |
| Avg Daily Volume (past mo.) | 0.25 |

### Quarterly EPS Performance

| Date | IBES Est | Actual | Suprise |
|---|---|---|---|
| 3/98 | (0.27) | (0.27) | - |
| 12/97 | | (0.38) | |

### Annual Fundamentals

| | 12/96 | 12/97 |
|---|---|---|
| Revenue | 1.4 | 9.4 |
| Growth | | 594% |
| Gross Sales | (1.4) | 1.5 |
| Operating Income | (11.0) | (19.1) |
| Net Income | (10.2) | (19.2) |

## Quarterly Fundamentals

| | 6/96 | 9/96 | 12/96 | 3/97 | 6/97 | 9/97 | 12/97 | 3/98 |
|---|---|---|---|---|---|---|---|---|
| Revenue | 0.2 | 0.4 | 0.6 | 1.3 | 2.2 | 2.6 | 3.3 | 4.0 |
| Seq'l Growth | | 52% | 54% | 120% | 78% | 16% | 26% | 22% |
| Y/Y Growth | | | | | 814% | 593% | 466% | 216% |
| Gross Sales | (0.3) | (0.4) | (0.6) | (0.2) | 0.5 | 0.6 | 0.6 | 1.2 |
| Operating Income | (2.1) | (2.8) | (4.6) | (4.4) | (4.3) | (4.1) | (6.3) | (6.0) |
| Net Income | (2.0) | (2.6) | (4.2) | (3.6) | (3.6) | (5.5) | (6.5) | (5.2) |

# VRSN — Electronic Commerce

| Gross Margins | NM | -97% | -12% | 23% | 23% | 18% | 29% | NM | 17% |
|---|---|---|---|---|---|---|---|---|---|
| Operating Margin | NM | NM | NM | NM | NM | NM | NM | NM | NM |
| Net Margin | NM | NM | NM | NM | NM | NM | NM | NM | NM |
| Cash & S-T Invest. | 30.0 | NA | NA | NA | 13.6 | 11.9 | 49.2 | 30.0 | 11.9 |
| L-T Debt | - | NA | NA | NA | - | - | - | - | - |
| StkHldrs Equity | 28.6 | NA | NA | NA | 15.9 | 12.5 | 51.2 | 28.6 | 12.5 |
| Op. Cash Flow | NA | NA | NA | NA | NA | (1.7) | (5.6) | (6.0) | (13.6) |
| **Per Share Data** | | | | | | | | | |
| Shares Out | 6.38 | NA | NA | NA | 6.57 | 20.15 | 20.74 | 6.38 | 7.12 |
| Net Income | (0.67) | NA | NA | NA | (0.84) | (0.32) | (0.25) | (1.61) | (2.70) |
| Cash & S-T Inv. | 4.70 | NA | NA | NA | 2.07 | 0.59 | 2.37 | 4.70 | 1.67 |
| Book Value | 4.48 | NA | NA | NA | 2.42 | 0.62 | 2.47 | 4.48 | 1.75 |

## Earnings Estimates & Valuation:

| | IBES EPS | Price Multiple |
|---|---|---|
| Current Yr Est | (0.85) | NM |
| Fwd Yr. Est. | (0.04) | NM |
| Last FY End | 97.12 | |
| # IBES Estimates | 5.00 | |

| | Growth | P/E to LT Growth |
|---|---|---|
| EPS Growth | -95.3% | NM |
| IBES L-T Growth | 75.0% | NM |

Misc:

| | |
|---|---|
| Employees | 184 |
| IPO Date | 1/30/98 |
| First Day Close | $25.50 |

## Company Description

VRSN is a leading and highly visible certificate authority (CA). As a CA, VRSN provides digital IDs or certificates, which are used to unique identify computer users. The Company issues certificates directly to consumers under its own brand, as well as through private label arrangements. Additionally, it offers organizations the tools and services to act as their own CA when managing intranets, extranets and other network applications. A successful IPO in 1/98 generated $25MM and much enthusiasm for this company.

Sources: Piper Jaffray Research, FactSet, IBES, Compustat, Company Reports
Figures in millions, except per share amounts

Piper Jaffray Equity Research
Electronic Commerce

# Company Profile:
## V-ONE CORP

# VONE

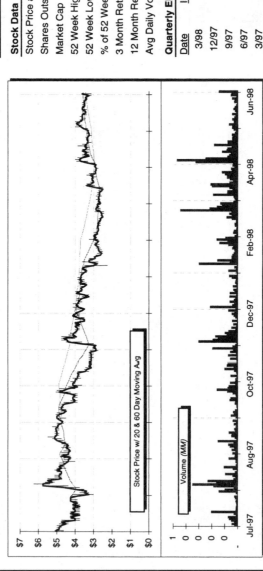

Stock Price w/ 20 & 60 Day Moving Avg

Volume *(MM)*

## Stock Data

| | 6/30/98 | |
|---|---|---|
| Stock Price as of | 6/30/98 | $3.63 |
| Shares Outstanding | | 13.76 |
| Market Cap | | $50 |
| 52 Week High | | $6.25 |
| 52 Week Low | | $2.25 |
| % of 52 Week High | | 58% |
| 3 Month Return | | 38% |
| 12 Month Return | | -28% |
| Avg Daily Volume (past mo.) | | 0.03 |

## Quarterly EPS Performance

| Date | IBES Est | Actual | Suprise |
|---|---|---|---|
| 3/98 | (0.14) | (0.12) | 0.02 |
| 12/97 | 0.02 | (0.41) | (0.43) |
| 9/97 | (0.01) | (0.03) | (0.02) |
| 6/97 | (0.05) | (0.19) | (0.14) |
| 3/97 | (0.05) | (0.07) | (0.02) |

## Annual Fundamentals

| | 12/96 | 12/97 |
|---|---|---|
| Revenue | 6.3 | 9.4 |
| Growth | | 50% |
| Gross Sales | 4.2 | 7.2 |
| Operating Income | (6.3) | (8.9) |
| Net Income | (6.7) | (9.4) |

## Quarterly Fundamentals

| | 6/96 | 9/96 | 12/96 | 3/97 | 6/97 | 9/97 | 12/97 | 3/98 |
|---|---|---|---|---|---|---|---|---|
| Revenue | 1.4 | 1.7 | 2.2 | 2.4 | 2.1 | 2.8 | 2.1 | 2.5 |
| Seq'l Growth | | 27% | 26% | 11% | -12% | 29% | -24% | 20% |
| Y/Y Growth | | | | | 58% | 61% | -4% | 4% |
| Gross Sales | 0.9 | 1.2 | 1.5 | 1.9 | 1.8 | 2.1 | 1.5 | 2.1 |
| Operating Income | (3.2) | (0.8) | (1.4) | (1.0) | (2.4) | (0.5) | (5.0) | (1.5) |
| Net Income | (3.4) | (1.0) | (1.3) | (0.9) | (3.2) | (0.4) | (4.9) | (1.5) |

| | | | | | | | | | | |
|---|---|---|---|---|---|---|---|---|---|---|
| Gross Margins | 65% | 70% | 67% | 77% | 85% | 75% | 72% | 83% | 68% | 77% |
| Operating Margin | NM | NM | -64% | -41% | NM | -18% | NM | -62% | NM | -95% |
| Net Margin | NM | -57% | -61% | -36% | NM | -16% | NM | -59% | NM | -100% |
| | | | | | | | | | | |
| Cash & S-T Invest. | 2.5 | 1.0 | 10.9 | 8.0 | 6.4 | 4.0 | 6.2 | 4.5 | 10.9 | 6.2 |
| L-T Debt | 0.1 | 0.2 | 0.1 | 0.1 | 0.3 | 0.3 | 0.3 | 0.3 | 0.1 | 0.3 |
| StkHldrs Equity | 2.0 | 1.0 | 14.0 | 13.2 | 10.8 | 10.7 | 9.9 | 8.8 | 14.0 | 9.9 |
| Op. Cash Flow | NA | (0.1) | (2.7) | (2.6) | (2.2) | (2.5) | (1.7) | (1.6) | (5.1) | (9.0) |
| **Per Share Data** | | | | | | | | | | |
| Shares Out | 8.46 | 8.30 | 12.66 | 12.67 | 12.88 | 13.01 | 13.07 | 13.32 | 12.66 | 13.07 |
| Net Income | (0.40) | (0.12) | (0.11) | (0.07) | (0.24) | (0.03) | (0.38) | (0.11) | (0.53) | (0.72) |
| Cash & S-T Inv. | 0.30 | 0.12 | 0.86 | 0.63 | 0.50 | 0.31 | 0.47 | 0.34 | 0.86 | 0.47 |
| Book Value | 0.23 | 0.12 | 1.11 | 1.04 | 0.84 | 0.82 | 0.76 | 0.66 | 1.11 | 0.76 |

**Earnings Estimates & Valuation:**

| | IBES EPS | Price Multiple |
|---|---|---|
| Current Yr Est | (0.41) | NM |
| Fwd Yr. Est. | NA | NM |
| Last FY End | 97.12 | |
| # IBES Estimates | 1.00 | |

| | Growth | P/E to LT Growth |
|---|---|---|
| EPS Growth | NA | NM |
| IBES L-T Growth | 35.0% | NM |

**Misc:**

| | |
|---|---|
| Employees | 71 |
| IPO Date | 10/24/96 |
| First Day Close | $5.00 |

## Company Description

VONE is the developer of SmartGate, a client/server smart card based security solution, that enables fully authenticated, network wide access security, encryption and privileges management. With its SmartGate Enterprise solution, V-ONE has developed a virtual private network (VPN) solution that provides secure remote access across multiple layers, between diverse user platforms, and utilizing all open network environments. The Company also offers a firewall solution called SmartWall. Customers consist largely of major financial, health care and government institutions.

Sources: Piper Jaffray Research, FactSet, IBES, Compustat, Company Reports
Figures in millions, except per share amounts

Piper Jaffray Equity Research
Electronic Commerce

# Index

# About the Author

Bill Burnham is the senior research analyst covering the Electronic Commerce industry for Crédit Suisse First Boston's Technology Group. As the first analyst on Wall Street to cover the Electronic Commerce industry, Mr. Burnham pioneered the study of this industry from an investor's perspective. Mr. Burnham is the author of several studies in the area of Electronic Commerce and is a frequent speaker and writer on the topic. Mr. Burnham's work has been chronicled by national and international media, and he is frequently quoted as an industry expert on the topic.

Prior to joining Crédit Suisse First Boston, Mr. Burnham was the senior research analyst for Electronic Commerce at the investment bank of Piper Jaffray Inc. While at Piper Jaffray he edited "EC Update," a monthly newsletter on the industry, and "EC Investor," an Internet site focused on investing in the Electronic Commerce industry. Prior to Piper Jaffray, Mr. Burnham was a senior associate in the Financial Services Group at the management consulting firm of Booz, Allen & Hamilton in New York where he led the firm's global efforts to understand the impact of the Internet on the world's financial system.

Mr. Burnham attended Washington University where he graduated summa cum laude, Phi Beta Kappa.

Piper Jaffray Inc., founded in 1895, has built a reputation as one of the nation's premier financial services firms by providing investment advice and services to individuals, institutions, and businesses. Piper Jaffray Inc.'s investment banking business has grown exponentially in the last several years by focusing on the needs of emerging growth companies in the healthcare, technology, financial, consumer, and industrial growth sectors. Piper Jaffray Inc. is one of the largest regional retail brokerages in the nation, and also has a national reputation for its expertise in debt financing. Securities products and services are offered through Piper Jaffray Inc., member SIPC and NYSE, Inc., a subsidiary of U.S. Bancorp. Through U.S. Bank, Piper Jaffray clients can access a full range of commercial and retail banking products. Nondeposit investment products are not insured by the FDIC, are not deposits or other obligations of or guaranteed by U.S. Bank National Association or its affiliates, and involve investment risks, including possible loss of the principal amount invested. For more information, visit our Web site at *www.piperjaffray.com.*